Everyman, I will go with thee,
and be thy guide

FEMALE PLAYWRIGHTS
OF THE RESTORATION
FIVE COMEDIES

Edited by
PADDY LYONS and
FIDELIS MORGAN

EVERYMAN
J. M. DENT · LONDON
CHARLES E. TUTTLE
VERMONT

Introduction and other critical apparatus
© J. M. Dent 1991

First published in Everyman in 1991
This edition 1994

J. M. Dent
Orion Publishing Group
Orion House,
5 Upper St Martin's Lane, London WC2H 9EA
and
Charles E. Tuttle Co. Inc.
28 South Main Street, Rutland, Vermont
05701, USA

Printed in Great Britain by
The Guernsey Press Co. Ltd, Guernsey, C.I.

British Library Cataloguing-in-Publication Data
is available upon request.

ISBN 0 460 87427 6

CONTENTS

NOTE ON THE PLAYWRIGHTS

Aphra Behn

Aphra Behn's earliest known writings are encoded intelligence reports, preserved in the Public Records Office; dating from 1666–7, they were written from abroad, while she was engaged in undercover operations against the Dutch, as a special agent for the British Secret Service. The story they tell is far from glamorous. She sent sound information about political intrigue and naval manoeuvres to her controllers in London, Thomas Killigrew and Sir Henry Bennett (Lord Arlington); they neglected to make use of what she communicated, and then fell behind in paying her keep and her wages. It all ended in impoverishment and tears, as she found herself needing to sell off her jewellery to eat, and had to borrow money for the fare home. By 1668, to keep out of debtors' prison, she was petitioning the King and sending begging letters to Killigrew.

As spy stories go, hers is not unusual. What is not clear is how an educated girl got into spying in the first place. Back in 1663, out in Surinam, which was then a British colony and was later to give Aphra Behn the setting for her novel *Oroonoko* (1688), one William Scot was remarked on as besotted with a young woman referred to as *Astraea*; *Astraea* was Aphra Behn's code-name while she was spying, and later on she used it as a literary pen-name. One of her tasks in Antwerp was to make contact with this Scot, who was then working as a double-agent, and to serve as go-between in negotiating his pardon and safe-conduct back to England. If, as the name Behn suggests, she had been married to a Dutchman, and if recent widowhood gave her business to see to in Antwerp, she had ready-made cover for this mission. But there are no documents to fill the gaps or convert to fact the speculative 'ifs' which begin to multiply.

Her Mr Behn may have married her in 1664, only to die in the plague of 1665, but this is guess-work. The girl that he married may well have been an Eaffry Johnson who was baptised at Harbledown in Kent in 1640. Such is the case advanced, convincingly, by Maureen Duffy,[1] who has been thorough in sifting through parish archives. But it is to presume that Aphra Behn was born a Protestant. Extensive bibliographical investigation has persuaded Mary Ann O'Donnell that the net should be cast wider, to allow that Aphra Behn may have been born a Catholic; she proposes that the search for antecedents be extended to recusant and colonial birth registers.[2] The recent discovery of further manuscript material in Aphra Behn's handwriting[3] encourages still more the view that what is known so far may not be all there is to be known about her.

Aphra Behn's first play, *The Forced Marriage*, was staged in 1670 at the Duke of York's theatre, which was then under female management, in the control of the widowed Lady Davenant. It was staged hot on the heels of another play by a female playwright, Frances Boothby, whose tragedy *Marcelia* had been performed by the rival company at Theatre Royal Drury Lane, where the manager was the same Thomas Killigrew who had left Aphra Behn penniless in Antwerp. Though she was to remain with the Duke's company and stay clear of working with Killigrew, he was to play a part in her professional recognition, all unwittingly.

In 1677 the Duke's company staged *The Rover*, a tight, bright comedy based on a rambling autobiographical ten-act piece, *Thomaso the Wanderer*, which Killigrew had penned years previously. *The Rover* was at first produced and published anonymously, and it was an immediate success. An unsigned postscript has some droll remarks about its borrowings: 'as for the words and characters, I leave the reader to judge and compare 'em with *Thomaso*, to whom I recommend the great entertainment of reading it'. Whether because she mocked his play with lightness and notable restraint, or because her play was so

[1]Maureen Duffy, *The Passionate Shepherdess: Aphra Behn 1640–1689* (London 1977), pp. 19–23.
[2]Mary Ann O'Donnell, *Aphra Behn: a bibliography of primary and secondary sources* (New York 1986), p. 2.
[3]Patrick Lyons, *Aphra Behn: Plays, Poems and other writings* (1991).

popular that to take the huff would look silly and lose him the chance to bask in her glory, Killigrew gave no sign of being offended. *The Rover* was a smash hit, and was reprinted later the same year with a new title-page, crediting 'Mrs A Behn' as the author. She was at a peak of confidence and added a touch more sarcasm to 'her postscript, standing up for women with a jibe against 'critics who are naturally so kind to any that pretend to usurp their dominion, especially of our sex'. *The Rover* became a stock piece and was revived constantly till well into the next century.

For a decade or so Aphra Behn wrote plays as if her livelihood depended on it, and it probably did. As she had for *The Rover*, she often began by restructuring and building inventively on out-moded pieces, but she seems not to have drawn on any existing play for *The Feigned Courtesans* (1679). Here she was especially reliant on her knowledge of the actors, with a subplot tailored to fit the three comic men who were stars of the Duke's company: Nokes, Underhill, and Leigh, who played Sir Signal, Mr Tickletext, and Petro – the parts that call for consummate clowns. Overall it is a play built around balance, the knockabout mirroring and thereby querying the postures and anxieties of the witty lovers. If the love-intrigues seem infuriatingly complex, that is the simple point. Though the women are not actually courtes-ans, but only feigning, the underlying issue is one of who loves whom as what, the embarrassments are real enough, and the conclusion is designed to display neatness rather than answers. Neither rank, gender, nor even Englishness settles anything. While the buffoons are plainly and laughably ridiculous, there is no corresponding guarantee that the witty lovers have got it all quite right. The territory is that of *Cosi Fan Tutte*, but here the double standard for the sexes is seen to be based on relations of power and economic circumstance, and not assumed to be somehow inherent, or natural. The play was favourably received at its opening, and there are records of successful revival as late as 1716.

In the 1680s, in the wake of the Popish Plot, London had become unsettled; times were harsher, and theatre felt the chill. Aphra Behn adjusted, and wrote comedies that faced up to the nastiness of being hard up – notably, *The City Heiress* (1682). But in that year the two London theatre companies finally merged into a single United Company, and as competition gave way to monopoly there were fewer commissions for new plays. Again Aphra Behn adjusted, turning her energies first to translation and editing, and then to narrative fiction. In her last years she was to make a come-back in the theatre with two outstanding plays. *The Lucky Chance* (performed 1686) is a black comedy about sex and the lack of money, and it raises but never resolves a question as to whether there is any connection whatsoever between the sexual acts people engage in and those going on in their heads. *The Emperor of the Moon* (1687) is an adroit and inventive farce, with characters from *commedia dell'arte* – very much actors' theatre. For years afterwards it was the play staged whenever the thirteenth of a month fell on a Friday.

Illness scarred Aphra Behn's's final years, but she retained her courage. Her last work was a political poem addressed to the Reverend Dr Burnet, who was earning himself a bishopric by legitimising the installation of William of Orange as King of England. Aphra Behn had remained a Jacobite, and this is a poem firmly refusing support to the new regime, all the more barbed for its careful tones of modulated politeness. She died on 16 April 1689; later that year William Canning, who had published this last poem, was arrested for putting oppositional literature into circulation.

Throughout her career Aphra Behn held to her principles. She argued for female equality through a steady critique against whatever set women apart or aside. In opposing exclusion, her stance was broad, democratic and even-handed. However, egaliterian feminism was not to hold sway in the following centuries, when a cult of 'femininity' would prove an effective mechanism for diminishing women, by defining as particularly worthy in a woman attributes perceived as generally less valuable in people at large. The requirement that a female writer be conspicuously 'feminine' was ultimately to cut Aphra Behn out of English Literature. For a half century or so after her death, her fame remained securely based on her work: her plays were revived and her books reprinted regularly. Defoe went on the record as ranking her with Milton and Rochester, among the 'great wits' of her era. But by the later eighteenth and nineteenth centuries, this placing was resented and seen as an insubordination; her biography was then combed and reconstructed for hints of 'unfeminine' behaviour that would damn her as indecent – and these were used to fuel campaigns to keep her work out of print. In retrospect, her real offence seems to have been the even-handedness of her comedy, where men are never ridiculed any less than women. Nothing stands still: in the past decade her plays have been performed more often than they were throughout the preceding two hundred years.

'Ariadne'

Nothing whatever is known about 'Ariadne'. There has been some footless speculation: Germaine Greer thinks she was a man;[4] 'Kendal' suggests she was Mary Pix.[5] But there is no evidence that any male author of the 1690s thought it worth his while to present himself as a female playwright; and it is clear from the preface to her first play that Mary Pix only began her writing career in 1696, the year after the stage success of *She Ventures and He Wins*.

Whoever 'Ariadne' was, the fact is that she wrote a lively play which was performed by an all-star cast at Lincoln's Inn Fields theatre in September 1695. Aphra Behn was six years dead, and in London not one play by any Englishwoman apart from Mrs Behn had been performed for over twenty years. Après 'Ariadne' le déluge . . .

Mary Pix

In the satirical play *The Female Wits*, Mary Pix is caricatured as Mrs Wellfed, 'a fat female author, a good sociable well-matured companion that will not suffer martyrdom rather than take three bumpers in a hand', and summed up as 'foolish and open-

---

[4] In *Kissing the Rod* (London 1988), p. 24.
[5] In *Love and Thunder* (London 1988), p. 156.

hearted'.[6] Casual negligence has obscured a background of letters and music which formed her as a playwright, although this can be re-established from local archives in Buckingham, Kent and Oxfordshire, from London parish registers and from the records of the Guild of Merchant Taylors.

Mary Pix was born Mary Griffith in 1666. Her father Roger Griffith (BA Balliol Oxon, 1664: MA Emanuel Cantab, 1669) was both rector of the Buckingham parish of Padbury and Master of the eminent Royal Latin (Free) School in Buckingham. (*The Female Wits* has Mrs Pix briefly display learning by trying to engage Mrs Manley and Mrs Trotter in 'a Latin dispute'[7] – but otherwise preferring to wear her learning lightly.) Her mother Lucy (née Berriman) was on her marriage (5 October 1665) described as a *soundesse*, or musician.

Although the Reverend Griffith died early in 1682, his widow and daughter lived on in the schoolhouse for some time after his death. Mary Griffith was courted by her father's successor, Thomas Dalby MA, a former pupil at the school. On a nocturnal visit to his girlfriend in February 1683, the house caught fire and burned to the ground. Dalby left Buckingham a year later, frightened by a local outbreak of smallpox. Mary Griffith also seems to have left town shortly after the fire destroyed her home for, in the London parish of St Savior's Benetfink, on 24 July 1684, Mary Griffith became Mary Pix, through her marriage to George Pix, a twenty-four-year-old merchant tailor.

George Pix had, on the death of his father in 1675 (also George, also a merchant tailor, and a churchwarden and distinguished soldier too) inherited Pix Hall in Kent, together with 243 acres of woodland, meadow, hopgardens, mills etc, and of course, the Pix coat of arms. It seems that George Jnr and his wife Mary were in residence shortly after their marriage, for their first son George was baptised there in June 1689. Unfortunately, the child died, and was buried in the local cemetery of Hawkhurst in September 1690. The following year George and Mary Pix were back in London, where their son William was baptised at St Andrew's Holborn on 12 November 1691. The couple were then described as being of Southampton Buildings, a street between High

[6]*The Female Wits*, ed. Fidelis Morgan (London 1981), p. 392 and p. 394.
[7]*The Female Wits*, p. 402.

Holborn and Chancery Lane – only a garden away from Lincoln's Inn Fields and the theatre.

Mary Pix's first play was performed in 1696, by the Drury Lane company. In 1697, after being satirised by that company in *The Female Wits*, she moved to Lincoln's Inn Fields, and over the next ten years wrote as many plays for that company. One contemporary dramatic handbook[8] declared 'she has boldly given us an essay of her talent . . . and not without success, though with little profit to herself'. Another more cheekily asserted that she had 'written her husband into debt'.[9]

The performance of Centlivre's *The Busybody* given on Saturday 28 May 1709 was advertised as for the benefit of Mrs Pix's executor. This indicates that she had died some time previously, and that her will was being processed. The will, however, has not been traced, and it is probable that, as a benefit was being held, something had gone drastically wrong, and the executor was out-of-pocket as a result. Possibly Mrs Pix had written away money which legally belonged to her husband and his family, possibly her generosity outmatched her funds. Whichever, her widower George Pix remarried in June 1709.

She is said to have collaborated with Centlivre; according to *The Post Boy* for 26–28 May 1709, the greater part of *The Busybody* was by Pix.

Susanna Centlivre

There are two versions of everything known of Mrs Centlivre's life before she became the most successful female playwright until Agatha Christie.

Susanna Centlivre was born either Rawkins[10] or Freeman[11] between 1667 and 1677. Her father is said to have died when she was an infant;[12] he is also said to have survived her mother, and

[8]Langbaine (& Gildon), *Lives and Characters of the English Dramatic Poets* (1699).
[9]Joseph Trapp, *The Players turned Academics* (1703).
[10]According to an obituary by her friend and early collaborator Abel Boyer, in *The Political Register of Great Britain* (1723).
[11]According to Giles Jacob, in *The Poetical Register* (1719), published during her lifetime.
[12]Jacob.

remarried while Susanna was in her teens, when she was driven by her new stepmother to leave home.[13] She then either joined a group of strolling players,[14] or dressed up as a man and went to Cambridge.[15]

Next comes a string of men: she was married 'or something like it'[16] to a nephew of Sir Stephen Fox,[17] who died, or something like it, within a year. She married a soldier named Carroll,[18] who died within two years.

There is no disagreement that as Susanna Carroll she was active in Whig literary circles, wrote eight plays which were performed and published, and went on tour with some travelling actors in 1706. Then she met and married Joseph Centlivre, Yeoman of the Mouth (i.e. cook) to Queen Anne. He had been attracted to her when he saw her perform the part of Alexander the Great in a touring production of Lee's *The Rival Queens* at Windsor Castle.

More importantly, between 1700 and her death in 1723, she wrote nineteen plays altogether, of which several have had a more distinguished stage history than Wycherley's *The Country Wife*, or Congreve's *The Way of the World*. Indeed there were command performances of her plays for the English royals through to and including Queen Victoria.

David Garrick, whose standards in theatre were famously high, kept two of her plays, *The Busybody* and *The Wonder* in his repertoire – and gave his final farewell performance as Don Felix in the latter play. Celebrated actors – from Garrick and Kitty Clive, through Edward Shuter, Henry Woodward, Charles Kemble, John Philip Kemble, Charles Matthews, Robert Elliston and Madame Vestris – frequently chose her plays for their own benefit performances, knowing that they offered good parts and, more to the point, were popular with the paying public.

[13]According to John Mottley, who claimed to have contributed to her play *A Bold Stroke for a Wife* (1718), and gives a notable circumstantial account of her in Thomas Whincop's *Scanderberg* (1747).

[14]According to the retired prompter, William Rufus Chetwood, *The British Theatre* (1750).

[15]Where she was installed in the rooms of the future MP Anthony Hammond, according to Mottley.

[16]Mottley.

[17]Jacob.

[18]Boyer describes him as 'her first husband', Jacob as married to her 'afterwards', and Mottley has it that he simply 'succeeded in her affections'.

The Busybody was almost ruined by the actors during rehearsal. Robert Wilkes threw the script into the pit and 'swore that nobody would bear to sit to hear such stuff'. It was 'a silly thing wrote by a woman, that the players had no opinion of'.[19] At the first performance 'there was a very poor house, scarce charges. Under the circumstances, it cannot be supposed that the play appeared to much advantage, the audience only came there for want of another place to go, but without any expectation of being much diverted; they were yawning at the beginning of it, but were agreeably surprised, more and more every act, till at last the house rang with as much applause as was possible to be given by so thin an audience.'[20]

The huge success of *The Busybody* led to confused theorising about the capacities of female playwrights, even from the play's champions. According to Richard Steele, playwright and essayist: 'the plot and incidents of the play are laid with that subtlety of spirit which is peculiar to females of wit, and is very seldom well performed by those of the other sex, in whom craft in love is an act of invention, and not, as with women, the effect of nature and instinct.'[21]

Mrs Centlivre died in December 1723. Her plays were to hold the stage for at least another century-and-a-half. A contemporary noted her legacy as solid because 'she could show (which I believe few other poets could who depended on their pen) a great many jewels and pieces of plate, which were the product of her labour.'[22]

[19]Mottley. His account of preproduction prejudice and difficulty is confirmed in *The Female Tatler* (1709).

[20]Mottley. His account of the play's early triumph is extended further by Richard Steele in *The Tatler No 15* (May 14, 1709).

[21]*The Tatler No 19* (May 24, 1709).

[22]Mottley, for whom brass was brass.

NOTE ON THE EDITORS

PADDY LYONS lectures in English at Glasgow University. He is a translator of Althusser and has written extensively on literary theory. His published work on the Restoration includes *Congreve's Comedies* (1982) and *Aphra Behn: Plays, Poems and other Writings* (1991).

FIDELIS MORGAN is an actress and playwright whose published work includes *The Female Wits* (1981), *A Woman of No Character* (1986), *The Well-Known Trouble maker: A Life of Charlotte Charke* (1988) and *The Misogynist's Sourcebook* (1989). She lives in London.

INTRODUCTION

To anyone who listens to radio plays or watches television, the existence of female playwrights is regularly announced and credited. For several decades, newspapers have advertised the fact that London's longest-running play was not written by a man, but by Agatha Christie.[1] Nonetheless, without some qualification to the contrary, the word 'playwright' means a man. Common usage thereby flies in the face of everyday observation, and is complicit with a silent misogyny. The strategy of forwarding women's writing as distinctively womanly now faces ready dismissal as overworked advocacy, as special pleading which is itself a sure sign of the second-rate. Coming from the past, the female playwrights of the Restoration challenge bias from another direction, from history that has been overlooked. From these writers' biographies it is plain that, to contemporary audiences, the plays included in this volume were every bit as successful as those by male playwrights of their times.

Women first gained significant access to the English stage as theatre-managers, as performers and as playwrights during the half-century following the Restoration of the monarchy in 1660. It was not an era otherwise remarkable for progress towards social equality of the sexes; ground won during the Commonwealth years was by then being lost, even in movements where egalitarianism was central. 'Although Quakers continued to advocate women's right to prophesy,' it has been noted, 'their official stance on the subject became ever more guarded.'[2] Theatre had no policy for equal opportunities to keep it apart from this tendency and it was by a diversity of routes that women came to be employed in crucial aspects of theatre work.

Royal warrant reopened the theatre in 1660 and brought

[1] *The Mousetrap* opened in 1952, and is billed as 'still running'.
[2] Elaine Hobby, *Virtue of Necessity: English Women's Writing 1649–88* (London 1988), p. 45.

actresses on stage, an innovation that broke with English tradition. From the founding of London's first public theatre in the 1570s to the closure of the theatres by Parliamentary edict in 1642, performers were exclusively male, and female roles had either been played by boy actresses (Portia, for example) or as dame parts taken by grown men (all the Merry Wives of Windsor, for example). But in the years while the theatres were closed, acting troupes had disbanded, skills were lost, training was abandoned, and the boys had become men. New acting companies had to be built up almost from scratch, and they looked to Europe rather than to the past, taking their practice from France where it was customary that female roles were played by women. From the first, English audiences were delighted with the new actresses, and became particularly fond of those who displayed a talent for caricaturing men, in 'breeches parts' – a novelty highlighting the break with earlier convention.

Continuity is, however, of concern in management, and it was to avoid a disruption of continuity that a woman first took charge of a theatre company. When Sir William Davenant died in 1668, his controlling interest in the Duke of York's company passed to his son Charles, who was then a minor and under the guardianship of his mother, Davenant's widow. No doubt to protect and maintain an inheritance which neglect would surely ruin, Lady Davenant took over the theatre, and was noted for her competence and her exercise of 'rule and dominion.'[3] Coming from the old nobility, Lady Davenant was well-familiar with theatrical planning: women from the aristocracy had always been privileged in that they could, away from the public stage, indulge theatrical aspirations. A noblewoman could write and publish a dramatic piece, once it was composed for reading aloud and not for actual performance,[4] she would perform in a masque, at home or at Court,[5] and in 1656 Lady Davenant had assisted in the produc-

[3]By the prompter, John Downes, *Roscius Angelicanus*, ed. Montague Summers (London, 1929), p. 31.

[4]For instance, *Antonie* (1592) by the Countess of Pembroke. Her niece, Lady Mary Wroth (to whom Ben Jonson dedicated *The Alchemist*) published a sonnet sequence and a *roman à clef*, but it is pertinent to note that *Love's Victory*, her solid dramatic piece, remained in manuscript and was not printed or performed.

[5]Most outlandishly: Jonson's *Masque of Blackness*, given at Court in 1605; it was specially commissioned by the Queen so that she, along with a band of ladies-in-waiting which included Lady Mary Wroth, could blacken up as negresses. With

tion at Rutland House of her husband's ten-act opera *The Siege of Rhodes*. She had an eye for talent and knew how to delegate, appointing the actor Thomas Betterton to see to day-to-day matters and to oversee the building of a new playhouse. It is testimony to Lady Davenant's acumen that her company was to produce Aphra Behn's first plays. Her commitment to continuity and to the future was strong, and in her retirement, Lady Davenant took under her care a young woman named Elizabeth Barry, who was to become the outstanding actress of her era and later would herself enter into theatre-management along with Betterton.

None of the female playwrights of this age came from the aristocracy,[6] and – Susanna Centlivre apart – none had any working background in theatre. In the eighteenth century the more able female playwrights were from theatrical families or were themselves actresses, but their Restoration predecessors came to playwrighting from outside the theatre, and had little in common other than literacy in English and middle-class affiliations. That women of their social placement were not to enjoy such opportunity in the following century is an outcome of a larger historical shift which was to bring sharp alteration in the lives of middle-class women. For the middle-classes in Restoration England, the ideal of the one-breadwinner family had not yet become dominant. Though the sexes were far from equal in legal standing, labour relations were not then so heavily differentiated across gender lines as they would become in the eighteenth century. The coming of the industrial revolution would then reinforce a pattern whereby a man worked, his wife kept servants and wages paid to female workers were pitifully low. But Restoration wives and husbands worked side-by-side in enterprises which maintained them both, as their forebears had done. It was still usual for widows and unmarried daughters to run businesses independently; female shop-keepers and tradespeople, bakers and printers, booksellers and brewers, were taken for granted. Female playwrights of the

restraint: Milton's *Comus*, in which the part of the Lady was written for fifteen-year-old Lady Alice Bridgewater; *Comus* was performed at Ludlow Castle in 1634 before Lady Alice's father, who was then Governor-General of Wales.

[6] Margaret Cavendish, Duchess of Newcastle was adamant that the plays she wrote and published were not designed for acting – a point that hardly seems to need insistence.

Restoration could work under the same conditions and for the same pay as male colleagues, because that was how women then worked. Only later would it seem transgressive for a woman to undertake 'man's work', showing a lack of 'femininity', or something worse.

Opportunity on its own never made a playwright, but talent needs support if it is to thrive. The first piece by a female playwright to appear on the public stage was a translation of Corneille's *Pompée* (1663) by Katherine Philips; she could not have completed the work, she was to insist, without the encouragement she met with while staying in Dublin.[7] How Aphra Behn's first script reached Lady Davenant's desk is not known, but her long and prolific career was sustained by a well-documented talent for friendship with the writers of her time.[8] Aphra Behn was the sole female playwright active in the middle decades of this period, and it was not until well after her death that a new forcing-house for theatrical talent was to emerge.

In 1695 Betterton established a breakaway theatre company and involved a group of leading actors in its management. These included Elizabeth Barry, who was the former protegée of Lady Davenant and long-time friend of Aphra Behn, and Ann Bracegirdle, who was confidante to the playwright Congreve. The need of the new company for new plays was met by new playwrights, who found their way by enabling these two great actresses to play opposite each other. In *She Ventures and He Wins*, the breeches part of Charlotte was taken by Ann Bracegirdle, and the more vigorous comic role of Urania by Elizabeth Barry. In Mary Pix's *The Beau Defeated* they again teamed in counterpoint, as Lady Landsworth and Mrs Rich. The effect of this pairing is especially noticeable on the work of playwrights who wrote only occasionally for the company: it brought out the best in both Catherine Trotter and Delarivier Manley.[9] It translated into tragedy as a double-act not unlike that of Snow White and the Wicked Queen,

[7] Fidelis Morgan, *The Female Wits* (London 1981), p. 8.

[8] Anne Wharton was discouraged by her relation Dr Burnett from accepting Aphra Behn's help; though she completed a play, *Love's Martyr*, which was entered in the Stationers' Register in 1686, it was never published or performed.

[9] *The Royal Mischief*, Delarivier Manley (1696); *The Fatal Friendship*, Catherine Trotter (1698).

and thereby brought success to otherwise undistinguished plays –
Antiochus the Great (1701) by Jane Wiseman, and *The Unnatural
Mother* (1698) by an anonymous 'young lady'.

More than fifty plays attributed to female playwrights appeared
in print during the half century from 1660–1710; and as publishers
generally bothered only with plays that had achieved a measure of
success, it is quite possible that a greater number were written,
performed and either forgotten or published anonymously. Before
1710, copyright was vested in the playhouse and the publisher, not
in the author. Till the close of the period, authorship was not
generally advertised on playbills, nor always proclaimed when
plays were printed. There is, therefore, much casual anonymity.
The Rover (1677), Aphra Behn's first great hit, was unattributed in
its first printing; plays known to be by Mary Pix and by Susanna
Centlivre also came into print without bearing their author's name.
This indifference may now seem strange, but it is indicative of a
time when plays were valued according to how they performed and
not by who wrote them. When authorship – female or otherwise –
remained a matter of passing interest, female playwrights were in
an open and equal market with their male colleagues.

In selecting the plays that comprise this volume we have focussed
on pieces which were successful with their contemporary audiences and also hold an appeal for theatre-goers today. The texts
have been established with reference to first editions, and retain
their original punctuation insofar as that seemed consistent with
clarity. The position of stage-directions has been regularised, and
obvious errors corrected. Spelling is modernised throughout except where a special pronunciation is to be inferred, or where words
and phrases have been garbled to give the effect of pidgin Italian,
school-room Spanish, or cod Latin. Unless otherwise stated, all
dates refer to first performances, and are given in New Style.

We wish to acknowledge kindness and assistance from staff at
the Bodleian Library, The British Library, Glasgow University
Library, the National Library of Scotland, and the Public Records
Office. Irene Kennedy and Elizabeth Watson of Glasgow University Library were especially helpful. Particular thanks are due
to Laurance Rudic for his investigations on our behalf in the
library of Lambeth Palace. Our early labours were lightened by
the typing skills of Flloyd Kennedy.

PADDY LYONS AND FIDELIS MORGAN

The Feigned Courtesans

OR

A NIGHT'S INTRIGUE

BY

APHRA BEHN

(1679)

DRAMATIS PERSONAE

WOMEN

LAURA LUCRETIA,	*a young lady of quality, contracted to Julio, in love with Galliard, and sister to Octavio.*
MARCELLA and CORNELIA,	*sisters to Julio, and nieces to Morosini, passing for courtesans by the name of Euphemia and Silvianetta.*
PHILLIPA,	*their woman.*
SABINA,	*confidante to Laura Lucretia.*

ITALIANS

MOROSINI	*an old count, uncle to Julio.*
JULIO,	*his nephew, contracted to Laura Lucretia.*
OCTAVIO,	*a young count, contracted to Marcella, deformed, revengeful.*
CRAPINE,	*Morosini's man.*
PETRO,	*supposed pimp to the two courtesans.*
SILVIO,	*page to Laura Lucretia.*

ENGLISH

SIR HARRY FILLAMOUR,	*in love with Marcella.*
GALLIARD,	*in love with Cornelia.*
SIR SIGNAL BUFFON,	*a fool.*
TICKLETEXT,	*his governor.*

Various pages, musicians, footmen and bravos.

SETTING   ROME, late evening to early morning.

Dedication

TO MRS ELLEN GWYNN

Madam,

'Tis no wonder that hitherto I followed not the good example of the believing poets, since less faith and zeal than you alone can inspire had wanted power to have reduced me to the true worship: your permission, madam, has enlightened me, and I with shame look back on my past ignorance, which suffered me not to pay an adoration long since, where there was so very much due, yet even now though secure in my opinion, I make this sacrifice with infinite fear and trembling, well-knowing that so excellent and perfect a creature as yourself only differs from the divine powers in this: the offerings made to you ought to be worthy of you, whilst they accept the will alone; and how madam, would your altars be loaded, if like heaven you gave permission to all that had a will and desire to approach 'em who now at distance can only wish and admire, which all mankind agree to do; as if, madam, you alone had the patent from heaven to engross all hearts; and even those distant slaves whom you conquer with your fame pay an equal tribute to those that have the blessing of being wounded by your eyes, and boast the happiness of being wounded by you daily; insomuch that succeeding ages who shall with joy survey your history shall envy us who lived in this, and saw those charming wonders which they can only read of, and whom we ought in charity to pity, since all the pictures pens or pencils can draw will give 'em but a faint idea of what we have the honour to see in such absolute perfection; they can only guess She was infinitely fair, witty, and deserving, but to what vast degrees in all, they can only judge who lived to gaze and listen; for besides, madam, all the charms and attractions and powers of your sex, you have beauties peculiar to yourself, an eternal sweetness, youth and air, which never dwelt in any face but yours, of which not one unimitable grace could be ever borrowed or assumed, though with never so much industry, to adorn another; they cannot steal a look or smile from you to enhance their own beauties' price, but all the world will know it yours; so natural and so fitted are all your charms and excellencies to one another, so entirely designed and created to make up in you alone the most perfect lovely thing in the world; you never appear but you glad the hearts of all that have the happy fortune to see you, as if you were made on purpose to put the whole world into good humour; whenever you look abroad, and when you speak, men crowd to listen to you with that awful reverence as to holy oracles or divine prophecies, and bear away the precious words to tell at home to all the attentive family the graceful things you uttered, and cry, 'But oh she spoke with such an air, so gay, that half the beauty's lost in the repetition'. 'Tis this that ought to make your sex vain enough to despise the malicious world that will allow a woman no wit, and bless ourselves for living in an age that can produce so wondrous an argument as your undeniable self, to shame those boasting talkers who are judges of nothing but faults.

But how much in vain, madam, I endeavour to tell you the sense of all mankind with mine, since to the utmost limits of the universe your mighty conquests are made known: and who can doubt the power of that illustrious beauty, the charms of that tongue, and the greatness of that mind, who has subdued the most powerful and glorious monarch of the world: and so well you bear the honours you were born for, with a greatness so unaffected, and affability so easy, an humour so soft, so far from pride or vanity, that the most envious and most disaffected can find no cause or reason to wish you less, nor can heaven give you more, who has expressed a particular care of you every way, and above all in bestowing, on the world and you, two noble branches, who have all the greatness and sweetness of their royal and beautiful stock; and who give us too a hopeful prospect of what their future braveries will perform, when they shall shoot up and spread themselves to that degree, that all the lesser world may find repose beneath their shades; and whom you have permitted to wear those glorious titles which you yourself generously neglected, well knowing with the noble poet, 'tis better far to merit titles than to wear 'em.

Can you then blame my ambition, madam, that lays this at your feet, and begs a sanctuary where all pay so great a veneration? 'Twas dedicated yours before it had a being, and overbusy to render it worthy of the honour made it less grateful; and poetry like lovers often fares the worse by taking too much pains to please; but under so gracious an influence my tender laurels may thrive, till they become fit wreaths to offer to the rays that improve their growth: which madam, I humbly implore, you still permit her ever to do, who is, madam,

Your most humble and most obedient servant,
A. Behn.

Act One

SCENE ONE

Enter LAURA LUCRETIA, *and* SILVIO *richly* dressed, ANTONIO *attending, coming all in haste.*

SILVIO: Madam, you need not make such haste away, the stranger that followed us from St Peter's Church pursues us no longer, and we have now lost sight of him. Lord, who would have thought the approach of a handsome cavalier should have possessed Donna Laura Lucretia with fear?

LAURA: I do not fear, my Silvio, but I would have this new habitation which I have destined for love, known to none but him to whom I've destined my heart: – [*aside*] ah, would he knew the conquest he has made. – Nor went I this evening to church with any other devotion, but that which warms my heart for my young English cavalier, whom I hoped to have seen there, and I must find some way to let him know my passion, which is too high for souls like mine to hide.

SILVIO: Madam, the cavalier's in view again, and hot in the pursuit.

LAURA: Let's haste away then, and Silvio, do you lag behind: 'twill give him an opportunity of enquiring, whilst I get out of sight, – be sure you conceal my name and quality, and tell him – anything but truth – tell him I am La Silvianetta, the young Roman courtesan, or what you please to hide me from his knowledge. [*Exeunt* LAURA *and* ANTONIO]

Enter JULIO *and* PAGE *in pursuit*

JULIO: Boy fall you into discourse with that page, and learn his lady's name – whilst I pursue her farther. [*Exit* JULIO]

[PAGE *salutes*[1] SILVIO, *who returns it, they go out as talking to each other*.]

[1] *Salutes*: greets

Enter SIR HARRY FILLAMOUR *and* GALLIARD

FILLAMOUR: He follows her close, whoe'er they be: I see this trade of love goes forward still.

GALLIARD: And will whilst there's difference in sexes. But Harry, the woman, the delicate women I was speaking of?

FILLAMOUR: Prithee tell me no more of thy fine women, Frank, thou hast not been in Rome above a month, and thou'st been a dozen times in love, as thou call'st it: to me there is no pleasure like constancy.

GALLIARD: Constancy! And wouldst thou have me one of those dull lovers who believe it their duty to love a woman till her hair and eyes change colour, for fear of the scandalous name of an inconstant! No, my passion like great victors hates the lazy stay, but having vanquished, prepares for new conquests.

FILLAMOUR: Which you gain as they do towns by fire, lose 'em even in the taking – thou ought grow penitent and weary of these dangerous follies.

GALLIARD: But I am yet too young for both: let old age and infirmity bring repentance, – there's her feeble province, and even then too we find no plague like being deprived of dear woman-kind.

FILLAMOUR: I hate playing about a flame that will consume me.

GALLIARD: Away with your antiquated notions, and let's once hear sense from thee: examine but the whole world Harry, and thou wilt find a beautiful woman the desire of the noblest, and the reward of the bravest.

FILLAMOUR: And the common prize of coxcombs: times are altered now, Frank, why else should the virtuous be cornuted,[2] the coward be caressed, the villain roll with six, and the fool lie with her ladyship.

GALLIARD: Mere accident, sir: and the kindness of Fortune, but a pretty witty young creature, such as this Silvianetta, and Euphemia, is certainly the greatest blessing this wicked world can afford us.

FILLAMOUR: I believe the lawful enjoyment of such a woman, and honest too, would be a blessing.

[2]*cornuted*: cuckolded

GALLIARD: Lawful enjoyment! Prithee what's lawful enjoyment, but to enjoy 'em according to the generous indulgent Law of Nature; enjoy 'em as we do meat, drink, air and light, and all the rest of her common blessings; — therefore prithee dear knight, let me govern thee but for a day, and I will show thee such a signiora, such a beauty, another manner of piece than your so admired Viterboan, Donna Marcella, of whom you boast so much.

FILLAMOUR: And yet this rare piece is but a courtesan, in coarse plain English, a very whore! — who filthily exposes all her beauties to him can give her most, not love her best.

GALLIARD: Why, faith, to thy comfort be it spoken, she does distribute her charms at that easy rate.

FILLAMOUR: Oh, the vast distance between an innocent passion, and a poor faithless lust!

GALLIARD: Innocent passion at Rome! Oh, 'tis not to be named but in some northern climate: to be an anchorite[3] here, is to be an epicure in Greenland; impossibilities, Harry. Sure thou hast been advising with Sir Signal Buffoon's governor! That formal piece of nonsense and hypocrisy.

FILLAMOUR: No faith, I brought the humour along with me to Rome, and for your governor I have not seen him yet, though he lodge in this same house with us, and you promised to bring me acquainted with him long since.

GALLIARD: I'll do't this very minute.

FILLAMOUR: No, I'm obliged not to engage myself this evening, because I expect the arrival of Count Julio, whose last letters assured me it would be tonight.

GALLIARD: Julio! What, the young Italian Count you made me acquainted with last summer in England?

FILLAMOUR: The same, the Ambassador's nephew, a good youth, and one I esteem.

Enter JULIO

JULIO: I hope my page will bring intelligence who this beauty is.

FILLAMOUR; Hah, Julio! Welcome, dear friend.

[*embraces him*]

JULIO: Sir Harry Fillamour! How glad am I to meet you in a country where I have power to repay you all those friendships I

---

[3]*anchorite*: recluse

received when I was a stranger to yours. Monsieur Galliard too, nay then I'm sure to want no diversion whilst I stay in Rome.   [*salutes* GALLIARD]

FILLAMOUR: But pray, what made you leave England so soon?

JULIO: E'en the great business of mankind, matrimony. I have an uncle here who has provided me fetters which I must put on; he says they will be easy. I liked the character of my mistress well enough, a brave masculine lady, a Roman of quality, Donna Laura Lucretia, till as luck would have it, at my arrival this evening, stepping into St Peter's Church, I saw a woman there that fired my heart, and whom I followed to her house; but meeting none that could inform me who she was, I left my page to make the discovery, whilst I with equal impatience came to look you out; whose sight I prefer even to a new amour, resolving not to visit home, to which I have been a stranger this seven years, till I had kissed your hands, and gained your promise to accompany me to Viterbo.

FILLAMOUR: Viterbo! Is that your place of residence?

JULIO: Yes; 'tis a pretty town, and many noble families inhabit there, stored too with beauties, at least 'twas wont to be: have you not seen it?

GALLIARD: Yes, and a beauty there too lately for his repose, who has made him sigh and look so like an ass ever since he came to Rome.

JULIO: I am glad you have so powerful an argument to invite you back, I know she must be rare, and of quality that could engage your heart.

FILLAMOUR: She's both; it most unluckily fell out, that I was recommended by a person of quality in England to a nobleman at Viterbo, who being a man of a temper frank and gallant, received me with less ceremony than is usual in Italy. I had the freedom of the house, one of the finest villas belonging to Viterbo, and the pleasure to see and converse at a distance with one of the loveliest persons in the world, a niece of this old count's.

JULIO: Very well, and could you see her but at a distance, sir?

FILLAMOUR: Oh no, 'twas all I durst desire, or she durst give; I came too late to hope; she being before promised in marriage to a more happy man, the consummation of which waits only the arrival of a brother of hers, who is now at the Court of France, and every day expected.

 Enter PETRO *dressed as a Barber*

GALLIARD: Hah! Signior Petro.

FILLAMOUR: Come sir, we'll take a turn i'ith' gallery, for this pimp never appears, but Francis desires to be in private.

GALLIARD: Thou wrong'st an honest ingenious fellow, to call him pimp.

PETRO: Ah, signior, what his worship pleases!

GALLIARD: That thou art I'll be sworn, or what any man's worship pleases; for let me tell ye Harry, he is capacitated to oblige in any quality: for sir, he's your brokering Jew, your fencing, dancing, and civility-master, your linguist, your anti-quary, your bravo,[4] your pathic,[5] your whore, your pimp, and a thousand more excellencies he has to supply the necessities of the wanting stranger. – Well sirrah – what design now upon Sir Signal and his wise governor; – what do you represent now?

PETRO: A barber, sir.

GALLIARD: And why a barber, good Signior Petro?

PETRO: Oh sir, the sooner to take the heights of their judg-ments; it gives handsome opportunities to commend their faces, for if they are pleased with flattery, the certain sign of a fool is to be most tickled when most commended, I conclude 'em the fitter for my purpose; they already put great confidence in me, will have no masters but of my recommending, all which I supply myself, by the help of my several disguises; by which and my industry, I doubt not but to pick up a good honest painful livelihood, by cheating these two reverend coxcombs.

GALLIARD: How the devil got'st thou this credit with 'em?

PETRO: Oh, easily, sir, as knaves get estates, or fools employ-ments.

FILLAMOUR: I hope amongst all your good qualities you forgot not your more natural one of pimping.

PETRO: No, I assure you sir, I have told Sir Signal Buffoon, that no man lives here without his inamorata:[6] which very word has so fired him, that he's resolved to have an *inamorata* whatever it cost him, and as in all things else I have in that too promised my assistance.

[4]*bravo*: hired assassin [5]*pathic*: rent boy [6]*inamorata*: lady-love

GALLIARD: If you assist him no better than you have done me he may stay long enough for his inamorata.

PETRO: Why faith sir, I lie at my young lady night and day, but she is so loath to part with that same maidenhead of hers yet — but tomorrow night sir there's hopes. —

GALLIARD: Tomorrow night! Oh 'tis an age in love! Desire knows no time but the present: 'tis now I wish, and now I would enjoy, a new day ought to bring a new desire.

PETRO: Alas, sir, I'm but an humble bravo.

GALLIARD: Yes, thou'rt a pimp, yet want'st the art to procure a longing lover the woman he adores, though but a common courtesan. — Oh confound her maidenhead — she understands her trade too well to have that badge of innocence.

PETRO: I offered her her price sir, —

GALLIARD: Double it, give anything, for that's the best receipt I ever found to soften women's hearts.

PETRO: Well sir, she will be this evening in the garden of Medici's Villa, there you may get an opportunity to advance your interest — I must step and trim⁷ Mr Tickletext, and then am at your service. [*Exit* PETRO]

JULIO: What is this knight and his governor, who have the blessed fortune to be managed by this squire?

FILLAMOUR: Certain fools Galliard makes use of when he has a mind to laugh: and whom I never thought worth a visit since I came to Rome: and he's like to profit much by his travels, who keeps company with all the English, especially the fops.

GALLIARD: Faith, sir, I came not abroad to return with the formality of a judge; and these are such antidotes against melancholy as would make thee fond of fooling. — Our knight's father is even the first gentleman of his house, a fellow, who having the good fortune to be much a fool and knave, had the attendant blessing of getting an estate of some eight thousand a year, with this coxcomb to inherit it; who (to aggrandise the name and family of the Buffoons) was made a knight, but to refine throughout and make a complete fop, was sent abroad under the government of one Mr Tickletext, his zealous father's chaplain, as arrant a blockhead as a man would wish

⁷*trim*: fit out

to hear preach: the father wisely foreseeing the eminent danger that young travellers are in of being perverted to Popery.

JULIO: 'Twas well considered.

GALLIARD: But for the young spark, there is no description can reach him; 'tis only to be done by himself; let it suffice 'tis a pert, saucy, conceited animal, whom you shall just now go see and admire, for he lodges in the house with us.

JULIO: With all my heart, I never longed more for a new acquaintance.

FILLAMOUR: And in all probability shall sooner desire to be rid on't. Allons. [*Exeunt*]

SCENE TWO

[*The scene draws off and discovers* MR TICKLETEXT *a-trimming, his hair under a cap, a cloth before him, and* PETRO *snaps his fingers, takes away the basin, and goes to wiping his face.*]

PETRO: Ah che bella! Bella! I swear by these sparkling eyes and these soft plump dimpled cheeks, there's not a *signiora* in all Rome, could she behold 'em, were able to stand their temptations, and for La Silvianetta, my life on't she's your own.

TICKLETEXT: Tace, tace, speak softly! — But honest Barberacho, do I, do I indeed look plump, and young, and fresh and — hah!

PETRO: Aye sir, as the rosy morn, young as old Time in his infancy, and plump as the pale-faced moon.

TICKLETEXT: Hey — Why this travelling must needs improve a man, [*aside*] — why how admirably well-spoken your very barbers are here, — but, Barberacho, did the young gentlewoman say she liked me? Did she, rogue? Did she?

PETRO: A-doated on you signior, doated on you.

TICKLETEXT: [*aside*] Why, and that's strange now, in the autumn of my age too, when nature began to be impertinent, as a man may say, that a young lady should fall in love with me. — Why, Barberacho, I do not conceive any great matter of sin only in visiting a lady that loves a man, hah.

PETRO: Sin sir, 'tis a frequent thing nowadays in persons of your complexion.

TICKLETEXT: Especially here at Rome too, where 'tis no scandal.

PETRO: Aye signior, where the ladies are privileged, and fornication licensed.

TICKLETEXT: Right! And when 'tis licensed 'tis lawful, and when 'tis lawful it can be no sin: besides Barberacho, I may chance to turn her, who knows?

PETRO: Turn her signior, alas any way, which way you please.

TICKLETEXT: Hey, hey, hey! There thou wert knavish, I doubt – but I mean convert her – nothing else I profess, Barberacho.

PETRO: True signior, true, she's a lady of an easy nature, and an indifferent argument well handled will do't – ha – here's your head of hair – [*combing out his hair*] – here's your natural friz! And such an air it gives the face! – So, signior – now you have the utmost my art can do.   [*takes away the cloth, and bows*]

TICKLETEXT: Well, signior: – and where's your looking-glass?

PETRO: My looking-glass?

TICKLETEXT: Yes signior, your looking-glass! An English barber would as soon have forgotten to have snapped his fingers, made his leg,[8] or taken his money, as have neglected his looking-glass.

PETRO: Aye, signior, in your country the laity have so little honesty, they are not to be trusted with the taking off your beard unless you see't done, – but here's a glass, sir.

   [*Gives him the glass.* TICKLETEXT *sets himself and smirks in the glass.* PETRO *standing behind him, making horns and grimaces, which* TICKLETEXT *sees in the glass, gravely rises, turns towards* PETRO.]

TICKLETEXT: Why how now, Barberacho, what monstrous faces are you making there?

PETRO: Ah, my belly, my belly, signior: ah, this wind-colic! this hypocondria does so torment me! Ah –

TICKLETEXT: Alas poor knave; certo, I thought thou hadst been somewhat uncivil with me, I profess I did.

PETRO: Who I sir, uncivil? – I abuse my patrone? – I that have almost made myself a pimp to serve you?

---

[8] *made his leg*: take a bow

TICKLETEXT: Tace, tace, honest Barberacho! No, no, no, all's well, all's well: – but hark ye – you will be discreet and secret in this business now, and above all things conceal the knowledge of this gentlewoman from Sir Signal and Mr Galliard.

PETRO: The rack, signior, the rack shall not extort it.

TICKLETEXT: Hold thy hand – [*gives him money*] there's somewhat for thee, but shall I, rogue – shall I see her tonight? –

PETRO: Tonight, sir, meet me in the Piazza dì Spagna, about ten o'clock, – I'll meet you there, – but 'tis fit, signior – that I should provide a collation,[9] – 'tis the custom here sir. –

TICKLETEXT: Well, well, what will it come to, – here's an angel. –

PETRO: Why sir 'twill come to – about – for you would do't handsomely – some twenty crowns. –

TICKLETEXT: How man, twenty crowns?

PETRO: Aye, signior, thereabouts.

TICKLETEXT: Twenty crowns – Why 'tis a sum, a portion, a revenue.

PETRO: Alas signior, 'tis nothing with her, – she'll look it out in an hour, – ah, such an eye! So sparkling, with an amorous twire[10] – then, sir, – then she'll kiss it out in a moment, – such a lip, so red, so round, and so plump, so soft, and so –

TICKLETEXT: Why has she, has she, sirrah – hah – here, here, prithee take money, here, and make no words on't – go, go your way, go – but to entertain Sir Signal with other matter, pray send his masters to him; if thou can't help him to masters, and me to mistresses, thou shalt be the good genius of us both: but see where he comes. –

   Enter SIR SIGNAL

SIR SIGNAL: Hah! Signior Illustrissimo Barberacho, let me hug thee, my little Miphistophiloucho – d'ye see here, how fine your brokering Jew has made me, Signior Rabbi Manaseth-Ben-Nebiton, and so forth; hah – view me round –   [*turns round*]

TICKLETEXT: I profess 'tis as fit as if it had been made for you.

SIR SIGNAL: Made for me – Why sir, he swore to me by the old law, that 'twas never worn but once, and that but by one High-German Prince – I have forgot his name – for the devil can never remember these damned Hogan-Mogan[11] titles.   [*A fart.*]

[9]*collation*: meal   [10]*twire*: leer   [11]*Hogan-Mogan*: Dutch

TICKLETEXT: No matter, sir.

SIR SIGNAL: Aye, but I should be loath to be in any man's clothes, were he never so high a German prince – except I knew his name though.

TICKLETEXT: Sir, I hold his name unnecessary to be remembered, so long as 'twas a princely pennyworth. – Barberacho get you gone, and send the masters.   [*Exit* PETRO]

SIR SIGNAL: Why how now governor? How now, Signior Tickletext! Prithee how camest thou so transmogrified, ha? Why thou look'st like any new-fledged Cupid.

TICKLETEXT: Do I? Away, you flatter, do I?

SIR SIGNAL: As I hope to breathe, your face shines through your powdered hairs, like you-know-what on a barn-door in a frosty morning.

TICKLETEXT: What a filthy comparison's there for a man of my coat?

SIR SIGNAL: What, angry – corpo di me, I meant no harm, – come, shall's to a bonaroba,[12] where thou shalt part with thy pusilage[13], and that of thy beard together?

TICKLETEXT: How mean you sir, a courtesan, and a Romish courtesan?

SIR SIGNAL: Now my tutor's up, ha, ha, ha, – and ever is when one names a whore; be pacified man, be pacified, I know thou hat'st 'em worse than beads[14] or holy-water.

TICKLETEXT: Away, you are such another knight – but leave this naughty discourse, and prepare for your fencing and civility-masters,[15] who are coming.

SIR SIGNAL: Aye, when, governor, when, oh, how I long for my civility-master, that I may learn to out-compliment all the dull knights and squires in Kent, with a 'Servitore Hulichimo' – 'No Signiora Bellissima, base le mane de vos Signiora scusa mia illustrissimo, caspeto de Bacco',[16] and so I'll run on, hah, governor, hah! won't this be pure?

TICKLETEXT: Notably ingenious, I profess.

SIR SIGNAL: Well I'll send my staffière[17] for him

---

[12]*bonaroba*: loose woman   [13]*pusilage*: insignificance
[14]*beads*: rosary   [15]*civility-masters*: etiquette teachers
[16]*'Servitore Hulichimo . . . Bacco'*: garbled greeting   [17]*staffière*: groom

incontinente.[18] – Hey, Jack-a-caso, what a damned English name is Jack? Let me see – I will call him Giovanni, which is as much as to say John! – Hey Giovanni.

Enter JACK

TICKLETEXT: Sir, by your favour, his English protestant name is John Pepper; and I'll call him by ne'er a Popish name in Christendom.

SIR SIGNAL: I'll call my own man sir, by what name I please sir; and let me tell you, Reverend Mr Tickletext, I scorn to be served by any man whose name has not an -acho or an -oucho, or some Italiano at the end on't – therefore Giovanni Pepperacho is the name by which you shall be distinguished and dignified hereafter.

TICKLETEXT: Sir Signal, Sir Signal, let me tell you, that to call a man out of his name is unwarrantable, for Peter is called Peter, and John John, and I'll not see the poor fellow wronged of his name for ne'er a Giovanni in Rome.

SIR SIGNAL: Sir I tell you that one Italian name is worth any two English names in Europe, and I'll be judged by my civility-master.

TICKLETEXT: Who shall end the dispute, if he be of my opinion?

SIR SIGNAL: Multo voluntiero, which is as much as to say, with all my heart.

JACK: But sir, my grandmother would never own me if I should change the cursen[19] name she gave me with her own hands, an't please your worship.

SIR SIGNAL: Hey bestia! I'll have no more of 'your worship', sirrah, that old English sir-reverence,[20] let me have you call me 'Signior Illustrissimo' or 'Padrona Mea' – or –

TICKLETEXT: Aye, that I like well enough now: – but hold, sure this is one of your masters.

Enter PETRO *dressed like a French fencing-master*

PETRO: Signior Barberacho has sent me to teach you de art of fencing.

SIR SIGNAL: Illustrissimo Signior Monsieur, I am the person who am to learn.

TICKLETEXT: Stay sir stay, – let me ask him some few questions

---

[18]*incontinente*: immediately   [19]*cursen*: Christian   [20]*sir-reverence*: title

first, for sir I have played at back-sword and could have handled ye a weapon as well as any man of my time in the university.

SIR SIGNAL: Say you so Mr Tickletext, and faith, you shall have a bout with him.

[TICKLETEXT *gravely goes to* PETRO]

TICKLETEXT: Hum – hum – Mr Monsieur – pray what are the guards that you like best?

PETRO: Monsieur, eder de quart or de tierce, dey be both French and Italian; den for your parades, degagements, your advancements, your eloignements and retierments:[21] dey be de same.

TICKLETEXT: Cart and horse, what new-found inventions and words have we here, – sir, I would know, whether you like St George's Guard or not.

PETRO: Allons – Monsieur, mettez-vous en guard! Take de flurette.[22]

SIR SIGNAL: Nay, faith and troth, governor, thou shalt have a rubbers[23] with him.

TICKLETEXT: [*smiling, refuses*] Nay, certo, Sir Signal, – and yet you shall prevail; – well, sir, come your ways?

[*takes the flurette*]

PETRO: Set your right foot forward, turn up your hand so – dat be de quart – now turn it dus – and dat be de tierce.

TICKLETEXT: Hocus pocus, hicksius doxius – here be de cart and here be de horse – why, what's all this for, hah sir – and where's your guard all this while?

SIR SIGNAL: Aye sir, where's your guard sir, as my governor says, sir, hah?

TICKLETEXT: Come, come, sir, I must instruct you I see – come your ways sir. –

PETRO: Attendez attendez un peu, – thrust de right hand and de right leg forward together. –

TICKLETEXT: Aye marry sir, that's a good one indeed! What shall become of my head then, sir, what guard have I left for that good Mr Monsieur, hah?

PETRO: Ah morbleu, is not dis for every ting?

TICKLETEXT: No marry is not it, sir, St George's guard is best for the head whilst you live, – as thus sir –

---

[21]fencing terms   [22]*flurette*: flourish   [23]*a rubbers*: a series of games

PETRO: Dat sir, ha ha – dat be de guard for de back-sword.

TICKLETEXT: Back-sword sir, yes, back-sword, what should it be else?

PETRO: And dis be de single-rapier.

TICKLETEXT: Single-rapier with a vengeance, there's a weapon for a gentleman indeed; is all this stir about single-rapier?

PETRO: Single-rapier! What will you have for de gentleman, de cudgel for de gentleman?

TICKLETEXT: No sir, but I would have it for de rascally Frenchman who comes to abuse persons of quality with paltry single-rapier. – Single-rapier! Come sir, come, – put yourself in your cart and your horse as you call it, and I'll show you the difference.

[*Undresses himself till he appears in a ridiculous posture.*]

PETRO: Ah Monsieur, me shall run you two three times through de body, and den you break-a me head, what care I for dat: – [*aside*] Pox on his ignorance.

TICKLETEXT: Oh ho sir, do your worst, sir, do your worst, sir.

[*They put themselves into several guards, and* TICKLETEXT *beats* PETRO *about the stage.*]

Enter GALLIARD, FILLAMOUR *and* JULIO

PETRO: Ah monsieur, monsieur, will you kill-a me?

TICKLETEXT: Ah monsieur where be your carts now and your horse, Mr Monsieur, hah? – And your single-rapier, Mr Monsieur, hah? –

GALLIARD: Why how now Mr Tickletext, what mortal wars are these? Ajax and Ulysses contending for Achilles his armour?[24]

PETRO: [*aside*] If I be not revenged on him, hang me.

SIR SIGNAL: Aye, why who the devil would have taken my governor for so tall a man of hands, but corpo de me Mr Galliard, I have not seen his fellow.

TICKLETEXT: Ah sir, time was, I would have played ye a match at cudgels with e'er a sophister[25] in the college, but verily I have forgotten it, but here's an impudent Frenchman that would have passed single-rapier upon us.

GALLIARD: How, nay a 'my word' then he deserved to be

[24]a reference to the *Iliad*   [25]*sophister*: student

chastised for't – but now all's at peace again; pray know my kinsman, Sir Harry Fillamour.

SIR SIGNAL: Yo baco les manos, Signior Illustrissimo Cavaliero, – and yours, signior, who are multo bien venito.[26]

TICKLETEXT: Oh Lord sir, you take me sir, in such a posture sir, as I protest I have not seen in this many years.

                                    [*dressing himself whilst he talks*]

FILLAMOUR: Exercise is good for health, sir.

GALLIARD: Sir Signal, you are grown a perfect Italian? Well, Mr Tickletext, you will carry him home a most accomplished gentleman I see.

TICKLETEXT: Hum, verily sir though I say it, for a man that never travelled before, I think I have done reasonably well; –I'll tell you, sir – it was by my directions and advice that he brought over with him – two English knives, a thousand of English pins, four pair of Jersey stockings, and as many pair of buckskin gloves.

SIR SIGNAL: Aye sir, for good gloves you know are very scarce commodities in this country.

JULIO: Here sir at Rome, as you say, above all other places.

TICKLETEXT: Certo mere hedging-gloves[27] sir, and the clouterlest[28] seams. –

FILLAMOUR: Very right sir, – and now he talks of Rome, – pray sir give me your opinion of the place – are there not noble buildings here? Rare statues, and admirable fountains?

TICKLETEXT: Your buildings are pretty buildings, but not comparable to our university buildings; your fountains I confess are, pretty springs, – and your statues reasonably well carved – but, sir, they are so ancient they are of no value! Then your churches are the worst that ever I saw – that ever I saw.

GALLIARD: How sir, the churches, why I thought Rome had been famous throughout all Europe for fine churches.

FILLAMOUR: What think you of St Peter's Church sir, is it not a glorious structure?

TICKLETEXT: St Peter's Church sir, you may as well call it St Peter's Hall sir; it has neither pew, pulpit, desk, steeple, nor ring of bells, and call you this a church, sir? No, sir, I'll say that for little England, and a fig for't, for churches, easy pulpits –

---

[26] garbled compliment
[27] *hedging-gloves*: gardening gloves   [28] *clouterlest*: patchiest

SIR SIGNAL: And sleeping pews.

TICKLETEXT: They are as well ordered as any churches in Christendom: and finer rings of bells sir, I am sure were never heard.

JULIO: Oh sir there's much in what you say.

FILLAMOUR: But then sir, your rich altars, and excellent pictures of the greatest masters of the world, your delicate music and voices, make some amends for the other wants.

TICKLETEXT: How sir! Tell me of your rich altars, your gewgaws[29] and trinkets, and Popish fopperies! With a deal of sing-song — when I say, give me sir five hundred close changes rung by a set of good ringers, and I'll not exchange 'em for all the anthems in Europe: and for the pictures sir, they are superstition, idolatrous and flat Popery.

FILLAMOUR: I'll convince you of that error that persuades you harmless pictures are idolatrous.

TICKLETEXT: How sir, how sir, convince me, talk to me of being convinced, and that in favour of Popery! No, sir, by your favour I shall not be convinced, convinced, quoth-a — no sir, fare you well an' you be for convincing, come away Sir Signal, fare you well sir, fare you well — convinced.   [*goes out*]

SIR SIGNAL: Ha, ha, ha, so now is my governor gone in a fustian-fume,[30] well, he is ever thus when one talks of whoring and religion, but come sir, walk in, and I'll undertake my tutor shall beg your pardon and renounce his English ill-bred opinion; nay, his English churches too — all but his own vicarage.

FILLAMOUR: I have better diversion sir, I thank you — come Julio, are you for a walk in the garden of Villa Medici, 'tis hard by? —

JULIO: I'll wait on you —   [*Exeunt* FILLAMOUR *and* JULIO]

SIR SIGNAL: How in the garden of Villa Medici? — But, hark ye, Galliard, will the ladies be there, the courtesans, the bonarobas, the inamoratas, and the bell'ingratas, hah?

GALLIARD: Oh, doubtless sir.   [*Exit* GALLIARD]

SIR SIGNAL: I'll e'en bring my governor thither to beg his pardon, on purpose to get an opportunity to see the fine women; it may be I may get a sight of my new mistress, Donna Silvianetta whom Petro is to bring me acquainted with.   [*Exeunt*]

---

[29]*gewgaws*: gaudy ornaments   [30]*fustian-fume*: bombastic temper

Act Two

SCENE ONE

Enter MOROSINI *and* OCTAVIO

OCTAVIO: By heaven I will not eat, nor sleep, nor pray for anything but swift and sure revenge, till I have found Marcella, that false deceiving beauty, or her lover, my hated rival Fillamour! Who wantons in the arms of the fair fugitive, laughs at my shameful easiness, and cries, these joys were never meant for tame Octavio.

Enter CRAPINE

MOROSINI: How now Crapine! What, no news, no news of my nieces yet, Marcella nor Cornelia?

CRAPINE: None sir.

OCTAVIO: That's wondrous strange, Rome's a place of that general intelligence, methinks thou might'st have news of such trivial things as women, amongst the cardinals' pages; I'll undertake to learn the religion de stato, and present juncture of all affairs in Italy, of a common courtesan.

MOROSINI: Sirrah, sirrah, let it be your care to examine all the nunneries, for my own part not a petticoat shall escape me. –

OCTAVIO: [*aside*] My task shall be for Fillamour.

MOROSINI: I'll only make a visit to your sister, Donna Laura Lucretia, and deliver her a letter from my nephew Julio, and return to you presently. – [*going out, is stayed by* OCTAVIO]

OCTAVIO: Stay sir, defer your visit to my sister Laura, she is not yet to know of my being in town, 'tis therefore I have taken a lodging in an obscure street, and am resolved never to be myself again till I've redeemed my honour. Come, sir, let's walk –

Enter to them as they are going out, MARCELLA *and* CORNELIA, *dressed like courtesans,* PHILIPPA *and attendants.*

MOROSINI: Stay, stay, what women are these?

OCTAVIO: Whores sir, and so 'tis ten to one are all the kind, only these differ from the rest in this, they generously own their trade of sin, which others deal by stealth in: they are courtesans.

[*Exeunt* MOROSINI *and* OCTAVIO]

MARCELLA:

> The evening's soft and calm, as happy lovers thoughts:
> And here are groves where the kind meeting trees
> Will hide us from the amorous gazing crowd.

CORNELIA:

> What should we do there? Sigh till our wandering breath
> Has raised a gentle gale amongst the boughs;
> To whose dull melancholy music, we
> Laid on a bed of moss, and new-fallen leaves,
> Will read the dismal tale of Echo's love!

— No, I can make better use of famous Ovid. (*snatches a little book from her*) And prithee what a pox have we to do with trees, flowers, fountains, or naked statues?

MARCELLA: But prithee mad Cornelia, let's be grave and wise, at least enough to think a little.

CORNELIA: On what? Your English cavalier, Fillamour, of whom you tell so many dull stories of his making love! Oh how I hate a civil whining coxcomb!

MARCELLA: And so do I, I'll therefore think of him no more.

CORNELIA: Good Lord! What a damnable wicked thing is a virgin grown up to woman.

MARCELLA: What, art thou such a fool, to think I love this Fillamour?

CORNELIA: It may be not at Rome, but at Viterbo, where men are scarce, you did; and did you follow him to Rome, to tell him you could love no more?

MARCELLA: A too-forward maid Cornelia, hurts her own fame, and that of all her sex.

CORNELIA: Her sex, a pretty consideration by my youth, an oath I shall not violate this dozen year: my sex should excuse me, if to preserve their fame they expected I should ruin my own quiet: in choosing an ill-favoured husband, such as Octavio before a young handsome lover, such as you say Fillamour is.

MARCELLA: I would fain persuade myself to be of thy mind, — but the world, Cornelia —

CORNELIA: Hang the malicious world –

MARCELLA: And there's such charms in wealth and honour too!

CORNELIA: None half so powerful as love, in my opinion; 'slife sister thou art beautiful, and hast a fortune too, which before I would lay out upon so shameful a purchase as such a bed-fellow for life as Octavio, I would turn arrant keeping courtesan, and buy my better fortune.

MARCELLA: That word too startles me.

CORNELIA: What courtesan, why, 'tis a noble title and has more votaries than religion, there's no merchandise like ours, that of love my sister! – And can you be frighted with the vizor, which you yourself put on?

MARCELLA: 'Twas the only disguise that could secure us from the search of my uncle and Octavio, our brother Julio is by this too arrived, and I know they'll all be diligent – and some honour I was content to sacrifice to my eternal repose.

CORNELIA: Spoke like my sister, a little impertinent honour we may chance to lose, 'tis true, but our downright honesty, I perceive you are resolved we shall maintain through all the dangers of love and gallantry; – though to say truth I find enough to do, to defend my heart against some of those members that nightly serenade us and daily show themselves before our window, gay as young bridegrooms and as full of expectation.

MARCELLA: But is't not wondrous, that amongst all these crowds we should not once see Fillamour; I thought the charms of a fair young courtesan might have obliged him to some curiosity at least.

CORNELIA: Aye! And a English cavalier too, a nation so fond of all new faces.

MARCELLA: Heaven, if I should never see him, and I frequent all public places to meet him; or if he be gone from Rome, if he have forgot me, or some other beauty have employed his thoughts! –

CORNELIA: Why; if all these if's and or's come to pass, we have no more to do than to advance in this same glorious profession, of which now we only seem to be: – in which to give it its due, there are a thousand satisfactions to be found, more than in a dull virtuous life! Oh the world of dark-lantern-men we should have; the serenades, the songs, the sighs, the vows, the presents, the quarrels, and all for a look or a smile, which you have been hitherto so covetous of, that Petro swears our lovers begin to suspect us for some honest jilts; which by some is accounted much the lewder scandal of the two, – therefore I think faith we must e'en be kind a little, to redeem our reputations.

MARCELLA: However we may rally, certainly there's nothing so hard to woman, as to expose herself to villainous man.

CORNELIA: Faith sister, if 'twere but as easy to satisfy the nice scruples of religion, and honour, I should find no great difficulty in the rest, – besides, another argument I have, our money's all gone, and without a miracle can hold out no longer honestly. –

MARCELLA: Then we must sell our jewels!

CORNELIA: When they are gone, what jewel will you part with next?

MARCELLA: Then we must –

CORNELIA: What, go home to Viterbo, ask the old gentleman pardon, and be received to grace again, you to the embraces of the amiable Octavio; and I to St Teresa's, to whistle through a grate like a bird in a cage, – for I shall have little heart to sing: – but come let's leave this sad talk, here's men – let's walk and gain new conquest, I love it dearly –

[*They walk down the garden.*]

Enter GALLIARD, FILLAMOUR *and* JULIO, *and see the women.*

GALLIARD: Women! And by their garb for our purpose too – they're courtesans, let's follow 'em.

FILLAMOUR: What shall we get by gazing but disquiet? If they are fair and honest, we look and perhaps may sigh in vain; if beautiful and loose, they are not worth regarding.

GALLIARD: Dear notional knight, leave your satirical fopperies, and be at least good-humoured, and let's follow 'em.

JULIO: I'll leave you in the pursuit, and take this opportunity to write my uncle word of my arrival, and wait on you here anon.

FILLAMOUR: Prithee do so: hah, who's that with such an equipage?

[*Exit* JULIO, FILLAMOUR *and* GALLIARD *going after.*]

[*Just as she is entering,* MARCELLA *and* CORNELIA *meet* LAURA, *who is dressed like a man, with her equipage.*]

GALLIARD: Pox, let the tradesmen ask, who cringe for such gay customers, and follow us the women!

[*Exit* FILLAMOUR *and* GALLIARD *down the scene,* LAURA
looking after 'em.]

LAURA: 'Tis he, my cavalier, my conqueror: Antonio, let the
coaches wait, – and stand at distance all! Now Silvio, on thy life
forget my sex and quality, forget my useless name of Laura
Lucretia, and call me Count of –

SILVIO: What, madam?

LAURA: Madam! Ah, foolish boy, thy feminine courage will
betray us all: – but – call me Count – Sans Coeur; – and tell me,
Silvio, how is it I appear? How dost thou like my shape – my
face and dress? My mien and equipage, may I not pass for man?
Looks it en prince and masculine?

SILVIO: Now as I live, you look all over what you wish; and
such as will beget a reverence and envy in the men, and passion
in the women. But what's the cause of all this transformation?

LAURA: Love! Love! Dull boy, couldst thou not guess 'twas
love? That dear Englese I must enjoy, my Silvio.

SILVIO: What, he that adores the fair young courtesan?

LAURA:

> That very he; my window joins to hers,
> And 'twas with charms which he'd prepared for her,
> He took this heart,
> Which met the welcome arrows in their flight,
> And saved her from their dangers.
> Oft I've returned the vows he's made to her
> And sent him pleased away;
> When through the errors of the night, and distance,
> He has mistook me for that happy wanton,
> And gave me language of so soft a power,
> As ne'er was breathed in vain to listening maids.

SILVIO: But with permission, madam, how does this change of
petticoat for breeches, and shifting houses too, advance that
love?

LAURA: This habit, besides many opportunities 'twill give me,
of getting into his acquaintance, secures me too from being
known by any of my relations in Rome; then I have changed my
house for one so near to that of Silvianetta's, and so like it too,
that even you and I have oft mistook the entrance; by which
means Love, Fortune, or Chance, may with my industry

contrive some kind mistake that may make me happier than the rest of womankind.

SILVIO: But what shall be reserved then for Count Julio, whose last letters promise his arrival within a day or two, and whom you're then to marry?

LAURA:
Reserved for him! A wife! A wife, my Silvio,
That unconcerned domestic necessary,
Who rarely brings a heart, or takes it soon away. —

SILVIO: But then your brother Count Octavio, do you not fear his jealousy?

LAURA:
Octavio! Oh, nature has set his soul and mine at odds,
And I can know no fear, but where I love.

SILVIO: And then that thing which ladies calls their honour. —

LAURA:
Honour, that hated idol, even by those
That set it up to worship: no,
I have a soul my boy, and that's all love!
And I'll the talent which heaven lent improve.

[*Going out, meets* MARCELLA *and* CORNELIA *followed by*
GALLIARD *and* FILLAMOUR.]

SILVIO: Here be the courtesans, my lord.

LAURA: Hah, Silvianetta and Euphemia! Pursued too by my cavalier, I'll round the garden, and mix myself amongst 'em.

[*Exit with her train*]

MARCELLA: Prithee sister, let's retire into the grove, to avoid the pursuit of these cavaliers.

CORNELIA: Not I, by these killing eyes! I'll stand my ground were there a thousand, all armed with conquering beauty.

MARCELLA: Hah — now on my conscience yonder's Fillamour!

CORNELIA: Hah! Fillamour!

MARCELLA: My courage fails me at the sight of him — I must retire.

CORNELIA: And I'll to my art of love.

[MARCELLA *retires, and leans against a tree,* CORNELIA
walks about reading.]

GALLIARD: 'Tis she, 'tis Silvianetta! Prithee advance, that thou mayst behold her and renounce all honest women: since in that one young sinner there are charms that would excuse even to thee all frailty.

FILLAMOUR: The forms of angels could not reconcile me to women of her trade.

GALLIARD: This is too happy an opportunity, to be lost in convincing thy singularity, –

[GALLIARD *goes bowing by the side of* CORNELIA. FILLAMOUR *walks about in the scene.*]

GALLIARD: – if creatures so fair and charming as yourself, had any need of prayer, I should believe by your profound attention you were at your evening's devotion.

CORNELIA: That you may find your mistake in the opinion of my charms, pray believe I am so, and ought not to be interrupted.

GALLIARD: I hope a man may have leave to make his devotions by you, at least, without danger or offence.

CORNELIA: I know not that, I have reason to fear your devotion may be ominous, like a blazing star, it comes but seldom, – but ever threatens mischief, – pray heaven, I share not in the calamity.

GALLIARD: Why I confess madam, my fit of zeal does not take me often, but when it does, 'tis very harmless and wondrous hearty. –

CORNELIA: You may begin then, I shall not be so wicked as to disturb your orisons.[31]

GALLIARD: Would I could be well assured of that, for mine's devotion of great necessity, and the blessing I pray infinitely for, concerns me; therefore in Christian charity keep down your eyes, and do not ruin a young man's good intentions, unless they would agree to send kind looks, and save me the expense of prayer.

CORNELIA: Which would be better laid out, you think, upon some other blessing.

GALLIARD: Why, faith, 'tis good to have a little bank upon occasion, though I hope I shall have no great need hereafter, – if the charming Silvianetta be but kind, 'tis all I ask of heaven.

CORNELIA: You're very well acquainted with my name, I find.

GALLIARD:
        Your name! 'Tis all I have to live on!

[31] *orisons*: prayers

Like cheerful birds, 'tis the first tune I sing,
To welcome in the day:
The groves repeat it, and the fountains purl it,
And every pretty sound that fills my ear,
Turns all to Silvianetta.

[FILLAMOUR *looks awhile on* MARCELLA.]

FILLAMOUR: Galliard, look there – look on that lovely woman;
'tis Marcella! The beautiful Marcella!

[*offers to run to her,* GALLIARD *holds him*]

GALLIARD: Hold! Marcella! Where?

PAGE: That lady there! Didst ever see her equal?

GALLIARD: – Why faith as you say Harry, that lady is beautiful
–and, make us thankful – kind, why 'tis Euphemia sir, the very
courtesan I would have showed you. –

FILLAMOUR: Forebear, I am not fit for mirth.

GALLIARD: Nor I in humour to make you merry; I tell ye –
yonder woman – is a courtesan.

FILLAMOUR: Do not profane, nor rob heaven of a saint.

GALLIARD: Nor you rob mankind of such a blessing, by giving
it to heaven before its time. – I tell thee 'tis a whore! A fine
desirable expensive whore.

FILLAMOUR: By heaven it cannot be! I'll speak to her, and call
her my Marcella, and undeceive thy lewd opinion.

[*offers to go,* GALLIARD *holds him back*]

GALLIARD: Do, salute her in good company for an honest
woman – do and spoil her markets: – 'twill be a pretty civil
spiteful compliment, and no doubt well taken; – come I'll
convince ye, sir. (*goes and pulls* PHILIPPA] – Hark ye thou
kind helpmeet for man – thou gentle child of night – what is the
price of a night or two of pleasure with yonder lady –
Euphemia, I mean, that Roman courtesan –

FILLAMOUR: Oh heavens! A courtesan!

PHILIPPA: Sure you're a great stranger in Rome, that cannot
tell her price.

GALLIARD: I am so – name it, prithee, here's a young English
purchaser – come forward, man, and cheapen for yourself. –

[*pulls him*]

PHILIPPA: [*flings away*] Oh, spare your pains, she wants no
customers. –

FILLAMOUR:
>No no, it cannot, must not be, Marcella!
>She has too much divinity about her,
>Not to defend her from all imputation,
>Scandal would die to hear her name pronounced.

PHILIPPA: Believe me, madam, he knows you not, I overheard all he said to that cavalier, and find he's much in love!

MARCELLA: Not know me, and in love! Punish him heaven for falsehood! But I'll contribute to deceive him on, and ruin him with perjury.

FILLAMOUR: I am not yet convinced, I'll try her farther. [*goes to her bowing*] – But, madam, is that heavenly beauty purchasable? I'll pay a heart, rich with such wounds, and flames –

GALLIARD: Not forgetting the money too good lad, or your wounds and flames will be of little use.

>[GALLIARD *goes to* CORNELIA]

MARCELLA: He tells you truth, sir, we are not like the ladies of your country, who tire out their men with loving upon the square, heart for heart, till it becomes as dull as matrimony, to women of our profession there's no rhetoric like ready money, nor billet-doux[32] like bill of exchange.[33]

FILLAMOUR: Oh! That heaven should make two persons so resembling, and yet such different souls. [*looks on her*]
>– 'Sdeath, how she darts me through with every look,
>But if she speak she heals the wound again.

Enter OCTAVIO, *with followers*

OCTAVIO: Hah, my rival Fillamour here! Fall on – draw sir, – and say, I gave you one advantage more and fought thee fairly.

>[*Draws on* FILLAMOUR, *who fights him out; the ladies run off:* GALLIARD *falls on the followers, with whom whilst he is engaged, enters* JULIO, *draws and assists him, and* LAURA *at the same time on the other side.*]

Enter PETRO *dressed like a civility-master:* SIR SIGNAL *and* TICKLETEXT. SIR SIGNAL *climbs a tree,* TICKLETEXT *runs his head into a bush, and lies on his hands and knees,* PETRO *assists* GALLIARD *and fights out the bravos.* PETRO *re-enters*

LAURA: Hah, my cavalier engaged amongst the slaves.

PETRO: My ladies' lovers! And set upon by Octavio! We must be

[32]*billet-doux*: love letter   [33]*bill of exchange*: note of money

diligent in our affairs! Sir Signal, where are ye! Signior Tickletext! – I hope they have not miscarried in the fray.

SIR SIGNAL: Oh vos servitor, vos signiora.

[comes down from the tree]

PETRO: No, the fool has wit enough to keep out of harm's way – *[Sees* TICKLETEXT *in a bush, pulls him out by the heels.]* Oh very discreetly done, signior. –

SIR SIGNAL: Why how now governor, what, afraid of swords?

TICKLETEXT: No sir, I am not afraid of swords, but I am afraid of danger.

Enter GALLIARD *embracing* LAURA; *after 'em,* JULIO *and* FILLAMOUR. FILLAMOUR *looks about.*

GALLIARD: This bravery, sir, was wondrous!

LAURA: 'Twas only justice sir, you being oppressed with odds.

FILLAMOUR: She's gone! She's gone in triumph with my soul.

JULIO: What was the matter sir, how came this mischief?

FILLAMOUR: Oh easily sir; I did but look, and infinitely loved!

JULIO: And therefore were you drawn upon, or was it some old pique?

FILLAMOUR:
   I know not sir, oh tell me not of quarrels.
   The woman, friend, the woman has undone me.

GALLIARD: Oh a blessed hearing! I'm glad of the reformation sir, you were so squeamish forsooth, that a whore would not down with ye! No, 'twould spoil your reputation. –

FILLAMOUR: A whore! Would I could be convinced she were so, 'twould call my virtue home, and make me man again!

GALLIARD: Thou liest – thou'rt as weak a brother as the best of us, and believe me Harry, these sort of damsels are like witches, if they once get hold of a man, he's their own till the charm be ended; you guess what that is, sir?

FILLAMOUR: Oh, Frank, hadst thou then felt how tenderly she pressed my hand in hers; as if she would have kept it there forever, it would have made thee mad, stark mad in love! *[aside]* – and nothing but Marcella could have charmed me.

GALLIARD: Aye gad, I'll warrant thee, – well, thou shalt this night enjoy her.

FILLAMOUR: How!

GALLIARD: How, why faith Harry, e'en the old way, I know no other. Why thou shalt lie with her, man! Come let's to her.

FILLAMOUR: Away, let's follow her instantly.
[*Going out is stopped by* SIR SIGNAL. *Enter* SIR SIGNAL,
    TICKLETEXT, PETRO.]
SIR SIGNAL: Signior, I have brought Mr Tickletext, to beg your
pardon – sir.
FILLAMOUR: I've other business, sir.   [*goes out*]
GALLIARD: Come let's follow him, and you my generous
cavalier, must give me leave to beg the honour of your
friendship.
LAURA: My inclinations sir, have given you more – pray let me
wait on you to your lodgings, lest a farther insolence should be
offered you.
GALLIARD: Sir, you oblige too fast.   [*they go out*]
SIR SIGNAL: Ah che diavilo ails these hot-brained fellows, sure
they're drunk.
PETRO: On fie signior, drunk, for a man of quality – 'tis
intolerable.
SIR SIGNAL: Aye: why how so, Signior Morigoroso?
PETRO: Imbriaco had made it a fine speech indeed.
SIR SIGNAL: Why, faith, and so it had, as thus, – 'ah che diavilo
ails, these hot-brained fellows, sure they are imbriaco, – now
would not I be drunk for a thousand crowns: imbriaco sounds
cinquante per cent better. – Come noble signior, let's andiamo a
casa, which is as much as to say, let's amble home. –
TICKLETEXT: In troth, wondrous expert – certo signior, he's an
apt scholar.
SIR SIGNAL: Ah sir, you shall see, when I come to my
civilities. –
PETRO: Where the first lesson you shall learn, is, how to give
and how to receive, with a bone grâce.
TICKLETEXT: That receiving lesson I will learn myself.
PETRO: This unfrequented part of the garden, signior, will fit
our purpose as well as your lodgings, – first then – signiors,
your address –
    [*Puts himself in the middle.* PETRO *bows on both sides, they
        do the like.*]
    – Very well! That's at the approach of any person of quality;
after which you must take out your snuff-box.
SIR SIGNAL: Snuff-box: why, we take no snuff signior.
PETRO: Then sir, by all means you must learn: for besides the

mode and gravity of it, it inviveates the pericranium! That is, sapientates the brain, – that is, inspires wit, thought, invention, understanding, and the like – you conceive me signiors –

[*bowing*]

SIR SIGNAL: Most profoundly, signior. – [*bowing*]

PETRO: – Then, signiors, it keeps you in confidence, and countenance! And whilst you gravely seem to take a snush,[34] you gain time to answer to the purpose, and in a politic posture – as thus – to any intricate question.

TICKLETEXT: Hum – certo, I like that well; and 'twere admirable if a man were allowed to take it when he's out in's sermon.

PETRO: Doubtless signior you might, it helps the memory better than rosemary, therefore I have brought each of you a snuffbox.

SIR SIGNAL: By no means: excuse me signior.

[*refuses to take 'em*]

PETRO: Ah, bagatelles signior, bagatelles, and now signiors, I'll teach you how to take it, with a handsome grace, signior your hand; – and yours signior. [*Lays snuff on their hands.*] – So now draw your hand to, and fro under your noses, and snuff it hard up: – excellent well.

[*They daub all their noses, make grimaces, and sneeze.*]

SIR SIGNAL: Methinks signior, this snuff stinks most damnably: pray, what scent do you call this?

PETRO: Cackamarda Orangate, a rare perfume I'll assure ye, sir.

SIR SIGNAL: Cackamarda Orangate, and 'twere not for the name of Cackamarda, and so forth, a man had as good have a sir-reverence at his nose. [*sneezes often and cries out*] Bonprovache!

PETRO: Bonprovache – signior, you do not understand it yet, bonprovache.

SIR SIGNAL: Why sir 'tis impossible to endure this same Cackamarda; why asafoetida[35] is odoriferous to it. [*sneezing*]

PETRO: 'Tis your right dulce piquante, believe me: – but come signiors, wipe your noses and proceed to your giving lesson.

SIR SIGNAL: As how signior?

PETRO: Why – present me with something – that – diamond on your finger! To show the manner of giving handsomely,

[34] *snush*: a pinch of snuff   [35] *asafoetida*: ill-smelling gum resin

[SIR SIGNAL *gives it him*] – Oh fie, signior – between your finger and thumb – thus – with your other fingers at a distance – with a speech, and a bow. –

SIR SIGNAL: Illustrissimo Signior, the manifold obligations, –

PETRO: Now a fine turn of your hand – thus – oh that sets off the present, and makes it sparkle in the eyes of the receiver. –

SIR SIGNAL: [*turns his hand*] – which you have heaped upon me, –

PETRO: There flourish again.

SIR SIGNAL: [*flourishes*] – oblige me to beg your acceptance of this small present, which will receive a double lustre from your fair hand. [*gives it him*]

PETRO: Now kiss your fingers ends, and retire back with a bow.

TICKLETEXT: Most admirably performed.

SIR SIGNAL: Nay sir I have docity[36] in me, though I say't: come governor, let's see how you can out-do me in the art of presenting.

TICKLETEXT: Well, sir, come, your snuff-box will serve instead of my ring, will it not?

PETRO: By no means sir, there is such a certain relation between a finger and a ring, that no present becomes either the giving or the receiving half so well.

SIR SIGNAL: Why 'twill be restored again, 'tis but to practise by.

PETRO: Aye signor, the next thing you are to learn is to receive.

TICKLETEXT: Most worthy signior, I have so exhausted the cornucopia of your favours [*flourishes*] – and tasted so plenteously of the fullness of your bounteous liberality, that to retaliate with this small gem – is but to offer a spark, where I have received a beam of superabundant sunshine. – [*gives it*]

SIR SIGNAL: Most rhetorically performed, as I hope to breathe, tropes and figures[37] all over.

TICKLETEXT: Oh Lord, Sir Signal.

PETRO: Excellent – now let's see if you can refuse as civilly as you gave, which is by an obstinate denial; stand both together.

---

[36]*docity*: gumption   [37]*tropes and figures*: figures of speech

— Illustrious signiors, upon my honour my little merit has not entitled me to the glory of so splendid an offering; trophies worthy to be laid only at your magnanimous feet.

SIR SIGNAL: Ah signior, no, no.

PETRO: Signior Tickletext.

> [*He offers, they refuse going backward.*]

TICKLETEXT: Nay certo signior.

PETRO: With what confidence can I receive so rich a present: Signior Tickletext, ah — Signior —

SIR SIGNAL: I vow, signior — [*still going backwards*] — I'm ashamed you should offer it.

TICKLETEXT: [*following* SIR SIGNAL *backwards*] In verity, so am I.

PETRO: Pardio! Bacchus, most incomparable. —

TICKLETEXT: But when signior are we to learn to receive again? —

PETRO: Oh sir that's always a lesson of itself: — but now signiors, I'll teach you how to act a story.

SIR SIGNAL: How! How signior, to act a story?

PETRO: Aye, sir, no matter for words or sense, so the body perform its part well.

SIR SIGNAL: How, tell a story without words, why, this were an excellent device for Mr Tickletext, when he's to hold forth to the congregation, and has lost his sermon-notes — why this is wonderful. —

PETRO: Oh sir, I have taught it men born deaf and blind: — look ye, stand close together, and observe — [*gets between them*] — closer yet. A certain Ecclesiastico, [*makes a sign of being fat*] plump and rich — [*galloping about the stage*] riding along the road, — meets a paver strapiao — un pavero strapiao, paure strapiao: [*puts himself into the posture of a lean beggar, his hands right down by his sides — and picks both their pockets*] — strapiao — strapiao — strapiao — elemosuna per un paure strapiao, par a moure de dievos — at last he begs a julio — [*makes the fat bishop*] neinte — [*lean*] the paure strapiao begs a mezo julio — [*fat*] neinte — [*lean*] une bacio — [*fat*] neinte — at last he begs his blessing — and see how willingly the Ecclesiastico gave his benediction — [*opening his arms, hits them both in the face*] — scusa, scusa mea, patronas —   [*begs their pardons*]

SIR SIGNAL: Yes, very willingly, which by the way he had never done had it been worth a farthing.

TICKLETEXT: Marry I would he had been a little sparing of that too at this time – [*sneezes*] a shame on't, it has stirred this same Cackamarda again most foully.

PETRO: Your pardon signior; – but come Sir Signal – let's see how you will make this silent relation – come stand between us two –

SIR SIGNAL: Nay, let me alone for a memory – come.

PETRO: I think I have revenged my backsword-beating.

[*goes off*]

SIR SIGNAL: Un paureo strapado – plump and rich, – no, no, the Ecclesiastico meet un paureo strapado – and begs a julio.

TICKLETEXT: Oh no sir, the strapado begs the julio.

SIR SIGNAL: Aye, aye, and the Ecclesiastico cries niente – [*snaps his nail*] un meze julio! – niente – un bacio, niente, your blessing then Signior Ecclesiastico.

[*Spreads out his arms to give his blessing – and hits* TICKLETEXT.]

TICKLETEXT: Odds me, you are all a little too liberal of this same benediction.

SIR SIGNAL: Hah – but where's Signior Morigoroso? What, is he gone? – but now I think on't, 'tis a point of good manners to go without taking leave.

TICKLETEXT: It may be so, but I wish I had my ring again, I do not like the giving lesson without the taking one, why this is picking a man's pocket certo.

SIR SIGNAL: Not so governor, for then I had had a considerable loss: look ye here, – how – how [*feeling in his pocket*] – how – [*in another*] – how – gone? Gone as I live! My money, governor! All the gold Barberacho received of my merchant today – all gone. –

TICKLETEXT: Hah – and mine – [*aside*] all my stock, the money which I thought to have made a present to the gentlewoman, Barberacho was to bring me to – Undone, undone – villians, cutpurses – cheats, oh run after him.

SIR SIGNAL: A pox of all silent stories: rogue, thief – undone.

[*Exeunt*]

Act Three

SCENE ONE

Enter JULIO *and his* PAGE

JULIO: How! The lady whom I followed from St Peter's Church a courtesan?

PAGE: A courtesan my lord, fair as the morning, and as young.

JULIO: I know she's fair and young, but is she to be had boy?

PAGE: My lord, she is – her footman told me, she was a zittella.

JULIO: How a zittella! – A virgin, 'tis impossible.

PAGE: I cannot swear it sir, but so he told me; he said she had a world of lovers: her name is Silvianetta sir, and her lodgings –

JULIO: I know't, are on the Corso; a courtesan! And a zittella too? A pretty contradiction! But I'll bate her the last, so I might enjoy her as the first; whate'er the price be, I'm resolved upon the adventure; and will this minute prepare myself –

[going off]

Enter MOROSINI *and* OCTAVIO

JULIO: – hah, does the light deceive me, or is that indeed my uncle, in earnest conference with a cavalier: – 'tis he – I'll step aside till he's past, lest he hinders this night's diversion.

[goes aside]

MOROSINI: I say 'twas rashly done, to fight him unexamined.

OCTAVIO: I need not ask, my reason has informed me, and I'm convinced, wheree'er he has concealed her, that she is fled with Fillamour.

JULIO: *[aside]* Who is't they speak of?

MOROSINI: Well well, sure my ancestors committed some horrid crime against nature, that she sent this pest of woman-kind into our family, – two nieces for my share, – by heaven, a proportion sufficient to undo six generations.

JULIO: *[aside]* Hah! Two nieces, what of them?

MOROSINI: I am like to give a blessed account of 'em to their brother Julio my nephew, at his return, there's a new plague now, – but my comfort is I shall be mad and there's an end on't.

                                                      [*weeps*]

JULIO: [*aside*] My curiosity must be satisfied. – Have patience noble sir, –

MOROSINI: Patience is a flatterer sir, – and an ass sir, and I'll have none on't – hah, what art thou?

JULIO: Has five or six years made ye lose the remembrance of your nephew – Julio?

MOROSINI: Julio! Would I had met thee going to thy grave.

                                                      [*weeps*]

JULIO: Why so, sir?

MOROSINI: Your sisters sir, your sisters are both gone.–[*weeps*]

JULIO: How gone, sir?

MOROSINI: Run away sir, flown, sir.

JULIO: Heavens! Which way?

MOROSINI: Nay, who can tell the ways of fickle women, – in short sir, your sister Marcella was to have been married to this noble gentleman, – nay was contracted to him, fairly contracted in my own chapel, but no sooner was his back turned, – but in a pernicious moonlight night she shows me a fair pair of heels, with the young baggage your other sister Cornelia, who was just come from the monastery where I bred her, to see her sister married.

JULIO: A curse upon the sex, why must man's honour depend upon their frailty. – Come –

    Give me but any light which way they went,
    And I will trace 'em with that careful vengeance –

OCTAVIO:

    Spoke like a man, that understands his honour,
    And I can guess how we may find the fugitives.

JULIO: Oh name it quickly, sir!

OCTAVIO:

    There was a young cavalier – some time at Viterbo,
    Who I confess had charms heaven has denied to me,
    That trifle beauty, which was made to please
    Vain foolish woman, which the brave and wise
    Want leisure to design. –

JULIO: And what of him!

OCTAVIO:
> This fine gay thing came in your sister's way,
> And made that conquest nature meant such fools for:
> And, sir, she's fled with him.

JULIO:
> Oh, show me the man, the daring hardy villain,
> Bring me but in the view of my revenge, –
> And if I fail to take it,
> Brand me with everlasting infamy.

OCTAVIO: That we must leave to Fortune, and our industry, –
come sir, let's walk and think best what to do. –
>>>>>>>>>>>>>>>>>>>>>>>>>>> [*going down the stage*]

Enter FILLAMOUR *and* GALLIARD

FILLAMOUR: Is not that Julio? – Boy, run and call him back.
>>>>>>>>>>>>>>>>>> [*Exit boy, re-enters with* JULIO]

JULIO: Oh, Fillamour, I've heard such killing news since last I
left thee.

FILLAMOUR: What, prithee?

JULIO:
> I had a sister, friend – dear as my life,
> And bred with all the virtues of her sex;
> No vestals at the holy fire employed themselves
> In innocenter business than this virgin;
> Till love, the fatal fever of her heart,
> Betrayed her harmless hours:
> And just upon the point of being married,
> The thief stole in, and robbed us of this treasure:
> She's left her husband, parents, and her honour,
> And's fled with the base ruiner of her virtue.

FILLAMOUR: And lives the villain durst affront ye this?

JULIO: He does!

GALLIARD: Where, in what distant world?

JULIO: I know not.

FILLAMOUR: What is he called?

JULIO:
> I know not neither, – some god direct me to the ravisher!
> And if he 'scape my rage!
> May cowards point me out for one of their tame herd.

FILLAMOUR: In all your quarrels I must join my sword.

GALLIARD: And if you want, – here's another sir, – that though
it be not often drawn in anger, nor cares to be, shall not be idle
in good company.

JULIO: I thank you both, and if I have occasion, will borrow
their assistance, but I must leave you for a minute, I'll wait on
you anon. –   [*They all three walk as down the street, talking.*]
   Enter LAURA, *with her Equipage*

LAURA:
> Beyond my wish, I'm got into his friendship,
> But oh how distant friendship is from love!
> That's all bestowed on the fair prostitute!
> – Ah Silvio, when he took me in his arms,
> Pressing my willing bosom to his breast,
> Kissing my cheek, calling me lovely youth,
> And wondering how such beauty, and such bravery,
> Met in a man so young! Ah, then, my boy!
> Then in that happy minute,
> How near was I to telling all my soul,
> My blushes and my sighs, were all prepared,
> My eyes cast down, my trembling lips just parting, –
> But still as I was ready to begin,
> He cries out 'Silvianetta'!
> And to prevent mine, tells me all his love! –
> But see – he's here. –
>   [FILLAMOUR *and* GALLIARD *coming up the scene*]

GALLIARD: Come, lay by all sullen unresolves! For now the
hour of the berger[38] approaches, night, that was made for
lovers! – Hah! My dear Sans-Coeur? My life! My soul! My joy!
Thou art of my opinion!

LAURA: I'm sure I am whate'er it be.

GALLIARD: Why my friend here, and I, have sent and paid our
fine for a small tenement of pleasure, and I'm for taking present
possession; – but hold – if you should be a rival after all. –

LAURA:
> Not in your Silvianetta! My love has a nice appetite,
> And must be fed with high uncommon delicates.
> I have a mistress sir, of quality;

---

[38]*berger*: shepherd's or lover's hour

Fair! As imagination paints young angels!
Wanton and gay as was the first Corinna,
That charmed our best of poets,
Young as the spring, and cheerful as the birds
That welcome in the day!
Witty as fancy makes the revelling gods,
And equally as bounteous when she blesses!

GALLIARD: Ah for a fine young whore, with all these charms!
But that same quality allays the joy, there's such a damned ado
with the obligation, that half the pleasure's lost in ceremony.
— Here for a thousand crowns I reign alone,
Revel all day in love without control.
— But come, to our business, I have given order for music, dark
lanterns, and pistols.

[*All this while* FILLAMOUR *stands studying.*]

FILLAMOUR: [*pausing aside*] Death, if it should not be
Marcella now!

GALLIARD: Prithee no more considering, — resolve and let's
about it.

FILLAMOUR:
I would not tempt my heart again! For love
Whate'er it may be in another's breast,
In mine, 'twill turn to a religious fire!
And so to burn for her! A common mistress,
Would be an infamy below her practice!

GALLIARD: Oh, if that be all, doubt not Harry, but an hour's
conversation with Euphemia will convert it to as lewd a flame
as a man would wish.

LAURA: What a coil's here about a courtesan! What ado to
persuade a man to a blessing all Rome is languishing for in vain!
— Come sir, we must deal with him, as physicians do with
peevish children, force him to take what will cure him.

FILLAMOUR: And like those damned physicians, kill me for
want of method; no, I know my own distemper best, and your
applications will make me mad.

GALLIARD: Pox on't, that one cannot love a woman like a man,
but one must love like an ass.

LAURA: 'Sheart, I'll be bound to lie with all the women in Rome,
with less ado than you are brought to one.

GALLIARD: Hear ye that Henry, 'sdeath, art not ashamed to be instructed by one so young! – But see

   MARCELLA *and* CORNELIA *enter above*

GALLIARD: – the star there appears, – the star that conducts thee to the shore of bliss. – She comes, let's feel thy heart, she comes!

So breaks the day on the glad eastern hills!
Or the bright god of rays from Thetis'[39] lap: –
A rapture now dear lad, and then fall to, for thou art old dog at a long grace.

FILLAMOUR: [*aside*] Now I'm mere man again, with all his frailties – Bright lovely creature! –

GALLIARD: Damn it, how like my lady's eldest son was that.

FILLAMOUR: May I hope my sacrifice may be accepted by you? – [*aside*] By heaven it must be she! Still she appears more like.

MARCELLA:
I've only time to tell you night approaches,
And then I will expect you.

   Enter CRAPINE, *gazing on the ladies*

CRAPINE: 'Tis she, Donna Marcella on my life, with the young wild Cornelia! – Hah – yonder's the English cavalier too; nay then, by this hand I'll be paid for all my fruitless jaunts: for this good news – stay let me mark the house. –

MARCELLA: Now to my disguise.   [*Exit* MARCELLA]

GALLIARD: And have you no kind message to send to my heart; cannot this good example instruct you how to make me happy?

CORNELIA: Faith stranger, I must consider first, she's skilled in the merchandise of hearts, and has dealt in love with so good success hitherto, she may lose one venture, and never miss it in her stock, but this is my first, and should it prove to be a bad bargain, I were undone for ever.

GALLIARD: I dare secure the goods sound –

CORNELIA: And I believe will not lie long upon my hands.

GALLIARD: Faith, that's according as you'll dispose on't madam – for let me tell you – gad, a good handsome

---

[39] *Thetis*: sea nymph

proper fellow, is as staple a commodity as any's in the nation, — but I would be reserved for your own use! Faith take a sample tonight, and as you like it, the whole piece, and that's fair and honest dealing I think, or the devil's in't.

CORNELIA: Ah stranger, — you have been so over-liberal of those same samples of yours, that I doubt they have spoiled the sale of the rest, — could you not afford think ye, to throw in a little love and constancy; to inch out that want of honesty of yours.

GALLIARD:
Love! Oh in abudance!
By those dear eyes, by that soft smiling mouth;
By every secret grace thou hast about thee,
I love thee with a vigorous, eager passion,
— Be kind, dear Silvianetta — prithee do,
Say you believe, and make me blessed tonight.

CRAPINE: [*aside*] Silvianette! so, that's the name she has rifled for Cornelia, I perceive.

CORNELIA: If I should be so kind-hearted! What good use would you make of so obliging an opportunity?

GALLIARD: That which the happy night was first ordained for.

CORNELIA: Well signior 'tis coming on, and then I'll try what courage the darkness will inspire me with: — till then — farewell. —

GALLIARD: Till then a thousand times adieu. —
[*blowing up kisses to her*]

PHILIPPA: Ah madam we're undone, — yonder's Crapine, your uncle's valet.

CORNELIA: Now a curse on him; shall we not have one night with our cavaliers — let's retire, and continue to outwit him, or never more pretend to't. — Adieu, Signior Cavalier — remember night. —

GALLIARD: Or may I lose my sense to all eternity.
[*Kisses his fingers and bows, she returns it for a while. Exit* CRAPINE.]

LAURA: [*aside*]
Gods, that all this that looks at least like love,
Should be dispensed to one insensible!
Whilst every syllable of that dear value,
Whispered on me, would make my soul all ecstacy.

[*to* GALLIARD]– Oh, spare that treasure for a grateful purchase;
       And buy that common ware with trading gold,
       Love is too rich a price: – [*aside*] I shall betray myself. –

GALLIARD:
       Away, that's an heretical opinion and which
       This certain reason must convince thee of;
       That love is love, wherever beauty is,
       Nor can the name of whore make beauty less.
     Enter MARCELLA *like a man, with a cloak about her.*

MARCELLA: Signior, is your name Fillamour?

FILLAMOUR: It is, what would you, sir? –

MARCELLA: I have a letter for you – from Viterbo, and your
Marcella, sir.   [*gives it him*]

FILLAMOUR:
       Hah – Viterbo! – And Marcella!
       It shocks me like the ghost of some forsaken mistress,
       That met me in the way to happiness,
       With some new longed-for beauty!   [*opens it, reads*]

MARCELLA: [*aside*] Now I shall try thy virtue, and my fate.

FILLAMOUR: What is't that checks the joy, that should surprise
me at the receipt of this!

GALLIARD: How now! What's the cold fit coming on?

FILLAMOUR: [*pauses*]
       I have no power to go – where this – invites me –
       By which I prove,
       'tis no increase of flame that warms my heart,
       But a new fire just kindled from those – eyes –
       Whose rays I find more piercing than Marcella's.

GALLIARD: – Aye gad, a thousand times – prithee, what's the
matter?

MARCELLA: [*aside*] Oh this false-souled man – would I had
leisure to be revenged for this inconstancy!

FILLAMOUR: – But still she wants that virtue I admire.

GALLIARD: Virtue! 'Sdeath thou art always fumbling upon that
dull string that makes no music: – what letter's that?   [*reads*]
       If the first confession I ever made of love be grateful to
         you, come armed tonight with a friend or two; and
         behind the garden of the fountains, you will receive –
       hah, *Marcella!*

– Oh damn it, from your honest woman! – Well, I see the devil's never so busy with a man, as when he has resolved upon any goodness! 'Sdeath, what a rub's here in a fair cast, – how is't man? Allegrementa! Bear up, defy him and all his works.

FILLAMOUR:
But I have sworn, sworn that I loved Marcella;
And honour, friend, obliged me to go,
Take her away and marry her,
– And I conjure thee to assist me too.

GALLIARD: What, tonight, this might, that I have given to Silvianetta! And you have promised to the fair – Euphemia!

LAURA: [*aside*] If he should go, he ruins my design, – nay if your word sir – be already past –

FILLAMOUR: 'Tis true, I gave my promise to Euphemia! But that to women of her trade, is easily absolved.

GALLIARD: Men keep not oaths for the sakes of the wise magistrates to whom they're made, but their own honour Harry: and is't not much a greater crime to rob a gallant, hospitable man of his niece, who has treated you with confidence, and friendship, than to keep touch with a well-meaning whore, my conscientious friend?

LAURA: Infinite degrees sir.

GALLIARD: Besides, thou'st an hour or two good, between this and the time required to meet Marcella.

LAURA: Which an industrious lover would manage to the best advantage.

GALLIARD: That were not given over to virtue, and constancy – two of the best excuses I know for idleness.

FILLAMOUR: – Yes – I may see this woman.

GALLIARD: Why God-a-mercy lad.

FILLAMOUR: – And break my chains, – if possible.

GALLIARD: Thou wilt give a good essay to that I'll warrant thee, before she part with thee! Come let's about it.

[*They are going out on either side of* FILLAMOUR *persuading him.*]

MARCELLA: [*aside*]
He's gone! The courtesan has got the day,
Vice has the start of virtue, every way,
And for one blessing honest wives obtain,

The happier mistress does a thousand gain!
I'll home – and practise, all their art to prove,
That nothing is so cheaply gained as love!   [*Exit*]

Enter SIR SIGNAL. TICKLETEXT *with his cloak tied about him, a great inkhorn tied at his girth, and a great folio under his arm:* PETRO *dressed like an antiquary.*

GALLIARD: [*as the others offer to go*] Stay, what farce is this – prithee let's see a little. – How now, Mr Tickletext, what, dressed as if you were going a pilgrimage to Jerusalem?

TICKLETEXT: I make no such profane journeys, sir.

GALLIARD: But where have you been Mr Tickletext?

SIR SIGNAL: Why sir, this most reverend and renowned anti-quary has been showing us monumental rarities and antiquities.

GALLIARD: 'Tis Petro, that – rogue.

FILLAMOUR: But what folio have you gotten there, sir, Knox,[40] or Cartwright?[41]

PETRO: [*aside*] Nay if he be got into that heap of nonsense, I'll steal off and undress.   [*Exit*]

TICKLETEXT: [*opening the book*] A small volume sir, into which I transcribe the most memorable and remarkable transactions of the day.

LAURA: That doubtless must be worth seeing.

FILLAMOUR: [*reads*] April the twentieth, arose a very great storm of wind, thunder, lightning, and rain, – which was a shrewd sign of foul weather. The twenty-second, nine of our twelve chickens getting loose, flew over-board, the other three miraculously escaping, by being eaten by me, that morning for breakfast.

SIR SIGNAL: Harkee Galliard – thou art my friend, and 'tis not like a man of honour to conceal anything from one's friend, – know then I am the most fortunate rascal that ever broke bread, – I am this night to visit sirrah – the finest, the most delicious young harlot, mum – under the rose – in all Rome! Of Barberacho's acquaintance.

GALLIARD: [*aside*] – Hah – my woman, on my life! And will she be kind?

SIR SIGNAL: Kind! Hang kindness, man, I'm resolved upon conquest by parly or by force.

[40]*John Knox*: Scottish religious reformer
[41]*Thomas Cartwright*: Puritan divine

GALLIARD: Spoke like a Roman of the first race, when noble rapes not whining courtship, did the lover's business.

SIR SIGNAL: 'Pshaw rapes man! I mean by force of money, pure dint of gold, faith and troth: for I have given five hundred crowns entrance already, and par dios Bacchus 'tis tropo caro — tropo caro, Mr Galliard.

GALLIARD: And what's this high-prized lady's name sir?

SIR SIGNAL: La Silvianetta, — and lodges on the Corso,[42] not far from St James's of the Incurables — very well situated in case of disaster — hah —

GALLIARD: Very well, — and did not your wide worship know this Silvianetta was my mistress?

SIR SIGNAL: How! His mistress! What a damned noddy[43] was I to name her! [aside]

GALLIARD: D'ye hear fool! Renounce me this woman instantly, or I'll first discover it to your governor, and then cut your throat sir.

SILVIO: Oh, doucement — dear Galliard — renounce her, — corpo de mi that I will soul and body, if she belong to thee man. —

GALLIARD: No more — look to't, — look you forget her name — or but to think of her — farewell —   [nods at him]

SIR SIGNAL: Farewell, quoth ye — 'tis well I had the art of dissembling after all, here had been a sweet broil upon the coast else. —

FILLAMOUR: Very well, I'll trouble myself to read no more, since I know you'll be so kind to the world to make it public?

TICKLETEXT: At my return sir, for the good of the nation, I will print it, and I think it will deserve it.

LAURA: This is a precious rogue, to make a tutor of.

FILLAMOUR: Yet these mooncalfs[44] dare pretend to the breeding of our youth, and the time will come, I fear, when none shall be reputed to travel like a Man of Quality, who has not the advantage of being imposed upon, by one of these pedantic novices, who instructs the young heir, in what himself is most profoundly ignorant of.

GALLIARD: Come, 'tis dark, and time for our design, — your servant, signiors.   [Exeunt FILLAMOUR and GALLIARD]

[42]Via del Corso, main thoroughfare of Rome
[43]noddy: simpleton   [44]mooncalfs: dolts

LAURA: I'll home, and watch the kind deceiving minute, that
may conduct him by mistake to me.   [*Exit*]
   Enter PETRO, *dressed as Barberacho, just as* TICKLETEXT
    and SIR SIGNAL *are going out.*

SIR SIGNAL: Oh Barberacho, we are undone! Oh, the diavilo
take that master you sent me?

PETRO: Master, what master?

SIR SIGNAL: Why Signior Morigoroso!

PETRO: Mor-oso – what should he be?

SIR SIGNAL: A civility-master he should have been, to have
taught us good manners, – but the cornuto cheated us most
damnably, and by a willing mistake taught us nothing in the
world but wit.

PETRO: Oh abominable knavery! Why what a kind of man was
he? –

SIR SIGNAL: – Why – much such another as yourself. –

TICKLETEXT: Higher, signior, higher!

SIR SIGNAL: Aye somewhat higher – but just of his pitch.

PETRO: Well sir, and what of this man?

SIR SIGNAL: Only picked our pockets, that's all.

TICKLETEXT: Yes, and cozened us of our rings.

SIR SIGNAL: Aye, and gave us Cackamarda Orangata for snuff.

TICKLETEXT: And his blessing to boot when he had done.

SIR SIGNAL: A vengeance on't, I feel it still.

PETRO: Why this 'tis to do things of your own heads; for I sent
no such Signior Moroso – but I'll see what I can do to retrieve
'm – I am now a little in haste, farewell. –   [*offers to go*]

TICKLETEXT: [*going out by* PETRO *and jogging him*] Remember to meet me – farewell, Barberacho.   [*goes out*]

SIR SIGNAL: [*pulling* PETRO] Barberacho – is the lady ready?

PETRO: Is your money ready?

SIR SIGNAL: [*aside*] Why now, though I am threatened, and
killed, and beaten, and kicked about, this intrigue I must
advance. – But dost think there's no danger?

PETRO: What, in a delicate young amorous lady, signior?

SIR SIGNAL: No, no, mum, I don't much fear the lady; but this
same mad fellow Galliard, I hear, has a kind of a hankering
after her – [*aside*] Now dare not I tell him what a discovery I
have made.

PETRO: Let me alone to secure you, meet me in the Piazza dì Spagna, as soon as you can get yourself in order; – [*aside*] where the two fools shall meet, and prevent either's coming.

SĪR SIGNAL: Enough, – here's a bill for five hundred crowns more upon my merchant, you know him by a good token, I lost the last sum you received for me, a pox of that handsel,[45] away here's company. [*Exit* PETRO. *Enter* OCTAVIO *and* CRAPINE.]

SIR SIGNAL: Now will I disguise myself, according to the mode of the Roman inamoratos; and deliver myself upon the place appointed. [*Exit*]

OCTAVIO: On the Corso didst thou see 'em?

CRAPINE: On the Corso, my lord, in discourse with three cavaliers, one of which has given me many a pistole, to let him into the garden a-nights at Viterbo, to talk with Donna Marcella, from her chamber window, I think I should remember him.

OCTAVIO: [*aside*] Oh, that thought fires me with anger fit for my revenge. – And they are to serenade 'em, thou say'st?

CRAPINE: I did my lord! And if you can have patience till they come, you will find your rival in this very place, if he keep his word.

OCTAVIO: I do believe thee, and have prepared my bravos to attack him: if I can act but my revenge tonight, how shall I worship Fortune! Keep out of sight, and when I give the word be ready all. I hear some coming, let's walk off a little. –

Enter MARCELLA *in man's clothes, and* PHILIPPA *as a woman, with a lantern.*

[OCTAVIO *and* CRAPINE *go off the other way.*]

MARCELLA: Thou canst never convince me, but if Crapine saw us, and gazed so long upon us, he must know us too, and then what hinders but by a diligent watch about the house, they will surprise us, ere we have secured ourselves from 'em.

PHILIPPA: And how will this exposing yourself to danger prevent 'em?

MARCELLA: My design now is, to prevent Fillamour's coming into danger, by hindering his approach to this house: I would preserve the kind ingrate with any hazard of my own: and 'tis

---

[45] *handsel*: deal

better to die than fall into the hands of Octavio. – I'm desperate with that thought, – and fear no danger! However be you ready at the door, and when I ring admit me. – Ha – who comes here?

Enter TICKLETEXT *with a periwig and cravat of* SIR SIGNAL'S. *A sword by his side, and a dark lantern:* PHILIPPA *opens hers, looks on him and goes out.*

TICKLETEXT: A man! Now am I though an old sinner, as timorous as a young thief, 'tis a great inconvenience in these Popish countries, that a man cannot have liberty to steal to a wench without danger; not that I need fear who sees me except Galliard, who suspecting my business, will go near to think I am wickedly inclined, Sir Signal I have left hard at his study, and Sir Henry is no nocturnal inamorato, unless like me he dissemble it. – Well certo 'tis a wonderful pleasure to deceive the world: and as a learned man well observed, that the sin of wenching lay in the habit only: I having laid that aside, Timothy Tickletext, principle Holder-forth of the Covent Garden Conventicle, Chaplain of Buffoon Hall in the County of Kent, is free to recreate himself.

Enter GALLIARD *with a dark lantern*

GALLIARD: Where the devil is this Fillamour? And the music? Which way could he go to lose me thus? (*looks towards the door*] – He is not yet come. –

TICKLETEXT: Not yet come, – that must be Barberacho! – Where are ye honest Barberacho, where are ye?

                                        [*groping towards* GALLIARD]

GALLIARD: [*aside*] Hah! Barberacho? That name I am sure is used by none but Sir Signal and his coxcomb tutor, it must be one of those. – Where are ye signior, where are ye? [*Goes towards him, and opens the lantern – and shuts it straightaway.*] – [*aside*] Oh, 'tis the knight, – are you there, signior?

TICKLETEXT: Oh, art thou come, honest rascal – conduct me quickly, conduct me to the beautiful and fair Silvianetta.

                                                [*gives him his hand*]

GALLIARD: Yes, when your dogship's damned. Silvianetta! 'Sdeath, is she a whore for fools?   [*draws*]

TICKLETEXT: Hah, Mr Galliard, as the devil would have it: – I'm undone if he sees me.   [*he retires hastily*]

GALLIARD: [*groping for him*] Where are you, fop? Buffoon! Knight!

[TICKLETEXT *retiring hastily runs against* OCTAVIO, *who is just entering, almost beats him down.*
OCTAVIO *strikes him a good blow, beats him back and draws.*
TICKLETEXT *gets close up in a corner of the stage.*
OCTAVIO *gropes for him, as* GALLIARD *does, and both meet and fight with each other.*]

GALLIARD: — What, dare you draw, — you have the impudence to be valiant then in the dark. [*they pass*]

GALLIARD: I would not kill the rogue, — 'sdeath, you can fight then, when there's a woman in the case!

OCTAVIO: [*aside*] I hope 'tis Fillamour! — You'll find I can, and possibly may spoil your making love tonight.

GALLIARD: Egad sweetheart and that may be, one civil thrust will do't: — and 'twere a damned rude thing to disappoint so fine a woman, — therefore I'll withdraw whilst I'm well.

[*he slips out*]

Enter SIR SIGNAL, *with a masquerading coat over his clothes, without a wig or cravat, with a dark lantern.*

SIR SIGNAL: Well, I have most neatly escaped my tutor; and in this disguise defy the devil to claim his own, — Ah, caspeto de diavilo! — What's that?

[*Advancing softly, and groping with his hands, meets the point of* OCTAVIO'S *sword, as he is groping for* GALLIARD.]

OCTAVIO: Traitor, darest thou not stand my sword?

SIR SIGNAL: Hah! Swords! No, signior — scusa mea signior, —

[SIR SIGNAL *hops to the door: and feeling for his way with his outstretched arms, runs his lantern in* JULIO'S *face who is just entering; finds he's opposed with a good push backward, and slips aside into a corner over against* TICKLETEXT. JULIO *meets* OCTAVIO *and fights him.* OCTAVIO *falls.* JULIO *opens his lantern, and sees his mistake.*]

JULIO: Is it you sir?

OCTAVIO: Julio! From what mistake grew all this violence?

JULIO: That I should ask of you, who meet you armed against me.

OCTAVIO: I find the night has equally deceived us; and you are fitly come! To share with me the hopes of dear revenge!

[*gropes for his lantern, which is dropped*]

JULIO:
>I'd rather have pursued my kinder passion,
>Love! And desire! That brought me forth tonight.

OCTAVIO: I've learnt where my false rival is to be this evening, and if you'll join your sword, you'll find it well employed.

JULIO: Lead on, I'm as impatient of revenge as you. –

OCTAVIO: Come this way then, you'll find more aids to serve us.   [*they go out*]

TICKLETEXT: – So! Thanks be praised all's still again, this fright were enough to mortify any lover of less magnanimity than myself. – Well of all sins, this itch of whoring is the most hardy, – the most impudent in repulses, the most vigilant in watching, most patient in waiting, most frequent in dangers: in all disasters but disappointment, a philosopher! Yet if Barberacho come not quickly, my philosophy will be put to't, *certo*.

>[*All this while* SIR SIGNAL *is venturing from his post, listening, and slowly advancing towards the middle of the stage.*]

SIR SIGNAL: The coast is once more clear, and I may venture my carcase forth again, – though such a salutation as the last, would make me very unfit for the matter in hand. – The batoon[46] I could bear with the fortitude and courage of a hero: but these dangerous sharps[47] I never loved; what different rencounters have I met withal tonight, *corpo de me*; a man may more safely pass the Gulf of Lyons, than convoy himself into a bawdy-house in Rome; but I hope all's past, and I will say with Alexander: – Vivat Esperance en despetto del Fato.
>   [*advances a little*]

TICKLETEXT: Sure I heard a noise, – no 'twas only my surmise!
>[*They both advance softly, meeting just in the middle of the stage, and coming close up to each other. Both cautiously start back, and stand on tiptoe in the posture of fear; then gently feeling for each other (after listening and hearing no noise) draw back their hands at touching each other's; and shrinking up their shoulders, make grimaces of more fear.*]

TICKLETEXT: Que equesto.

SIR SIGNAL: Hah a man's voice! [*aside*] – I'll try if I can fright

---

[46]*batoon*: truncheon   [47]*sharps*: cheats

him hence. [*in a horrible voice*] – Una maladette spirito incarnate.

TICKLETEXT: [*aside*] Hah, spirito incarnate! That devil's voice I should know.

SIR SIGNAL: [*in the same tone*] See, signior! *Una Spirito*, which is to say, *un spiratalo, immortallo, incorporallo, inanimate, immateriale, philosophicale*, invisible – unintelligible – diavilo!

TICKLETEXT: Aye, aye, 'tis my hopeful pupil! Upon the same design with me, my life on't, – cunning young whore-master! – I'll cool your courage – good Signior Diavilo! If you be the diavilo, I have una certaina immateriale invisible conjuratione, that will so neatly lay your inanimate unintelligible diavilo-ship –   [*pulls out his wooden sword*]

SIR SIGNAL: How! He must needs be valiant indeed that dares fight with the devil. [*Endeavours to get away.* TICKLETEXT *beats him about the stage.*] – Ah signior, signior sia! Ah – caspeto de Bacchus – hey cornuto, I am a damned silly devil that have no dexterity in vanishing.

[SIR SIGNAL *gropes about and finds the door – going out, meets just entering* FILLAMOUR, GALLIARD *with all the musicians – he retires, and stands close.*]

SIR SIGNAL: – Hah, – what have we here, new mischief? – [TICKLETEXT *and he stands against each other, on either side of the stage.*]

FILLAMOUR: Prithee how came we to lose ye?

GALLIARD: I thought I had followed ye, – but 'tis well we are met again. Come tune your pipes, –   [MUSICIANS *play a little*] *Enter* MARCELLA *dressed as before*

MARCELLA: This must be he.   [*goes up to them*]

GALLIARD: Come come, your song boy, your song.

SONG
Crudo Amore, crudo Amore,
Il mio core non fa per te
Soffrir non vo tormenti
Senza mai sperar merce
Beltà che sia tiranna,
Beltà che sia tiranna

Dal mio offerto recetto non è
Il tuo rigor s'inganna
Se le pene
Le catene
Tenta avolgere al mio piè
Sì sì cruedel' Amore,
Il mio core non fa per te

Lusinghiero, lusinghiero,
Piu non credo alta tua fè
L'incendio del tuo foco
Nel mio core piu vivo non è
Beltà che li diè luoco
Beltà che li diè luoco
Ma il rigor l'ardore sbande
Io non sato tuo gioco
Ch' il veleno
Del mio seno
Vergoroso fallito se n'e
Sì sì crudel Amore,
Il mio core non fa per te.

Whilst this is being sung, enter OCTAVIO, JULIO, CRAPINE, *and bravos*

OCTAVIO: 'Tis they we look for, draw and be ready. –

TICKLETEXT: [*aside*] Hah, draw – then there's no safety here, *certo.*

[OCTAVIO, JULIO *and their party draw, and fight with* FILLAMORE *and* GALLIARD. MARCELLA *engages on their side; all fight, the musicians confusedly amongst them:* GALLIARD *loses his sword, and in the hurry gets a bass viol, and happens to strike* TICKLETEXT *, who is getting away – his head breaks its way quite through, and it hangs about his neck; the fighting moves offstage.*]

Enter PETRO *with a lantern.* SIR SIGNAL *stands close still*

TICKLETEXT: Oh undone, undone, where am I, where am I?

PETRO: Hah – that's the voice of my amorous Ananias, – or I am mistaken – what the devil's the matter? [*Opens his lantern*] – Where are ye, sir? – Hah, cuts so – what new-found pillory have we here?

TICKLETEXT: Oh honest Barberacho, undo me, undo me quickly.

PETRO: So I design sir, as fast as I can – or lose my aim – there sir, there: all's well – I have set you free, come follow me the back way, into the house.   [*Exit* PETRO *and* TICKLETEXT]

    Enter FILLAMOUR *and* MARCELLA, *with their swords drawn,* GALLIARD *following.*

GALLIARD: A plague upon 'em, what a quarter's here for a wench, as if there were no more i'th' nation, – would I'd my sword again.   [*gropes for it*]

MARCELLA: Which way shall I direct him to be safer? – How is it sir? I hope you are not hurt.

FILLAMOUR: Not that I feel, what art thou ask'st so kindly?

MARCELLA: A servant to the Roman courtesan, who sent me forth to wait your coming sir, but finding you in danger shared it with you. – Come let me lead you into safety sir –

FILLAMOUR: Thou'st been too kind to give me cause to doubt thee.

MARCELLA: Follow me sir, this key will give us entrance through the garden.   [*Exeunt*]

    Enter OCTAVIO *with his sword in his hand*

OCTAVIO: Oh! What damned luck had I so poorly to be vanquished. When all is hushed, I know he will return, – therefore I'll fix me here, till I become a furious statue – but I'll reach his heart.

SIR SIGNAL: Oh lamentivolo fato – what bloody villains these Popish Italians are!

    Enter JULIO

OCTAVIO: Hah – I hear one coming this way – hah – the door opens too, – and he makes toward it – pray heaven he be the right: for this I'm sure's the house? – Now luck, an't be thy will, –   [*follows* JULIO *towards the door softly*]

JULIO:

    The rogues are fled but how secure I know not, –
    And I'll pursue my first design of love,
    And if this Silvianetta will be kind. –

    Enter LAURA *from the house in a night-gown*

LAURA: Whist – who is't names Silvianetta?

JULIO: A lover, and her slave –

LAURA: Oh is it you, – and are you escaped unhurt? Come to my
bosom – and be safe forever. –   [*she takes him by the hand*]

JULIO: 'Tis love that calls, and now revenge must stay. – This
hour is thine, fond boy, the next that is my own I'll give to
anger. –

OCTAVIO: Oh ye pernicious pair, – I'll quickly change the scene
of love into a rougher and more unexpected entertainment.

    [*She leads* JULIO *in.* – OCTAVIO *follows close, they shut the
door upon 'em.* SIR SIGNAL *thrusts out his head to
hearken, hears nobody and advances.*]

SIR SIGNAL: Sure the devil reigns tonight, would I were
sheltered and let him rain fire and brimstone, for pass the streets
I dare not – this should be the house – of hereabouts I'm sure
'tis. – Hah – what's this – a string – of a bell I hope – I'll try to
enter; and if I am mistaken 'tis but crying 'con licentia.' [*rings*]

    Enter PHILIPPA

PHILIPPA: Who's there?

SIR SIGNAL: 'Tis I, 'tis I, let me in quickly. –

PHILIPPA: Who – the English cavalier?

SIR SIGNAL: The same – I am right – I see I was expected.

PHILIPPA: I'm glad you're come, – give me your hand. –

SIR SIGNAL: I am fortunate at last, – and therefore will say with
the famous poet.

    – No happiness like that achieved with danger,
    Which once o'ercome – I'll lie at rack and manger.

                            [*Exeunt*]

Act Four

SCENE ONE

Enter FILLAMOUR *and* GALLIARD *as in Silvianetta's apartment*

FILLAMOUR:
>How splendidly these common women live,
>How rich is all we meet with in this palace;
>And rather seems th' apartment of some prince,
>Than a receptacle for lust and shame.

GALLIARD: You see Harry, all the keeping fools are not in our dominions; but this grave, this wise people, are mistress-ridden too.

FILLAMOUR: I fear we have mistook the house, and the youth that brought us in may have deceived us, on some other design, however whilst I've this – [*draws his sword*] – I cannot fear.

GALLIARD: A good caution, and I'll stand upon my guard with this – [*pulls a pistol out of his pocket*] – but see – here's one will put us out of doubt.

FILLAMOUR: Hah! The fair enchantress.

Enter MARCELLA *richly and loosely dressed*

MARCELLA:
>What, on your guard, my lovely cavalier!
>Lies there a danger in this face and eyes,
>That needs that rough resistance?
>– Hide, hide that mark of anger from my sight,
>And if thou wouldst be absolute conquerer here,
>Put on soft looks, with eyes all languishing,
>Words tender, gentle sighs, and kind desires.

GALLIARD: Death! With that unconcern he hears all this? Art thou possessed – pox why dost not answer her?

MARCELLA: [*aside*]
>I hope he will not yield – He stand unmoved –

Surely I was mistaken in this face,
And I believe in charms that have no power.
GALLIARD: 'Sdeath, thou deservest not such a noble creature, –
[*aside*] – I'll have 'em both myself.
FILLAMOUR: [*pausingly*]
– Yes, thou hast wondrous power,
And I have felt it long.
MARCELLA: How!
FILLAMOUR:
– I've often seen that face – but 'twas in dreams:
And sleeping loved extremely!
And waking – sighed to find it but a dream,
The lovely phantom vanished with my slumbers,
But left a strong idea on my heart;
Of what I find in perfect beauty here,
– But with this difference, she was virtuous too!
MARCELLA: What silly she was that!
FILLAMOUR: She whom I dreamed I loved.
MARCELLA:
You only dreamt that she was virtuous too!
Virtue itself's a dream of so slight force,
The very fluttering of love's wings destroys it,
Ambition, or the meaner hope of interest, wakes it to
      nothing,
In men a feeble beauty shakes the dull slumber off. –
GALLIARD: Egad, she argues like an angel, Harry!
FILLAMOUR:
– What haste thou'st made, to damn thyself so young!
Hast thou been long thus wicked?
Hast thou sinned past repentance,
Heaven may do much, to save so fair a criminal,
Turn yet and be forgiven!
GALLIARD: What a pox dost thou mean by all this canting?
MARCELLA:
A very pretty sermon, and from a priest so gay,
It cannot choose but edify.
Do holy men of your religion signior, wear all this habit,
Are they thus young, and lovely? Sure if they are,
Your congregation's all composed of ladies,
The laity must come abroad for mistresses.

FILLAMOUR: Oh that this charming woman were but honest!

GALLIARD: 'Twere better thou wert damned; honest! Pox, thou dost come out with things so mal-à-propos –

MARCELLA:
> Come leave this mask of foolish modesty,
> And let us haste where love and music calls;
> Music! That heightens love! And makes the soul
> Ready for soft impressions!

GALLIARD: So, she will do his business with a vengeance!

FILLAMOUR:
> Plague of this tempting woman, she will ruin me:
> I find weak virtue melt from round my heart,
> To give her tyrant image a possession:
> So the warm sun thaws rivers icy tops,
> Till in the stream he sees his own bright face!

GALLIARD: Now he comes on apace, – how is't my friend? Thou stand'st as thou'dst forgot thy business here! – The woman Harry! The fair courtesan! Canst thou withstand her charms? I've business of my own, prithee fall to – and talk of love to her.

FILLAMOUR:
> Oh I could talk eternity away,
> In nothing else but love! – Couldst thou be honest?

MARCELLA:
> Honest! Was it for that you sent two thousand crowns.
> Or did believe that trifling sum sufficient,
> To buy me to the slavery of honesty?

GILLIARD Hold there my brave virago.

FILLAMOUR:
> No, I would sacrifice a nobler fortune,
> To buy thy virtue home!

MARCELLA: What should it idling there?

FILLAMOUR:
> Why – make thee constant to some happy man,
> That would adore thee for't.

MARCELLA:
> Unconscionable! Constant at my years?
> – Oh 'twere to cheat a thousand!
> Who between this and my dull age of constancy
> Expect the distribution of my beauty.

GALLIARD: [*aside*] 'Tis a brave wench –
FILLAMOUR:
> Yet charming as thou art, the time will come
> When all that beauty, like declining flowers,
> Will wither on the stalk, – but with this difference,
> The next kind spring brings youth to flowers again,
> But faded beauty never more can bloom.
>   –If interest make thee wicked, I can supply thy pride. –

MARCELLA:
> Curse on your necessary trash! – Which I despise
> But as 'tis useful to advance our love!

FILLAMOUR:
> Is love thy business? Who is there born so high,
> But love and beauty equals,
> And thou mayst choose from all the wishing world?
> This wealth together would enrich one man,
> Which dealt to all would scarce be charity.

MARCELLA:
> Together! 'Tis a mass would ransom kings!
> Was all this beauty given for one poor petty conquest;
> – I might have made a hundred hearts my slaves,
> In this lost time of bringing one to reason.
> – Farewell, thou dull philosopher in love;
> When age has made me wise, – I'll send for you again.
>   [*offers to go,* GALLIARD *holds her*]
GALLIARD: By this good light a noble glorious whore.
FILLAMOUR:
> Oh, stay, – I must not let such beauty fall,
> – A whore – consider yet the charms of reputation:
> The ease, the quiet and content of innocence,
> The awful reverence all good men will pay thee,
> Who as thou art will gaze without respect,
> – And cry – 'What pity 'tis she is – a whore –'

MARCELLA:
> Oh you may give it what coarse name you please;
> But all this youth and beauty ne'er was given,
> Like gold to misers, to be kept from use.   [*going out*]
FILLAMOUR: Lost, lost – past all redemption.
GALLIARD: Nay, gad, thou shalt not lose her so, – I'll fetch her
  back, and thou shalt ask her pardon.   [*runs out after her*]

FILLAMOUR:

> By heaven, 'twas all a dream! An airy dream!
> The visionary pleasure disappears, – and I'm myself again,
> – I'll fly before the drowsy fit o'ertake me.   [*going out*]

Enter GALLIARD *and then* MARCELLA

GALLIARD:

> Turn back – she yields, she yields to pardon thee.
> – Gone! – Nay, hang me if ye part.
>
>> [*runs after him, his pistol still in his hand*]

MARCELLA: Gone! I have no leisure now for more dissembling.
>> [*takes the candle, and goes in*]

Enter PETRO, *leading in* TICKLETEXT, *as by dark*

PETRO: Remain here signior, whilst I step and fetch a light.

TICKLETEXT: Do so, do so honest Barberacho! – Well, my escape even now from Sir Signal was miraculous, thanks to my prudence and prowess! Had he discovered me, my dominion had ended; and my authority been of none effect, certo.

>> [PHILIPPA *at the door puts in* SIR SIGNAL]

PHILIPPA: Now signior you're out of danger, I'll fetch a candle, and let my lady know of your being here!   [*Exit* PHILIPPA]

> [SIR SIGNAL *advances a little. Enter* PETRO *with a light, goes between 'em and starts.*]

TICKLETEXT: Sir Signal! –

SIR SIGNAL: My governor!

PETRO: The two fools met! A pox of all ill luck: now shall I lose my credit with both my wise patrons: my knight I could have put off with a small harlot of my own, but my levite[48] having seen my Lady Cornelia, that is La Silvianetta, – none but that Susanna would satisfy his eldership:[49] but now they both saved me the labour of a farther invention to dispatch 'em.

SIR SIGNAL: I perceive my governor's as much confounded as myself; – I'll take advantage by the forelock, be very impudent and put it upon him faith, – Ah governor, will you never leave your whoring! Never be staid, sober and discreet, as I am.

TICKLETEXT: So, so, undone, undone! Just my documents to him. –   [*walks about,* SIR SIGNAL *follows*]

SIR SIGNAL: And must I neglect my precious studies, to follow you, in pure zeal and tender care of your person! Will you never

---

[48]*levite*: clergyman
[49]Biblical tale of Susanna and the Elders (The Apocrypha)

consider where you are? In a lewd Papish country! Amongst the Romish heathens, – and for you, a governor, a tutor, a director of unbridled youth, a gownman,⁵⁰ a politician, for you I say, to be taken at this unrighteous time of the night, in a flaunting cavaliero dress, an unlawful weapon by your side, going the high way to Satan, to a courtesan! And to a Romish courtesan! Oh abomination, oh scandalum infinitum!

TICKLETEXT: Paid in my own coin!

PETRO: So, I'll leave the devil to rebuke sin, and to my young lady, for a little of her assistance, in the management of this affair.   [*Exit*]

TICKLETEXT: – I do confess, – I grant ye I am in the house of a courtesan, and that I came to visit a courtesan, and do intend to visit each night a several courtesan: – till I have finished my work. –

SIR SIGNAL: Every night one! Oh glutton!

TICKLETEXT: My great work of conversion, – upon the whole nation, generation, and vocation of this wicked provoking sort of womankind: called courtesans: – I will turn 'em – yes I will turn 'em, – for 'tis a shame that man should bow down to those that worship idols! And now I think sir, I have sufficiently explained the business in hand, – as honest Barberacho is my witness! – And for you – to – scandalise – me – with so naughty an interpretation – afflicteth me wonderfully. –
                        [*pulls out his handkerchief, and weeps*]

SIR SIGNAL: – Alas poor Mr Tickletext, now as I hope to be saved it grieves my heart to see thee weep; – faith and troth now, I thought thou hadst some carnal assignation; – but ne'er stir: I beg thy pardon, and think thee as innocent as myself, that I do – but see the lady's here – 'slife dry your eyes, man!

    Enter CORNELIA, PHILIPPA *and* PETRO

CORNELIA: I could beat thee for being thus mistaken, – and am resolved to flatter him into some mischief, to be revenged on 'em for this disappointment; go you, and watch for my cavalier the while.

TICKLETEXT: Is she come? – Nay then turn me loose to her. –

CORNELIA: [*addressing* SIR SIGNAL] My cavalier!
                        [TICKLETEXT *pulls him by, and speaks*]

TICKLETEXT: – Lady –

    ⁵⁰*gownman*: university student

SIR SIGNAL: You sir, why who the devil made you a cavalier, – most Potentissima Signiora, I am the man of title, by name Sir Signal Buffoon, sole son and heir to eight thousand pound a year. –

TICKLETEXT: Oh sir, are you the man she looks for?

SIR SIGNAL: I sir, no sir, I'd have ye know sir, I scorn any woman be she never so fair, unless her design be honest and honourable!

CORNELIA: The man of all the world I've chosen out, from all the wits and beauties I have seen, – [*aside*] – to have most finely beaten.

SIR SIGNAL: How! In love with me already, – [*aside*] – she's damnable handsome too, now would my tutor were hanged a little for an hour or two, out of the way.

CORNELIA:
Why fly you not into my arms, [*she approaching, he shunning*]
These arms that were designed for soft embraces?

SIR SIGNAL: Aye, and if my tutor were not here, the devil take him that would hinder 'em – and I think that's civil egad.

TICKLETEXT: [*aside to* PETRO] Why, how now Barberacho, what am I cozened then, and is Sir Signal the man in favour?

PETRO: Lord signior, that so wise a man as you cannot perceive her meaning; – [*aside*] – for the devil take me if I can. – Why this is done to take off all suspicion from you – and lay it on him; – don't you conceive it signior?

TICKLETEXT: Yes honest rogue, – Oh the witty wag-tail, – I have a part to play too, that shall confirm it – young gentlewoman. –

CORNELIA:
Ah, Bell' Ingrato, is't thus you recompense my suffering love?
To fly this beauty so adored by all,
That slights the ready conquest of the world
To trust a heart with you.
–Ah – traditor crudele.

SIR SIGNAL: Poor heart, it goes to the very soul of me to be so coy and scornful to her that it does, but a pox on't her over-fondness will discover all.

TICKLETEXT: Fly, fly, young man, whilst yet thou hast a spark of virtue shining in thee, fly the temptations of this young hypocrite; the love that she pretends with so much zeal and

ardour, is indecent, unwarrantable, and unlawful! First indecent, as she is woman – for thou art woman – and beautiful
woman – yes, very beautiful woman! On whom nature hath
showed her height of excellence in the out-work: but left thee
unfinished, imperfect and impure.

CORNELIA: Heavens, what have we here!

SIR SIGNAL: A pox of my Sir Domine, now is he beside his text,
and will spoil all.

TICKLETEXT: Secondly, unwarrantable; by what authority dost
thou seduce with the allurements of thine eyes, and the
conjurements of thy tongue, the wastings of thy hands, and the
tinklings of thy feet, the young men in the villages?

CORNELIA: Sirrah! How got this madman in? Seize him, and
take him hence.

SIR SIGNAL: Corpo de mi, my governor tickles her notably,
i'faith – but had he let the care of my soul alone tonight, and
have let me taken care of my body, 'twould have been more
material at this time.

TICKLETEXT: Thirdly, unlawful –

CORNELIA: Quite distracted! In pity take him hence, and lead
him into darkness, 'twill suit his madness best.

TICKLETEXT: How, distracted! Take him hence.

PETRO: This was lucky – I knew she would come again – take
him hence – yes, into her bed-chamber – pretty device to get you
to herself, signior.

TICKLETEXT: Why but is it? – Nay then I will facilitate my
departure – therefore I say, – [*beginning to preach again*] – Oh
most beautiful and tempting woman –

CORNELIA:
Away with him, give him clean straw and darkness,
And chain him fast, for fear of further mischief.

PETRO: She means for fear of losing ye. [*going to lead him off*]

TICKLETEXT: Ah baggage! As fast as she will in those pretty
arms.

SIR SIGNAL: Hold, hold man, mad said ye? – Ha, ha, ha – mad!
Why we have a thousand of these in England that go loose
about the streets, and pass with us for as sober discreet religious
persons as a man shall wish to talk nonsense withal.

PETRO: You are mistaken signior, I say he is mad – stark mad.

SIR SIGNAL: Prithee, Barberacho what dost thou mean?

PETRO: To rid him hence that she may be alone with you – 'slife sir, you're madder than he – don't you conceive? –

SIR SIGNAL: Aye, aye! Nay, I confess, Illustrissima Signiora, my governor has a fit that takes him now and then, a kind of frenzy, –a figary – a whimsy – a maggot that bites always at naming of Popery. [*Exit* PETRO *with* TICKLETEXT]

SIR SIGNAL: – So – he's gone. – Bellissima Signiora, – you have most artificially removed him – and this extraordinary proof of your affection is a sign of some small kindness towards me, and though I was something coy and reserved before my governor, Excellentissima Signiora, let me tell you, your love is not cast away.

CORNELIA: Oh sir, you bless too fast! But will you ever love me? –

SIR SIGNAL: Love thee! Aye and lie with thee too, most magnanimous signiora, and beget a whole race of Roman Julius Cæsars upon thee; nay, now we're alone, turn me loose to impudence, i'faith. [*ruffles her*]

Enter PHILIPPA *in haste, shutting the door after her*

PHILIPPA: Oh madam here's the young mad English cavalier got into the house, and will not be denied seeing you.

CORNELIA: This was lucky!

SIR SIGNAL: How the mad English cavalier! If this should be our young Count Galliard now – I were in a sweet taking – oh I know by my fears 'tis he; – oh prithee what kind of a manner of man is he?

PHILIPPA: A handsome – resolute – brave – bold –

SIR SIGNAL: Oh enough enough – madam, I'll take my leave –I see you are – something busy at present, – an' I'll –

CORNELIA: Not for the world, – Philippa – bring in the cavalier – that you may see there's none here fears him signior.

SIR SIGNAL: Oh hold hold, – madam, you are mistaken in that point, for to tell you the truth, I do fear, – having – a certain – aversion of antipathy – to – madam – a gentleman – why, madam they're the very monsters of the nation, they devour every day a virgin. –

CORNELIA: Good heavens! And is he such a fury?

SIR SIGNAL: Oh and the veriest Beelzebub, – besides madam

he vowed my death, if ever he catched me near this house, and he ever keeps his word in cases of this nature, – oh that's he,

                   [*knocking is heard at the door*]

SIR SIGNAL: – I know it by a certain trembling instinct about me, – oh what shall I do? –

CORNELIA: Why – I know not, – can you leap a high window?

SIR SIGNAL: He knocks again, – I protest I am the worst vaulter in Christendom, – have ye no moderate danger – between the two extremes of the window or the mad count? No closet? – Fear has dwindled me to the scantling of a mousehole.

CORNELIA: Let me see, – [*aside*] – I have no leisure to pursue my revenge farther, and will rest satisfied with this, – for this time. – Give me the candle, – and whilst Philippa is conducting the cavalier to the alcove by dark, – you may have an opportunity to slip out, – [*aside*] – perhaps there may be danger in his being seen – farewell, fool –   [*Exit* CORNELIA *with the candle*]

    PHILIPPA *goes to the door, lets in* GALLIARD, *takes him by the hand.*

GALLIARD: Pox on't, my knight's bound for Viterbo, and there's no persuading him into safe harbour again, – he has given me but two hours to dispatch matters here, – and then I'm to embark with him upon this new discovery of honourable love, as he call it, whose adventurers are fools, and the returning cargo, that dead commodity called a wife! A voyage very suitable to my humour, – Who's there? –

PHILIPPA: A slave of Silvianetta, sir give me your hand. –

                      [*Exit over the stage*]
                   [SIR SIGNAL *goes out softly*]

SCENE TWO

The scene changes to a bed-chamber alcove

                [PETRO *leading in* TICKLETEXT]

PETRO: Now signior you're safe and happy in the bed-chamber of your mistress – who will be here immediately, I'm sure. I'll fetch a light and put you to bed in the meantime. –

TICKLETEXT: Not before supper I hope, honest Barberacho.

PETRO: Oh signior that you shall do lying, after the manner of the ancient Romans.

TICKLETEXT: Certo, and that was a marvellous good lazy custom. [*Exit* PETRO]

Enter PHILIPPA *with* GALLIARD *by dark.*

PHILIPPA: My lady will be with you instantly – [*goes out*]

TICKLETEXT: [*advancing forward*] Hah, sure I heard somebody come softly in at the door: I hope 'tis the young gentlewoman.

GALLIARD: [*in a soft tone*]
Silence! And night, Love, and dear opportunity!
Join all your aids to make my Silvia kind,
For I am filled with the expecting bliss,
[TICKLETEXT *thrusts his head out to listen*]
And much delay, or disappointment kills me.

TICKLETEXT: Disappointment kills me, – and me too certo – 'tis she – [*gropes about*]

GALLIARD:
Oh haste my fair, haste to my longing arms, –
Where are you, dear and loveliest of your sex?

TICKLETEXT: That's I, that's I, mi alma! mea core, mea vita!
[*groping and speaking low*]

GALLIARD: Hah – art thou come my life! My soul! My joy! –
[*goes to embrace* TICKLETEXT, *they meet and kiss*]
'Sdeath what's this, a bearded mistress! Lights lights there, quickly lights! Nay curse me if thou 'scapest me.
[TICKLETEXT *struggles to get away, he holds him by the cravat and periwig.*]

Enter PETRO *with a candle*

GALLIARD: Barberacho, – confound him, 'tis the fool! Whom I found this evening about the house, hovering to roost him here! – Hah – what the devil have I caught – a Tartar? Escaped again! The devil's his confederate. –
[PETRO *puts out the candle, comes to* TICKLETEXT, *unties his cravat behind, and he slips his head out of the periwig, and gets away, leaving both in* GALLIARD's *hands.*]

PETRO: Give me your hand, I'll lead you a back-pair of stairs through the garden.

TICKLETEXT: Oh any way to save my reputation – oh –

GALLIARD: Let me but once more grasp thee, and thou shalt find more safety in the devil's clutches! None but my mistress serve ye.

[*Gropes after him.* PETRO *with* TICKLETEXT *running over the stage,* GALLIARD *after 'em, with the cravat and periwig in one hand, his pistol in t'other.*]
Enter PHILIPPA *with a light.*

PHILIPPA: Mercy upon us, what's the matter – [*a pistol goes off*] – what noise is this – hah a pistol – what can this mean?
   Enter SIR SIGNAL *running.*

SIR SIGNAL: Oh save me, gentle devil, save me, the stairs are fortified with cannons and double culverins;[51] I'm pursued by a whole regiment of armed men! Here's gold, gold in abundance! Save me –

PHILIPPA: What cannons? What armed men?

SIR SIGNAL: Finding myself pursued as I was groping my way through the hall, and not being able to find the door, I made towards the stairs again, at the foot of which I was saluted with a great gun – a pox of the courtesy.

GALLIARD: [*offstage*] Where are ye, knight, buffoon, dog[52] or Egypt?[53]

SIR SIGNAL: Thunder and lightning! 'Tis Galliard's voice. –

PHILIPPA: Here, step behind this hanging[54] – there's a chimney which may shelter ye till the storm be over, – if you be not smothered before.   [*puts him behind the arras*]
   Enter GALLIARD *as before, and* CORNELIA *at the other door*

CORNELIA: Heavens! What rude noise is this?

GALLIARD:
   Where have you hid this fool, this lucky fool?
   He whom blind change, and more ill-judging woman
   Has raised to that degree of happiness
   That witty men must sigh and toil in vain for?

CORNELIA: What fool, what happiness?

GALLIARD:
   Cease, cunning false one to excuse thyself,
   See here the trophies of your shameful choice,
   And of my ruin, cruel – fair – deceiver!

CORNELIA: Deceiver sir, of whom – in what despairing minute did I swear to be a constant mistress? – To what dull whining lover did I vow and had the heart to break it?

---

[51]*double culverins*: huge cannons   [52]*dog*: worthless fellow
[53]*Egypt*: gypsy   [54]*hanging*: curtain

GALLIARD: Or if thou hadst, I know of no such dog as would
believe thee: no, thou art false to thy own charms, and hast
betrayed them to the possession of the vilest wretch That ever
Fortune cursed with happiness;
>   False to thy joys, false to thy wit and youth,
>   All which thou'st damned with so much careful industry
>   To an eternal fool,
>   That all the arts of love can ne'er redeem thee!

SIR SIGNAL: Meaning me, meaning me.
>   [*peeping out of the chimney, his face blacked*]

CORNELIA: A fool! What indiscretion have you seen in me,
should make ye think I would choose a witty man for a lover,
who perhaps loves out his month in pure good husbandry, and
in that time does more mischief than a hundred fools; ye
conquer without resistance, ye treat without pity, and triumph
without mercy; and when you are gone, the world cries – she
had not wit enough to keep him, when indeed you are not fool
enough to be kept! Thus we forfeit both our liberties and
discretion with you villanous witty men; for wisdom is but
good success in things, and those that fail are fools!

GALLIARD:
>   Most gloriously disputed!
>   You're grown a Machiavellian in your art.

CORNELIA: Oh necessary maxims only, and the first politics we
learn from observation. – I've known a courtesan grown
infamous, despised, decayed, and ruined, in the possession of
you witty men, who when she had the luck to break her chains,
and cast her net for fools, has lived in state, finer than brides
upon their wedding-day, and more profuse than the young
amorous coxcomb that set her up an idol.

SIR SIGNAL: Well argued of my side, I see the baggage loves me!
>   [*peeping out with a face more smutted*]

GALLIARD:
>   And hast thou! Oh, but prithee jilt me on,
>   And say thou hast not destined all thy charms
>   To such a wicked use;
>   Is that dear face and mouth for slaves to kiss:
>   Shall those bright eyes be gazed upon, and serve
>   But to reflect the images of fools?

SIR SIGNAL: [*peeping, more black*] That's I still.

GALLIARD:

>   Shall that soft tender bosom be approached,
>   By one who wants a soul, to breathe in languishment,
>   At every kiss that presses it?

SIR SIGNAL: Soul, what a pox care I for soul – as long as my person is so amiable.

GALLIARD:

>   No, renounce that dull discretion that undoes thee,
>   Cunning is cheaply to be wise, leave it to those that have
>   No other powers to gain a conquest by,
>   It is below thy charms; –
>   – Come swear, – and be foresworn most damnably,
>   Thou hadst not yielded yet; say 'twas intended only,
>   And though thou liest, by heaven, I must believe thee, –
>   – Say, – hast thou – given him – all?

CORNELIA:

>   I've done as bad, as we have discoursed th' affair,
>   and 'tis concluded on. –

GALLIARD:

>   As bad! by Heaven, much worse! discoursed with him!
>   Art thou so wretched, so deprived of sense,
>   To hold discourse with such an animal?
>   Damn it! The sin is ne'er to be forgiven.
>   – Hadst thou been wanton to that lewd degree,
>   By dark he might have been conducted to thee;
>   Where silently he might have served thy purpose,
>   And thou hast had some poor excuse for that!
>   But bartering words with fools admits of none.

CORNELIA: I grant ye, – had I talked sense to him, – which had been enough to have lost him for ever.

SIR SIGNAL: [*aside*] Poor devil, how fearful 'tis of losing me!

GALLIARD:

>   That's some atonement for thy other sins, –
>   Come break thy word and wash it quite away.

SIR SIGNAL: That cogging⁵⁵ won't do my good friend, that won't do.

---

⁵⁵*cogging*: manipulation

GALLIARD:
>Thou shalt be just and perjured,
>And pay my heart the debt of love you owe it.

CORNELIA: And would you have the heart – to make a whore of me?

GALLIARD: With all my soul, and the devil's in't if I can give thee a greater proof of my passion.

CORNELIA: I rather fear you would debauch me, into that dull slave called a wife.

GALLIARD:
>A wife! Have I no conscience, no honour in me!
>Prithee believe I would not be so wicked, –
>No, – my desires are generous! And noble,
>To set thee up, that glorious insolent thing,
>That makes mankind such slaves! Almighty courtesan!
>– Come! To thy private chamber let us haste,
>The sacred temple of the God of Love;
>And consecrate thy power!   [*offers to bear her off*]

CORNELIA: Stay, do you take me then for what I seem!

GALLIARD: I am sure I do! And would not be mistaken for a kingdom! But if you art not, I can soon mend that fault, and make thee so, – come – I'm impatient to begin the experiment.
>   [*offers again to carry her off*]

CORNELIA: Nay then I am in earnest, – hold, mistaken stranger! – I am of noble birth! And should I in one hapless loving minute, destroy the honour of my house, ruin my youth and beauty! And all that virtuous education, my hoping parents gave me?

GALLIARD: Pretty dissembled pride and innocence! and wounds no less than smiles! – Come let us in, – where I will give thee leave to frown and jilt, such pretty frauds advance the appetite.   [*offers again*]

CORNELIA:
>By all that's good I am a maid of quality!
>Blessed with a fortune equal to my birth!

GALLIARD:
>I do not credit thee; or if I did,
>For once I would dispense with quality,
>And to express my love, take thee with all these faults.

CORNELIA: And being so, can you expect I'll yield?

GALLIARD:
    The sooner for that reason if thou'rt wise;
    The quality will take away the scandal, –
    Do not torment me longer –   [*offers to lead her again*]

CORNELIA: Stay and be undeceived, – I do conjure ye. –

GALLIARD: Art thou no courtesan?

CORNELIA: Not on my life nor do intend to be.

GALLIARD: No prostitute! Nor dost intend to be?

CORNELIA: By all that's good, I only feigned to be so.

GALLIARD:
    No courtesan! Hast thou deceived me then?
    Tell me thou wicked – honest cozening beauty!
    Why didst thou draw me in, with such a fair pretence,
    Why such a tempting preface to invite,
    And the whole piece so useless and unedifying?
    – Heavens! not a courtesan!
    Why from thy window didst thou take my vows,
    And make such kind returns? Oh, damn your quality,
    What honest whore but would have scorned thy cunning?

CORNELIA: I make ye kind returns!

GALLIARD: Persuade me out of that too! 'Twill be like thee!

CORNELIA: By all my wishes I never held discourse with you –
but this evening, since I first saw your face.

GALLIARD: [*in passion*]
    On, the impudence of honesty and quality in woman!
    A plague upon 'em both, they have undone me,
    Bear witness, oh thou gentle queen of night,
    Goddess of shades, adored by lovers most;
    How oft under thy covert she has damned herself,
    With feigned love to me!

CORNELIA: [*angry*] Heavens! This is impudence, that power I
call to witness too, how damnably thou injurest me.

GALLIARD: You never from your window talked of love to me?

CORNELIA: Never.

GALLIARD: So, nor you're no courtesan?

CORNELIA: No by my life.

GALLIARD: So, nor do intend to be, by all that's good.

CORNELIA: By all that's good, never.

GALLIARD: So, – and you are real honest, and of quality?

CORNELIA: Or may I still be wretched.

GALLIARD: So, then farewell honesty and quality! – 'Sdeath, what a night, what hopes, and what a mistress, have I all lost for honesty and quality!   *[offers to go]*

CORNELIA: Stay. –

GALLIARD: I will be racked first, – *[in fury]* – let go thy hold! – *[in a soft tone]* – unless thou wouldst repent.

CORNELIA:
    I cannot of my fixed resolves for virtue!
    – But if you could but – love me – honourably –
    For I assumed this habit and this dress –

GALLIARD: To cheat me of my heart the readiest way! And now, like gaming rooks,[56] unwilling to give o'er till you have hooked in my last stake, my body too, you cozen me with honesty, – oh damn the dice – I'll have no more on't I, the game's too deep for me unless you played upon the square, or I could cheat like you. – Farewell, Quality! –   *[goes out]*

CORNELIA:
    He's gone, Philippa run and fetch him back;
    I have but this short night allowed for liberty!
    Perhaps tomorrow I may be a slave?   *[Exit PHILIPPA.]*

CORNELIA: – Now o' my conscience there never came good of this troublesome virtue – hang't I was too serious, but the devil on't he looks so charmingly – and was so very pressing I durst trust my gay humour and good nature no farther!
                          [she walks about]
             [SIR SIGNAL peeps and then comes out]

SIR SIGNAL: He's gone! – so, ha, ha, ha. – As I hope to breathe madam, you have most neatly dispatched him; poor fool – to compare his wit and his person to mine –

CORNELIA: Hah, the coxcomb here still. –

SIR SIGNAL: Well, this countenance of mine never failed me yet.

CORNELIA: Ah –

[Looking about on him, sees his face black, squeaks and runs away.]

SIR SIGNAL: Ah, why what the diavilo's that for, – why 'tis I, 'tis I most *Serenissima Signiora!*

[56]*rooks*: cheats

[GALLIARD *returns with* PHILIPPA]

GALLIARD: What noise is that, or is't some new design to fetch me back again?

SIR SIGNAL: How! Galliard returned!

GALLIARD: Hah! What art thou? A mortal or a devil?

SIR SIGNAL: How! Not know me? Now might I pass upon him most daintily for a devil, but that I have been beaten out of one devilship already, and dare venture no more conjurationing.

GALLIARD: Dog, what art thou – not speak! Nay then I'll inform myself, and try if you be flesh and blood.   [*kicks him*]

SIR SIGNAL: [*avoiding the kick*] No matter for all this – 'tis better to be kicked than discovered, for then I shall be killed! – And I can sacrifice a limb or two to my reputation at any time!

GALLIARD: Death, 'tis the fool, the fool for whom I am abused and jilted, 'tis some revenge to disappoint her cunning, and drive the slave before me. – Dog! Were you her last reserve. –
                                                                   [*kicks him*]

SIR SIGNAL: [*keeping in his cry*] Still I say mum!

GALLIARD: The ass will still appear through all disguises, nor can the devil's shape secure the fool –   [*kicks him*]

   SIR SIGNAL *runs out, as* CORNELIA *enters and holds*
   GALLIARD

CORNELIA: Hold tyrant –

GALLIARD:

Oh women! Women! Fonder in your appetites
Than beasts; and more unnatural!
For they but couple with their kind, but you
Promiscuously shuffle your brutes together,
 The fop of business with the lazy gown-man – the learned ass
with the illiterate wit. – The empty coxcomb with the politician,
as dull and insignificant as he; from the gay fool made more a
beast by fortune to all the loathed infirmities of age!
   – Farewell – I scorn to crowd with the dull herd!
Or graze upon the common where they batten –[*goes out*]

CORNELIA:

I know he loves, by this concern I know it,
And will not let him part dissatisfied!   [*goes out*]
By all that's good I love him more each moment;
And know he's destined to be mine. –

Enter MARCELLA

CORNELIA: – What hopes Marcella? What is't we next shall do?

MARCELLA: Fly to our last reserve, come let's haste and dress in that disguise we took our flight from Viterbo in, – and something – I resolve!

CORNELIA: My soul informs me what! – I ha't! A project worthy of us both – which whilst we dress I'll tell thee, – and by which,

> My dear Marcella, we will stand or fall,
> 'Tis our last stake we set; and have at all. –   [*Exeunt*]

Act Five

SCENE ONE

Enter PETRO, TICKLETEXT, *from the garden*

TICKLETEXT: Haste honest Barberacho, before the day discover us to the wicked world, and that more wicked Galliard!

PETRO: Well signior, of a bad turn it was a good one, that he took you for Sir Signal! The scandal lies at his door now sir, – so the ladder's fast, you may now mount and away. –

TICKLETEXT: Very well go your ways, and commend me, honest Barberacho, to the young gentlewoman! And let her know, as soon as I may be certain to run no hazard in my reputation, I'll visit her again!

PETRO: I'll warrant ye signior for the future!

TICKLETEXT: So, now get you gone lest we be discovered!

PETRO: Farewell signior, et bon voyage.   [*Exit* PETRO]

TICKLETEXT: [*descending*] 'Tis marvellous dark, and I have lost my lantern in the fray! [*groping*] – hah – whereabouts am I – hum – what have we here! – ah help help help! [*Stumbles at the well, gets hold of the rope, and slides down in the bucket.*] I shall be drowned! Fire, fire, fire, for I have water enough! Oh for some house, – some street, nay, would Rome itself were a second time in flames, that my deliverance might be wrought by the necessity for water, – but no human help is nigh – oh.

Enter SIR SIGNAL *as before*

SIR SIGNAL: Did ever any knight-adventurer run through so many disasters in one night! My worshipful carcase has been cudgelled most plentifully, first banged for a coward, which by the way was none of my fault, I cannot help nature! Then clawed away for a diavilo! There I was the fool! But who can help that too! Frighted with Galliard's coming into an ague, then chimneyed into a fever, where I had a fine regale of soot, a perfume which nothing but my Cackamerde Orangate could excell! And which I find by [*snuffs*] my smelling has defaced nature's image, and a second time made me be suspected for a devil! – Let me see – [*opens his lantern and looks on his hands*] –'tis so – I am in a cleanly pickle! If my face be of the same hue, I am fit to scare away old Beelzebub himself i'faith: [*wipes his face*] – aye – 'tis so – like to like, quoth the devil to the collier! Well I'll home, scrub myself clean if possible, get me to bed, devise a handsome lie to excuse my long stay to my governor, and all's well, and the man has his mare again!

[*shuts his lantern and gropes away, runs against the well*] – Que questo [*feels gently*] Make me thankful 'tis substantial wood, by your leave – [*opens his lantern*] How! A well! Sent by providence that I may wash myself, lest people smoke me by the scent, and beat me anew for stinking.

[*Sets down his lantern, pulls off his masquing-coat, and goes to draw water.*]

'Tis a damnable heavy bucket! Now do I fancy I shall look when I am washing myself, like the sign of the Labour-In-Vain.

TICKLETEXT: So my cry is gone forth, and I am delivered by miracle from this dungeon of death and darkness: this cold element of destruction –

SIR SIGNAL: Hah – sure I heard a dismal hollow voice. –

[TICKLETEXT *appears in the bucket above the well.*]

TICKLETEXT: What, art thou come in charity. –

SIR SIGNAL: Ah, le diavilo! Le diavilo! Le diavilo!

[*Lets go the bucket, and is running frighted away.*]

Enter FILLAMOUR *and* PAGE. SIR SIGNAL *returns*

SIR SIGNAL: – How, a man! Was ever wretched wight so miserable, the devil at one hand, and a Roman night-walker at the other! Which danger shall I choose! –

[*gets to the door of the house*]

TICKLETEXT: So, I am got up at last – thanks to my knight, for I am sure 'twas he! Hah, he's here – I'll hear his business.

[*goes near to* FILLAMOUR]

FILLAMOUR:

Confound this woman! This bewitching woman,
I cannot shake her from my sullen heart,
Spite of my soul I linger hereabouts;
And cannot to Viterbo.

TICKLETEXT: Very good! A dainty rascal this!

Enter GALLIARD *with a lantern, as from* SILVIO's *house, held by* PHILIPPA

FILLAMOUR: — Hah who's this coming from her house, perhaps 'tis Galliard.

GALLIARD: No argument shall fetch me back, by heaven.

FILLAMOUR: 'Tis the mad rogue!

TICKLETEXT: Oh Lord, 'tis Galliard! And angry too, now could I but get off, and leave Sir Signal to be beaten, 'twere a rare project — but 'tis impossible without discovery.

PHILIPPA: But will you hear her signior!

GALLIARD: That is, will I lose more time about her! Plague on't, I have thrown away already such songs and sonnets, such madrigals and posies, such night-walks, sighs, and direful lovers-looks, as would have mollified any woman of conscience and religion! And now to be popped i'th' mouth with Quality! Well, if ever you catch me lying with any but honest well-meaning damsels hereafter, hang me: — farewell old secret farewell. [*Exit* PHILIPPA]
— Now am I ashamed of being cozened so damnably, Fillamour that virtuous rascal, will so laugh at me! 'Sheart, could I but have debauched him, we had been on equal terms, — but I must help myself with lying, and swear I have — a —

FILLAMOUR: You shall not need, I'll keep your counsel sir.

GALLIARD: Hah — êtes-vous là! —

TICKLETEXT: How — Fillamour all this while — some comfort yet, I am not the only professor that dissembles! But how to get away. —

GALLIARD: Oh Harry, the most damnably defeated!

[*a noise of swords*]

FILLAMOUR: Hold! What noise is that! Two men coming this way as from the house of the courtesans.

Enter JULIO *backwards, fighting* OCTAVIO *and bravos*

GALLIARD: Hah, on retreating, — 'sdeath I've no sword!

FILLAMOUR: Here's one, I'll take my page's.

[*takes the boy's sword*]

Re-enter JULIO *and* OCTAVIO, *fighting*

GALLIARD: Now am I mad for mischief, here, hold my lantern, boy!

[*They fight on* JULIO's *side, and fight* OCTAVIO *out at the other side. Enter* LAURA *and* SABINA *at the foredoor, where* SIR SIGNAL *stands:* TICKLETEXT *groping up that way, finds* SIR SIGNAL *just entering in:* LAURA *and* SABINA *pass across the stage.*]

SIR SIGNAL: Hah a door open! I care not who it belongs to, 'tis better dying within doors like a man, than in the street like a dog. [*going in*]

TICKLETEXT: [*in great fear comes up and pulls* SIR SIGNAL] Signior! Ah gentle signior, whoe'er ye are that owns this mansion, I beseech you to give protection to a wretched man! Half dead with fear and injury!

SIR SIGNAL: Nay, I defy the devil to be more dead with fear than I! – Signior, you may enter! Perhaps 'tis somebody that will make an excuse for us both, – but hark, they return!

[*They both go in, just after* LAURA *and* SABINA *and* SILVIO *enter.*]

LAURA:
He's gone! He's gone! Perhaps forever gone, –
Tell me, thou silly manager of love!
How got this ruffian in, how was it possible
Without thy knowledge – he could get admittance?

SABINA: Now as I hope to live and learn I know not madam! Unless he followed you when you let in the cavalier, which being by dark he easily concealed himself; no doubt some lover of Silvianetta's who mistaking you for her took him too for a rival!

LAURA:
'Tis likely, and my Fortune is to blame,
My cursed Fortune, who like misers,
Deals her scanty bounties with so slow a hand,
That or we die before the blessing falls,
Or have it snatched ere we can call it ours!
[*raving*]To have him in my house, to have him kind!
Kind as young lovers when they meet by stealth:
As fond as age to beauty! And as soft,
As love and wit could make impatient youth,
Preventing even my wishes and desires,
– Oh gods! And then! Even then to be defeated,
Then from my o'erjoyed arms to have him snatched;
Then when our vows had made our freedom lawful!
What maid could suffer a surprise so cruel!

        — The day begins to break, — go search the streets,
        And bring me news he's safe or I am lost.
    Enter GALLIARD, FILLAMOUR *and* JULIO

FILLAMOUR: Galliard! Where art thou!

GALLIARD: Here safe and by thy side. —

LAURA: 'Tis he!

JULIO: Who'er he were, the rogue fought like a fury, and but for your timely aid I'd been in some danger.

FILLAMOUR: But Galliard, thou were telling me thy adventure with Silvianetta! There may be comfort in't.

LAURA: [*aside*] So, now I shall hear with what concern he speaks of me.

GALLIARD: Oh damn her, damn her!

LAURA: Hah!

GALLIARD: The veriest jilt that ever learnt the art.

LAURA: Heavens!

GALLIARD: Death, the whore took me for some amorous English elder brother! And was for matrimony in the devil's name! Thought me a loving fool, that ne'er had seen so glorious a sight before! And would at any rate enjoy!

LAURA: [*aside*] Oh heaven! I am amazed! How much he differs from the thing he was but a few minutes since.

GALLIARD: And to advance her price, set up for quality! Nay, swore she was a maid! And that she did but act the courtesan!

LAURA: Which then he seemed to give credit to, — oh the forsworn dissembler.

GALLIARD: But when I came to the matter then in debate, she was for honourable love forsooth, and would not yield no marry would she, not under a licence from the parson of the parish.

JULIO: Who was it prithee, 'twere a good deed to be so revenged on her!

GALLIARD: Pox on her no, I'm sure she's a damned gipsy, for at the same time she had her lovers in reserve, lay hid her bed-chamber.

LAURA:
        'Twas that he took unkindly.
        And makes me guilty of that rude address!

FILLAMOUR: Another lover had she?

GALLIARD: Yes, our coxcomb knight Buffoon, laid by for a relishing bit, in case I proved not seasoned to her mind.

LAURA: Hah! He knew him then!

GALLIARD: But damn her, she passes with the night, the day will bring new objects.

FILLAMOUR: Oh I do not doubt it Frank!

LAURA: [*aside* to SILVIO] False and inconstant! Oh I shall rave Silvio.

Enter CORNELIA *in man's clothes with a letter*

CORNELIA: Here be the cavaliers! Give me kind heaven but hold of him, and if I keep him not, I here renounce my charms of wit and beauty? – Signiors, is there a cavalier amongst ye, called Fillamour?

FILLAMOUR: I own that name; what would you, sir?

CORNELIA: Only deliver this signior.

[FILLAMOUR *goes aside, opens his lantern, and reads.* JULIO *and* GALLIARD *talk aside.*]

FILLAMOUR: [*reads*] *I'll only tell you I am brother to that Marcella whom you have injured; to oblige you to meet me an hour hence, in the Piazza dì Spagna! I need not say with your sword in your hand, since you will there meet, Julio Sebastiano Morosini.*

[*aside*] – Hah! her brother sure returned from travel. –

[*to* CORNELIA] – Signior – I will not fail to answer it as he desires.

[*aside*] I'll take this opportunity to steal off undiscovered.

[*going out*]

CORNELIA: So I've done my sister's business, now for my own.

GALLIARD: But my good friend, pray what adventure have you been on tonight.

JULIO: Faith sir, 'twas like to have proved a pleasant one, I came just now from the Silvianetta, – the fair young courtesan.

CORNELIA: [*aside*] Hah! What said the man – came from me!

GALLIARD: How sir, you with Silvianetta! When?

JULIO: Now, all the dear livelong night.

CORNELIA: [*aside*] A pox take him, who can this be?

GALLIARD: This night! This night! That is not yet departed!

JULIO: This very happy night: – I told you I saw a lovely woman at St Peter's Church.

GALLIARD: You did so.

JULIO: I told you too I followed her home, but could learn neither her name nor quality, but my page getting into the acquaintance of one of hers, brought me news of both: her name Silvianetta, her quality a courtesan!

CORNELIA: I at church yesterday! Now hang me if I had any such devout thoughts about me, why, what a damned scandalous rascal this?

JULIO: Filled with hopes of success, at night I made her a visit, and under her window had a skirmish with some rival, who was then serenading her.

GALLIARD: [*aside*] Was't he that fought us then? – But it seems you were not mistaken in the house, – on with your story pray – [*aside*] – death, I grow jealous now, – you came at night you said? –

JULIO: Yes, and was received at the door by the kind Silvianetta, who softly whispered me, 'Come to my bosom, and be safe for ever!' And doubtless took me for some happier man.

LAURA: [*aside, raving*] Confusion on him, 'twas my very language!

JULIO: Then led me by dark, into her chamber!

CORNELIA: [*aside*] Oh, this damned lying rascal! I do this? –

JULIO: But oh the things, the dear obliging things, the kind the fair young charmer said and did.

GALLIARD: To thee!

JULIO: To me.

GALLIARD: Did Silvianetta do this, Silvianetta the courtesan?

JULIO: That passes sir, for such, but is indeed of quality.

CORNELIA: This stranger is the devil! How should he know that secret else.

JULIO: She told me too 'twas for my sake alone, whom from the first minute she saw, she loved! She had assumed that name and that disguise, the sooner to invite me.

LAURA: 'Tis plain, the things I uttered! – Oh, my heart!

GALLIARD: Curse on that public jilt, the very flattery she would have passed on me.

CORNELIA: [*aside*] Pox take him, I must draw on him, I cannot hold!

GALLIARD: Was ever such a whore!

LAURA: [*aside*]
Oh that I knew this man, whom by mistake!
I lavished all the secrets of my soul to!

JULIO:
> I pressed for something more than dear expressions,
> And found her yield apace,
> But sighing, told me, of a fatal contract,
> She was obliged to make to one she never saw,
> And yet if I would vow to marry her, when she could prove
> To merit it, she would deny me nothing.

LAURA: 'Twas I, by heaven, that heedless fool was I.

JULIO:
> Which I with lover's eager joy performed,
> And on my knees uttered the hasty words,
> Which she repeated o'er, and gave me back!

GALLIARD: [*aside*] So, he has swallowed with a vengeance the very bait she had prepared for me, or anybody that would bite.

JULIO:
> But ere I could receive the dear reward of all my vows,
> I was drawn upon by a man that lay hid in her chamber:
> Whether by chance or design I know not, who fought me out,
> And was the same you found me engaged with.

CORNELIA: A pleasant rascal this, as e'er the devil taught his lesson to.

GALLIARD: So, my comfort is, she has jilted him too most damnably.

CORNELIA: 'Slife, I have anger enough to make me valiant, why should I not make use on't, and beat this lying villain whilst the fit holds?

GALLIARD: And you design to keep these vows, though you're contracted to another woman?

JULIO:
> I neither thought of breaking those, or keeping these,
> My soul was all employed another way.

LAURA: — It shall be so, — Silvio, — I've thought upon a way that must redeem all, — hark and observe me.
> [*takes* SILVIO *and whispers to him*]

JULIO: But I'm impatient to pursue my adventure, which I must endeavour to do, before the light discover the mistake; — farewell sir. [*Exit* JULIO]

GALLIARD: Go and be ruined quite, she has the knack of doing it.

SILVIO: I'll warrant ye madam for my part.   [*Exit* LAURA]

GALLIARD: I have a damned hankering after this woman, why could I not have put the cheat on her, as Julio has? I stand as little on my word as he! A good round oath or two had done the business, – but a pox on't I loved too well to be so wise.

[SILVIO *comes up to him*]

SILVIO: Con licentia, signior! Is your name Galliard?

GALLIARD: I am the man sweetheart, – let me behold thee – hah – San-Coeur's page.

SILVIO: [*aside*] A deuce of his lantern, what shall I say now? – Softly signior, I am that page whose chiefest business is to attend to my lord's mistress sir.

CORNELIA: [*aside, listening closely*] His mistress: whose mistress, what mistress? 'Slife how that little word has nettled me!

GALLIARD: [*aside, hugging himself*] Upon my life, the woman that he boasted of – A fair young amorous – noble – wanton – a – And she would speak with me my lovely boy?

SILVIO: You have prevented the commands I had! But should my lord know of it –

GALLIARD:
    Thou wert undone! I understand thee –
    And will be secret as a confessor –
    As lonely shades, or everlasting night –
Come, lead the way –

CORNELIA: [*aside*] Where I will follow thee, though to the bed of her thou'rt going to, and even prevent thy very business there.

[*Exeunt*]

SCENE TWO

A chamber

Enter LAURA *as before, in a night-gown*

LAURA:
    Now for a power that never yet was known
    To charm this stranger quickly into love,
    Assist my eyes, thou god of kind desires;
    Inspire my language with a moving force
    That may at once gain and secure the victory.
Enter SILVIO

SILVIO: Madam, your lover's here: your time's but short, consider too Count Julio may arrive!

LAURA:

> Let him arrive! Having secured myself of what I love, ---
> I'll leave him to complain his unknown loss
> To careless winds as pitiless as I – Sabina, see the rooms
> Be filled with lights! Whilst I prepare myself to entertain him.
> Darkness shall ne'er deceive me more –

Enter to SILVIO, GALLIARD *gazing about him*, CORNELIA *peeping at the door*

GALLIARD:

> All's wondrous rich, – gay as the Court of Love,
> But still and silent as the shades of death;
>
> > [*soft music whilst they speak*]
>
> – Hah – music! and excellent! Post on't – but where's the woman – I need no preparation. –

CORNELIA: No you are always provided for such encounters and can fall to *sans* ceremony, – but I may spoil your stomach.

> > [*a song is heard tuning*]

GALLIARD:

> A voice too, by heaven and 'tis a sweet one:
> Grant she be young and I'll excuse the rest.
> Yet vie for pleasure with the happiest Roman!
> [*The song is sung offstage, as if by* LAURA, *after which soft music till she enters.*]

SONG
(by a Person of Quality)

Farewell the world and mortal cares,
The ravished Strephon cried,
As full of joy and tender tears
He lay by Phillis' side:
Let others toil for wealth and fame,
Whilst not one thought of mine,
At any other bliss shall aim,
But those dear arms, but those dear arms of thine.

Still let me gaze in thy bright eyes,
And hear thy charming tongue,

> I nothing ask t'increase my joys
> But thus to feel 'em long;
> In close embraces let us lie,
> And spend our lives to come,
> Then let us both together die
> And be each other's, be each other's tomb.

GALLIARD: — Death, I'm fired already with her voice —
CORNELIA: So, I am like to thrive, —
    Enter JULIO.
JULIO:

> What mean these lights in every room,
> As if to make the day without the sun:
> And quite destroy my hopes! —
  Hah, Galliard here!

CORNELIA: A man! Grant it some lover, or some husband,
heaven! Or anything that will but spoil the sport. The lady!
Oh, blast her! How fair she is!
    Enter LAURA *with her lute, dressed in a careless rich dress,*
    followed by SABINA *to whom she gives her lute.*
JULIO: Hah! 'tis the same woman.
LAURA: [*sees* JULIO *and is startled*] A stranger here! What art
can help me now. —   [*she pauses*]
GALLIARD: By all my joys a lovely woman 'tis.
LAURA: Help me Deceit, Dissembling, all that's Woman —
    [*She starts and gazes on* GALLIARD, *pulling* SILVIO.]
CORNELIA: Sure I should know that face. —
LAURA:

> Ah look my Silvio! Is't not he! — It is!
> That smile, that air, that mien, that bow is his!
> 'Tis he by all my hopes, by all my wishes!

GALLIARD:

> He, yes, yes, I am a he, I thank my stars!
> And never blessed 'em half so much for being so,
> As for the dear variety of woman!

CORNELIA: Curse on her charms, she'll make him love in
earnest.
LAURA: [*going towards him*] It is my brother! And report was
false!

GALLIARD: How, her brother! Gad, I'm sorry we are so near
akin, with all my soul; for I'm damnably pleased with her!

LAURA:
Ah why do you shun my arms – or are ye air?
And not to be enclosed in human twines –
Perhaps you are the ghost of that dead lord!
That comes to whisper vengeance to my soul.

GALLIARD: [*aside*] 'Sheart! A ghost! This is an odd preparative
to love.

CORNELIA: 'Tis Laura! My brother Julio's mistress, and sister
to Octavio!

GALLIARD: Death, madam, do not scare away my love, with
tales of ghosts, and fancies of the dead. I'll give ye proofs I'm a
living loving man, as arrant an amorous mortal as heart can
wish – [*aside*] – I hope she will not jilt me too.

CORNELIA: So! He's at his common proof for all arguments, if
she should take him at his word now, and she'll be sure to do't.

LAURA:
Amiable stranger, pardon the mistake!
And charge it on a passion for a brother!
Devotion was not more retired than I,
Vestals, or widowed matrons when they weep,
Till by a fatal chance I saw in you;
The dear resemblance of a murdered brother!   [*weeps*]

JULIO: [*aside*] What the devil can she mean by this?

LAURA:
I durst not trust my eyes, yet still I gazed,
And that increased my faith you were my brother,
But since they erred, and he indeed is dead,
Oh give me leave to pay you all that love,
That tenderness and passion that was his.   [*weeping*]

CORNELIA: So, I knew she would bring matters about some
way or other, oh mischief mischief help me! 'Slife, I can be
wicked enough when I have no use on't, and now I have I'm as
harmless as a fool.

    [*As* GALLIARD *is earnestly talking to* LAURA, JULIO *pulls
    him by the sleeve.*]

LAURA: Oh save me, save me from the murderer!

JULIO: Hah!

GALLIARD: A murderer where?

LAURA: I faint, I die with horror of the sight!

GALLIARD: Hah – my friend a murderer! Sure you mistake him madam, he saw not Rome till yesterday – an honest youth madam and one that knows his distance upon occasion! – 'Slife, how cam'st thou here – prithee be gone and leave us.

JULIO: Why do you know this lady sir?

GALLIARD: Know her! – a – aye, aye – man – and all her relations, she's of quality: – withdraw withdraw – madam – a – he is my friend and shall be civil. –

LAURA: I have an easy faith for all you say, – but yet however innocent he be or dear to you, I beg he would depart – he is so like my brother's murderer, that one look more would kill me –

JULIO: A murderer! Charge me with cowardice, with rapes or treason – gods a murderer!

CORNELIA: A devil on her! She has robbed the sex of all their arts of cunning.

GALLIARD: Pox on't, thou'rt rude! Go, in good manners go. –

LAURA:
> I do conjure ye, torture me no more,
> If you would have me think you're not that murderer,
> Be gone – and leave your friend to calm my heart
> Into some kinder thoughts.

GALLIARD: Aye, aye, prithee go! I'll be sure to do thy business for thee.

CORNELIA: Yes, yes, you will not fail to do a friendly part no doubt –

JULIO: 'Tis but in vain to stay – I see she did mistake her man last night, and 'twas to chance I am in debt for that good fortune! – I will retire to show my obedience, madam.

> [*Exit* JULIO. GALLIARD *going to the door with him*]

LAURA: [*aside*]
> He's gone, and left me mistress of my wish!
> Descend ye little winged gods of Love,
> Descend and hover round our bower of bliss,
> Play in all various forms about the youth;
> And empty all your quivers at his heart.

[GALLIARD *returns, she takes him by the hand.*]

LAURA:
> — Advance, thou dearer to my soul than kindred,
> Thou more than friend or brother.
> Let meaner souls base-born conceal the god!
> Love owns his monarchy within my heart,
> So kings that deign to visit humble roofs:
> Enter disguised, but in a noble palace,
> Own their great power, and show themselves in glory.

GALLIARD:
> I am all transport with this sudden bliss,
> And want some kind allay to fit my soul for recompence.

CORNELIA: Yes, yes, my forward friend, you shall have an allay, if all my art can do't, to damp thee even to disappointment.

GALLIARD:
> My soul's all wonder now, let us retire,
> And gaze till I have softened it to love.
>> [*going out is met by* CORNELIA]

CORNELIA: Madam!

LAURA: More interruption! —Hah — [*turns*]

CORNELIA: My master the young Count Julio —

LAURA: Julio!

GALLIARD: [*aside*] What of him?

CORNELIA: — being just now arrived at Rome —

LAURA: [*aside*] Heavens, arrived!

CORNELIA: — sent me to beg the honour of waiting on you.

LAURA: Sure, stranger, you mistake! —

CORNELIA: If madam you are Laura Lucretia! —

GALLIARD: [*aside*] Laura Lucretia! By heavens, the very woman he's to marry.

LAURA: [*aside*]
> This would surprise a virgin less resolved,
> But what have I to do with aught but love!
> — And can your lord imagine this an hour,
> To make a ceremonious visit in?

GALLIARD:[*aside*] Riddles by Love! Or is't some trick again?

CORNELIA: Madam, where vows are past, the want of ceremony may be pardoned!

LAURA:
> I do not use to have my will disputed,
> Be gone, and let him know I'll be obeyed.

CORNELIA: [*aside*]
> 'Slife, she'll out-wit me yet, –
> Madam, I see this niceness is not general,
> – You can except some lovers.

GALLIARD: My pert young confident, depart, and let your master know he'll find a better welcome from the fair vain courtesan, la Silvianetta! Where he has passed the night and given his vows.

LAURA: [*aside, smiling*] Dearly devised, and I must take the hint.

CORNELIA: [*aside*] He knows me sure, and says all this to plague me. My lord, my master with a courtesan! He's but just now arrived.

GALLIARD: A pretty forward saucy lying boy this! And may do well in time. – Madam, believe him not, I saw his master yesterday, – conversed with him, – I know him, he's my friend! – 'Twas he that parted hence but now, – he told me all his passion for a courtesan, scarce half an hour since.

CORNELIA: So!

LAURA: I do not doubt it, oh, how I love him for this seasonable lie,
[*to* CORNELIA]– And can you think I'll see a perjured man,
> Who gives my interest in him to another?

[*aside, laughing to* GALLIARD] – Do I not help ye out most artfully?

CORNELIA: I see they are resolved to outface me.

GALLIARD: Now vowed to marry her.

LAURA: Heavens to marry her!

CORNELIA: [*aside*] To be conquered at my own weapon too, – lying! 'Tis a hard case.

GALLIARD: Go boy you may be gone, you have won your answer child, and may depart – come madam let us leave him.

CORNELIA: Gone, no help, death I'll quarrel with him, – nay, fight him, – damn him, – rather than lose him thus. – [*pulls him*] – Stay signior. – You call me boy – but you may find yourself mistaken sir, – and know – I've that about me may convince ye. [*showing his sword*] – 'T has done some execution!

GALLIARD: Prithee, on whom or what? Small village curs! The
   barking of a mastiff would unman thee.   [*offers to go*]
CORNELIA:
       Hold – follow me from the refuge of her arms!
       As thou'rt a man, I do conjure thee do't:
   [*aside*]– I hope he will, I'll venture beating for't.
GALLIARD   Yes, my brisk – little rascal – I will a –
LAURA: By all that's good you shall not stir from hence, ho who
   waits there, Antonio, Silvio, Gaspero, –
       They all enter
LAURA: – take that fierce youth, and bear him from my sight.
CORNELIA   You shall not need, 'slife these rough rogues will be
   too hard for me, – I've one prevention left, – farewell,
       May'st thou supply her with as feeble art,
       As I should do, were I to play thy part.
                                          [*goes out with the rest*]
GALLIARD: He's gone! Now let's redeem our blessed minutes
   lost.   [*they go in*]

SCENE THREE

The scene changes to the street. – Piazza dì Spagna.

   Enter JULIO *alone*
JULIO: Now by this breaking day-light I could rave, I knew she
   mistook me last night which made me so eager to improve my
   lucky minutes, – sure Galliard is not the man, I long to know the
   mystery, – hah – who's here? – Fillamour.
       Enter FILLAMOUR *met by* MARCELLA *in man's clothes; they*
       pass by each other, cock[57] and jostle.
MARCELLA: I take it, you are he I look for, sir!
FILLAMOUR: My name is Fillamour.
MARCELLA: Mine, – Julio Sebastiano Morosini.
JULIO: [*aside*] Hah, my name, by heaven!
FILLAMOUR:
       I doubt it not, since in that lovely face
       I see the charming image of Marcella!
JULIO: Hah!

   [57]*cock:* swagger

MARCELLA: [*aside*]
>   You might, ere travel ruffled me to man,
>   – I should return thy praise whilst I survey thee,
>   But that I came not here to compliment – draw –   [*draws*]

FILLAMOUR: Why, 'cause thou'rt like Marcella?

MARCELLA:
>   That were sufficient reason for thy hate,
>   But mine's because thou hast betrayed her basely;
>   – She told me all the story of her love,
>   How well you meant, how honestly you swore,
>   And with a thousand tears imployed my aid:
>   To break the contract she was forced to make,
>   T'Octavio, and give her to your arms,
>   I did, and brought you word of our design,
>   – I need not tell ye what returns you made;
>   Let it suffice, my sister was neglected,
>   Neglected for a courtesan, – a whore!
>   I watched, and saw each circumstance of falsehood.

JULIO: Damnation! what means this?

FILLAMOUR:
>   I scorn to save my life by lies or flatteries,
>   But credit me, the visit that I made,
>   I durst have sworn had been to my Marcella!
>   Her face, her eyes, her beauty was the same,
>   Only the business of her language differed,
>   And undeceived my hope.

MARCELLA:
>   In vain thou think'st to flatter me to faith, –
>   When thou'dst my sister's letter in thy hand,
>   Which ended that dispute,
>   Even then I saw with what regret you read it:
>   What care you took to disobey it too, –
>   The shivering maid, half dead with fears and terrors of the
>   night,
>   In vain expected a relief from love or thee,
>   Draw that I may return her the glad news I have revenged
>   her.

JULIO:
>   Hold, much mistaken youth! 'Tis I am Julio,
>   Thou, Fillamour, know'st my name, know'st I arrived

But yesterday at Rome, and heard the killing news
Of both my sisters flights, Marcella, and Cornelia, –
[*to* MARCELLA] And thou art some imposture.

MARCELLA: [*aside*] If this now should be true, I were in a fine
condition.

FILLAMOUR: Fled! Marcella fled!

JULIO:
    'Twas she I told thee yesterday was lost,
    But why art thou concerned, – explain the mystery!

FILLAMOUR:
    I loved her more than life! Nay even than heaven!
    And dost thou question my concern for her,
    Say how! And why! And whither is she fled!

JULIO:
    Oh, would I knew, that I might kill her in her lover's arms,
    Or if I found her innocent, restore her to Octavio

FILLAMOUR:
    To Octavio! And is my friendship of so little worth,
    You cannot think I merit her.

JULIO:
    This is some trick between 'em! But I have sworn
    Most solemnly, have sworn by heaven and my honour
    To resign her, and I will do't or die, –
[*to* MARCELLA]– Therefore declare quickly, declare where she is,
    Or I will leave thee dead upon the place.

MARCELLA: So, death or Octavio, a pretty hopeful choice this!

FILLAMOUR: Hold! by heaven, you shall not touch a single
hair, thus – [*puts himself between 'em and draws*] – will I guard
the secret in his bosom.

JULIO: 'Tis plain thou'st injured me, – and to my honour I'll
sacrifice my friendship, follow me.

[*Exeunt* JULIO *and* FILLAMOUR]

    Enter PETRO *and* CORNELIA

MARCELLA: Ah, Petro, fly, fly, swift and rescue him. –

[*Exit* PETRO *with his sword in his hand*]

CORNELIA: Oh have I found thee, fit for my purpose too. Come
haste along with me, – thou must present my brother Julio
instantly, or I am lost, and my project's lost, and my man's lost,
and all's lost.

Enter PETRO

PETRO: Victoria, victoria, your cavalier and conqueror! The other, wounded in his sword-hand, was easily disarmëd.

MARCELLA: Then let's retire, if I am seen I'm lost, – Petro, stay here for the cavalier, and conduct him to me to this house;– I must be speedy now. –

CORNELIA: [*pointing to* MARCELLA] Remember this is Julio!

PETRO: I know your design, and warrant ye my part: – hah, Octavio. [*Exeunt* PETRO, MARCELLA *and* CORNELIA]

Enter OCTAVIO, MOROSINI *and* CRAPINE.

OCTAVIO: Now cowardice, that everlasting infamy, dwell ever on my face, that men may point me out that hated lover, that saw his mistress false, stood tamely by whilst she repeated vows! Nay was so infamous, so dully tame, to hear her swear her hatred and aversion, yet still I calmly listened! Though my sword were ready, and did not cut his throat for't.

MOROSINI: I though, you'd said you'd fought.

OCTAVIO:
Yes, I did rouse at last and waked my wrongs;
But like an ass, a patient fool of honour,
I gave him friendly notice I would kill him;
And fought like prizers,[58] not as angry rivals.

MOROSINI: Why that was handsome, – I love fair play; what would you else have done!

OCTAVIO:
Have fallen upon him like a sudden storm,
Quick, unexpected in his height of love:

Enter PETRO *and* FILLAMOUR

OCTAVIO: – See – see yonder; or I'm mistaken by this glimmering day or that is Fillamour; now entering at her door, 'tis he by my revenge! – What say you sir.

MOROSINI: By th' mass I think 'twas he, –

Enter JULIO

OCTAVIO:
Julio, I've caught the wantons in their toil,
I have 'em fast, thy sister and her lover. [*embraces him*]

[58]*prizers*: contestants in boxing match

JULIO: Eternal shame light on me if they 'scape then.

OCTAVIO: Follow me quick, – whilst we can get admittance.

JULIO: Where – here?

OCTAVIO: Here, – come all and see her shame and my revenge.

JULIO: And are you not mistaken in the house?

OCTAVIO: Mistaken! I saw the ravisher enter just now, thy uncle saw it too, oh, my excessive joy, come if I lie – say I'm a dog, a villain. [*Exeunt as into the house*]

SCENE FOUR

Scene changes to a chamber

Enter SIR SIGNAL – *groping a little*

SIR SIGNAL: There's no finding my way out, – and now does fear make me fancy, – this some enchanted castle. –

Enter TICKLETEXT, *listening*

TICKLETEXT: Hah, an enchanted castle!

SIR SIGNAL: Belonging to a monstrous giant! Who having spirited away the King of Tropicipopican's daughter, keeps her here enclosed, and that I wandering knight am by fickle fortune sent to her deliverance.

TICKLETEXT: [*aside, listening*] How's that! spirited away the King of Tropicipopican's daughter! Bless me, what unlawful wickedness is practised, in this Romish heathenish country!

SIR SIGNAL: And yet the devil of any dwarf squire or damsel have I met with yet, – would I were cleanlily off o' this business, – hah, lights as I live, and people coming this way! – Bless me from the giant, – oh Lord what shall I do. – [*Falls on his knees*]

TICKLETEXT: I fear no giants, having justice on my side, but reputation makes me tender of my person! – Hah – what's this, a curtain: I'll wind myself in this, it may secure me!

[*winds himself in a window curtain*]

SIR SIGNAL: – They're entering, what shall I do – hah – here's a corner! Defend me from a chimney.

[SIR SIGNAL *creeps to the corner of the window, and feels a space between* TICKLETEXT'S *legs and the corner: creeps in, and stands up just behind* TICKLETEXT.]

Enter GALLIARD *leading* LAURA. SABINA *with lights just after 'em.* JULIO, OCTAVIO, MOROSINI *and* CRAPINE.

OCTAVIO: Just in the happy minute.

GALLIARD: I've sworn by every god! By every power divine! To marry thee! And save thee from the tyranny of a forced contract, – nay gad if I lose a fine wench for want of oaths this bout, the devil's in me.

OCTAVIO: What think ye now sir?

JULIO:
        Damnation on her, set my rage at liberty!
        That I may kill 'em both.   [MOROSINI *holds him*]

MOROSINI: I see no cause for that, she may be virtuous yet.

OCTAVIO:
        Do ye think as such to pass her off on me,
        Or that I'll bear the infamy of your family,
        No, I scorn her now, but can revenge my honour on a rival!

MOROSINI: Nay then I'll see fair play, – [*goes to* GALLIARD *who turns*] – turn and defend thy life.

JULIO:
        Whilst I do justice on the prostitute:
        – hah –   [*he gazes, she runs to* GALLIARD]
        Defend me, 'tis the woman that I love.

LAURA: Octavio!

OCTAVIO: Laura! My sister! Perfidious! Shameful! –
                          [*offers to kill her*]

JULIO: Hold! Thy sister this? that sister I'm to marry!

LAURA: Is this then Julio? And do all the powers conspire to make me wretched?

OCTAVIO: May I be dumb for ever!
    [OCTAVIO *holds his sword down, and looks sadly.* JULIO *holds* LAURA *by one hand, pleads with* OCTAVIO *with the other.*]

    Enter FILLAMOUR *and* PETRO

FILLAMOUR: Hah, Galliard! In danger too!
    [FILLAMOUR *draws, and steps to them:* MOROSINI *puts himself between them.*]

OCTAVIO: Fillamour here! how now, what's the matter, friend?
          [*they talk whilst enter* MARCELLA *and* CORNELIA]

CORNELIA: Hah, new broils, sure the devil's broke loose tonight! – My uncle as I live!
       [MOROSINI *pleads between* FILLAMOUR *and* OCTAVIO]

MARCELLA: And Octavio! Where shall we fly for safety?

CORNELIA: I'll even trust to my breeches! 'Tis too late to retreat! – 'Slife, here be our cavaliers too, nay then ne'er fear falling into the enemies' hands.

FILLAMOUR: I, I fled with Marcella! Had I been blessed with so much love from her, I would have boasted on't i'th' face of heaven.

MARCELLA: [*to* OCTAVIO] Look ye, sir.

FILLAMOUR:
> The lovely maid, I own I have a passion for,
> But by the powers above the flame was sacred,
> And would no more have passed the bounds of honour,
> Or hospitality! Than I would basely murder!
> And were she free,
> I would from all the world make her forever mine.

MARCELLA: Look ye sir, a plain case this.

GALLIARD: He tells ye simple truth sir.

OCTAVIO: Was it not you, this scarce-past night I fought with here, in the house by dark, just when you had exchanged your vows with her!

LAURA: [*aside*] Heavens! Was it he?

FILLAMOUR: This minute was the first I ever entered here!

JULIO: 'Twas I, sir, was that interrupted lover, – and this the lady!

LAURA: [*aside*] And must I yield at last?

OCTAVIO: Wonders and riddles!

GALLIARD: [*slyly*] And was this the Silvianetta sir, you told the story of?

JULIO:
> The same whom inclination, friends, and destiny,
> Conspire to make me blessed with.

GALLIARD: So many disappointments in one night would make a man turn honest in spite of nature.

SIR SIGNAL: [*peeping from behind*] Some comfort yet, that I am not the only fool defeated! Ha! Galliard!

OCTAVIO: [*to* FILLAMOUR] I'm satisfied – [*to* GALLIARD] – but what could move you sir – to injure me! One of my birth and quality?

GALLIARD: Faith sir I never stand upon ceremony when there's

a woman in the case, – nor knew I 'twas your sister: or if I had I
should ha' liked her ne'er the worse for that, had she been kind.

JULIO:
    It is my business to account with him,
    And I am satisfied he has not injured me!
    He is my friend!

GALLIARD: That's frankly said! And uncompelled I swear she's
innocent!

OCTAVIO:
    If you're convinced! I too am satisfied!
    And give her to you whilst that faith continues!
                                            [*gives him her*]

LAURA: [*aside*]
    And must I, must I force my heart to yield!
    And yet his generous confidence obliges me!

OCTAVIO: [*kneels*]
    And here I vow by all the sacred powers,
    That punish perjury, never to set my heart
    On faithless woman! – Never to love nor marry!

[*rises*] Travel shall be my business, – [*to* JULIO] thou my heir!

SIR SIGNAL: So, poor soul, I'll warrant he has been defeated
too!

MARCELLA: Marcella sir will take ye at your word!

FILLAMOUR: Marcella!

MARCELLA: Who owns with blushes truths should be concealed, but to prevent more mischief. – [*to* OCTAVIO] That I
was yours sir was against my will, my soul was Fillamour's ere
you claimed a right in me; though I ne'er saw or held discourse
with him, but at an awful distance, – nor knew he of my flight.

OCTAVIO: I do believe, and give thee back my claim, I scorn the
brutal part of love! The noblest body where the heart is
wanting.

        [*They all talk aside,* CORNELIA *comes up to* GALLIARD.]

CORNELIA: Why how now cavalier! How like a discarded
favourite do you look now, who whilst your authority lasted
laid about ye; domineered huffed and blustered, as if there had
been no end on't: now a man may approach ye without terror!
– You see the meat's snatched out of your mouth sir, the lady's
disposed on! Whose friends and relations you were so well
acquainted with.

GALLIARD: Peace, boy, I shall be angry else. –

CORNELIA: Have you never a cast mistress, that will take compassion on you: faith, what think ye of the little courtesan now?

GALLIARD: As ill as e'er I did! What's that to thee?

CORNELIA: Much more than you're aware on sir, – and faith to tell you truth I'm no servant to Count Julio! But e'en a little mischievous instrument she sent hither to prevent your making love to Donna Laura.

GALLIARD: [*aside*] 'Tis she herself, – how could that beauty hide itself so long from being known! – Malicious little dog-in-a-manger, that would neither eat, nor suffer the hungry to feed themselves! What spiteful devil could move thee to treat a lover thus! But I am pretty well revenged on ye!

CORNELIA: On me!

GALLIARD: You think I did not know those pretty eyes! That lovely mouth I have so often kissed in cold imagination.

CORNELIA: Softly tormentor!   [*they talk aside*]

MARCELLA: In this disguise we parted from Viterbo! Attended only by Petro and Philippa! At Rome we took the title and habit of two courtesans; both to shelter us from knowledge, and to oblige Fillamour to visit us, which we believed he would in curiosity, and yesterday it so fell out as we desired.

FILLAMOUR: Howe'er my eyes might be imposed upon, you see my heart was firm to its first object, can you forget and pardon the mistake?

JULIO: She shall! And with Octavio's – and my uncle's leave, – thus make your title good. –   [*gives her to* FILLAMOUR]

OCTAVIO: 'Tis vain to strive with destiny!   [*gives her*]

MOROSINI: With all my heart, – but where's Cornelia all this while!

GALLIARD: Here's the fair straggler sir.
                                        [*leads her to* MOROSINI]

MOROSINI: [*holding his cane up at her*] Why thou baggage, thou wicked contriver of mischief, what excuse had'st thou for running away! Thou had'st no lover?

CORNELIA: 'Twas therefore sir I went to find one! And if I am not mistaken in the mark, 'tis this cavalier I pitch upon for that use and purpose.

GALLIARD: Gad I thank ye for that, – I hope you'll ask my leave first, I'm finely drawn in i'faith! – Have I been dreaming all this night of the possession of a new-gotten mistress, to wake and find myself noosed to a dull wife in the morning.

FILLAMOUR: Thou talk'st like a man that never knew the pleasures thou despisest; faith try it, Frank, and thou wilt hate thy past loose way of living.

CORNELIA: And to encourage a young setter-up, I do here promise to be the most mistress-like wife. – You know, signior, I have learnt the trade, though I had not stock to practise, and will be as expensive, insolent, vain, extravagant, and inconstant, as if you only had the keeping part, and another the amorous assignations, what think ye sir?

FILLAMOUR: Faith, she pleads well! And ought to carry the cause!

GALLIARD: She speaks reason! And I'm resolved to trust good nature! – Give me thy dear hand. –

[*They all join to give it him, he kisses it.*]

MOROSINI: And now you are both sped, pray give me leave to ask ye a civil question! Are you sure you have been honest, if you have, I know not by what miracle you have lived.

PETRO: Oh sir as for that, I had a small stock of cash in the hands of a couple of English bankers, one Sir Signal Buffoon –

SIR SIGNAL: [*peeping*] Sir Signal Buffoon! What a pox does he mean me trow?

PETRO: – and one Mr Tickletext!

TICKLETEXT: How was that, – certo my name!

[TICKLETEXT *peeps out, and both he and* SIR SIGNAL *see each other, their faces being close together, one at one side the curtain, and the other at the other.*]

GALLIARD & FILLAMOUR: Ha ha ha!

SIR SIGNAL: And have I caught you i'faith Mr Governor! Nay ne'er put in your head for the matter, here's none but friends mun.

GALLIARD: How now what have we here!

SIR SIGNAL: Speak of the devil and he appears.

[*pulls his governor forward*]

TICKLETEXT: I am undone! – but good Sir Signal do not cry whore first! As the old proverb says!

SIR SIGNAL: And good Mr Governor, as another old proverb says, do not let the kettle call the pot black-arse! –

FILLAMOUR: How came you hither gentlemen!

SIR SIGNAL: Why! Faith sir, divining of a wedding or two forward, I brought Mr Chaplain to give you a cast of his office, as the saying is.

FILLAMOUR: What, without book Mr Tickletext.

CORNELIA: How now! Sure you mistake, these are two lovers of mine.

SIR SIGNAL: How sir your lovers! We are none of those sir, we are Englishmen.

GALLIARD: You mistake Sir Signal, this is Silvianetta.

SIR SIGNAL & TICKLETEXT: [*aside*] How!

GALLIARD: Here's another spark of your acquaintance, – do you know him?

TICKLETEXT: How Barberacho! Nay, then all will out. –

GALLIARD: Yes, and your fencing and civility-master.

SIR SIGNAL: Aye, – why what was it you that picked our pockets then, – and cheated us!

GALLIARD: Most damnably, – but since 'twas for the supply of two fair ladies, all shall be restored again.

TICKLETEXT: Some comfort that.

FILLAMOUR: Come, let's in and forgive all, 'twas but one night's intrigue, in which all were a little faulty!

SIR SIGNAL: And Governor, pray let me have no more domineering and usurpation! But as we have hitherto been honest brothers in iniquity, so let's wink hereafter at each other's frailties!

> Since love and women easily betray man,
> From the grave gown-man to the busy lay-man.

She Ventures
and
He Wins

by

'ARIADNE'

(a young lady)

1695

DRAMATIS PERSONAE

WOMEN

CHARLOTTE,	*a rich heiress*
JULIANA,	*her cousin, in love with Sir Charles Frankford*
BELLASIRA,	*in love with Sir Roger Marwood*
URANIA,	*wife to Freeman*
DOWDY,	*wife to Squire Wouldbe, pretending to rule her husband, yet always jealous and uneasy*
MRS BELDAM,	*her mother, a pawnbroker*
DOLL,	*Urania's maid*

MEN

SIR CHARLES FRANK-FORD,	*brother to Charlotte, in love with Juliana*
SIR ROGER MARWOOD,	*friend to Sir Charles*
LOVEWELL,	*a younger brother of small fortune*
FREEMAN,	*a vintner, husband to Urania*
SQUIRE WOULDBE,	*a proud pragmatical coxcomb of poor extraction, husband to Dowdy.*

Servants, waiters, chairmen, bailiffs, etc.

When first performed at the New Theatre in Little Lincoln's Inn Fields in September 1695, a prologue announced it as 'a woman's treat'. When the play appeared in print in 1696, it was described on the title-page as 'written by a young lady'; the author continued to conceal her identity, signing her preface with only a *nom de plume*, 'Ariadne'.

PREFACE

I dare not venture to send this play barefaced into the world, without saying something in its defence: I am very sensible of the many nice judgments I expose myself to, who may justly find an infinite number of faults in it; which, I profess ingenuously, I am not able to mend; for, indeed, I am altogether unacquainted with the stage and those dramatic rules, which others have with so much art and success observed. It was the first I ever made public by appearing on the stage, which, (with the advantage it met with, of admirable acting) is all the recommendations I have for exposing it, in its own naked simplicity, without any ornaments of language or wit; therefore, I believe, the best apology I can make for myself and play is, that 'tis the error of a weak woman's pen, one altogether unlearned, ignorant of any, but her mother-tongue, and very far from being a perfect mistress of that too; and confess I have but just wit enough to discern I want it infinitely; yet these reasons which should have dissuaded me, could not conquer the inclinations I had for scribbling from my childhood. And when our island enjoyed the blessing of the incomparable Mrs Behn, even then I had much ado to keep my muse from showing her impertinence; but, since her death, has claimed a kind of privilege; and, in spite of me, broke from her confinement.

The plot was taken from a small novel; which, I must needs own, had design and scope enough to have made an excellent play, had it met with the good fortune to have fallen into better hands; but, as it is, I venture to send it abroad, where, if it finds but a favourable reception from my own sex, and some little encouragement from the other, I will study in my next to deserve it. Which then, perhaps, may make me ambitious enough to be known; but, in the meantime, I humbly beg the favour to borrow the name of

ARIADNE

PROLOGUE

Spoken by Mrs Bowman, in man's clothes.

This is a woman's treat y'are like to find;
Ladies, for pity; men, for love be kind;
Else here I come, her champion, to oppose
The two broadsides of dreadful wits and beaux:
'Tis odd indeed; but if my sword won't do,
I can produce another weapon too, –
But to my task. – Our author hopes indeed,
You will not think, though charming Aphra's dead,
All wit with her, and with Orinda's fled.
We promised boldly we would do her right,
Not like the other house, who, out of spite
Trumped up a play upon us in a night.
And it was scarcely thought on at the most,
But *Hey-Boys Presto!* conjured on the post.
These champions bragged they first appeared in field,
Then bid us tamely, *article and yield*;
So did the French, and thought themselves secure;
But, to their cost, have fairly lost Namur.
And so much, gentlemen, by way of satire,
Now I am come t'examine your good nature:
Since 'tis a Lady hopes to please tonight,
I'm sure you Beaux will do the ladies right.
Clap every scene; and do yourselves the honour,
Loudly to boast the favours you have done her.
So may the Play-house, Park, and Mall befriend you,
And no more Temple-Garden broils attend you.

EPILOGUE

Written by Mr Motteux

Spoken by Mr Dogget, dressed as a Beau.

Our poetess is troubled in her mind,
Like some young thing, not so discreet as kind,
Who, without terms, has her dear toy resigned.
You all are wild to bring her to the touch;
You beg, you press, you swear, and promise much;
'Twere well if your performances were such:
Our authoress now is in, at your devotion,
Though she, perhaps to please you, wants the notion,
Be generous once, she'll quickly mend her motion.
For, pray take notice, 'tis her maidenhead,
(That of her brain I mean) and you that wed
Feel seldom easy joys, till that is fled.
If you are kind, she's willing to go on;
But if you turn her off, the nymph turns nun;
And what a scandal would be to the nation,
Should some for want of trade leave their vocation,
And, among friars pray for occupation?
I'm much afraid a woman's like a play,
You'd have 'em new and pretty every day,
Or, else, your servant, 'gad I cannot stay.
'Tis true, you wait awhile in expectation
(When up the curtain flies) of recreation;
But you all go, when ere the play is done;
Then down the curtain drops, and whip you're gone,
And thence to tell ungrateful truths you run.
Be kinder: let our unknown fair appease ye,
Though you mistake her play, her ★ ★ ★ may please ye:
She hides it now, yet she mislikes the task,

But knows how much you love a vizard mask.
Yet sure she must be safe among you here;
We Beaux can ne'er be critics on the fair:
As for you, judges, if I rightly know ye,
You should think that ungrateful task below ye.
Ye braves, that made your campaign at the Wells,
Storming the breach of some fair citadels,
If kind, may chance to find out where she dwells.
Ladies, for your own sakes you must be kind;
Lest, while we scarce one writing beauty find,
Vain men deny your sex the graces of the mind.
Take you her part, the men of course submit,
And so your beauty shall secure her wit.
Let all these reasons kindly draw you in,
And safely then She Ventures, and We Win.

Act One

SCENE ONE

Enter CHARLOTTE *and* JULIANA *in men's clothes*

JULIANA: Faith, Charlotte, the breeches become you so well 'tis almost pity you should ever part with 'em.

CHARLOTTE: Nor will I, till I can find one can make better use of them to bestow 'em on, and then I'll resign my title to 'em for ever.

JULIANA: 'Tis well if you find it so easy, for a woman once vested in authority, though 'tis by no other than her own making, does not willingly part with it. But, prithee child, what is thy design? For I am yet to learn.

CHARLOTTE: Why, to ramble the town till I can meet with the man I can find in my heart to take for better for worse. These clothes will give us greater liberty than the scandalous world will allow to our petticoats, which we could not attempt this undertaking in without hazard to our modesty. Besides, should I meet with the man whose outside pleased me, 'twill be impossible by any other means to discover his humour; for they are so used to flatter and deceive our sex, that there's nothing but the angel appears, though the devil lies lurking within, and never so much as shows his paw till he has got his prey fast in his clutches.

JULIANA: Methinks you that have so true a notion of that treacherous sex, should be afraid to venture for fear of being yourself deceived.

CHARLOTTE: No, my dear Julia, to avoid it is the scope of my design; for, though by laziness and ease the generality of mankind is degenerated into a soft effeminacy, unworthy of the noble stamp was set upon their soul, there still remains a race retains the image Heaven made them in, virtuous, and just, sincere and brave: and such a one I'll find, if I search to the Antipodes for him, or else lead apes in Hell.

JULIANA: But, dear child, will not every one think you stark mad for a husband, to take this extravagant course for one?

CHARLOTTE: No sure: none can think one of my youth and fortune can want the tenders of hearts enough; I'm not obliged to follow the world's dull maxims, nor will I wait for the formal address of some ceremonious coxcomb, with more land than brains, who would bargain for us as he would for his horse, and talks of nothing but taxes and hard times, to make me a good housewife; or else some gay young fluttering thing, who calls himself a Beau, and wants my fortune to maintain him in that character: such an opinionated animal, who believes there needs no more to reach a lady's heart than a bon mien, fine dress, the periwig well adjusted, the hand well managed in taking snuff, to show the fine diamond ring, if he's worth one; sometimes a conceited laugh, with the mouth stretched from one ear to t'other, to discover the white teeth, with sneak and cringe in an affected tone, cries, 'Damn me, Madam, if you are not the prettiest creature my eyes ere saw! 'Tis impossible for me to live if you are so cruel to deny me,' with a world of such foolish stuff, which they talk all by rote. No, my Julia, I'll have one who loves my person as well as gold, and please myself, not the world, in my choice.

JULIANA: If there's any such thing as real love in that false sex, none sure is so capable to inspire it, as the charming Charlotte: your person is indeed infinitely taking, your humour gay, and wit refined, and beauty enough to tempt a hermit; yet, after all, you'll find it a difficult business to distinguish, which the most zealous adorations are paid to, your beauty, or gold.

CHARLOTTE: I warrant thee, child, I'll take care of that: but come, to our affairs in hand.

JULIANA: Where's your brother?

CHARLOTTE: He's safe enough, he dined today at Sir Roger Marwood's, where, 'tis twenty to one, he'll be engaged the evening.

JULIANA: Suppose he should meet us in our rambles, he'd certainly know us.

CHARLOTTE: You're so full of your suppositions; suppose he should, which there's no great danger of, but at the play-house, where we'll first steer our course: he's too discreet to discover us, and too good humoured to be angry, but will think it one of my mad frolics, without other design, but a little diversion. But I know from whence your fear proceeds; which, if you put any more scruples into my head, I'll discover; therefore look to your good behaviour.

JULIANA: [*sighs*] I confess you have me at an advantage, but that has now no part in my design, to serve you with that little wit I have; there's a coach waits us at the garden gate.

CHARLOTTE: Allons, my dear, now love be propitious.

[*Exit* CHARLOTTE *and* JULIANA]

SCENE TWO

Enter FREEMAN *and* URANIA, *with a letter in her hand*

URANIA: Nay, prithee Freeman, be not in such a rage at a thing so contemptibly ugly, that is not worth raising the passion of a man: you must trust to my honesty after all you can do; and if I designed you foul play, I would not acquaint you thus freely, as I do, with all the coxcomb's proceedings. Pray leave him to my management, and for once trust a woman's revenge; I'll warrant you I'll handle him so as shall give you more pleasant satisfaction than any you can propose; nothing so sharpens our sex's invention, as revenge, the darling delight of our nature; and, if I do not pursue mine home, may the curse of being thought dishonest, without knowing the pleasure of it, fall upon me.

FREEMAN: Urania, I do not suspect you of any design to abuse me; but, as I believe you honest, I would have the world do so too. Besides, there is no fort so impregnable, that may not one time or other, with long assaults or stratagem, be taken. But I will have patience, and see the result of your designs; and, if they do not satisfy me very well, will then take my own measures with him.

URANIA: Agreed, with all my heart. Here is the letter I just now received from him, and likewise my answer.

[*gives him two separate billets*]

FREEMAN: [*reads*] *Dear Mrs Honeysuckle, I don't know what a*
devil you have done to me, but I can neither eat, drink, or sleep,
for thinking of those dear, damned eyes that have set my heart
on fire; let me know when that troublesome property, your
husband, is out of the way, and I will fly to assure you, I am
your devoted slave, Squire Wouldbe.
   Familiar fancy fool! I know his impudence so well, I do not
wonder at him. But now for yours:
   [*reads again*] *'Tis impossible to gain any opportunity by my*
husband's being abroad, because then I am confined to the bar;
but, if you dare, for my sake, metamorphose your breeches into
petticoats, but avoiding the seeing of my husband, and you may
pass with all the security possible. Tonight, in play-time, will be
very convenient; it being a new one, we shall in all likelihood be
empty of company; so that you may have the opportunity, if
you desire it, of being alone, with your obliged humble servant.
   What mean you by this, Urania? Sure you mistook when you
gave me this letter? What is your design? The devil take me if I
can imagine.   [*looks surly*]
URANIA: Why, first to draw the woodcock into the net, and
then to use him as I think fit. Pray rely on me, and be not so
suspicious, for, if you are, you unravel my whole design.
FREEMAN: I can scarce confine my anger to a jest; but, for once,
I trust you; but if you play me false, and make me thus the
property, as he calls me, of my own disgrace, look to 't, by
heaven I'll murder thee.
URANIA: Your threats in no way terrify me, having no designs
that will give you any cause of displeasure: I'll dispatch away a
messenger to my gallant, and, in the meantime, give you your
instructions, for you must be assistant to me.
FREEMAN: Well, go in, I'll follow you immediately.
                                               [*Exit* URANIA]
FREEMAN: I never had the least reason to distrust her honesty,
though I'm not perfectly satisfied with this letter of hers; but I'll
watch her narrowly, and it shall 'scape me hard if she deceive
me.   [*Exit* FREEMAN]

SCENE THREE

St James's Park

Enter LOVEWELL *crossing the stage,* CHARLOTTE *and* JULIANA *following him, in men's clothes.*

CHARLOTTE: Thus far we have kept sight of him, see we don't lose him now.

JULIANA: No, he's turning again this way.

CHARLOTTE: Well, if I like his humour and sense as well as his person, my search is at an end: for this is my man. I believe he'll make an excellent frugal husband, he has led us a sweet jaunt; I am very weary, but must not complain. Oh, here he comes again. I'll accost him, and try what mettle he's made of.

JULIANA: Why sure thou art not stark mad; s'life he'll beat us, do you see how surly he looks.

CHARLOTTE: No parlying now; prepare to second me, whilst I give the onset.

JULIANA: Thou'rt a mad wench, but I'll not fly from my colours.

CHARLOTTE: Well said girl, now I like thee; but here he is.

Enter LOVEWELL, *as crossing the stage,* CHARLOTTE *stops him.*

CHARLOTTE: Give a stranger leave sir, to disturb your meditations, which seem to be as serious, as if you had just received the fatal nay, and were now breathing vengeance against fortune, love, and woman-kind.

[*All the while she speaks, he surveys her from head to foot*]

LOVEWELL: Indeed, you mistake young sir, I was thinking of no such trifles: these fooleries belong to your years, or at least are only then excusable. But I believe you're disposed to be merry, gentlemen, and at this time I am very unfit company for you; the serious humour I am in will not agree with yours.

JULIANA: Is it the effects of being crossed in some design makes you so, or your natural temper?

LOVEWELL: Neither sir, but why does it concern you to know.

CHARLOTTE: Because we would gladly divert it, sir, would

you accept of our endeavours towards it, by admitting us into your company.

JULIANA: There's nothing so pernicious to health as the indulging of melancholy, and we having a particular interest in yours, must by no means leave you with so dangerous a companion.

LOVEWELL: A particular interest in my health, for what end, sir?

CHARLOTTE: Oh, for several: my future happiness and all my joy on earth depends upon it; had I as many lives as Argus's eyes, I'd hazard 'em all for the preservation of yours.

LOVEWELL: Heyday! Whence grows this mighty kindness? I fear sir, you are mistaken; I do not remember I ever had the honour to see you before.

CHARLOTTE: I have evidences enough confirms me, you're the man that has cruelly robbed a near and dear relation of mine of her repose for ever, and except you restore it her by reciprocal love, I fear the worst effects of this unhappy passion.

LOVEWELL: Oh sir, I find you design to divert yourself instead of me. [LOVEWELL *makes to walk off*]

CHARLOTTE: [*catching hold of him*] By honour, trust, and all that's sacred, I'm serious.

LOVEWELL: Well sir, bring me to the lady; I'm not so cruelly inclined to let a pretty woman languish for any civil kindness I can do her.

CHARLOTTE: [*aside to* JULIANA] Oh heavens! Julia! If he should be married! I dare not proceed till I know. Do you ask him the question, for I have not courage.

JULIANA: Never fear it, he has not the slovenly air of a married man; but you shall soon be satisfied. [*to* LOVEWELL] Pray sir, give me leave to ask you an impertinent question. Are you married?

LOVEWELL: Heavens forbid, 'tis the only happiness I can boast.

CHARLOTTE: Perhaps you may find it a greater than you are aware of, before we part, if you use it to your advantage.

JULIANA: What think you, sir, of a young beautiful lady with a great fortune, who loves you well enough to throw herself into your arms? Could you find in your heart, think you, to refuse her?

LOVEWELL: Why, faith, my little acquaintance, these would all very well agree with a man under my circumstances; but pray gentlemen, unriddle, and let me know the good fortune you tantalize me with.

CHARLOTTE: Well sir, I will most faithfully discharge my message. I have as I told you, a relation that is infinitely dear to me, who is, if the world does not flatter her, not unhandsome. Young I'm sure she is, and not ill-humoured, but what supplies all defects, is a fortune not despicable, being by the death of her mother's father, who was a rich East-India merchant, possessed of £1500 a year, besides a considerable value in money and jewels; but what renders her most worthy of your affections, is that she passionately loves you, loves you to madness, from the first moment she saw you, and must be ever miserable to live without you.

JULIANA: Alas, it is not possible she can live at all, without a suitable return to her affection, you cannot sure sir, be cruel to a young lady.

LOVEWELL: [*looks surly*] Ah poor lady, it may be so. [*to* JULIANA] But you had best, sir, put your friend upon some other subject, for we shall not be company for each other long, if he proceeds in this. One of you I presume have been dabbling with your lady-mother's woman, and wants a convenient tool to cover shame. You were strangely ill- advised to pick me out: there be cullies[1] enough to serve your gross purpose. For whatever opinion you may have of your moving rhetoric, you'll find it no easy matter to impose upon a man who has had more experience of the town than your years will give you leave to know. 'Tis your youth indeed that best excuses your folly, in attempting a man you have no reason either from his character (if you ever heard it) or that conversation you had with him, to think a fool fit for the use I find you design me.

[*is walking off*]

CHARLOTTE: By heaven, and all that's good, you do me wrong: I'm sensible how hard a matter it would be to impose on you, or did she think you so, I'm sure would scorn you; may all the happiness I wish myself prove

[1] *cullies*: dupes

endless torments, if every word I have said, be not sincerely true. [CHARLOTTE *holds him and looks concerned*]

LOVEWELL: What! I warrant 'tis some good pious alderman's wife, that finding her husband defective, wants a drudge to raise an heir to the family; 'tis indeed the common game we younger brothers live by.

JULIANA: Sir, do our habits or addresses merit no better an opinion, than so sordid a thought of us? Besides, did we not tell you, she is a rich young heiress, and consequently unmarried.

LOVEWELL: Pardon me, sir, I had forgot that, but there follows a greater mischief; she's, I suppose, for honourable love: No, I'm for none of that. If she'll accept of a civil kindness or so, I'll do my best to please her.

CHARLOTTE: When I have told you sir, that this lady whom you please to be so witty upon, is sister to Sir Charles Frankford, think if you can hope for anything from her but what marriage, which you so much despise, entitles you to; if you do not know him, give yourself the trouble to enquire after him, and his sister Charlotte, whom perhaps you may not find so contemptible, as you imagine; or at least if she does not merit your love, she may a little more respect.

LOVEWELL: [*aside*] This looks very real, it may be true, and I like an unlucky dog be too incredulous. – Sir, I most earnestly entreat your pardon. Sir Charles Frankford I know very well, and have often heard of his beautiful sister, but yet you must give me leave to distrust my own merit, so much as to think she cannot cast away a thought, much less her love on so unworthy an object of it, as the unhappy Lovewell.

CHARLOTTE: You're as suspicious as an old lady that marries a young man is of a handsome chamber-maid. But no more doubts and scruples dear Infidel, but if you resolve to marry this kind-hearted lady, make me the messenger.

LOVEWELL: Well, conduct me to the lady – we shall make the best bargain. I hope you would not have me marry without seeing her.

CHARLOTTE: No sir. Be tomorrow morning, exactly at nine o'clock, at Rosamond's Pond,[2] she'll meet you there

---

[2]*Rosamond's Pond*: a famous spot for assignations in St James's Park

with one lady more, both masked. She that gives you her hand, accept with it her heart and person. But come not if you do not fully resolve to marry her; consider of it till tomorrow morning. Come cousin, I believe by this time we have tired the gentleman of our company.

JULIANA: But first, let's know your final resolution.

LOVEWELL: 'Tis to meet the lady however.

JULIANA: We may trust to her charms for the rest.

CHARLOTTE: Well sir, adieu. Remember nine.

LOVEWELL: Fear not, I'm too much pleased with the imagination of my approaching happiness to forget it.

CHARLOTTE: We'll set you down where you please.

LOVEWELL: With all my heart. I lodge in Leicester-fields.

CHARLOTTE: That's in our way, come sir.   [*Exeunt Omnes*]

Act Two

SCENE ONE

Enter SQUIRE WOULDBE, *with a letter in his hand, reading*

SQUIRE WOULDBE: I am the luckiest fellow that ever was born,
I was surely wrapped in my mother's smock, none of all the
weak sex can find in their heart to deny me: I have most
powerful charms, that's certain. But Oh, ye gods! That a man of
my parts should be born of such mean parents! I must hasten,
for 'tis near six.

Enter DOWDY. SQUIRE WOULDBE *puts the letter hastily up.*

SQUIRE WOULDBE: [*aside*] Pox on her, now shall I be plagued
with her impertinence.

DOWDY: [*running to him*] Nay, I will see that paper, what is it
you put up so hastily. Let me see, you rebel you, for I'm resolved
I will see it, that I will.

SQUIRE WOULDBE: See, what would you see? 'tis nothing but a
libel. [*gives her a wrong paper*] There, take it, bid the maid
bring my cloak and my sword; I'm just sent for out, to a client.

DOWDY: Is this all? [*Gives him the paper. Cries and snivels as
she speaks.*] Here take it again; but you shan't go out to ne'er
a client in England, that you shan't. Marry gip! Go to a
client, and leave me to sup alone, after I have got a hot
supper for you too. You don't care for my company, that
you don't. I don't care, I'll go and tell my mother, that I will,
I won't be used so.

SQUIRE WOULDBE: [*aside*] I must wheedle the fool; not that I
care for the mother more than the daughter, but I shall lose
many a good forfeited pawn in the year, if any complaints are
made.

DOWDY: What's that you mutter to yourself? I swear and
protest I will go to my mother, and make her fetch home all the
plate and linen in your house, you rebel you, and see where you

can get more. Was not I the making of you? Now you'd leave me, and a hot supper, for a client. Marry come up.

[She going off, he catches hold of her.]

SQUIRE WOULDBE: Nay, prithee Bunny, don't be angry; as true as I am God A'mighty's child, I'll come home to supper; pray Bunny, let I go.

[Makes a courtesy and looks simply.]

DOWDY: You shan't go, that you shan't, you rebel you.

[She pouts and looks surly.]

SQUIRE WOULDBE: If you won't let me go to my clients, how shall I be able to maintain my family? Let me go Bunny, and indeed and indeed I'll give you a fine new petticoat, such a one as your neighbour Mrs Whatyoucallun has.

DOWDY: But will you come home to supper then at eight o'clock?

SQUIRE WOULDBE: I will truly, Bunny – what have you got?

DOWDY: A most lovely buttock of beef and cabbage; do Puggy, pray come home. Ha, but will you?

[Fawns upon him, and kisses him.]

SQUIRE WOULDBE: 'Deed I will Mrs Honesuckle, tum dive I one, two, tee Busses, nay, one mo: 'bye Bunny.

DOWDY: You're a wicked man – well go, but make haste home.

SQUIRE WOULDBE: *[aside]* Heaven make thankful, I am at last rid of her nauseous fondness. 'Bye-bye, I'll take my cloak within.

[Exit SQUIRE WOULDBE]

DOWDY: 'Bye dear rogue. Oh 'tis a sweet natured man, he's strangely fond of me.

Enter MRS BELDAM

MRS BELDAM: How now daughter, where's my son?

DOWDY: He's just gone out, mother, but he'll come home again to supper.

MRS BELDAM: He'd best, or he may look for the Point Cravat[3] I have here for him – a Forfeited Pawn, of no less than one of the King's officers, Mr Constable of our Parish; 'tis almost spick and span new – he never wore it but of Sundays. But are you sure daughter, he'll come back to supper, or else I will not leave it.

DOWDY: Oh, I am sure he will, for he promised me, and he's never worse than his word. Poor rogue! Oh, he's the kindest

[3] *Point cravat*: lace neckerchief

wretch, mother, that ever was, he grows fonder and fonder every day than other. Won't you sup with us mother? Poor wretch, he longs to see you.

MRS BELDAM: No, daughter, I cannot stay. I have appointed a customer to be at home at seven, to take in a silver tankard, which I will send to you, for that you have is called home, and I am to return it tomorrow; this is one much of the same value, the change will hardly be perceived.

DOWDY: But you will bring it before you take the other home I hope; for my Puggy will drink out of nothing but silver.

MRS BELDAM: Aye, aye, that I will. Since you say my son is so good, you shall have anything. Here, take what I have brought for him; remember my love to him, and so goodnight, daughter; I must be gone.   [*Exit* MRS BELDAM]

DOWDY: Goodnight, forsooth, if you must. 'Tis a rare thing to have such a mother; she's always giving my Puggy one good thing or other, which makes him take care to please me. She will one time or other disgrace me, by coming in her everyday clothes: I am ashamed to call her mother in them.

[*Exit* DOWDY]

SCENE TWO

SIR CHARLES'S *garden*

Enter SIR CHARLES FRANKFORD *and* SIR ROGER MARWOOD, *with musicians.*

SIR CHARLES: I think Sir Roger, we must give my sister, and cousin Julia, an essay of our serenade; the song is pretty, and may properly be applied to any of the fair sex. But is it not very gallant to treat a sister thus?

SIR ROGER: I believe, Sir Charles, if Madam Juliana had not a greater share in it than your sister, she'd lose her part in this entertainment.

SIR CHARLES: I must own my fair cousin has charmed me; but I have of late observed her grown so thoughtful, I fear her heart already is engaged, which makes me fear to own any pretensions to it.

SIR ROGER: She cannot sure be insensible to the brother of

Charlotte, whom she so tenderly loves; advance your addresses, you have a good advocate.

SIR CHARLES: No, I'll see that mad sister of mine disposed of first: I'd give five hundred guineas to see her in love; for I dare not own my being so, till she's a little tamed. She'll only make me her sport, as she does all mankind besides.

SIR ROGER: I think Sir Charles you should rather give it to secure her from it if possible; for what assurance have you she will not, blind with that mad passion, be betrayed to match herself to one unworthy of her merit, and bring an alliance to your family, you'd blush to own.

SIR CHARLES: No, I dare swear for her; however frolicsome she is in her humour, she'd scorn to look on anything that was basely born: but I have often heard her declare she would, whenever she married, match herself where she found more merit than estate. I know so well her pride in that concern, I dare trust the honour of our family in the hands.

SIR ROGER: Then if she should throw herself away upon some well-born younger brother, not worth a groat, I find you would easily forgive her.

SIR CHARLES: She has a plentiful fortune, enough to make any man happy; she's free and absolute, and has as much right to dispose of herself and fortune as I of mine.

SIR ROGER: It argues but little kindness, for your sister to be so careless of her advantage.

SIR CHARLES: You need not instruct me in my kindness for my sister, she never found any want of it, nor shall she. But whence comes your concern for her, Sir Roger?

SIR ROGER: As she's the sister of my dearest friend. But come, let's have that song. Are you sure they're together?

SIR CHARLES: They seldom part so soon, you know. [To the MUSICIANS] Come, gentlemen, let's have the song.

SONG

Young Celinda's youthful charm,
    Fills the admiring town with wonder;
The stubbornest heart her eyes alarm,
    And makes them to her power surrender;

Face, and shape, and wit so rare!
        Heaven's masterpiece she was designed:
A graceful mien, and such an air,
        Nothing excels it but her mind.

Though women envy, men admire;
Her eyes, in all, do love inspire.

SIR ROGER: I think the door opens.

SIR CHARLES: Pray, gentlemen, retire a little, we'll come to you
immediately in the street.   [*Exit* MUSICIANS]
        Enter CHARLOTTE *and* JULIANA *in their own clothes, and*
        BETTY *with them.*

SIR CHARLES: 'Tis they, let's get behind this arbor,[4] from whence
we may discover what they say; they certainly will go in there; 'tis
the usual place of discoursing their secrets in. Perhaps I may pay
for my listening; but I cannot resist so sweet a temptation.

        [SIR CHARLES *and* SIR ROGER *go behind the arbor*]
        [CHARLOTTE *and* JULIANA *go into the arbor:* BETTY *stays
        outside.*]

CHARLOTTE: [*speaking as she enters the arbor*] I told you 'twas
but your fancy; I was sure no music, nor no one else but my
brother, would enter here, and he is not at home. Now, my dear
Julia, do not you applaud my happy fortune? Is it not better,
thus to choose for one's self amongst a multitude, than out of a
few, whose interest, more than love, solicits me? If all things
prove but successful to my wishes in this affair, I shall be
perfectly happy; if my dear Julia was but so, I could not wish
myself another joy.

JULIANA: Nothing would more alleviate my grief than constantly to see you so; which is the hearty wish of your unhappy
friend.

CHARLOTTE: You heighten your own trouble by your obstinate
refusal to let him know what I am sure he'd accept with joy. For
heaven's sake let me tell him, I'm confident he'll bless me for't,
and so will you hereafter.

JULIANA: I'll sooner yield my body to the stake than own a
passion for a man thinks me not worth his taking notice of. No,

---

[4] *arbor:* tree

my dear Charlotte, I beg you to conceal it, as you would do a fatal secret that would betray my life; for, the first minute he discovers it, I'll put it out of his power ever to see me more.

CHARLOTTE: It grieves my soul to see you thus afflicted, and will not give me leave to ease your pain; but, be assured, I never will betray the least of all your thoughts without your free consent.

JULIANA: No matter what becomes of wretched Juliana, so my dear Charlotte's happy.

CHARLOTTE: Take by the same method, and you may be so too; for, should my designs fail the way I've laid them, I'll openly own them, and then I do not fear being denied; though 'twould vex me heartily to miss the pleasure of knowing whether I'm beloved or not.

JULIANA: Alas! Your passion's but in jest: you do not yet know the torments, to wake whole nights with restless thoughts.

CHARLOTTE: No, no, never will; where're I loved, I'd tell him so, and break that useless piece of modesty, imposed by custom, and gives so many of us the pip.[5]

JULIANA: I wish I had your merry heart; but I am now so serious, that the least jest is unsavoury to me. Prithee Betty, sing the last new song I gave you.

CHARLOTTE: Nay, if thou'rt come to rhyming, thou'rt in love indeed.

SONG

Restless in thoughts, disturbed in mind,
　　Short sleep's deep sighs: ah much, I fear,
The inevitable time, assigned
　　By fate, to love's approaching near.

When the dear object present is,
　　My flutt'ring soul is all on fire:
His sight's a heaven of happiness;
　　And, if he stays, I can't retire.

Tell me, someone, in love well read,
　　If these be symptoms of that pain.
Alas, I fear, my heart is fled,
　　Enslaved to love, and love in vain.

[5] *gives the pip*: makes us sick

CHARLOTTE: That's your own fault. But come, let's in, the air grows cool.

JULIANA: I'll wait on you to your chamber, and there leave you to your repose.   [*Exit* CHARLOTTE, JULIANA *and* BETTY]

[SIR CHARLES *comes forward and speaks*]

SIR CHARLES: Well, what think you now, Sir Roger, had I not reason for my suspicion? I have paid for my curiosity; but I am only too well assured of what I feared before.

SIR ROGER: Suppose, Sir Charles, you should prove the man? I dare believe I guess not much amiss – who should your sister take such liberty with, as to offer to declare a business of that nature to, but to you?

SIR CHARLES: I wish no happier fortune. But much I fear my stars are not so kind.   [*sighs*]

SIR ROGER: We forget our music; or, at least, they'll think so.

SIR CHARLES: Come, let's to 'em.

[*Exit* SIR CHARLES *and* SIR ROGER]

SCENE THREE

· *A tavern kitchen*

Enter FREEMAN, URANIA *and* COOK-MAID

URANIA: Doll, do you be sure to keep the kitchen clear; we must be as quick as possible for fear of interruption by companies coming in.

FREEMAN: Plague on him! If he would but make haste, there is now but one company in the house.

DOLL: Oh he's here, sir, just got out of a chair.

URANIA: Run you, Doll, and bring him in here; and get you gone, Freeman, you know your end.   [*Exit* DOLL]

FREEMAN: I warrant I'll remember it with a vengeance.

[*Exit* FREEMAN]

[DOLL *returns with* SQUIRE WOULDBE *in woman's clothes, and exits.*]

SQUIRE WOULDBE: [*makes a curtsey, and goes up to her*] Your servant, sweet Mrs Strawberry, am not I a pretty gentlewoman? Now tum dive I a buss.[6]

[6] *a buss*: a kiss

URANIA: Fie sir, what do you mean, you know there's always capitulation before a surrender; you must promise constancy, secrecy, and a thousand other things beside, before we come to the main point.

SQUIRE WOULDBE: Hark you dear child, is this a place to make conditions in? What a devil made you bring me into the kitchen, your chamber had been a properer place for what we have to say and do?

URANIA: Aye, but to have sent you up alone, or carried you up directly, might have given cause of suspicion to my servants, which now I avoid by taking you from hence.

SQUIRE WOULDBE: Let's lose no time, dear child, but go where love and beauty calls. [*aside*] Egad, this was a high touch if it passes for my own. [*to her*] Come, come, do not delay my bliss, your house begins to fill; and we may lose this blessed opportunity.

URANIA: Well, come then, but you must be sure to be very civil.

SQUIRE WOULDBE: Aye, aye, as civil as you desire . . .
          [*leaves off amazedly on hearing* FREEMAN'S *voice*]

FREEMAN: [*loud, offstage*] A man, say you, in woman's clothes with my wife? Damn him, give me my sword, I'll stick him to the wall.

URANIA: O heavens what will you do, you're betrayed!

SQUIRE WOULDBE: [*shaking and showing great signs of fear*] 'Swounds, what shall I do? Here's ne'er a hole to creep in, as I see, that will hide a mouse.

FREEMAN: [*offstage*] Here, Sirrah, charge this pistol for me whilst I charge the other; perhaps he's armed for a surprise, but I'll maul the dog, I'll lay his lechery for him I warrant him.

URANIA: [*seeming in a great fright*] You're a dead man if you do not do something presently. [*looking about, she sees the cistern*] Here, here, get into the cistern; there is as it happens but very little water in it.

SQUIRE WOULDBE: Ah lord, anywhere, so I may but save my dear life; well this is a judgment upon me for coveting my neighbour's wife: if I had been at home with my own, I need not have feared anybody.   [*gets into the cistern*]

    Enter FREEMAN, *armed, looking about*

FREEMAN: What have you done with your metamorphosed gallant? Produce him you'd best, for if he escape my fury you shall feel it, you Jezebel you!

URANIA: What is't you mean, are you mad to make me and yourself ridiculous? I know of never a gallant that I have; if you do you had best find him out. Who is it puts these crotchets in your crown? You never had reason to believe ill of me, and why should you hearken to every fool's tale?

FREEMAN: Why, had not you a man with you in women's clothes?

URANIA: I have had nobody with me but my midwife, and if you had come sooner you might have examined, if you pleased.

FREEMAN: Indeed Urania, I am to blame to suspect you upon every idle story; but I was told that Squire Wouldbe was with you in women's clothes; pray forgive my passion.

URANIA: Indeed you are unkind, but I can forgive you more than this.

FREEMAN: Have an eye to the bar, for I am sent for out but will not stay. [*Exit* FREEMAN]

[SQUIRE WOULDBE *peeps out*]

SQUIRE WOULDBE: Is he gone? I'm almost drowned, the water's come in ever since I've been here.

URANIA: He is, you may venture forth. [*aside*] Pray heaven I hold from laughing.

[SQUIRE WOULDBE *comes out dripping wet*]

SQUIRE WOULDBE: What shall I do, I shall catch my death, with all these wet clothes about me?

URANIA: Here, take this key, and go up to the Star, there's a bed provided for you, and as soon as I can secure my husband, I'll come to you.

SQUIRE WOULDBE: Dear kind charming creature, how you revive me? But are you sure he's gone now, and the coast clear, for 'tis impossible I can take sanctuary in the same place again, for by this time 'tis full of water.

URANIA: You'll have no more occasion, I hope, but if you should, I think you must hide there in the feather tub; [*pointing to a feather tub*]

SQUIRE WOULDBE: I wish I had seen that before, t'would have saved me a ducking.

URANIA: Alas, I forgot it in my fright, but you had best begone for fear of a surprise again.

[*Just as he goes to the door, he hears trampling within, returns in a great fright, and jumps into the feather-tub, and stays.*]

SQUIRE WOULDBE: Aye Lord, he's here again!

URANIA: This was such an unexpected jest, I shall burst with laughing. [*she goes to him*] 'Tis only your fear, here's no body coming, my husband's gone out, and will not return this hour.

SQUIRE WOULDBE: [*comes out all over feathers*] For the Lord's sake don't let me stay here, I shall be frighted out of my wits.

URANIA: Go as soon as you please, lock yourself in, and put the key under the door against I come.

SQUIRE WOULDBE: See, see, is there nobody stirring?

URANIA: Not a mouse, go make haste.

[*Exit* SQUIRE WOULDBE]

Enter FREEMAN, *laughing*

FREEMAN: So I think I have had my jest too, to make him go into the feather tub.

URANIA: You heard me mention it, did you?

FREEMAN: Yes, and I knew his fear would make him take to it upon the least noise; are all things in readiness above?

URANIA: Aye, never fear, let me alone for mischief.

[*Exit* FREEMAN *and* URANIA]

Act Three

SCENE ONE

SQUIRE WOULDBE *is discovered, undressing himself to go to bed.*

SQUIRE WOULDBE: My fright's almost over, but I'm plaguey wet and cold, pox confound the cockold. [*going towards the bed with the candle in his hand, he falls in a trap-door up to his neck and puts his candle out.*] Hey! What the devil's come to me now; am I going quick to hell?

Enter two DEVILS *with torches, and point at him.*

SQUIRE WOULDBE: Help! Help! Will nobody come to my rescue? The devil's come for me indeed.

[*Dance. Enter two more* DEVILS, *who join in a dance with other two, frightening and seizing him. He cries out, and shows great signs of fear after the dance; two more enter and sing:*]

DEVIL:
> Say brother divel say, what must be done
> With this wicked mortal, whose glass is now run?
> We'll dip him in Styx to abate his hot lust,
> Then headlong to hell we the lecher will thrust:
> We'll laugh at his torments and jest at his groans,
> The horns he designed he shall feel in his bones.
> Let's away with him then to great Pluto our king,
> Who expects before this the lewd victim we'll bring.

[*They take him up and carry him off.*]

SQUIRE WOULDBE: [*roaring out*] Help, the Devil, the Devil!

[*Exit*]

Enter FREEMAN *and* URANIA, *laughing*

FREEMAN: So, I think we have sufficiently frighted the fool, but what hast ordered them to do with him now?

URANIA: To carry him home just in the pickle he's in to his wife.

FREEMAN: Sure the coxcomb will never venture hither again?

URANIA: If he do, my next revenge shall be more home.

FREEMAN: I would at any time lose a night's sleep for so much sport. 'Tis time to raise the rest of the family, and then try to get a little sleep.

URANIA: With all my heart, my head aches a'laughing.

[*Exeunt*]

SCENE TWO

MR LOVEWELL *knocks at a door. Enter a* SERVANT.

LOVEWELL: Is Sir Roger Marwood within?

SERVANT: Yes, sir, I'll acquaint him you are here, if you please to walk in.   [*Exit* SERVANT, *followed by* LOVEWELL]
   [LOVEWELL *returns with* SIR ROGER, *who is dressed to go out.*]

LOVEWELL: Sir Roger, your servant. You're an early riser I see; I thought I had been time enough to your levee?

SIR ROGER: That you might have been, had not Sir Charles Frankford sent in great haste to speak with me; for early rising is not a fault I am often guilty of.

LOVEWELL: You are very happy, Sir Roger, to have so free access where so much beauty is your daily entertainment; how is it possible to defend your heart from so many charms the lovely Charlotte, they say, is mistress of. But is she so beautiful as the town reports? For I never saw her.

SIR ROGER: She is indeed beyond imagination, but of so strange and fantastical a humour no one can please her; you have more right to pretend to her favours than I, for she so much declares against a man of an estate, I dare not think of addressing.

LOVEWELL: That can be only an extravagant way of talking; she cannot think an estate, where 'tis but an embellishment to both qualifications, a fault.

SIR ROGER: Sir Charles indeed is of your opinion, but I am much mistaken if he does not quickly find it, the real sentiments of her heart; for last night we heard she and Madam Juliana her cousin discoursing in the garden; she talked of love and some design she had in hand today she feared being crossed in, but what that was Heaven knows.

LOVEWELL: [*aside*] Hah, this absolutely confirms me, 'tis real: I am impatient till I see her. – Well Sir Roger, I'll take my leave of you; I hinder your intended visit.

SIR ROGER: I must confess, I am very eager to see Sir Charles in hopes to hear more of his sister's design.

LOVEWELL: Shall I see you anywhere in the evening, Sir Roger?

SIR ROGER: With all my heart.

LOVEWELL: Where?

SIR ROGER: I shall be at Lockets[7] from eight to ten or later.

LOVEWELL: I will, if possible, wait on you there.   [*Exeunt*]

SCENE THREE

St James's Park

Enter CHARLOTTE *and* JULIANA, *masked*

JULIANA: I see you'll really meet him then?

CHARLOTTE: Aye, and marry him too, if he has courage enough to venture on me.

JULIANA: 'Tis a strange resolution, Heaven send you may never have reason to repent it; think well, my dear, what you do, consider it is irrevocable.

CHARLOTTE: Prithee forbear; thy serious notions almost spoil my design; but know my Juliana, I have given him my heart, and will my person, for I passionately love him.

JULIANA: I wish him worthy of his happy fortune; the time draws near; does not your heart go a-pit a-pat?

CHARLOTTE: Yes, for fear he'll not come.

JULIANA: [*looking out*] That care is at an end, prepare for the combat, for yonder comes your antagonist.

CHARLOTTE: 'Tis he indeed, my courage almost fails me, but 'tis too late to retreat; I'll stand the brunt, let what will be the event.

   Enter LOVEWELL, *and gazes on them:* CHARLOTTE *advances towards him, pulls off her glove and gives him her hand, which he kisses.*

LOVEWELL: If the whole piece prove as beautiful as this sample, I find I'm undone already; come unmask, dear madam, and kill me quite.

JULIANA: Not to show a better face, but better nature; I'll give her my sample.[8]   [*pulls off her mask*]

LOVEWELL: 'Twas kindly said and done. [*To* CHARLOTTE]

---

[7] *Lockets*: a fashionable coffee house   [8] *sample*: example

But egad madam, if you mean to preserve the conquest of my heart entirely to yourself, you'd best put by that cloud, for there are dangerous eyes. [*Looking at* JULIANA]

JULIANA: She'll soon reduce the rebel to his obedience, convince him of the truth, by showing him a prospect of that heaven which is allotted for him.

CHARLOTTE: No, I'll leave it to his imagination, which perhaps may be to my advantage; and if you have courage enough to venture on me as you see me, here's my hand and heart, and all that's mine to be entirely yours.

LOVEWELL: 'Tis a large proffer; but I'm for none of fortune's blind bargains; come upon the square, dear lady, and I am for you. I ever had an aversion to a vizor-mask; it shall be one of my articles,⁹ that from this day forward you shall never wear one.

CHARLOTTE: With all my heart, conditionally that this day the only one in which I must reign, I may wear it at pleasure.

LOVEWELL: After you have discovered that face which is to charm me out of my liberty, I'll agree to all you desire.

CHARLOTTE: [*pulling off her mask*] As you're a man of honour, stand to your word, for now I claim you as my own.

LOVEWELL: [*eagerly kissing her hand*] By heavens, an angel! Dear charming creature, dispose of your happy slave for ever; I am now no more the cautious illnatured fellow I have been all this time; I am all o'er love and rapture. Come lovely creature, let's away to church, where I may make you mine without danger of ever losing you.

CHARLOTTE: [*laughing*] Mercy on me! What an alteration's here! From whence proceeds this mighty change?

LOVEWELL: Could you expect less from that bewitching face, enough to tempt Diogenes from his tub,¹⁰ and make that surly stoic turn epicure! Heaven never made such dazzling beauty but to do miracles. I'm now love's convert. [*Aside*] So I find I'm a woman's ass already, I am downright damnably in love, and will through this matrimonial gulf, if I perish in the attempt.

CHARLOTTE: You're very serious sir, pray don't consider too much: I may chance to lose a husband by it.

⁹*articles*: rules   ¹⁰*Diogenes*: cynic philosopher said to have lived in a tub

LOVEWELL: I am thinking how very happy I shall be when the divine Charlotte's mine; come dear madam, I will delay my bliss no longer.

CHARLOTTE: Aye, for heavens sake, let's away while this passion lasts, this violence will soon be over, and then the tide will turn.

LOVEWELL: It never, never shall, dear charming angel.

CHARLOTTE: [*to* JULIANA] Come cousin, you must be our witness.

JULIANA: I wish I may be ever so to all that makes you happy.

[*Exeunt omnes*]

SCENE FOUR

Enter SQUIRE WOULDBE *and* DOWDY

SQUIRE WOULDBE: Nay, pray dear Bunny, don't be nangry indeed and indeed; I was taken up by the watch[11] and carried to the Round-house.[12]

DOWDY: Yes, yes, a likely matter, and how came you out pray?

SQUIRE WOULDBE: Why the devil sent four of his life-guard, and took me out by main force.

DOWDY: Don't think to make a fool of me, but tell me the truth, you'd best, you rebel you: who was it brought you home? They looked like devils indeed; but how come you in this pickle to come home without your clothes?

SQUIRE WOULDBE: [*aside*] What the devil shall I say now? [*pauses a little*] Why indeed Bunny, I cannot tell, for I was damnable drunk, and did not know I was in the Round-house till I woke this morning and found myself there: pray Bunny, forgive I, as true as I am God Almighty's child, I won't do so no more. [*kneels and makes pitiful faces*]

DOWDY: Get you gone, you fool, and don't make yourself such an ass; you are like to wear your old clothes till Easter, for you shall have no new ones.

SQUIRE WOULDBE: Nay, pray Bunny now don't be so nangry; indeed I do love Bunny. [*rises, kisses and fawns on her*]

[11]*watch*: night watchman [12]*Round-house*: his lock-up

DOWDY: You have such a way with you, well, come then but will you be good?

SQUIRE WOULDBE: I will indeed Bunny, go and bid the maid warm my bed, for I am very weary with my last night's lodging; if anybody comes to speak with me, let me not be disturbed.

DOWDY: I will my dear, poor wretch, I'll go and make you some buttered ale[13] too. [*Exit* DOWDY]

SQUIRE WOULDBE: Aye do, so I have appeased one fool. I'm damned mad at this disappointment, if I thought Urania had a hand in it, I'd be revenged of her, by publishing to the town I had lain with her; I did verily believe the devil had run away with me, till I discovered one of them to be Ben the Drawer;[14] 'twas certainly a contrivance of Freeman's. I'll return it to him with the honourable badge of a pair of horns. I'll sleep three or four hours, and then write to her for another appointment, I doubt not but the kind soul is willing. [*Exit* SQUIRE WOULDBE]

SCENE FIVE

The Blue Posts in the Haymarket

Enter LOVEWELL, CHARLOTTE *and* JULIANA

LOVEWELL: Now, my dear Charlotte, that I can call you mine; how much I prize the blessing you shall find by the great value I shall set on you.

CHARLOTTE: You are wonderous devout, but 'twill ne'er last long: the saucy name of husband will in short time claim its lawful authority. But pray Mr Lovewell, hasten dinner.

Enter SERVANTS *with dinner*

JULIANA: 'Tis here you are always happy; you can but wish and have.

LOVEWELL: Come ladies, fall to, if you have any appetite; I must restrain mine, though grace is said.

CHARLOTTE: If you have any to what's here let's sit – Remember this is my day of power; and being the last that I must reign, you must expect me to be very tyrannical.

---

[13]*buttered ale*: warm ale mixed with butter, sugar and cinnamon
[14]*drawer*: tapster

JULIANA:　All happiness to you both, and may it ever continue.
　[*drinks to 'em*]
CHARLOTTE:　As much to dear Juliana in the man she loves.
LOVEWELL:　Success and happiness attend us all. What think
　you of a song, ladies, 'twill give us time to eat.
CHARLOTTE:　With all my heart.
LOVEWELL:　Call in the music there!
　　　　　　　　　[*Exit* WAITER *and re-enter with* MUSICIANS]
LOVEWELL:　[*to the* MUSICIANS] Come, pray oblige us with a
　song.

A Dialogue by a man and a woman

WOMAN:

　　　　Oft have you told me that you loved,
　　　　And asked how I your flame approved;
　　　　Of love and flames I've heard 'tis true,
　　　　Yet never till it came from you.
　　　　But I would know what 'tis so called,
　　　　Before my heart in't be involved.

MAN:

　　　　'Tis a desire in the mind,
　　　　A pleasing pain, and joy refined.
　　　　Life is a dull insipid thing,
　　　　Where love its blessings does not bring.
　　　　The Gods themselves, who joys dispense,
　　　　Have felt its mighty influence.

WOMAN:

　　　　If Gods that power have owned, alas! I fear
　　　　I strive in vain to keep my freedoms here.

MAN:

　　　　Resign it then, and bless me with your love,
　　　　A glory I'd not change to move
　　　　The brightest star in all the orb above.

WOMAN:

　　　　If you will promise ever to be true,
　　　　My heart and freedom I'll give up to you.

MAN:

　　　　As well the needle from his pole may move,
　　　　As I to love and thee unfaithful prove.

CHORUS TOGETHER:
>In love and in pleasure we'll pass all our nights,
>And each day we'll revel with some new delights;
>Thus we'll live, and love on, till together we die;
>And in each other's arms to Elysium will fly.
>
>[*Exit* MUSICIANS]

CHARLOTTE: Now, Mr Lovewell, you must give my cousin and I permission to leave you for a little time, to go to the Exchange to provide some necessaries; and because I will not leave you idle, pray take pains to tell[15] that purse of gold.

LOVEWELL: Since it must be so, what you please. But I hope you will not make it long before you return.

CHARLOTTE: You shall not stay for us half an hour.

LOVEWELL: Where will you go when you come back?

CHARLOTTE: We'll discourse of that when we meet again; farewell. Come cousin. [*Exit* CHARLOTTE *and* JULIANA]
[LOVEWELL *waits on them to the door, returns, sits down, and counts the gold.*]

LOVEWELL: Five hundred pieces; a pretty sum, and not unwelcome at this time. Egad I was a very lucky fellow to have a pretty rich young lady thus thrown into my arms, just in the ebb of my fortune.

Enter WAITER *with a letter*

WAITER: Here's a note, sir, left for you at the bar, as they went out. [*Exit* WAITER]

LOVEWELL: Ha! What should be the meaning of this! [*opens, and reads*] – *Dispose of yourself as your humour serves you, when you have done with the employment I left you; for you will meet at this time with no other entertainment from your Bride.* [DRAWER *ready*] Death, hell, and furies! what can this mean! Am I thus jilted at last by some lewd woman! Oh sot! that I could think one of Charlotte's birth and fortune would marry at that wild rate. She only took up that name to gull the easy coxcomb, unthinkful fool; I could curse myself, her, the sex, and all the world. What shall I do, o dear damned imposter! By heaven I love her so, I can scarce repent I have

---

[15]to tell: to count

made her mine; were she but honest, which much I fear, I would
not change her for the world's Empress. But why do I flatter
thus a senseless passion? This toad, for ought I know a lewd
prostitute, who only has drawn me in to go to gaol for her. Oh
there it is! Some false fair devil, forsaken by her keeper, that
wanted only a husband for that use, or else to father somebody's child. But however, she is no very poor whore. [*shows
the purse*] But this is no place to expostulate in. – here, Drawer!

Enter DRAWER

DRAWER: Did you call, sir?

LOVEWELL: Aye, what's to pay?

DRAWER: All's paid, sir, by the ladies.   [*Exit* DRAWER]

LOVEWELL: So that's some comfort still; come, cheer thy heart,
Lovewell; all yet may be well. They're jilts of quality, however. I
believe it is e'en some lady-errant that's run mad reading of Don
Quixote; but hang't, jesting is a little unsavoury at this time. I'll
see if I can find out Sir Roger Marwood, who may tell me some
tidings of the true Charlotte, though not of my fair damned
devil. Oh, curse of my credulity.

Well; since this damned jilt is gone;
I am fairly rid of all the sex in one.   [*Exit* LOVEWELL]

Act Four

SCENE ONE

Enter LOVEWELL, *and* DRAWER

LOVEWELL: Is Sir Roger Marwood here?

DRAWER: Yes, sir.

LOVEWELL: Who's with him?

DRAWER: Only Sir Charles Frankford.

LOVEWELL: Tell them Lovewell desires to know if he may have admittance to them.

Enter SIR ROGER

DRAWER: Yes, sir, I will.

LOVEWELL: 'Sdeath, what shall I do? Tell him I'm married, he'll only laugh at me, as all the world will do besides. He's here! Heavens, what shall I say?

SIR ROGER: Why so ceremonious, Mr Lovewell, to your friends? Come, come in, we are all alone, and shall be glad of a third person to make us company.

LOVEWELL: Mine will be but very indifferent at this time; for I'm cursedly out of humour.

SIR ROGER: I'm sorry for that, and much more so, if you have any just occasion; but come, we'll endeavour to divert you.

LOVEWELL: [*aside*] 'Twill be ineffectual at this time – Call Drawer. I'll follow you, sir.

[*Exeunt* SIR ROGER *and* LOVEWELL]

The scenery draws open, and SIR CHARLES FRANKFORD *is discovered, writing at a table. Glasses and bottles.*

Enter to him SIR ROGER MARWOOD *and* LOVEWELL

SIR CHARLES: Mr Lovewell, your servant. You'll pardon me I did not wait on you. I was writing an excuse to my sister, whom I promised to fetch home from Kensington[16] this evening, but an unexpected business is fallen out which hinders me. You'll give me leave to make an end. [*sits down*]

[16]*Kensington*: then a village outside London

LOVEWELL: Aye, pray Sir Charles. [*to him*] Has Madam
   Charlotte been long out of town, Sir Charles? [*aside*] So I find
   I'm indeed ruined, she's out of town. Oh! I could curse!

SIR CHARLES: She went but this morning to make a visit to a
   relation we have there, who she brings home with her; I'm
   sending my coach for her, she would go this morning into a
   hackney.[17]

LOVEWELL: [*aside*] Ha! some hopes still. [*to* SIR CHARLES] If
   your coach goes empty, pray, Sir Charles, give me leave to make
   use of it, for I am obliged to be at Kensington tonight to mount
   the guard.

SIR CHARLES: With all my heart; 'tis at your service.

LOVEWELL: I'll lose no time then, for fear the ladies should stay
   for it.

SIR CHARLES: I'm sorry to lose your good company so soon,
   but I'm likewise engaged. Here, who waits?
      Enter DRAWER

SIR CHARLES: Bid one of my servants come to me.

DRAWER: Yes, Sir.   [*Exit* DRAWER]
      Enter FOOTMAN

SIR CHARLES: Here, give this letter to the coach-man, and bid
   him carry it to my sister at my Aunt Treaters, and wait on the
   gentleman where he pleases.

LOVEWELL: Sir Charles, your servant. Sir Roger, yours. [*aside*]
   So now if I can but get this letter from the coach-man, which I
   suppose will be no hard matter to effect, I shall certainly find
   whether it be my Charlotte or no.   [*Exit* LOVEWELL]

SIR ROGER: This Lovewell's a pretty gentleman. I have often
   thought he's in all circumstances the very man I have heard
   your sister wish for to meet in a husband. But how goes the
   business with your fair cousin Juliana? I dare believe she loves
   you.

SIR CHARLES: I dare believe so too, but only as she is a relation.
   I fear some happier man is the subject of her sight.

SIR ROGER: That you may soon resolve yourself, by discovering
   your passion to your sister, who knows the deepest secrets of
   her heart.

---

[17]*a hackney*: a hired coach

SIR CHARLES: 'Tis true, I may: But I so much fear the discovery will not be to my advantage, that I find some pleasure in being unresolved, to hope the best.

SIR ROGER: Take courage, sir, and try: my life on't 'tis you, and only you that takes up all her thoughts.

SIR CHARLES: Well, I'll venture, let the event be what it will: But come, Sir Roger, we shall outstay our time, 'tis now near six, the hour which we appointed to be at Whitehall.

[*Exeunt* SIR CHARLES *and* SIR ROGER]

SCENE TWO

Enter FREEMAN *and* URANIA *from separate doors*

URANIA: I find there is no getting rid of this opinionated blockhead's saucy importunities, but by exposing him to the whole town, which I'll venture bearing a share in to be revenged of him. Hast the letter Freeman?

FREEMAN: Yes, here it is. I warrant old Madam Beldam catches at it as greedily as she would a client for her son.

[URANIA *takes it, and reads*]

URANIA: [*reading*] *Madam, I cannot see so much goodness as your virtuous daughter is possessed with, abused so grossly by the lewdness of her husband, without (if it is possible) making you sensible of it; if you will be further informed, be this evening at seven o'clock in St James's Park, where you may be convinced how great a brute he is to her, by finding him with a wench. Your friend unknown.*

You have adapted it to her capacity; but I thought you would have writ it to Madam Dowdy herself.

FREEMAN: Oh no, it might have lighted in the husband's hands, and that would spoil all. But have you answered his letter?

URANIA: Yes; and appointed him to be here at nine, to come in boldly, and call for a room, and to let me alone with the rest, which I'd contrive for him. I warrant him I'll be as good as my word; be sure to get some Cherry Bounce[18] for them, you know they are all souls.

---

[18]*Cherry Bounce*: cherry brandy

FREEMAN: I'll warrant I'll have that shall do their business for
'em. I'll put the letter into the penny post myself.

URANIA: And I'll go and see the chamber prepared for him.

[*Exeunt*]

SCENE THREE

Enter CHARLOTTE, JULIANA, BELLASIRA, *with a* SERVANT

CHARLOTTE: A gentleman, say you, come in my brother's coach
with a letter for me?

SERVANT: Yes, madam.

CHARLOTTE: Do you know his name?

SERVANT: Yes, madam, 'tis I think Mr Lovewell.

CHARLOTTE: Go tell him I'll wait on him presently.

[*Exit* SERVANT]

CHARLOTTE: Now, my dear girl, you must assist me, or all my
designs are crossed.

BELLASIRA: What it you would have us do?

CHARLOTTE: Come in, and I will tell you.   [*Exeunt omnes*]

Enter LOVEWELL, *and* SERVANT

SERVANT: Please, sir, to stay one moment here, my lady will
come to you presently.

LOVEWELL: Thank you honest friend. I have easily compassed
the letter; but never was poor unfortunate lover upon a rack as I
am this minute, between hope and fear.

Enter BELLASIRA

LOVEWELL: [*aside*] By heavens I am lost! It is not my Charlotte. I
am so confounded I know not what to say. [*goes to her, and
salutes her*] Madam, Sir Charles made me so happy to be the
messenger of this to his fair sister, Madam Charlotte, whom I
presume you are. [*gives her the letter*]

BELLASIRA: My name is Charlotte, and sister to Sir Charles
Frankford; but I am amazed why he should give a gentleman the
trouble his meanest servant could have performed.

LOVEWELL: [*aside*] Ruined and lost! Cursed, cursed, deluded
fool! [*to* BELLASIRA] Madam, 'twas at my earnest entreaty to
have an opportunity to make me welcome where I could hope
none, but from such an introducer. [*aside*] I'm so distracted I
know not what I say, or do.

BELLASIRA: You seem disordered. Sir, are you not well? Please you to sit?

LOVEWELL: No, madam; I'm taken on the sudden with a strange dizziness in my head, nothing but the air will do me good. Madam, your most humble servant.   [*Exit* LOVEWELL]

BELLASIRA: So this is but one part over, the greatest yet remains behind. I'll in and dispatch this letter after him.

[*Exit* BELLASIRA]

Enter MRS BELDAM *and* DOWDY

DOWDY: I don't care, I will tell him that I will; and I'll tear his eyes out, a rebel as he is. [*blubbering and crying*]

MRS BELDAM: Nay, pray daughter be persuaded, that will make him be upon the march; let us go into this St James's Park, and catch him there, and then we'll swinge him off both together.

DOWDY: But don't go in that pickle, mother; 'twill disgrace me now I am a gentlewoman. Oh, oh, oh! That he should cuckold me that have been the making of him.

MRS BELDAM: Have patience, daughter; perhaps it is a story laid upon him. I'll go home, and put on my best clothes, and come presently.   [*Exit* MRS BELDAM]

DOWDY: Well, I will go and see whether he is there, or no; but I'll up for a dram of comfort, for my spirits are cast quite down.

[*Exit* DOWDY]

SCENE FOUR

Enter LOVEWELL *reading*

LOVEWELL: [*reading*] *If it may be permitted me to hope any thing from the disorder I see in you at our last conversation, I would gladly believe it to my advantage; the sight of you has given me an infinite deal of disquiet, but your absence an insupportable pain. I conjure you to return to me with all speed you can, that I may know what reception my heart may find with you, upon whom I have bestowed it unasked. I demand yours in return, upon which depends the felicity of – Charlotte.* [*sighing*] I would it was in my power to give. What has my cursed fortune reserved me for! Must I ever be her sport! I'm jilted by a false Charlotte, when I might have had the true one.

But that is not the worst of my misery; for to complete it, and make me truly wretched, I love this false, unknown, beyond my reason, and all things. Here she comes, and I'm more out of countenance than she'll pretend to be.

Enter BELLASIRA

LOVEWELL: To answer your commands, madam, I am come; not that I dare with anything from the hopes you give me here. [*shows the letter*] Such blessings does not belong to the unhappy Lovewell, who serves only for the sport of fortune, and all the world besides.

BELLASIRA: I believe you found nothing in my letter, sir, (though I must blush to own it) but what looks too sincere to give the least mistrust it was not real. Heaven is not truer than that Charlotte loves, languishes, and without a grateful sense of her unbounded passion, dies for you.

LOVEWELL: Heaven has not now another curse in store to make me more unhappy.

BELLASIRA: Is then my youth and fortune so contemptible, that it would only heap up miseries upon the man I love? The generous offer I make you of my heart is not a common prize; no, my dear Lovewell, [*she sighs*] for I must call you so, 'tis unacquainted in love's wide labyrinth, and there will lose its way.

LOVEWELL: Forbear, dear madam, to distract me with this angel's goodness, I am not worthy of the least of all this mighty kindness, I wish 'twere in my power to give my heart to her that best deserves it, for none has so just a claim as the divine Charlotte. You have treated me with that sincerity, that 'twould be a baseness I never should forgive myself to betray you with such hopes, (pardon the expression) I cannot justly give; in short madam, to my eternal confusion I speak it, I am not master of my inclinations, I love with all the ardour of prevailing passion, a false ungrateful woman, and what renders my folly inexcusable, one I know not, nor ever perhaps may see again.

BELLASIRA: And can you be so unjust to yourself, and cruel to me, to scorn my real love for a chimera?[19]

LOVEWELL: Express my cursed misfortune by some gentler

---

[19]*a chimera*: a fanciful idea

term, I beg you, that does not suit with the respect that I will
always pay you.

BELLASIRA: If you will still prefer a base ungrateful woman
before the truest love that e'er possessed a tender virgin's
breast, yet grant me this one boon, that I may always know
where to hear of you. I mean no wrong to your ingrate, or to
trouble you with the persecution of my unwelcome love.

LOVEWELL: Be assured, dear madam, you always shall command me in that, and all things else, that lies within my power.

BELLASIRA: Well sir, I will not detain you longer in this uneasy
entertainment.

LOVEWELL: [*kisses her hand*] Adieu, dear madam, you shall
very speedily hear of the unhappy Lovewell. [*Exit* LOVEWELL]

BELLASIRA: So I think I have done pretty well for a young
beginner, but I must give an account of my success, that I
believe they have heard it all.   [*Exit* BELLASIRA]

SCENE FIVE

St James's Park

Enter BELDAM *and* DOWDY. BELDAM *dressed in an old
fashioned point coif,*[20] *a laced Mazarine hood*[21] *over her
face, an a-la-mode scarf laced round, ruffled full behind.
Both masked.*

MRS BELDAM: I wonder how the misses, as they call 'em do,
that wear these masks. I never wore one before. I am all in a
sweat with it, how can you bear yours?

                     [*pulls off her mask and wipes her face*]

DOWDY: Oh, I have learnt to wear one since I was a gentlewoman.

   [*Several men and women cross the stage*]

MRS BELDAM: What a world of fine folks here is, but I don't see
my son yet?

DOWDY: He may be a t'other side, let us go round.

   Enter FREEMAN

[20]*point coif*: lace headwear
[21]*Mazarine hood*: style of hood worn by Charles II's mistress, the Duchess de
Mazarin (i.e., *very* old hat)

FREEMAN: So, there's my game. [*to them*] You seem ladies, to be in search of somebody, can I assist you?

DOWDY: You? Why, what are you?

FREEMAN: A knight adventurer, to serve all pretty ladies.

MRS BELDAM: What, I warrant you, you take us for misses now, because we have got masks; but I'd have you know my daughter and I are not for your turn, we are none of this-end-of-the-town folks.

FREEMAN: Pray good angry old gentlewoman, I mean no harm, nor do not take you for any of this-end-of-the-town ladies; but would perhaps, if you would accept the service, help you to a sight of him you come to find.

DOWDY: Why, how do you know who we come to find?

FREEMAN: Know, why I know by the stars, not only that, but all your most secret thoughts. Did you never hear of Partridge?[22]

MRS BELDAM: Yes, he that makes almanacs, I always buy his, because he nosticates, as they call it, what will come to pass.

FREEMAN: Why, I am he, I can tell you now what you come here for.

DOWDY: Oh mother! He may tell me perhaps where we may find my rebel.

FREEMAN: Aye, that's a small matter in my art, to let you see I perfectly know your concerns: you come here expecting to find your husband with his miss at Rosamond's Pond.

MRS BELDAM: Oh daughter, this is certainly Dr Partridge, and he can tell this by 'strology; maybe he may tell us where to find him.

DOWDY: Pray sir, be so kind if you can.

FREEMAN: Can, that's a good one. Why, I'll carry you to the very house; nay, the very room where he is, if you'll go with me.

DOWDY: Your servant good sir, I'll go with all my heart, shan't us mother?

MRS BELDAM: Yes, if the learned doctor pleases; but will you go with us, good Sir Doctor?

FREEMAN: Yes, that I will. [*to* DOWDY] Let's see your hand lady. [*looks in her hand*] Ha, you were born under Vulcan, you must have a care of horns; I doubt you have been a little too

---

[22]*Partridge*: John Partridge, astrologer, and quack. Later exposed by Swift.

near his forge already by your complexion, let me see, you'll have seven children, as beautiful and wise as the mother, and as honest and modest as the father; you'll be a widow very speedily, that is, within these five or six years. Next husband shall keep a coach.

MRS BELDAM: Oh good sir, tell me if I shall live to see that day.
[*shows her hand to him*]

FREEMAN: Yes, you may, if you spare your brandy bottle a little more than you do.

MRS BELDAM: [*aside*] Oh Lord, I see he knows all I do, I wish he does not find out from whence I furnish my daughter's house with fine sugar, spice, etcetera, and candles, and make Mrs Lockup the house-keeper be turned out of her place.

FREEMAN: Well, come ladies, shall I conduct you where I promised? I have set a spell upon him, that he cannot stir till I come.

DOWDY: Aye, come mother, I long to be at him.

MRS BELDAM: My fingers itch too, I'll pull off his point cravat again with a vengeance.

FREEMAN: Come ladies, I'll lead the way.   [*Exeunt omnes*]

SCENE SIX

Enter CHARLOTTE *and* JULIANA *from separate doors*

CHARLOTTE: Oh coz, Juliana, I was just seeking; I have a secret to discover to you gives me a great deal of pleasure; my brother is passionately in love, and just now confessed it to me, and has engaged me to be his advocate, will not you assist me?

JULIANA: Cruel Charlotte, why this to me? Do you triumph over my misfortune?

CHARLOTTE: Unkind Juliana, to think I would – 'tis you yourself has charmed him.

JULIANA: I fear 'twas gratitude, and not his choice, made him think on me; Unfaithful creature, to betray to him the dearest secret of my life, and force an inclination, perhaps he ne'er had thought of.

CHARLOTTE: By all that's good, my dear, you wrong me, he owned it to me with all the signs of fear your heart was prepossessed; he ever heard our late conversation in the garden, and charged me, if I knew you would not receive his addresses favourably, never to tell you the least tittle of it; I gave him so much encouragement as to revive his hopes.

JULIANA: And so your discourse ended, did it?

CHARLOTTE: No, I told him then of my marriage, which he was far from being angry at, but blamed me a little for using of him so; and promised to forgive me, upon condition I would prevail with you to accept his addresses.

JULIANA: You need not doubt succeeding: my heart too much pleads for him to need another advocate.

CHARLOTTE: Let's go to my cousin, Bell: I left her with my brother, and flew with all impatience to bring these happy tidings.   [*Exuent*]

Act Five

SCENE ONE

Enter CHARLOTTE *and* SIR ROGER MARWOOD

SIR ROGER: You could not, madam, have made a better choice, for Lovewell wants not virtues to make him in all things a complete gentleman, but an estate, which his elder brother was born to, and he best deserves. But why will you use him thus, madam?

CHARLOTTE: Only to find which he has most esteem for, my person or estate.

SIR ROGER: That was a trial to be made before, and not now; when 'tis not in your power to revoke what you have done.

CHARLOTTE: 'Tis, I own, a foolish curiosity; but pray Sir Roger, no more objections, but if you will oblige me, do as I desire.

SIR ROGER: Well, madam, I will, upon two conditions: first, that you use your interest with your pretty cousin, you have brought to town with you, to accept the prize she has made of my heart; and secondly, to put poor Mr Lovewell out of his pain tonight, by discovering his happiness to him.

CHARLOTTE: I engage my honour for both. Do but as I desire for two or three hours, and after I'll be guided by you.

SIR ROGER: I'll obey you, madam, but remember the conditions. [*Exit* SIR ROGER]

Enter JULIANA *and* BELLASIRA

CHARLOTTE: What have you done with my brother?

BELLASIRA: My aunt is entertaining him with politics, which we thought we had but little concern in; so have left them to settle the nation, whilst I come to settle my heart; but I find you have disposed of him whose hands I did design to put it in. Prithee what hast done with him? I shall grow monstrous jealous, if you do not give a very good account of him?

CHARLOTTE: Hey day! What, are you in love too! Sure the little god will empty his quiver in our family, for never was such a company of loving souls?

JULIANA: You see 'tis dangerous jesting with edge tools; you cannot, Charlotte, but in honour assist her, for 'twas you that screwed her up to a love key.

CHARLOTTE: I am glad to find her so inclined, for Sir Roger just now engaged me to be his intercessor.

BELLASIRA: You'll find it no hard task to persuade me to a good opinion of him; but have you engaged him in your affair?

CHARLOTTE: Yes, he is gone about it; but I have yet another part for you, and then I'll undeceive him.

BELLASIRA: I'll do anything you'd have me promise, but that; for I'll swear I am in pain for him.

CHARLOTTE: I do sincerely promise you I will. I wait but for Sir Roger's return, and then you shall know my farther design; come let's now in and release my brother.

> [*Exit* CHARLOTTE *and* BELLASIRA]
>   *Enter* LOVEWELL *and* SIR ROGER

LOVEWELL: Sir Roger, your most humble servant, you are the only man that now is only welcome to me; how can you have so much goodness to throw away a thought on one so wretched?

SIR ROGER: I ne'er forsake my friends in their distress. I wish I could bring comfort to your trouble; all I can say, is, still to hope the best: a day or two may perhaps unriddle the mystery, and you may yet be happy. But come, Mr Lovewell, you must go out with me, I will not leave you alone to your melancholy thoughts.

LOVEWELL: I am at your service, dispose of me as you please.

SIR ROGER: Are you ready?

LOVEWELL: Always to wait on you.   [*Exeunt*]

> *Enter again, as in the street,* SIR ROGER *and* LOVEWELL

SIR ROGER: [*aside*] It goes against my nature to betray this man, though 'tis but in a jest; here are the rascals coming.

> *Enter four* BAILIFFS. *They seize* LOVEWELL'S *sword before he sees them.*

SIR ROGER: Ha! What mean you hell-hounds?

FIRST BAILIFF: No harm to you, sir. Mr Lovewell? I arrest you at the suit of Alderman Saintly in an action of £10,000

LOVEWELL: I never heard of such a name.

SECOND BAILIFF: I suppose, sir, your lady does.

LOVEWELL: Oh does she so, hell confound her for it. Nay, hands off, I'll follow you upon my honour, where'er you'll carry me.

FIRST BAILIFF: Will you not send for bail, sir?

LOVEWELL: No sir, I'll directly to the gaol where I must lie.

SIR ROGER: Will not my bail be accepted? I'll willingly engage for one.

LOVEWELL: By no means, Sir Roger, I will not involve my friends in my misfortunes. They must e'en take my body for the debt, for I am not worth it no way else.

SIR ROGER: I'll straight away to this Alderman Saintly, and see what's to be done.   [*Exit* SIR ROGER]

LOVEWELL: Farewell sir, you'll find me at the gate house. Come sirs, conduct me where you will, I'll tamely follow; I think the mystery is now disclosed with a vengeance.   [*Exeunt omnes*]

   Enter SIR CHARLES FRANKFORD, CHARLOTTE, JULIANA
      and BELLASIRA

SIR CHARLES: Why should you delay my happiness, dear cousin, for the punctilio[23] of formal courtship; I have long loved you, let that atone for it; and if my sister does not flatter me, you do not hate me.

JULIANA: What would the world, and you yourself think of me, to catch at your first proffer, as if I feared you would recant? [*smiling*] I dare trust your constancy, and stay till 'tis convenient.

SIR CHARLES: To the world you may very well answer your conduct; for it is but confirming the reports which have been often of it, being so designed for me, 'tis what I beg of you; and what time's more convenient than now, at the consummating my sister's wedding?

JULIANA: Upon this condition, that you can oblige Sir Roger and my cousin Bellasira to marry at the same time, I'll promise you.

SIR CHARLES: Do you dispose her to it? I'll warrant him, for he's

---

[23] *punctilio*: delicate management

passionately in love with her. What say you, cousin, will you obstruct my bliss? For now it alone depends on you.

BELLASIRA: You know, Sir Charles, you may dispose of me, who are my guardian.

Enter SIR ROGER MARWOOD

CHARLOTTE: Now for some news from enchanted my esquire? [*she takes* SIR ROGER *aside*]

SIR ROGER: 'Tis done as you commanded; but 'tis well if you do not repent it, for I left him in a desperate humour.

CHARLOTTE: Good heaven forbid! Sir Roger, pray wait on my cousin Bellasira to him, but do not you appear; by that time she has done, we'll all be there, [*to* BELLASIRA] you have my full directions. [*Exit* SIR ROGER, *leading* BELLASIRA]

SIR CHARLES: Indeed, sister, you have gone too far, in thus imprisoning a man who shortly must command you. What is it you design now? If you play him any further pranks I'll betray you to him.

CHARLOTTE: I will not. I have only sent my cousin Bellasira to once more try him; after which, I, and Sir Roger, will go to him. You, and my cousins, shall be in hearing; and when you find we come to any agreement, then come in.

SIR CHARLES: Suppose he takes cousin Bellasira at her word, what think you then?

CHARLOTTE: Think! Why, I shall think him a man: But if he can resist the temptation, an angel.

SIR CHARLES: Come, let us go. I'm very impatient to see him disabused. [*Exeunt*]

Enter TURNKEY

TURNKEY: Sir, here is a gentlewoman desires to speak with you. Shall I let her in?

LOVEWELL: A gentlewoman! Aye, pray conduct her in; this is a pretty place to entertain ladies in, but 'tis her own seeking. Who should it be? My fair devil of a wife perhaps!

Enter BELLASIRA

LOVEWELL: This is indeed amazing goodness! How could you think of a lost wretch, dear madam, forsook by all the world?

BELLASIRA: Not all you see, no my dear Lovewell, I never will forsake you, but constantly attend your fortunes; mine cannot be favourable whilst yours are adverse; would you but make mine yours, as I will always espouse your concerns, there should not be a joy possessed by Charlotte, but what should be her Lovewell's, and all his griefs be hers.

LOVEWELL: Your generousity confounds me, I must not add so much to that vast heap of favours I stand indebted to you for; I'm incapable any way to make the least return.

BELLASIRA: Is it so hard to love? I have youth and fortune, is that no charm?

LOVEWELL: Your person is infinitely charming, and that more than angel's goodness, not to be resisted. But know, dear madam, [*sighs*] since I must tell you, to justify myself from that ingratitude, you justly might reproach me with: I am to my destruction married, married, dear lady; that's the cursed cause of all my misery.

BELLASIRA: Then I am lost indeed, a fatal moment that I saw you first. Why were we born to be both unhappy?

LOVEWELL: I could, dear madam, forever be blessed with you, but would not wrong your goodness to involve you in my wretched ruin.

BELLASIRA: This is mere excuse. But for all your cruelty to me, I'll free you from this uncomfortable place, and if you'll still persist in your ingratitude, expect the curse that follows that base sin of never being happy.   [*Exit*]

LOVEWELL: For heaven's sake, dear madam, stay and hear me speak. [*Following her to the door. He returns.*] She's gone, and much I fear, will keep her word; had I but known her before I was bewitched by that damned sorceress, how happy might we both have been? But I'll no longer cavil²⁴ with my fate, but by a tame submission to it baffle its utmost malice.

                                        [*sits down and reads*]

    Enter SIR ROGER MARWOOD *and* CHARLOTTE. LOVEWELL
    starts up and throws away his book.

LOVEWELL: Hah! What do I see! S'death 'tis the dear devil herself; now shall I play the fool and be again deluded, for I find I have not power to be heartily angry at her. But how came he with her?

CHARLOTTE: You seem surprised, sir, I fear my sight offends you.

²⁴*cavil*: frivolously argue

LOVEWELL: I wish it ne'er had pleased me. [*sighs*] False woman, of all the coxcombs that this town abounds with, why was I culled out to be your property! But tell me if thou hast so much grace left to once speak truth, how came he with you?

SIR ROGER: As a kind friend should do, to release thee of thy pains, and take them on myself. I love this lady with all the blindness which attends that passion, marry her at any rate, and sacrifice the world to give myself that satisfaction. She has prudently considered your equal want of fortunes will but make you both miserable.

CHARLOTTE: Therefore if you'll consent to make void our marriage, you shall this minute be released from this place; if not, stay till necessity compels you.

LOVEWELL: Treacherous man, how could you call me friend, and thus basely betray me?

CHARLOTTE: Well, what say you, sir?

LOVEWELL: Hell confound you both; no, I'll still keep thee to be revenged of thee, and plague thee for the wrongs thou hast done me, ungrateful creature, to torture thus a man thou knowest loved thee from the first moment he saw that damned bewitching face; wer't but honest, I could love thee still; but I will tear thee from my heart and never think of thee again, [*sighs*] if possible. [*she weeps*] Ah stop those crocodile's tears, for though I know them to be so, they pierce me to the soul.

CHARLOTTE: Can you forgive me, sir for all this usage? I long have loved you, which made me resolve some way or other to marry you; how I effected it, I need not tell you. I had no sooner done it but I repented, believing justly you would be provoked to use me ill, when once you found I had only borrowed the name of Charlotte – this made my fly your anger.

LOVEWELL: And to secure yourself, secured me. Ha! Was it so? I thank you kind wife, indeed 'twas wonderous love.

CHARLOTTE: Pray hear me out. Sir Roger here, who has long solicited me to his unlawful love, presuming on the scantiness of my fortune, when he found all other ways ineffectual to obtain me, proffered to marry me; which I likewise refused, acquainting him withal of my marriage with you, which made him clap this action on you, to drive you to the choice of either renouncing me or else to keep you here.

LOVEWELL: Oh heavens! That ever such a piece of villainy should harbour in that heart I always thought was noble. How could you call me friend, and thus betray me?

SIR ROGER: [*aside*] She makes me appear a pretty rogue, that's the truth of it; but I must let her run on. – You know, Mr Lovewell, love and friendship are not compatible, where the object of it is adored by both.

LOVEWELL: Then are thou honest? Come swear and damn thyself, you know I am credulous, and shall believe you.

CHARLOTTE: By heavens, and all that is sacred, I am chaste; and love thee at that extravagant rate, I'd quit a throne to dwell with thee in chains. Oh my dear Lovewell, could you meet mine with an equal passion, how happy might we be!

LOVEWELL: Yes, in some country where we could live by air and love; for I know not how we shall maintain a costlier diet.

CHARLOTTE: Providence will not let us starve, we must trust to that; I ask you nothing but your love, I will maintain myself. Indeed you wrong my virtue, I'm truly honest, and would not injure you, though in a thought to gain the world. Forgive what's past, and take me to your bosom.

LOVEWELL: [*holds her in his arms*] Heaven knows how willingly I could, yes I could love thee, dote on thee, and be thy fool. [*puts her from him*] Stand off, vain easy ass; what am I doing, trepanning²⁵ of myself again?

CHARLOTTE: You shall not throw me from ye, I'll follow thus, [*hangs on him*] and never will forsake you; and here I swear I will not leave this place, till you conduct me hence.

LOVEWELL: May I believe you serious?

CHARLOTTE: You must, you shall. I ever will be yours, with as much truth as ever turtle loved her dearest mate.

LOVEWELL: Well, I will live with thee, for heaven knows I love thee; and though you have used me thus, will always use you well.

SIR ROGER: [*smiling*] So madam, I see I'm quite forsaken.

Enter SIR CHARLES, JULIANA, BELLASIRA

SIR CHARLES: Here are more witnesses to your bargain, Mr

---

²⁵*trepanning*: ensnaring

Lovewell, than you are aware of; but methinks, my new brother, you might have asked me leave.

LOVEWELL: Oh, Sir, do not triumph over the easiness of a deluded man. I humbly ask your pardon for the wrong I did design in marrying this fair imposter, whom I did indeed believe your sister; my love for her transported me beyond all thoughts of what I owed you.

[SIR   CHARLES   *takes*   CHARLOTTE,   *and   gives   her   to*   LOVEWELL.]

SIR CHARLES: Here, Lovewell, take her; for my sake use her well: I'll leave it to her to justify her procedure to you. But upon my honour she is my only sister, the rich heiress, Charlotte, whom you first believed.

LOVEWELL: The happy sequel does indeed make a large amends for all I have suffered. But are you sure we do not dream? For I am so accustomed to misfortunes I cannot yet believe them real.

CHARLOTTE: But you were not so diffident, Mr Lovewell, before my estate was added by my brother's discovery.

LOVEWELL: An estate to one in my circumstances is no unwelcome addition. But be assured, dear madam, from the sincerity I ever used to you, 'tis the least part of my joy; but I have, by my knowledge who you are, an unquestioned proof of your virtue, and Sir Roger's being still my friend.

SIR ROGER: And so you shall always find me. [*to* BELLASIRA] For here's my pretentions.

BELLASIRA: Do you think, Sir Roger, I can so soon disengage my heart from cruel Mr Lovewell?

LOVEWELL: Fair cruel Lady! How could you torture so a wretched man not then himself, with a pretended love that gave me more disquiet than my own troubles? But now I am all joy, and will, unasked, forgive the world and fortune for all past injuries; now my dear Charlotte's mine, heaven has not another blessing left that I think worth the asking.

CHARLOTTE: You are wonderous zealous now, pray heaven it lasts.

LOVEWELL: It must, it ever shall. How can you distrust my love, who have given you such evident proofs of it?

SIR ROGER: Since heaven is in this bounteous humour of

dispensing blessings, why should it be only a niggard to me, and make me only a dull spectator of your happiness? Say; will not you join with me in my suit to your fair cousin here?

[*looking at* BELLASIRA]

SIR CHARLES: She is my charge, which I here resign to you. I know she'll be guided by my advice. [*gives her to* SIR ROGER] And now cousin Juliana, I claim your promise.

JULIANA: Methinks you might stay till tomorrow, 'tis time enough, considering how long it is to last.

SIR CHARLES: No, we'll not trust the treachery of another day; fortune is fickle, and may frown tomorrow.

JULIANA: Well then here's my hand, from this day forward, for better for worse, etc.

BELLASIRA: What think you of those words, Sir Roger, do they not make you tremble?

SIR ROGER: Yes, for fear of some fatal interruption before they come to be pronounced.

SIR CHARLES: Let's lose no time then; I have a friend will quickly dispatch the ceremony. [*Exeunt*]

Enter FREEMAN, URANIA, *and* DOLL

URANIA: Well, Doll, what have you done with the Squire?

DOLL: As you commanded, madam, conducted him to your chamber, with charge not to speak but in a whisper; and because I'd be sure he should discover nothing by his candle, I took it away with me, for fear I told him it might be seen at windows, which might occasion a suspicion, not being a room in use; he readily consented, and said, he could find the way to bed by dark, and slipped a crown into my hand to secure my master not coming up. [*Exit* DOLL]

FREEMAN: So 'tis well, there remains no more now; the house fills apace, but the company I design to entertain with this jest is Sir Charles Frankford, and Sir Roger Marwood, who have just sent to bespeak a supper here. I'm sure they bring company with 'em, they have ordered such a noble one; we had best take orders for it, and then we shall have time to entertain them.

Enter SIR CHARLES, SIR ROGER, LOVEWELL, CHARLOTTE, JULIANA, BELLASIRA, FREEMAN *and* URANIA

URANIA: I've used all methods to restrain his folly, by showing the scorn a virtuous woman could to a dishonest love: that but increased his persecutions till I was weary of being angry. I thought, by counterfeiting to return his kindness, which his vanity easily induced him to believe, I might draw him into some snare to betray his lewd intentions to the world, without the hazard of my own reputation, which is generally sacrificed to the malice of a disappointed coxcomb. And to perfect my revenge, I have contrived to let his wife be witness to't, and so leave the fool to her punishing, which he'll find plague enough.

FREEMAN: Call in Doll, and let's begin the farce.

Enter DOLL

FREEMAN: Come, Doll, to your post. [*aloud*] Where's your mistress, Doll? [DOLL *squeaks*] Ha! What are you frighted at?

DOLL: Nothing, sir, but I was almost asleep, and you surprised me.

FREEMAN: That will not serve your turn, mistress. What do you guard this door so close for, is anybody in that chamber?

DOLL: In this chamber, sir, no: who should be here?

FREEMAN: Where is your mistress, I say?

DOLL: My mistress, sir: in her chamber not well, and gone to bed.

FREEMAN: No, but she is not: for, missing her, I have been to seek her, not only there, but in all the rooms in the house, except this. Pray deliver the key, without more fooling; for I will see what you keep sentry for. [*aside*] So by this time I suppose the fool is frighted enough. [*aloud*] Deliver it me, I say, you had best.

DOLL: Pray, sir, don't fright me so, there it is.

[*Gives the key. Exit* FREEMAN *as into the room.*]

FREEMAN: [*within*] That shall not serve your turn: I'll fetch you out of the chimney here. Doll, bring my pistols presently.

SQUIRE WOULDBE: [*within*] Oh pray, Mr Freeman, spare me this time, and you shall never catch me in your house again, nor with your wife.

FREEMAN: Come down then, or I'll fetch you, with a pox to you.

SQUIRE WOULDBE: Oh pray, Mr Freeman, have a little patience, and I will.

Enter FREEMAN *pulling in* SQUIRE WOULDBE *wrapped in a blanket.*

FREEMAN: Nay, nay, no struggling; I must show the company my wife's gallant. [*they all laugh*]

SQUIRE WOULDBE: Who the devil have I been with all this time? Here's Urania, now I find she fools me. (*to* URANIA) How dare you thus expose me? Do not you fear my revenge?

URANIA: [*aloud*] Not at all. I have witnesses enough to prove both your intentions and mine. But I have one within you know not of, whom I'll fetch to you. [*Exit* URANIA]

FREEMAN: Well, Squire Wouldbe, I hope hereafter you'll leave my wife to such a poor clownish fellow as myself; you see she does not understand your merit, but thinks me good enough for her.

SQUIRE WOULDBE: I am ashamed of myself, that's the truth of it, which makes me silent.

Enter URANIA, *with* DOWDY *in a night-gown*

SQUIRE WOULDBE: My wife! Nay then I'm ruined past redemption. [*aside*] How the devil came she here? But that she has not sense enough for an intrigue, I should suspect she was as much mistaken in her bedfellow as myself.

DOWDY: Have I catched you, you rebel you; I warrant you I'll do your errand to my mother.

SQUIRE WOULDBE: Nay, good Bunny, not so fast; pray let me know first how you came here a-bed with me.

DOWDY: Why, Dr Partridge conjured me here on purpose to catch you.

SQUIRE WOULDBE: That's likely; you and I must come to a reckoning about it.

DOWDY: Reckon me no reckonings; there the doctor can tell you as much. [*pointing to* FREEMAN]

SQUIRE WOULDBE: This Dr Partridge! Why, this is Freeman, the master of this house. There is some trick in this. [*to* FREEMAN] I suppose you have been beforehand with me, and given me the horns I designed you.

DOWDY: What do you mean by horns? Do you think I'd be a whore?

FREEMAN: Faith, Squire, no: you may keep your dainty bit to yourself; when I have a mistress it shall be one that will have wit enough to conceal what we do; for o' my conscience, she'd tell.

DOWDY: [*aside*] I can't imagine how I came here to say truth; for I thought I had been a-bed at home, till that gentlewoman came and waked me, and bid me say what I did.

URANIA: You know, Esquire Wouldbe, how many disappointments I have given you just in the height of your expectations, which would never persuade you was done in scorn of your lewd design; this was the only way I thought would rid me of your saucy importunity. I did believe it very necessary to let your wife be an eye-witness of your faith to her, that she may hereafter take more than usual care to keep her coxcomb to herself. I will not give you the satisfaction to let you know how I effected it, but if she or her mother remembers, they may. I'll only add this: there has been no wrong offered to her honesty, which you may easily believe, if you consider the charms of her wit and person.

CHARLOTTE: I think 'tis great pity they should not be entirely each other's, for they are the best matched pair I ever saw.

JULIANA: Indeed, Urania, you are a woman of a singular virtue, that can resist the force of that tempting mein and air.

SIR ROGER: Faith sir, you'd better march off, these ladies will be too hard for you else.

SIR CHARLES: Aye, prithee Freeman, we have e'en enough of their companies, dispose of them as you please.

SQUIRE WOULDBE: Gad I'd be reveng'd of her if I live.

FREEMAN: [*to* SQUIRE WOULDBE] Well, sir, you may go if you please, and take your pretty lady with you, your clothes are in the bar-room where you may dress you, there you have your dismission from this company.

URANIA: And what can you leave your dear Mrs Honeysuckle? Tum dive I a buss, sure you cannot think but I love you strangely after all this proof of my kindness.   [*they all laugh*]

SQUIRE WOULDBE: [*aside*] Pox confound ye, I could cry for madness.   [*Exit*]

DOWDY: Ladies, your servant; I thank you for all your compliments, and shall be very glad to see you at my house. [*going*]
                                                              [*they all laugh*]

URANIA: Hark ye, pray take your booby home with you, and see to keep him there.

DOWDY: I'll have nothing to say to him, I'll go home to my
mother and tell her.   [*Exit* DOWDY]

SIR CHARLES: Prithee put out the coxcomb and bring some
music with you. What think you ladies of a dance?

CHARLOTTE: With all our hearts.

BELLASIRA: You see what constant things you men are to your
vows! I warrant this fellow swore as much faith and constancy
as any of you can.

CHARLOTTE: Hang the poor animals, disgrace not so the race
of men, to compare him to one; such senseless wretches are only
lumps of dirt, not fit for any nobler form.

Enter FREEMAN *with* MUSICIANS

LOVEWELL: So, here's the music. What shall we dance? The
Brawls?[26]

---

[26]*The Brawls*: an old French dance resembling the *Cotillon*, a country dance.

The Beau Defeated

OR

THE LUCKY YOUNGER BROTHER

BY

MARY PIX

1700

DRAMATIS PERSONAE

WOMEN

LADY LANDSWORTH,	*a rich widow from Yorkshire*
MRS RICH,	*a fantastic City widow*
BETTY,	*maid to Mrs Rich*
LUCINDA,	*niece to Mrs Rich*
GOVERNESS,	*to Lucinda*
MRS CLERIMONT,	*cousin to the Clerimont brothers*
MRS FIDGET,	*landlady to Younger Clerimont*
LADY LA BASSET,	*gamester*
MRS TRICKWELL,	*another gamester*

MEN

SIR JOHN ROVERHEAD,	*a beau*
ELDER CLERIMONT,	*a country squire*
YOUNGER CLERIMONT,	*his brother*
BELVOIR,	*friend to Younger Clerimont*
MR RICH,	*a citizen*
CHRIS,	*manservant to Sir John Roverhead*
TOBY and JACK,	*servants to the Clerimont brothers.*

Act One

SCENE ONE

Enter MRS RICH *with* BETTY, *her maid*

BETTY: What's the matter, madam? What has happened to you? What has anybody done to you?

MRS RICH: An affront? . . . Ah! I die: an affront! . . . I faint: I cannot speak. A chair quickly.

BETTY: [*giving a chair*] An affront! To you, madam, an affront! Is it possible?

MRS RICH: But too true, my poor Betty. Oh! I shall die. To disrespect me in the open street! What insolence!

BETTY: How, madam! Not to show respect to such a person as you? Madam Rich: the widow of an honest banker, who got two hundred thousand pounds in the King's service? Pray, madam, who has been thus insolent?

MRS RICH: A duchess: who had the confidence to thrust my coach from the wall, and make it run back above twenty yards.

BETTY: A very impertinent duchess. What! Madam, your person shining all o'er with jewels, your new gilt coach, your dappled Flanders with long tails, your coachman with cocking whiskers like a Swiss Guard, your six footmen covered with lace more than any on a Lord Mayor's day? I say, could not all this imprint some respect in the duchess?

MRS RICH: Not at all. And this beggarly duchess, at the end of an old coach, drawn by two miserable starved jades,[1] made her tattered footmen insult me.

BETTY: 'Slife! Where was Betty? I'd have told her what she was.

MRS RICH: I spoke to her with a mien[2] and tone proportionable to my equipage;[3] but she, with a scornful smile, cried, 'Hold thy peace, Citizen', struck me quite dumb.

[1] *jades*: worthless hags   [2] *mien*: bearing   [3] *equipage*: retinue

BETTY: Citizen! Citizen! To a lady in a gilt coach, lined with crimson velvet, and hung round with a gold fringe.

MRS RICH: I swear to thee, that I had not the force to answer to this deadly injury; but ordered my coachman to turn, and drive me home at full gallop.

BETTY: But, madam, pray consider things rightly, and take this as it was intended; for, I conceive, it was not against your person, but your name, that this affront was designed; and why do you not make haste to change it?

MRS RICH: That I have resolved; but I quarrel daily with my destiny, that I was not at first a woman of quality.

BETTY: Well, well, madam, you have no great reason to complain; and though you are not as yet a woman of quality, you are at least very rich; and you know, that with money you may buy quality, but birth very often brings no estate.

MRS RICH: That's nothing; there is something very charming in quality, and a great name.

BETTY: Yet sure you'd think yourself in a worse condition, madam, were you, as many great ladies in the world are, who want everything; and, in spite of their great name, are known, but by the great number of creditors, that are bawling at their doors from morning till night.

MRS RICH: That's the modish air, 'tis that distinguishes the people of quality.

BETTY: Methinks, madam, 'tis a great satisfaction, to dare to go out at the great gate, without being in danger of having your coach and horses seized by a troop of sergeants; what would you say, if you were obliged to return home in a filthy hack,[4] as several of quality have done?

MRS RICH: Ah! Would to heavens that had happened to me, and that I were a countess.

BETTY: But, madam, you don't imagine –

MRS RICH: Yes, yes, I do imagine, and I had rather be the beggarliest countess in the town, than the widow of the richest banker in Europe. Well, I am resolved; and, I will be a countess, cost what it will; and to that intent, I'll absolutely break all commerce with those little Cits,[5] by whose alliance I am debased; and first I'll begin with Mr Rich.

[4] *hack*: hired carriage   [5] *Cits*: citizens

BETTY: Mr Rich, madam, your brother-in-law?

MRS RICH: My brother-in-law! My brother-in-law! Thou simple wench! prithee know better!

BETTY: Pardon me, madam, I thought he had been your brother-in-law, because he was brother to your deceased husband.

MRS RICH: That's true, my husband's brother, but my husband being dead, fool, Mr Rich is now no more kin to me that my footman; nevertheless the fellow thinks himself of importance, and is continually a-censuring my conduct, and controlling my actions: nay, even the little minx his daughter, when we go in my coach together, places herself at the end by my side.

BETTY: Little ridiculous creature!

MRS RICH: But that which angers me the most, is, that with her little smiling, mimicking behaviour, she attracts the eyes of the whole town, and I have not so much as a glance.

BETTY: What a foolish town is this! Because she's young and pretty, they take more notice of her than you.

MRS RICH: It shall be otherwise, or I'll see her no more.

BETTY: Nay, your Ladyship will humble her, for of late you rarely suffer her to come near you.

MRS RICH: Well, I will have a title, and a name, that's resolved; a name that shall fill the mouth.

BETTY: Ah! Madam, a great name will become you extremely; but a name is not sufficient, I believe you must have a husband too; and you ought to take care what choice you make.

MRS RICH: I know the world well enough, and have in my eye one of the most accomplished gentlemen in the town.

BETTY: How, madam, already made your choice, and I know nothing?

MRS RICH: Sir John would not let me tell thee.

BETTY: What, Sir John? Sir John Roverhead of Roverhead Castle?

MRS RICH: He himself.

BETTY: Why, madam, speak seriously, is it Sir John Roverhead you design to marry?

MRS RICH: Prithee where's the wonder?

BETTY: Why pray consider, madam, Sir John is not worth a groat.[6]

[6]*groat*: a very small sum of money. The groat was by this time worthless and only minted as Maundy Money.

MRS RICH: I have sufficient for us both, and there is justice in
what I design. Mr Rich did not get his estate too honestly; and
'tis some kind of restitution, to raise up with what he has left
me, one of the ancient families in the north.

BETTY: Oh! Since 'tis a marriage of conscience I have no more
to say.

MRS RICH: Betty.

BETTY: Madam.

MRS RICH: Prithee what's thy surname?

BETTY: Has your Ladyship forgot?

MRS RICH: Dost imagine it worth a place in my memory?

BETTY: Cork, madam.

MRS RICH: Oh, filthy! From henceforth let me call thee *de la
Bette*; that has an air French, and agreeable.

BETTY: What you please, madam.

MRS RICH: De la Bette, whatever bills the mechanical fellows,
little trades-people bring ye, let 'em wait, let 'em walk for't, and
watch my levee; but if Monsieur comes that brought the
prohibited gloves, l'eau de fleur d'orange,[7] and the complexion,[8] you understand me, give him his price, and ready money.

BETTY: Yes, madam.

MRS RICH: And do ye hear, put a hundred guineas in the
embroidered purse for basset.[9]

BETTY: Bless me, madam! Have you lost all that I put in
yesterday morning?

MRS RICH: Impertinence! I am sufficiently recompensed in
learning the game, and the honourable company I am admitted
into.

BETTY: Indeed, madam, the footmen say, Mrs Trickwell is a
perfect female rook, lives upon gaming, nay, and keeps out
on't, they say, and they can tell.

MRS RICH: Hold your tongue, she is a woman of quality, knows
everybody at Court, all their intrigues, is as deep in affairs, and
keeps as many secrets, as Maintenon,[10] I'll be sworn; ma foi.[11]
What a word was there! But, as I was saying, she has told me,

---

[7]*l'eau de fleur d'orange*: orange flowerwater
[8]*complexion*: make-up   [9]*basset*: card game
[10]*Maintenon*: Madame de Maintenon, 2nd wife of Louis XIV
[11]*ma foi*: i'faith

and half a dozen ladies more, secrets six hours together; and such secrets *de la Bette*, let me die, were we not women of discretion, might reach the lives, or eternally disgrace, of some that shall be nameless.

BETTY: They are very happy, if they are in her power.

MRS RICH: Peace, has nobody sent a how-de-ye yet?

BETTY: No.

MRS RICH: 'Tis my horrid custom of getting up so early in a morning.

BETTY: Madam, 'tis past twelve.

MRS RICH: And I dressed, and have been abroad, abominable! I charge ye tomorrow don't bring my clothes till past two, if I am so mad to call for 'em.

BETTY: Won't your Ladyship inquire after my Lady Landsworth's health, methinks you neglect her, though she is rich, gay and beautiful, and honours your house with her choice of it whilst she's in town.

MRS RICH: Honours! Who are thou speaking to, sweetheart? I do not like her, she won't play; nay, will sit ye two hours together and speak ill of nobody; she is not fit for the conversation of quality.

Enter a BOY

BOY: Madam, Mrs Trickwell, and another lady, is come to teach your Ladyship, *Shembring*, I think they call it –

MRS RICH: Ombre[12], sot, I shall be rid of thee, thou fragment of the shop. *De la Bette*, I'll go to them, if Sir John comes, call me, not else.

[*Exit* MRS RICH *and* BOY]

Enter LADY LANDSWORTH

LADY LANDSWORTH: My dear Mrs Betty, I'm glad to find thee alone.

BETTY: Your Ladyship does me too much honour.

LADY LANDSWORTH: Thou art so discreet and obliging, I cannot love thee too well. Where's thy impertinent mistress?

BETTY: Gone to learn *ombre*, with a hundred guineas in her pocket.

LADY LANDSWORTH: Ha, ha, ha, her pride, ill-nature, and self-opinion, makes her follies unpitied. I'd fain be rid of the nauseous conversation this house abounds with.

[12]*Ombre*: card game

BETTY: Indeed my City Lady turning courtier has a hopeful flock of teachers: mistresses grown old, and then forsaken, who, in the tatters of their prosperity, pass upon her for decayed quality, female gamesters, and fools in abundance.

LADY LANDSWORTH: They are affected without beauty, or good clothes, though that alone's enough to spoil one that had both; their mirth is insipid, and their raillery abusive, and yet not poignant. For my part, I've almost lost my gay humour for fear of being like 'em; if I continue here one week longer I shall e'en exchange the town, where I expected such pleasure, for my old Yorkshire retirement.

BETTY: Could you but get Mrs Clerimont to ye, madam, she'd immediately introduce you to the beau monde, where wit, gallantry, and good breeding, are emulators. You say she's a relation.

LADY LANDSWORTH: She is so at a distance, but you see all my sending will not prevail with her to come at me, nor appoint a time when I shall wait upon her; what can be the reason?

BETTY: I know not, unless 'tis being here; for truly I fancy, though my mistress is fled to Covent Garden, she is as much despised by the real quality, as she is cajoled by the pretenders to it. You say you are not acquainted with Mrs Clerimont though related to her: so perhaps she guesses you of our stamp, and avoids ye. For heaven's sake, madam, how came ye hither?

LADY LANDSWORTH: Why, I'll tell thee, Betty, I was married a mere baby to a very old man, who, in his youth, having been a debauchee, and dealing only with the worst of our sex, had an ill opinion of all, kept me like a nun, broke off all commerce to London, or indeed with anybody, not excepting relations.

BETTY: And could you endure this?

LADY LANDSWORTH: Most patiently; never found fault with his woollen shirts or night-caps, lay all night to the music of his cough, or the rattling of his physic, writ nothing but receipts,[13] scarce ever opened my mouth, but out came, 'how do ye do, my dear; did the syrup I made last please ye?'

BETTY: Your Ladyship was a miracle.

LADY LANDSWORTH: And what do you think I got by doing thus?

[13]*receipts*: recipes

BETTY: I don't know, but I'm sure you deserved a great deal.

LADY LANDSWORTH: Even three thousand pounds a year, besides money, plate, and jewels. This Mrs Rich's husband was my old man's banker, and once I saw her in the country, besides she had money of mine in her hands, so to her, and this dear town I came; resolving to participate in all the innocent liberty my youth, my wealth, and sex desires.

BETTY: Ah, madam! Had our sex but your forbearance, they might all be happy.

LADY LANDSWORTH: I am of the mind that Fortune offers every mortal their share of satisfaction; but if they pluck the green fruit, forestall her purpose, or miss the ripened moment, they rarely have another prospect.

BETTY: Right, madam, and is it not the same in love? If a lady refuses the man she likes, all her adventures in that kind prove awkward and unlucky after it.

LADY LANDSWORTH: Say's thou so, Mrs Betty; well I am resolved to indulge my inclinations, and rather than not obtain the person I like, invert the order of nature, and pursue, though he flies.

BETTY: Impossible, one glance of yours subdues the proudest love-defier of them all.

LADY LANDSWORTH: Fo, you flatter; but seriously my dear confidante, being once condemned to matrimony without ever asking my consent, now I have the freedom to make my own choice, and the whole world the mart — I have the oddest whimsies.

BETTY: Then your Ladyship intends to venture on a second marriage?

LADY LANDSWORTH: Truly, Mrs Betty, I believe so, why should we dissemble when we are alone? — But such a husband I would have.

BETTY: What sort of a husband. Let's hear the marks, that I may try to find the man.

LADY LANDSWORTH: He should be genteel, yet not a beau; witty, yet no debauchee; susceptible of love, yet abhorring lewd women; learned, poetical, musical, without one dram of vanity; in fine, very meritorious, yet very modest; generous to the last degree, and master of no estate; mightily in love with me, and not so much as know I am worth the clothes I wear.

BETTY: Ha, ha, ha, to your romances again lady-fair, 'tis only there you can converse with those heroes; this town affords no such, I can assure you: modest, meritorious, and genteel, ha, ha, ha, your pardon, madam, why such a wight[14] would not get his daily bread, not rags to cover his nakedness; 'tis frontless impudence makes the grand appearance, and carries the world before it.

LADY LANDSWORTH: I suppose I shall increase your laughter, when I tell you I fancy I have found the man.

BETTY: Madam.

LADY LANDSWORTH: You know, throughly tired with the impertinence within, and not being fitted to give or receive visits, I have often rambled with my woman incognito – and have done the strangest things.

BETTY: What, for heaven's sake?

LADY LANDSWORTH: Even lost my heart; in love, Mrs Betty, desperately in love.

BETTY: With whom, dear madam?

LADY LANDSWORTH: Oh, a pretty gentleman, who has all those accomplishments I desire writ in his face, as plain as –

BETTY: The nose in't, I warrant.

LADY LANDSWORTH: Yes truly, for all your jesting: I sat by him in the playhouse, and discovered his sense as taking as his figure.

BETTY: But where was his modesty, when he attacked a mask?

LADY LANDSWORTH: That's your mistake, 'twas I gave the onset, nay, went farther, appointed him a meeting there again, enjoined him not to dog me, nor endeavour to learn who I was, which he punctually obeyed.

BETTY: And you performed your assignation.

LADY LANDSWORTH: Yes indeed, last night; and to try his generosity, when the door-keeper came into the side-box for money,[15] I seemed in a great fright, and said, I had left my purse at home, he immediately offered me a guinea, which though I accepted, by the melancholy air of his face, I guessed it had not a twin brother.

---

[14]*wight*: fellow   [15]*theatre audiences paid by act*

BETTY: Bless me, madam! That pretence, and taking his money, made you look like a woman of the town.

LADY LANDSWORTH: So I designed: I forced him to tell me his name and lodging, e'er I'd accept the favour, and now I have a game to play, wherein you must assist me.

BETTY: In what ever you desire. Oh! Madam, Sir John Roverhead is just upon us.

LADY LANDSWORTH: What luck is this! Is there no avoiding the fop?

   Enter SIR JOHN ROVERHEAD *and* CHRIS *his man*

SIR JOHN: Ha, Chris! The beautiful wealthy widow of the north.

CHRIS: Why, sir, she is not Mrs Rich.

SIR JOHN: Sagely discovered, but she's better, Mr Wisdom, more desirable, and deeper in my affections.

CHRIS: Your pardon, sir, I have done.

SIR JOHN: Stand back.   *[adjusting himself to* CHRIS]

LADY LANDSWORTH: What postures the thing uses, to make it more ridiculous than nature first designed it.

SIR JOHN: [*to* CHRIS] Now to be florid. [*to* LADY LANDSWORTH] —

   Sure some auspicious planet ruled today,
   For every star is witness,
   How often, when I have made my visit here,
   I have sighed to see your ladyship —

LADY LANDSWORTH:

   — Still taking coach, or chair.
   Have I not helped you out, sir?

SIR JOHN: Lord, madam, such beauty, wit and dress what man can bear?

LADY LANDSWORTH: Such affectation, folly and nonsense, what woman can endure?   [*Exit*]

SIR JOHN: Ah hey, Mrs — Betty, what's the meaning of this?

BETTY: The effect of her country ignorance.

SIR JOHN: It must be so, for I think Chris, I am nicely dressed today.

CHRIS: Aye, but perhaps she likes the inward man.

SIR JOHN: She's a fool, that's certain. But, Mrs Betty, I hope my affairs stand well with your lady; this was but a trifle whom I addressed too with my universal gallantry, which had she received, I should have laughed at; my valet knows 'tis my way to all that make an appearance.

CHRIS: Under fifty.

SIR JOHN: Or above, if they make an appearance.

BETTY: Aye, Sir John 'tis you alone have the bewitching way, court all the world, and catch my unwary mistress by the by; because 'tis like quality.

SIR JOHN: Like! that's degrading; I'd be an original, like nothing.

BETTY: Nothing sure can be like you.

SIR JOHN: A witty baggage this, we must engage her.

CHRIS: With all my heart, secure you the mistress, and let me alone for the maid.

SIR JOHN: Well, but Mrs Betty, after this idle chat shall we crave leave to see your mistress.

BETTY: You may, and you only; she's at cards.

SIR JOHN: I protest thou art charmingly dressed, and pretty, I vow; what design have you today?

BETTY: Is it to me you speak, sir?

SIR JOHN: To whom else?

BETTY: I thought, like a poet you were repeating,[16] and designed the compliment for the next of quality you met.

SIR JOHN: Fie, fie, let me die if you are not the prettiest, amiable creature I know: prithee who makes thy mantuas,[17] how modestly the little creature dresses her head too!

BETTY: Ha, ha, ha, this is excess of French breeding: but, Sir John, you forget my lady expects you.

SIR JOHN: I shall ever forget her when I look upon thee, my life, my soul,
[*sings*]She threw by her knotting in haste –
ho, ho, ho, come along Chris I've shot her flying.
[*sings*]And caught me about my well-shaped waist –
ho, ho, ho.   [*Exit singing*]

BETTY: So, this is the high top fool in my lady's equipage, the favoured fool, and she has enough in her train to give a man of sense the spleen but to hear her catalogue. Well, since Fortune

---

[16]*repeating*: reciting   [17]*mantuas*: dresses

has thrown me in this chamber-maid station, I'll revenge her
cruelty, and plague her favourites.

    No fool by me shall e'er successful prove,
My plots shall help the man of sense in love.   [*Exit*]

Act Two

SCENE ONE

Enter BELVOIR *meeting* JACK

BELVOIR: How now Jack, is thy master within?

JACK: No, sir.

BELVOIR: 'No sir'; let me come morning, noon, or night, still I am answered, 'No sir'; 'twas by accident I found his lodgings, and I plainly perceive he is denied; this is most injurious to our former friendship, quite contrary to the contract made when we were fellow students, when I was only Clerimont's, and Clerimont Belvoir's.

JACK: Aye, sir, my master's strangely altered; but I dare not tell.

BELVOIR: Come, for once I'll tempt thee to a breach of trust, I may do him service; I hear his father's dead.

JACK: Ah, sir! That's his grief, the very fountain of his discontentment.

BELVOIR: Trust me Jack, few young gentlemen use to break their hearts for such a loss.

JACK: Yes, if they are younger brothers, and left not worth a groat; 'twill go a great way with them, a great way indeed, sir.

BELVOIR: But he was the old lord's favourite, who had land enough without entail to make my Clerimont happy.

JACK: Alas! Mr Belvoir, I find you know not our story.

BELVOIR: Not the particulars, only what I've heard from fame; if thou believest me thy master's friend, hide nothing from me.

JACK: I do, so notwithstanding his commands, you shall hear our misfortunes. You know my master's elder brother is a perfect squire, on my conscience the product of two virginities, such an unaccountable blockhead, that though he gave the assured proof of spending his father's estate, and did it so ungenteely, that he was despised by men of sense, shunned by all but the unthinking rabble, ridiculous even below lampooning.

BELVOIR: Why Jack, the town improves thee beyond the university, thou growest witty.

JACK: No, 'tis the approach of poverty whets my spleen; egad if I am reduced to rags I'll spare ne'er an elder brother of them all, though he were a prince.

BELVOIR: Ah well-a-day, for the poor gentlemen in gilt coaches. But proceed to the matter, good friend John.

JACK: Why this dunce, I think I called him before, shatter-brains –

BELVOIR: Hold.

JACK: Whose sole delight lay in his kindred hounds, who for his hunting companions entertained all the lubbers[18] of the four adjacent parishes, till the country was going to petition the Parliament for labourers; this monster of the woods, this –

BELVOIR: Well, what of him.

JACK: Has got every penny of my old lord's estate, whilst my master, the most deserving of his race, (though I say it that should not) is left to starve, rob, drown, or what he pleases.

BELVOIR: But how came this to pass, Jack, ha?

JACK: Why that damned jilt Fortune, or her left-handed daughter, as blind as she, Chance.

BELVOIR: A mischance, upon my word.

JACK: A confounded one. My old lord lay long bedrid of the gout, and the wight I have described lived in an estate some few miles distant; one day hunting that way, he bethought himself, and made his sick father a visit; but knowing he could not sit a moment without talking to his beloved Jowler, Ringwood, etc. takes the whole kennel along with him into the chamber, whilst the t'other kennel below (I mean the peasants) were so sharp set, they scarce left my lord an unmauled dish to come to his table.

BELVOIR: Horrid, filthy brutes!

JACK: In fine, this so exasperated the old man that in a rage he burnt his will, designing to leave my master whatever was in his power; but the malicious fates decreed it otherwise, for that very night the angered father died suddenly, and all his wealth fell to that soft-headed fool in one swoop; and the devil, I say, do him good with it.

---

[18]*lubbers*: sturdy, though lazy, fellows

BELVOIR:　Foh, there must be application made to him, Jack, this must not be suffered.

JACK:　To his huntsman apply then, for he's his only oracle.

BELVOIR:　There's Mrs Clerimont in town, his first cousin, a vast fortune, and one who has a larger share of wit and goodness; she shall be consulted. What, a young gentleman shall never droop for missing a paltry fortune.

JACK:　Dear sir, do your best. But now I beg of you to be gone; I hear him coming, and he will be in such a passion if he discover I have been talking to you, or told he was at home; for 'tis his humour to hide from all his friends.

BELVOIR:　Well, I'll not cross him now, but certainly find out some way to assist him. Farewell, honest Jack, be sure you prove faithful and kind to him.

JACK:　Upon my veracity to my uttermost. I only wish to serve him —　　　　　[*Exit* BELVOIR. JACK *stands out of sight*]
　　Enter CLERIMONT *in mourning*

CLERIMONT:　Mine's not the mourning of an heir; oh my noble father, sure I should have grieved enough for thee, for thy unspeakable loss, without additional calamities. What will become of me, must I wait at proud men's doors, and cringe for an admittance? Can I flatter the puffed-up lord, and fawn for a vile office? Debase my immortal soul to feed this moulding clay? 'Tis impossible, 'tis more than man can bear!

JACK:　Sir.

CLERIMONT:　What.

JACK:　I thought you called.

CLERIMONT:　Thou art too officious; I have advised thee oft to leave me, and seek thy fortune where the Goddess smiles. I am a wretch that now is sinking lower than his own despairing thoughts can frame.

JACK:　Lord, sir, is this all the philosophy you have learned, I think I am the best proficient; starving frights not me half so much as parting; faith, though the world is crowded with knaves that an honest gentleman can scarce breathe, I'll jostle stoutly but you shall have elbow-room.

CLERIMONT:　Poor fellow! Thou differest from the common tribe of servants; they fly poverty worse than infection; or else with saucy impudence insult.

Enter a COACHMAN *with a letter*

COACHMAN: Is this Mr Clerimont's lodging?

JACK: Well, and what then, how came you here without calling me? What's your name, and what's your business?

COACHMAN: Not with you, sauce-box.

JACK: How, sirrah!

CLERIMONT: Peace; my name is Clerimont.

COACHMAN: Then, sir, there's a lady in my coach has sent you this, she says it requires no answer. [*gives a letter and goes off*]

CLERIMONT: Ha, gold! fly Jack, call him back.

JACK: [*pulling in the* COACHMAN] Hark-ye, you sneak-nose, hounds-face, you have affronted my master.

COACHMAN: Why fool, I brought him money.

JACK: I thought so, ye pimp, he scorns it.

CLERIMONT: Here, return this back; tell the lady she mistakes the man, and I'll wait upon her where she appoints, and convince her that she does.

COACHMAN: Gad, a notable mistake.

CLERIMONT: Rascal, no fingering. Follow you, and take the number of his coach; if you are not honest, sirrah, I shall find a time to cut your ears off.

JACK: I'll watch him, I warrant. Bring money to my master! Sirrah, get you gone.

COACHMAN: Sure they are all distracted!

CLERIMONT: 'From my mask in the playhouse.' By my life a very harlot. How few in my circumstances would refuse these offers; but my nature's quite otherwise. I cannot be obliged where I contemn, nor live so vile a way: Not but the temptation's doubly baited, profit and pleasure; for though the baggage is loose as the wanton winds, yet she is witty beyond her sex. What a medley's here.

[*reads*] *When I tell ye I am in love, by that modest air, and downcast look of yours, I guess you'll think me mad, and expect (according to the damsels in Romance) I should have a fit of sickness, been at the point of death, e'er I made the discovery. But women of my character are not so nice. I am a mistress, have abundance of money; if you have but little, a wise man may pick comfort out of this. I sent you a token, as an earnest of my future favours; agreeable to your wonted*

obedience come not to the coach, but meet me at four in the Park, and thank me with your acceptance.

Ha, ha, ha, ha, I see the devil's not wanting on his part, he'd have me a greater sinner e'er I come to despair. The postscript is the same mad stuff.

[*reads*] *You shall know me by an affected motion in my walk, and a bell toss with my head,* – humph!

    Enter JACK

JACK: The lady's gone, sir, and the money too: gad, sir, though to please you, I was in a passion, yet my mouth watered plaguily at the gold.

CLERIMONT: What said the creature?

JACK: The creature! Gad she was an angel. She pulled off her mask, I believe, to laugh freely, for she burst out vehemently; and when the man said you'd have none on't, she gave herself a swing, and cried, the more fool he, drive on coachman.

CLERIMONT: So merry! But 'tis her time whilst youth and beauty lasts; she'll have years enough of sorrow.

JACK: Sir, my landlady's a-coming, you have used her so to sack[19] and chocolate in a morning, that she'll ne'er fail you.

CLERIMONT: Pish, I am sick of her impertinence.

    Enter MRS FIDGET

MRS FIDGET: Good-morrow Mr Clerimont; good lord, still walking with that melancholy air! Well, well, were I such a pretty gentleman, I'd defy Fortune.

CLERIMONT: Prithee, landlady, what would you have me do; if you think the ladies will like me so well, take my picture and hang it out at your balcony; e'en make your best of me, if that will content ye.

MRS FIDGET: Fie, fie, you might have private chamber-practice enough, if you'd give your mind to't: 'uds my life, if the young handsome fellows were like you, there would never have come so many of them to their coach-and-six. Let me tell ye, Mr Clerimont, if I thought you had been of this reserved humour, I'd not have let my lodgings to you. I used to have women of quality to my fine gentlemen, and suppers dressed in my house have lasted my family a week; besides that put into my hand

---

[19]*sack*: Spanish wine

that shall be nameless, else I had ne'er lived in the credit you see me in these twenty years in the parish.

CLERIMONT: Good Mrs Fidget.

MRS FIDGET: Nay you shall hear me. Brought up my daughters, as I have done. As fine women, though I say it, as any that adorn Covent Garden church.

CLERIMONT: Church! I should rather have thought they'd adorn the playhouse.

MRS FIDGET: Now out upon you, Mr Clerimont, my daughters are never seen at the playhouse; I bring them up in the fear of heaven.

JACK: Yes, and they are both married in the fear of heaven too: for neither of them troubled the church in that affair, as I have been told.

MRS FIDGET: Well, saucy-face. But Mr Clerimont, what I have said is all for your good, and I hope you do take it into your consideration: for truly today there came a very pretty lady, and notwithstanding your order, I sent up the coachman: I am willing to bring you to preferment.

CLERIMONT: Bring me to the pox, and the devil —

MRS FIDGET: Marry gap, is this my thanks!

CLERIMONT: I tell ye, I am tired of these morning lectures, and if my lodgings cannot be free from noise and impertinence, I must quit them. Follow me, Jack, I'll take the air.   [*Exeunt*]

MRS FIDGET: So out-of-sorts, and gone without giving me my mornings-draught: why, Master John, Master John, give me the key of the closet, I must rummage it for a dram of the bottle: 'udsdeath I shan't be in a humour again this half-hour, the man's a fool, I think.

When beauty courts the charming pleasures shun,
Be virtuous, though he's sure to be undone;
He's mad, 'udsflesh! I'd sooner turn a nun.   [*Exit*]
[*The scenery opens and discovers* MRS RICH, MRS TRICK-
WELL, *and* LADY LA BASSET, *rising from play.*]

MRS TRICKWELL: [*to* MRS RICH] I protest your Ladyship plays to a miracle; but I would not have had you ventured money yet.

MRS RICH: Oh pardon me, madam, I should not have minded it else. But do you think I shall ever be capable?

LADY LA BASSET: Why, you are perfect already; a wonderful apprehension.

MRS RICH: Oh, fie! My Lady la Basset, you compliment in reality; may I hope to play at Court? I have a great ambition to play at Court. Oh my stars! I should torment our city ladies to death, to talk of honours done me at Court.

LADY LA BASSET: Yes, yes, you shall be introduced, and honoured at Court, I'll promise ye, or my interest fails me; and for setting it out let me alone, I'll make their ears tingle, i' faith.

MRS RICH: Oh, my dear, dear Lady Basset, let me embrace ye, the very conception on't is felicity to the highest degree. Mon Dieu! How we'll tease the little City creatures.

   Enter MRS BETTY

BETTY: Madam, Sir John Roverhead is come to wait on you, and has got some music to entertain your ladyships.

MRS RICH: Oh, heavens! That master of accomplishments! Instruct me, dear ladies, how to receive him.

LADY LA BASSET: Seem in a cabal,[20] then burst out a-laughing, and let fall some mysterious words that tend towards scandal.

MRS RICH: Good! Ridiculous to the highest degree, that ever a woman of her quality should make such a faux pas, the town will ring on't: Oh, my stars! 'Tis something so odd, ha, ha, ha, ha.

MRS TRICKWELL: Transportingly foolish! Yet it makes me laugh, ha, ha, ha, ha.

LADY LA BASSET: Who can forbear, ha, ha, ha.

   Enter SIR JOHN

SIR JOHN: Pardon; ladies, the interruption; may I participate; I die to laugh in comfort with women of your wit and merit.

MRS RICH: Oh fie! Sir John, 'tis a secret upon my word; we must be tender of our own sex; you are but too well acquainted with our weakness; scandal of an hour old is as much out of date with you, as a Gazette in the afternoon to the sots that hunt foreign news.

SIR JOHN: News! Gad madam, there's no such thing, there's nothing new under the sun; the world is a continual round of nauseous repetition; in the last generation, and this, young girls were mad for husbands, then mad to get rid of 'em; sharpers[21]

[20]*cabal*: plotting group   [21]*sharpers*: cheats

had their cullies;²² gamesters their fools; physicians killed their patients, and were paid for't; lawyers got estates, and their clients were undone with suing for 'em; courtiers' promises, and bullies' oaths, ever made a great noise, and signified nothing.

MRS RICH: Satirical, I vow! Why, you are in a mortifying way, Sir John.

SIR JOHN: Indeed scarce fit to appear before your ladyship: I have had a billet-doux²³ from a woman of sixty, which has given me the spleen to that degree, I could out-rail a hypocritical fanatic.

MRS RICH: Sixty! Pleasant, I protest.

SIR JOHN: She's a walking memento mori;²⁴ I have suffered some time under the persecution, and in bitterness and gall, instead of ink, have wrote a stanza, to show how awkwardly an old woman makes advances.

MRS RICH: Oh, dear Sir John, let us have it.

LADY LA BASSET: We are all petitioners.

SIR JOHN: You shall command me, ladies.   [*Sings*]

Della tired Strephon with her flame,
    While languishing she viewed him,
        The well-dressed youth despised the dame
        But still old Puss pursued him.

Some pity on a wretch bestow,
    That lies at your devotion:
        Perhaps near fifty years ago,
        Some might have liked the motion.

No heart like mine did ever burn,
    I'm rich too, I'll assure you;
        And I must tell you in return,
        You're uglier than a Fury.

If you, proud youth, my flame despise,
    I'll hang me in my garters:
        Why, then make haste to win the prize,
        Among love's foolish martyrs.

²²*cullies*: dupes   ²³*billet-doux*: love letter
²⁴*memento mori*: reminder of death

Can you see Delia brought so low,
And make her no requitals?
Delia may to the devil go
For Strephon, stop my vitals.

I'll be as constant as a dove,
And always we'll be billing:
No more damned stories of your love,
Your very breath is killing.

These eyes for you shall learn to shine,
That twinkle in their sockets.
I'll never in a cellar dine,
When I may go to Lockets.[25]

What in my charms and youth I want,
I'll make it up in duty.
Prithee leave off this foolish cant,
I'll stoop to nought but beauty.

MRS TRICKWELL: [*aside to* MRS RICH] Did you observe how my Lady la Basset eyed Sir John?
MRS RICH: Yes, and am pleased with it: I would not have a fellow pretend to me, that all the fine women in town are not fond of. – [*to* SIR JOHN] Our thanks in abundance, 'tis wonderful pretty.
SIR JOHN: Your pardon, harsh and untunable, like the subject.
    Enter MRS BETTY
BETTY: [*aside to* MRS RICH] Mr Rich will not be answered, madam, I had much ado to keep him out here.
MRS RICH: Ladies, let me beg you would take Sir John into the drawing-room, and entertain him a moment. A hideous Citizen will tease me about a little business, but I'll dispatch him in the third part of a minute, and rejoin the agreeable conversation.
SIR JOHN: We shall wait with impatience, madam.
                                                      [*Exeunt severally*]
    Enter MR RICH
BETTY: There he walks, madam, he would stay in spite of me.
MRS RICH: Ah, Mr Rich! What design brings you hither? Your

---

[25] *Lockets*: fashionable eating house

absence this day would have been very obliging; but since you are here, let's finish pray as soon as you can. Well, what's the business.

MR RICH: Hey—day! What's this? Good Madam Rich, my sister-in-law, how despisingly you talk? Hark ye, hark ye, this behaviour does not become ye; and without telling you what relates to me, you'll one day repent of your ridiculous way of living, and carriage.

MRS RICH: An elbow-chair, Betty, I foresee Mr Rich intends to talk me to sleep.

MR RICH: No, madam, on the contrary: for were you in your right senses, what I have to say would most terribly keep you awake.

MRS RICH: You strangely concern yourself with my conduct.

MR RICH: And who will concern himself, if I don't? You are my daughter's aunt, widow of Paul Rich my brother, and I will not have it laid upon the Exchange, that my brother's widow, and daughter's aunt is run stark mad.

MRS RICH: How mad! You lose all respect, Mr Rich; but I shall find a way to get rid of you, that I may hear no more such sottish unmannerly language, to which I scorn to answer.

MR RICH: Oh! 'Slife, Madam Rich, you ought to get rid of all your ridiculous airs of quality and greatness, that you may receive no more affronts equal to this days.

MRS RICH: You ought not, Mr Rich to reproach me of that, where I am only exposed, because I'm thought your sister-in-law; but there's an end of that, Mr Rich, I'll have it published in the Gazette, that since my widowhood, I am no more your sister, and so I renounce you for my brother-in-law, Mr Rich; and since hitherto my expenses, no noble manner of living, and what I every day practise, could never correct the fault of having once been a Citizen's wife. I do now pretend –

MR RICH: Zooks, Madam Rich, 'tis the best part of your history, that name of Rich; and had it not been for the good conduct of the poor deceased, you had not been in a condition for so much pomp and greatness. I would fain know –

MRS RICH: Courage, courage, Mr Rich, you do well, talk on, talk on 'tis your last time.

MR RICH: I would fain know, let me tell you, if it would not be more decent for you to have a good grave coach, lined with an olive-coloured cloth, a lean coachman in a dark brown coat, a little modest boy with short hair to open the door, and a pair of gentle geldings, than all this sumptuous equipage, that makes people enquire who you are; these modish prancing Flanders,[26] that dash the industrious people that walk; and all that useless numerous train, which makes you despised by the people of quality, envied by your equals, and cursed by the mob. You ought, Mrs Rich, to retrench all this greatness and folly with which you are surrounded.

BETTY: But, sir − [to MRS RICH who spits and coughs] What's the matter with you, madam?

MRS RICH: I take breath, Betty, is not Mr Rich come to his second point?

MR RICH: No, good Mrs Rich, and I return still to the equipage.

MRS RICH: Oh, the long-winded tiresome man!

MR RICH: Among the rest, what d'ye do with that huge bulky coachman, with his curling whiskers like a Dutch mastiff's tail? 'Zbud he looks as if he belonged to the Czar of Muscovy.

BETTY: But, sir, would you have my lady turn barber, and shave her coachman?

MR RICH: No, but she may turn him away, and take another.

MRS RICH: Well, sir, one word's as good as a thousand, I pretend to live as I please, and will have none of your counsel; I laugh at you and all your reproofs; I am a widow, and depend on nobody but myself. You come here and control me, as if you had an absolute authority over me. Oh, my stars! What rudeness are you guilty of? But it is your City breeding.

MR RICH: Still abusing the City, 'tis a shame, Mrs Rich, a burning shame. I tell thee, thou proud vain thing, thou gilt ginger-bread; the City is famous for men substantial in their persons, their purses, their credits, when your Limberhams,[27] this-end-of-the-town beaux, are the half product of nature, wretchedly pieced up by art, weak in their bodies, their brains, their everything; and 'udsbones! They have no more credit than they have religion; whilst as I said before the City is famous for −

[26]Flanders: horses
[27]Limberhams: Tame foolish keepers of women, character in Dryden's play, The Kind Keeper

MRS RICH: Cuckolds: good Mr Rich take my advice, and take breath; you have outdone one of our holders-forth, upon my word ye have.

MR RICH: [*mimicking her*] Upon my word ye have; what an affected tone's there? Gadzooks my brother Rich was a fool.

MRS RICH: That's no wonder; most Citizens are.

MR RICH: Yes, to their wives, ungrateful cockatrice; and he — blind, credulous man, to pretend to leave my daughter a fortune to your management, forsooth: Gadzooks, I had rather he had left her never a groat.

MRS RICH: So had I; there we agree once; put it down, Betty, for a miracle. Oh! Is it done? Have ye said all? Will you go out of my house, or must I go? Upon my word I have company waits for me, that are a thousand and a thousand times more engaging; will ye believe me, or no, Mr Rich?

MR RICH: What company? Fools, I warrant 'em.

MRS RICH: He must be convinced: perhaps, Betty, that will drive him hence, open the door.

[*Scenery opens and discovers* SIR JOHN, LADY LA BASSET, MRS TRICKWELL *and* VERMIN, *a footman.*]

MRS RICH: [*continues*] Oh! I am just suffocated with impertinence expiring under the heavy load of nonsense; dear Lady Basset revenge me, ridicule that lump of the City till he frets himself into shape: I'll introduce ye: look ye, sir, this is the honourable Lady Basset, this is the ingenious Mrs Trickwell; the gentleman I leave to speak for himself.

SIR JOHN: I am, sir.

MR RICH: [*roughly*] And what are you, sir?

SIR JOHN: Why, your humble servant, sir, that's all, sir.

LADY LA BASSET: I vow he nods like the statue in Don Juan, ha, ha, he, he.

MRS TRICKWELL: And looks like —

MRS RICH: A Citizen, and that's ridiculous enough of all conscience, he, he.

MR RICH: [*mimicking*] Good lack, he, he, he: gadzooks you are a parcel of tawdry insignificant butterflies; if ye provoke me, I'll draw your pictures with a vengeance.

SIR JOHN: Dawley has done mine at length already, much

more to my satisfaction; it hangs at Court in a duchess's bed-chamber, Cit.

MR RICH: The devil it does? The mop that cleans it set upright, and good drapery, would be a better figure.

LADY BASSET: Filthy simile.

MRS TRICKWELL: Why, *m'amie*, this is the reverse of Sir Courtly; a second surly, I protest.

MR RICH: Thou wretched woman, whom I justly shame to call sister, these are things that live on thee, prey on thy very substance, and have no more worth, or real quality than the ornament of pageants: look, here's the equipage of one, those lank cheeks are to be filled out at thy table; [*pulls* VERMIN *forward*] and thy pocket rooked at games thou dost not understand, for rigging.

LADY LA BASSET: Now out upon ye; stand back Vermin; see if the ill-natured man has not quite dashed the boy? 'Tis the filthy tailor's fault.

MR RICH: What, he'll trust no longer.

SIR JOHN: Fie, Mr Rich, this is prodigiously abusive, upon my honour; I presume you've never been at the Court.

MR RICH: Nor you at the Camp, which now's the only way to make a perfect courtier: I tell thee, fop, if thou art known there, 'tis only for thy folly; thy reputation lies in ruining others, which thou dost infallibly, by being once in their company; and thy chiefest accomplishment is taking snuff with a bel air, patching, painting, powdering like a woman, and squeaking like an eunuch, gadzooks.

SIR JOHN: Sir.

MR RICH: Look ye, if you are offended, or think the ladies so, as much a Citizen as I am, I wear a sword, and follow me ye caper-cutter if ye dare.

SIR JOHN: Some colonel of the train-bands, I warrant; I'll not disorder my dress. I am weary of this fulsome stuff; to the park my Angels, and let's breathe a little.

ALL: Aye, aye, to the Park, to the Park.

MRS RICH: With all my heart to the Park: lackeys, is the coach there? But my house is at your service: cool yourself sweet Sir John, whilst we laugh at this adventure; shall we not Lady Basset?

LADY LA BASSET: I cannot help it.

SIR JOHN: Nor I upon my honour.

[*Exeunt laughing.* MR RICH *and* BETTY *remain*]

MR RICH: Why what the devil's here to do, Betty?

BETTY: My mistress is run stark staring mad, but I humour her distraction till we can find a way to cure it.

MR RICH: Prithee let's in and consult; I placed thee here for that purpose, and trust in thee.

BETTY: I will ever prove faithful, sir.

MR RICH:

> Two powerful friends, lust and ambition reign
> In this rich, buxom widow's sickly brain;
> To lay them both, a husband must be had
> Beautiful and young, and sounding titles clad;
> But that shall be your care and mine, egad.   [*Exeunt*]

Act Three

SCENE ONE

Enter MRS CLERIMONT *and* BELVOIR

MRS CLERIMONT: This is strange news you tell me of my cousin; I heard indeed the unhappy accident of his father's sudden death, but thought he had been still in the country.

BELVOIR: No, he lives in town retired, shuns all his acquaintance; his noble mind surmounts his fortunes, and he disdains to be obliged; it affects me strongly, for I loved him with such a passion; loved him, that I thought till I beheld your beauteous self, it could never have been exceeded.

MRS CLERIMONT: When I reflect how cold our present friendships are, I needs must own 'tis nobly generous in you to seek and serve him in this distress; nor shall my assistance any way be wanting, let us but find the means.

BELVOIR: First we must endeavour to see him, reconcile him to the world, and try to cure his melancholy.

Enter LUCINDA

LUCINDA: Madam, there's a gentleman below who says his name is Clerimont.

BELVOIR: Clerimont!

LUCINDA: He seems of some far country by his dress and attendance.

MRS CLERIMONT: On my life the elder brother: This may prove lucky, bring him up: come, sir, we will have some contrivance how to make the younger easy.

BELVOIR: Such goodness and ingenuity as yours cannot fail, when 'tis employed for merit.

Enter the ELDER CLERIMONT *and* LUCINDA, *followed by* TOBY *leading two hounds coupled.*

ELDER CLERIMONT: [*speaks entering*] Nay, sweetheart, dan't fear your rooms, my dogs have been in ladies' chambers afore now, my lady mother would let 'em lie on her bed rather than cross me: love me, love my dog, as the saying is. Come along Toby.

MRS CLERIMONT: What a scene is here!

BELVOIR: Exactly as Jack described him.

ELDER CLERIMONT: Servant coz: Do ye see I am come to Lounnon: hey 'tis no matter for ceremony; I ha' just now been bussing[28] Jewel, might-hap you dan't care to be kissed after the dog.

MRS CLERIMONT: You are in the right on't, 'tis not material.

ELDER CLERIMONT: I have a free way, coz, you must excuse me.

MRS CLERIMONT: Oh, you are very welcome.

ELDER CLERIMONT: No for matter o'that I shan't trouble you, I shall lie in my inn. Here's Toby, my huntsman, he'd a main mind to see Lounnon, so I did it to please the booby; ha Toby.

TOBY: Nay, nay master, dan't; lay it awl upon me; an' any bad chance should happen, you were as forward as I, else we'd ne'er a' come; you are a little too stubborn, by the mess.

BELVOIR: Well said Toby; Toby has a free way too, I perceive, sir.

ELDER CLERIMONT: Yes marry I allow it him: he is a rare huntsman. Show thy parts Toby, hallow, hallow, Toby.

TOBY: Holla, holla, holla, etc.

MRS CLERIMONT: Oh! 'tis mighty well. But, good cousin, it goes quite through my head.

ELDER CLERIMONT: Might hap so, you are used not to it. Ha boys! He'll make the woods ring i'faith.

BELVOIR: 'Tis much better there, I believe.

ELDER CLERIMONT: Good lord! It offends your tender ears, does it? I warrant you are one of the zilken sparks a rough wind would blow to pieces. Pardon me coz, I must be merry.

MRS CLERIMONT: Oh! The gentleman will take nothing ill from a relation of mine.

ELDER CLERIMONT: Midhap he is your husband, or midhap he is your sweetheart, for he creeps main close to ye.

---

[28]*bussing*: kissing

BELVOIR: I am the humblest of the lady's servants.

ELDER CLERIMONT: Oh ho! Her humble servant, that's all one; in our country they call 'um sweethearts, or suitors; 'tis e'en all one.

MRS CLERIMONT: Pray cousin, give me leave to ask you if you are married yet, or not.

ELDER CLERIMONT: No, by my tackings,[29] I ha' e'en more wit than that comes to; I learned so much by my dogs.

MRS CLERIMONT: By your dogs?

ELDER CLERIMONT: Aye, by my dogs: see this couple now how they leer, how spitefully they look at one another. I tell thee coz, this is Jewel, and this is Beauty; the bitch is Beauty, do ye mark me, coz; there was not two dogs in the whole pack loved like these two, they played together like two kittens; nay, for all they are hounds, one would not eat without t'other, and now they are joined their hate is the same; one snarls, t'other bites, one pulls this way, t'other that; gadzooks! They'd either venture hanging to be parted; therefore no coupling for me, I say, ha, ha, ha, ha, coz.

MRS CLERIMONT: Ha, ha, ha, ha, ha.

TOBY: Nay, by the mess this is true, master has spoken all at once; master's a shrewd man, foth and troth.

ELDER CLERIMONT: Well, but coz, I come to Lounnon a purpose to see sports we han't i'th' country, and to spend my money, as ye see.

MRS CLERIMONT: What diversions are you for?

ELDER CLERIMONT: Why look ye, I'd vain see a good bear-baiting, and I'd see the tiger. Ah! That's a parlous beast; we will see the tiger shan't we Toby?

TOBY: Aye 'udslid, though I shall be a little avraid.

BELVOIR: You would not have the lady carry you to those places, I hope?

ELDER CLERIMONT: Aye, why not, sir? They'll see I'm a country man, and that wan't disgrace her, besides I have four thousand pounds a year, for all I wear my own hair, Monsieur Periwig.

BELVOIR: The more's the pity.

---

[29] *tackings*: harnesses

MRS CLERIMONT: Peace, Mr Belvoir, we shall lose our design else. Cousin, 'tis impossible for me to go to the bear-garden; if you'll oblige me, you shall spend this day with me, and participate of the pleasures I take, tomorrow some fitter companion shall show you what you like better.

ELDER CLERIMONT: A match! I dan't pass upon't, if I do throw away a day with you.

MRS CLERIMONT: We'll first to the Park; and then in the afternoon to the play.

TOBY: Aye, d'ye, master, do ye. 'Udslid, I ha' longed to zee a play, e'er since I zaw the poppet-show at our vare.

ELDER CLERIMONT: Come, my poor dogs! Evads, coz, you'll scarce think it, I'd as lieve kiss this poor creature, as e'er a lady in Christendom – I'm sure her breath's as sweet; they'll not like Lounnon; we must hasten down again, Toby.

TOBY: Aye, master; when we've zeen a little; here's rare vine voke!

MRS CLERIMONT: Lead, Mr Belvoir.

BELVOIR: We shall be the sport of the Park.

MRS CLERIMONT: No matter; my cousin shall gallant me.

ELDER CLERIMONT: Come on, i'faith! Follow, Toby!

SCENE TWO

The Park

Enter LADY LANDSWORTH *and* MRS BETTY

LADY LANDSWORTH: He refused it, my best confidante! Nobly despised the shining gold! By all my amorous stars, he has bravely won my heart! Panting and warm I feel him there! Oh! The dear god of my desire.

BETTY: In raptures, nay, then you are lost indeed! Ha! Here comes my lady, and her worthy train!

Enter MRS RICH, SIR JOHN, *etc.*

MRS RICH: My Lady Landsworth! Let us only make our honours en passent – Mon Dieu! I did not think't had been in her – I protest to a miracle!

[MRS RICH *courtesies to* LADY LANDSWORTH, *with ridiculous airs.* LADY LANDSWORTH *mimics her.*]

SIR JOHN: Shall we not address?

MRS RICH: No, no, no, no. Away to the Mall.

SIR JOHN: Ah me!

[*Looking amorously on* LADY LANDSWORTH]

LADY LANDWORTH: There's a foil to my hero! What a languishing air the fop put on! When such stuff as that enters into my thoughts, I shall turn girl again, and play with babies.

BETTY: See! Who walks there in mourning!

LADY LANDSWORTH: Bless me! You make me start: 'tis he! Yes; that's the shape, where manly majesty's triumphant! Who would not be in love with sorrow, when they see it in that face: who would not long to remove the cause; and dress it up in charming smiles: forgive me, virtue! Forgive me, love, if I a little farther make the trial – now to disguise my face and heart –

[*clasps on her mask, and walks carelessly off*]

Enter CLERIMONT *and* JACK

JACK: Do ye think ye shall know her, sir?

CLERIMONT: Know her! 'Tis impossible to mistake! Gay, as the gaudy sun, or distant flowery fields! She moves like air, and throws her charms around: But be not caught my soul! She is, what I would still abhor – a name, would blacken her lilied bosom, and wither all the roses that spread that face of beauty!

JACK: But, sir! If she has a world of money, sir –

CLERIMONT: Peace, fool!

JACK: I ha' done, sir! But abundance of money covers a multitude of faults – that's all, sir!

CLERIMONT: Blockhead! – Why so fast, fair lady? At this rate, by that time a man has overtaken ye, he'll have lost the breath he should employ, in saying fine things. – Will ye not stay?

LADY LANDSWORTH: Not stay! Yes, stay an age; fixed never to remove: an everlasting monument of love. I know you dote upon heroic: I have been reading three whining plays this morning, that I may love in your strain.

CLERIMONT: For heaven's sake, tell me truly, what thou art; for, sure, there's something in thee I so love and hate, that, were my fortune kind, I shall ne'er be happy more.

LADY LANDSWORTH: I'll tell ye, with a truth equal to the freedom I use; (for sincerity is all the virtue I pretend to.) It was my first fate to be kept by an alderman, but he was formal, stiff, and too suspicious for my humour; so I fled from him into the arms of a brisk, airy, young colonel; then the days were spent in revels. When he went to Flanders, I campaigned too; but, ah! As I had dressed my fluttering hero up, like any bridegroom, a saucy bullet came and spoiled the work of tailors, milliners, and fifty trades besides: down dropped the beau.

CLERIMONT: You speak without any concern.

LADY LANDSWORTH: Alas! Grieving for the dead would spoil us for the living. Now, I am a perquisite[30] of a country gentleman; a man of gravity, and one of the pious senators; a great stickler against wenching and profaneness. He allows me wealth enough, and liberty enough. Besides him, I have two or three interlopers, each fancying himself my particular, when, for my part, I care not a straw for any of 'em. But, ah! Amongst my numerous lovers, I know now how, Myrtillo has crept too near my heart; – that's meaning you, sir.

CLERIMONT: The relation freezes up my youthful blood, and checks desire with horror! Does none tell thee what a wretch thou art?

LADY LANDSWORTH: None. They call me Goddess, Angel, and court me with unbated fires; the first, the very earliest product of the year, dainties fit for queen's tables, still load the board; far-fetched wines, such as unbend the soul from cares, and lock up every thought that would disturb us; – yet amidst this flowing plenty, amidst this crowd of flatterers, my awkward fancy sickens at their offered loves, loathes their soft endearments, and builds its sole happiness in manly roughness like yours.

CLERIMONT: Thou art one of nature's favourites; formed when she was gay, and decked in her own smiles; yet me you cannot charm; there's a rustic, out-of-fashion grace, a modest innocence, which only takes my soul; nor can I value favours that may be bought with any other price than love.

LADY LANDSWORTH: [*aside*] He speaks, as my own heart had coined the words: I would not be too credulous. – Believe me, sir, I am not used to woo, or be refused; but, I perceive when once we love, we quit our pride; I can bear reproof from you; and rather than not see ye, see you still to chide me.

[30]*perquisite*: perk

CLERIMONT: No. I must fly, if I'd be safe; I cannot boast a virtue stoical enough to behold you with indifference; those eyes were made to conquer! Oh pity, that they scatter contagion only! I could crawl low as the earth to touch that beauteous hand; but when I reflect, a senseless fop, for some vain present, may riffle all those sweets; then, I could eat my lips, e'er join 'em to infection. – Farewell.

LADY LANDSWORTH: Stay but some moments longer; I have a few things more to offer; hear 'em; perhaps I ne'er may trouble you again.

CLERIMONT: I shall be fooled at last; believe her love; trust her, and be undone! – What would ye say?

LADY LANDSWORTH: Come this way, lest we are observed.

[*They walk backward.* JACK *and* BETTY *come forward.*]

JACK: Is thy lady so plaguy rich, say'st thou damsel?

BETTY: Rich! Why she values a hundred pounds, no more than I do a brass farthing. – She makes nothing to present a man, she likes, with a coach-and-six – and your master here, with his puling[31] modesty, will stand preaching morals, till he has baulked her fancy, and then 'twill be in vain to cry peccavi;[32] for she, like opportunity, when once she turns her back, leaves no grasping hold.

JACK: Hark ye, my dear, can ye keep a secret.

BETTY: As well as any of my sex; according as the nature of the secret is; if 'twill make no mischief; take away nobody's fame: in short, if 'twill do rather good than harm to divulge it; ten-to-one but it goes no farther for me.

JACK: Well, that's ingenious; and I'll trust thee. This master of mine is the veriest libertine the whole town affords; has tired vice in every one of her shapes; and now, forsooth, for variety turns hypocrite, that he may find their pleasures out.

BETTY: Ha! Is't possible?

JACK: True, upon my honour; though he'd kill me should he know I discovered it; and deny all, with a face as grave as a fanatic. – Oh! He's a rare mimic.

BETTY: But, how shall my lady be convinced he is such a rake, if he'll deny 't?

[31]*puling*: whining   [32]*peccavi*: sinner

JACK: Our landlady sells china, bring her thither; my master will never know: she'll tell you as much – [*aside*] I can make my landlady say what I will – Well Jack – thy brain shall still secure this cargo.

BETTY: If she thinks it worth her while to enquire, I'll tell her – look they are parting.

JACK: 'Udso, so they are indeed – I must after; ply him, my dear, and I'll ply thee.   [*Exeunt* CLERIMONT *and* JACK]

LADY LANDSWORTH: Oh my dear Betty! How shall I express my joys! Sure, such a man no age produced before! He's the phoenix of his kind!

BETTY: I wish he prove so.

LADY LANDSWORTH: Why?

BETTY: Hush! Here comes Mrs Clerimont, you have so often sent to.

LADY LANDSWORTH: Ha! Dear Betty, tell her who I am. – Now for an air of gravity, and quite another humour than what I have shown to her name-sake, lest they should find me out by description.

    Enter ELDER CLERIMONT, BELVOIR *and* MRS CLERIMONT

MRS CLERIMONT: – is it? Cousin, your most humble [BETTY *whispers to* MRS CLERIMONT] servant – I ask your pardon a thousand times, for my neglect to wait on you. I have designed it everyday; but –

LADY LANDSWORTH: No excuse, good madam; ladies in this town have too much business on their hands, to throw an hour upon a thing so insignificant as a country relation; one so remote too, that only claims that honour by marriage.

MRS CLERIMONT: Nay madam –

LADY LANDSWORTH: Besides, had you given yourself the trouble, 'twould have been but one, I am sure; for my conversation is only praises of the country; raving at every diversion here, because I understand it not; my discourse leaping perpetually into Yorkshire, and talking for ever of my turkeys, my dairy, and so forth.

BETTY: [*aside*] Hey! What maggot's[33] this? – Then am I the most deceived in the appearance of a woman, that ever I was in my life.

[33] *maggot*: whim

ELDER CLERIMONT: A shrewd gentlewoman this! I like her mainly: pray mistress, what made you come to Lounnon then?

LADY LANDSWORTH: Truly, sir, 'twas business, moneies left in banker's hands, by my dear husband deceased – oh!

ELDER CLERIMONT: Good soul! She weeps! So young, and weep for a dead husband! Good soul!

MRS CLERIMONT: Melancholy suits ill with such charming youth: cousin, you have been unfortunately by your affairs driven into a house, the rendezvous of fops, and senseless coquettes, who have entertained you with pleasures so insipid, they have given you a disgust to those more refined, that will reconcile you to the pretty epitome of our English world the town.

ELDER CLERIMONT: Marry gap! Dan't spoil the gentlewoman, coz, mahaps she likes the country best, why so do I; no offence, I hope coz.

BELVOIR: We must not suffer so fair an enemy. The playhouse, Hyde Park, everything shall contribute to force a kinder opinion from you.

LADY LANDSWORTH: I have seen it all, and despise it: at the theatre, am tired with the double-acted farce, on the stage and in the side-boxes; the noisy nonsense of the pit; the impudence of the orange-women renders the whole entertainment to me, a disagreeable medley: then, for Hyde Park, that's madness in perfection; and the poor lunatic that runs an eternal circle in his Bedlam apartment, has, in my judgement, equal pleasure.

MRS CLERIMONT: Oh fie, my Lady Landsworth, this cannot be your real thoughts.

LADY LANDSWORTH: To a tittle, I assure ye.

ELDER CLERIMONT: I'faykings, the young woman speaks rarely: why Toby, she has run down the Lounnoners – Toby! A Lard! Where is Toby and the two dogs? So ho, so ho!

MRS CLERIMONT: Peace, good cousin; I believe they are at the Park gate.

ELDER CLERIMONT: Oh my man? My dogs? where are they? I shall run mad? So ho, Toby!

LADY LANDSWORTH: Mrs Betty, let's steal off; I think I have dissembled enough for one day.

BETTY: And I hear you have been met with too – I follow madam.
                              [*Exeunt* LADY LANDSWORTH *and* BETTY]

ELDER CLERIMONT:　Why Toby! I say Toby! Speak to thy nown master, Toby!

BELVOIR:　Come, sir; we shall find 'em out.

ELDER CLERIMONT:　Ah never, I fear: Toby, Toby!

　　Enter TOBY *with his head broken*

TOBY:　What ails ye to bawl so? D'ye zee how I have been served: I went to come in with my hounds, and an ugly fellow in red knocked me down, and took the poor curs from me.

ELDER CLERIMONT:　Aye ye coward! where was the quarter-staff.

TOBY:　Why, he had a sword; zee how my head's broke.

ELDER CLERIMONT:　I had rather thy neck were broke than my dogs lost.

TOBY:　Zome wiser than some: Zo had I not – go out yonder, and ha'um again for a tester.

ELDER CLERIMONT:　Go then! Farewell, coz, you ne'er bring me hither again I'll warrant

　　　　　　　　　　　　　[Exeunt ELDER CLERIMONT *and* TOBY]

MRS CLERIMONT:　Let's after, we must not part thus; and as we go, I'll tell ye my opinion of Lady Landsworth.

BELVOIR:　I confess she is past my apprehension.　　*[Exeunt]*

　　Enter SIR JOHN ROVERHEAD *and* CHRIS

SIR JOHN:　With much ado, I have broke from the widow; I appointed to meet here the prettiest rose-bud; if her fortune equals the widow, she secures me.

CHRIS:　Ah sir! I wish the common fortune-hunter's fate be not yours, to take the worst as last.

SIR JOHN:　Fool! That genius that raised me to this, will, no doubt, preserve me conspicuous: the ornament of the town, and idol of the ladies. You must know dunce, I love the young creature, I am to meet now; and I'd marry the widow.

CHRIS:　Why then I should think you liked her.

SIR JOHN:　Incorrigible sot! I hate her as the devil – but has she not five thousand a year? Let that, for ever, stop thy mouth.

CHRIS:　Then 'tis the five thousand a year you'd marry – I ha' done, sir, I ha' done.

SIR JOHN:　She comes; remember I am the Lord – the title will strike an awe into her, and make her refuse me nothing.

　　Enter LUCINDA, *and* GOVERNESS

LUCINDA: But d'ye think he'll come, governess?

GOVERNESS: I hope his Lordship will.

LUCINDA: His Lordship! That sounds purely: I vow my aunt will love me, when I am a great Lady – look – here he is governess – Oh Gemini! 'Tis a dear man.

SIR JOHN: My little angel! This was kind! The place appeared gloomy as shades beneath, till your bright eyes, exceeding the stars, created a double day.

LUCINDA: O la! What fine words he has! Sir – My Lord I mean – I am a foolish girl, and know not how to answer, but I am young, and not unapt to learn.

GOVERNESS: Nay, I'll say that for miss – she was ever as forward as the best of 'em.

SIR JOHN: Pretty innocence! She shall not want instructions modelled by me, the world will own her perfect.

GOVERNESS: And truly, my Lord, she has enough to pay her teacher.

SIR JOHN: Hold, hold! Name not wealth; 'tis a dross I despise.

LUCINDA: Fie, governess! Do you think his Lordship values money?

SIR JOHN: Not I, upon my honour. [*aside to* CHRIS] Get it out of the old one, what she's worth; lest it prove not worth my while to follow her any longer.

CHRIS: Yes, sir, yes.

LUCINDA: Now, my Lord, the reason why I have a mind to be married, is, because I may have a little more freedom. I never go anywheres now, but that old woman's at my heels; and I have heard 'em say, wives go where they will and do what they will.

SIR JOHN: So shalt thou, my dear miss – [*aside*] Marry, quotha; more words than one to that bargain.

LUCINDA: But when will you meet me here again then, and run away with me? For I was told, I should be run away with: they say, most fortunes are.

CHRIS: [*to* SIR JOHN] Sir – twenty thousand pounds, when she is at age.

SIR JOHN: [*aside*] Very well! Gad I'll marry her; by that time, I shall have spent it; broke her heart; and be ready for another. – My dear blossom, how happy am I to have gained your affections! Though 'tis no wonder; for the universality of women die for me.

LUCINDA: For my part, you spoke to me, for that I like ye; else, truly Mr – (pish, my Lord –) I see as fine things walk here as you.

SIR JOHN: Oh fie!

CHRIS: This is true nature, a baby indeed; she has not yet learnt to dissemble.

SIR JOHN: Can ye get out in a morning, my dear?

LUCINDA: Yes, any time; I am left wholly to my governess, and you won her heart, t'other morning with some sack; promise her some more, and she'll bring me, I warrant.

SIR JOHN: There's that will buy sack: will ye bring miss tomorrow, by five o'clock?

GOVERNESS: Yes, yes, she shall wait on your honour, nobody minds us at home: but we'll serve em a trick.

CHRIS: Sir, sir, Mrs Rich, and the company you left, are just coming into this walk.

SIR JOHN: My dear, dear, farewell! – One of my relations, that I dare not see – Farewell this instant – keep these verses to remember me; and tomorrow –

LUCINDA: Oh Gemini! If I forget, I'll be hanged – I shan't sleep all night for thinking on't. Goodbye – Is he not a pure man, nurse?

[*Exeunt* SIR JOHN *and* CHRIS]

GOVERNESS: Aye, marry is he – they shan't think to thrust us up in a garret; we'll ha' money, and good things, as well as your proud aunt, and her folks.

LUCINDA: Oh la. Mum! Here's my aunt and all they upon our backs; what shall we say now.

Enter MRS RICH, LADY LA BASSET, *and* MRS TRICKWELL

MRS RICH: This was furiously odd; to desert us only with the whim to show us airs in bowing when we meet.

LUCINDA: Oh la! 'Furiously' – there's a hard word! I'll learn my aunt's words that I may appear agreeable to my Lord – furiously – remember, governess!

MRS RICH: Mrs Trickwell, I am sick of the Park; here's neither the beaux or the belle monde. Really when Sir John's gone we search in vain for gallantry or a good appearance.

LADY LA BASSET: I wonder how he durst quit the place, when I was here.

MRS RICH: You!

MRS TRICKWELL: Upon my life, madam, the ladies are all mad
   for this miracle of a knight: I wish your ladyship had him fixed
   in the matrimonial noose, that the rest may burst with envy.
MRS RICH: Fear not Mrs Trickwell, I have him with a double
   chain; love and interest – ha! This impertinent girl here!
LUCINDA: Pray don't be angry, aunt.
MRS RICH: In the first place, leave off that word aunt; and make
   use of madam: or stay at home with your father.
LUCINDA: But aunt, since you are my aunt, why may I not call
   you aunt?
MRS RICH: Why, I being a woman of quality, and you but a
   Citizen's daughter, I cannot, in decency, be your aunt, without
   degrading myself in some measure.
LUCINDA: Oh, good aunt, let not that concern you, for I shall be
   a woman of quality too in a little time.
MRS RICH: What says the girl?
LUCINDA: 'Tis in my power to be as great a Lady as you, aunt,
   at least.
MRS RICH: Child!
LUCINDA: I am acquainted with a Lord; the handsomest and
   most obliging in the world. I have met him several times in the
   Park; and he'll marry me when I please – therefore never
   trouble yourself, aunt, about my quality.
MRS RICH: And what's this Lord's name?
LUCINDA: They call him my Lord Fourbind; he's very rich, and
   of great quality, for he told me so.
MRS RICH: Truly, niece, I am very well pleased, that, notwithstanding the mean education your father bestowed on you, you
   have thoughts worthy the honour I do you, of suffering you to
   be my niece; and you are obliged to me, and my conversation
   for this.
LUCINDA: I have another obligation to desire, aunt.
MRS RICH: What is that?
LUCINDA: To marry as soon as 'tis possible, if you please aunt,
   the gentleman you love, that it may countenance my marriage
   with him I love; that when my father would chide me, I may
   answer him, I have not done worse than my aunt.
MRS TRICKWELL: You're in the right [*aside*] – what a terrible
   thing is example!

LUCINDA: But my aunt must make what haste she can; my Lord Fourbind, my lover, is most furiously impatient.

MRS RICH: Ah! Mrs Trickwell! Now can I be revenged of Mr Rich! His daughter is in love with a courtier, and a courtier with her; and she's distracted to be married to him – if the father and mother would but die with vexation, I should be rid of troublesome creatures.

MRS TRICKWELL: But, madam, are you resolved to assist your niece in her design?

MRS RICH: Certainly. And I would not for a thousand pound, lose this excellent occasion of sending Mr Rich to Bedlam.

MRS TRICKWELL: That is very charitable, truly.

MRS RICH: Come ladies, let's home to dinner; this news has pleased me.

> My niece, and I, will the example lead,
> Teach City-dames the way to mend their breed,
> Choose for ourselves; let our dull parents pray;
> Devoutly cheat; each other's lives betray:
> And whilst they drudge, we'll briskly throw away.

                                                    [*Exeunt*]

Act Four

SCENE ONE

Enter YOUNGER CLERIMONT

CLERIMONT: What a wretch am I! Forsook by Fate; abandoned
to want and misery; my soul denied to use her faculty; no
generous power to help the afflicted; and, as if this were not
enough, my virtue too, the last stake that I could boast of, is
going! I love this vicious creature, in spite of all her crimes. Her
charms have won my heart. Begone, thou soft intruder; thou
effeminate passion, only fit for lazy minds. Have I not wracks
without thee, to keep me waking? S'death! What a dog I am!
Going to be kept by a vile prostitute! Her drudge; unkennelled
for a fop, lord, or some wealthy fool; sent to my post of watching!
Confusion! I'll not endure it!   [*walks about distracted*]
     Enter BELVOIR, MRS CLERIMONT *and* JACK

JACK: There he is; I must not be seen.

BELVOIR: My dearest friend! My Clerimont! What have I done
to merit this unkindness? Why dost thou shun those friends,
who fondly love thee? This lady, your relation, begs to serve ye.

CLERIMONT: Alas! I am infectious! The detested plague
poverty's upon me! The meagre fiend approaches fast, with her
attendants, starving and rags! She'll render me so odious, I shall
fly, if possible, myself!

MRS CLERIMONT: Better fortune waits to crown your virtues;
believe me, cousin, it does: Your brother's in town; at my
house; send to him.

CLERIMONT: What, to be answered as I was last: if I would be
his bailiff, I might eat: curses, I'd sooner feed on my own flesh!
Sue to him, who never knew humanity!

BELVOIR: Well; grant him a churl;[34] there are a thousand ways
besides to advance your fortune.

[34]*churl*: ill-bred surly fellow

CLERIMONT: None, but such as I despise.

MRS CLERIMONT: Allow me one request; give me your company this day, and submit to my contrivance; I have thoughts at work, that may produce your future peace.

BELVOIR: My friend, I am sure, used to have more complaisance, than to deny a lady.

CLERIMONT: I am at your dispose; but remember, madam, nothing shall tempt me for bread to do an ill thing.

MRS CLERIMONT: Nor would I offer it.

BELVOIR: Come with us then; and shake off these melancholy looks.

CLERIMONT: Impossible! – Jack!

JACK: Sir?

CLERIMONT: Stay you at home; and, d'ye hear – [*whispers*] – if any messages come –

JACK: I shall, sir.

MRS CLERIMONT: Come, sir, uncloud that brow; we won't leave you in despair, though we found you so.

CLERIMONT:

>   Your kindness comes too late:
>   For if ye could the weight of Fate remove:
>   I'm dashed again; and cursed with guilty love.   [*Exeunt*]

JACK: Landlady! Landlady!

Enter MRS FIDGET

MRS FIDGET: Why, how now impudence! D'ye think you are in an alehouse?

JACK: I humbly beg your pardon, sweet Madam Fidget.

MRS FIDGET: Well, 'tis your ignorance, I excuse it: what humour's your hopeful master in now?

JACK: Oh these were his relations, I hope all will be amended: But, landlady, humph, madam, there's a plot you and I must carry on for his good.

MRS FIDGET: With all my heart, I love a plot extremely, I was ever good at plotting: but, dear brother plotter, let us do nothing rashly.

JACK: What, a glass of sack first; ye shall have it, ye shall have it.

MRS FIDGET: Truly, it helpeth invention.

JACK: Come here's prosperity to our honest endeavours.

MRS FIDGET: With all my spirit.

JACK: T'other glass to the success.

MRS FIDGET: Agreed; now let me know it.

JACK: There's a lady in love with my master.

MRS FIDGET: What, she that called in the coach?

JACK: The same.

MRS FIDGET: By my troth! A lovely woman; that there may come no worse news to England; fill my glass, sirrah.

JACK: Now this lady is not a whore, nor a married woman, nor a widow, nor a maid –

MRS FIDGET: I understand ye.

JACK: D'ye, faith; why, what is she, say you?

MRS FIDGET: A kept mistress, fool.

JACK: Right, egad; well, these Londoners are plaguey sharp, we should ne'er have guessed in the country: this damsel is worth thousands, and she'd fain throw away some upon my master: he, modest fool, (begging his pardon) he'll none on't, forsooth. So I, being cunning, have found out her humour by her appurtenance, her waiting gentlewoman, and lied my master into her good graces; told her he was a mere debauchee; she partly believed me, but comes to you to be confirmed; if you can lie, landlady.

MRS FIDGET: Mistrust me not, Jack, I warrant ye; but if he won't stand to it, what signifies our promises.

JACK: Oh, 'twill create a longer acquaintance, and truly I'll get some money out of her, if he won't; we must not perish; nor will I forsake him.

MRS FIDGET: Well, I'll do my best in an honest way.

JACK: Hark, a coach stops, bring 'em up to show your china, and I'll be there to confirm what you say.

MRS FIDGET: I run.   [*Exit* MRS FIDGET]

JACK: 'Tis a delicate age, by jingo, when the rake is the fine gentleman; and the fine gentleman is the lady's favourite, egad. Mum, she comes.

    Re-enter MRS FIDGET, *with* LADY LANDSWORTH *and* MRS BETTY.

LADY LANDSWORTH: Where d'ye lead me, madam.

MRS FIDGET: Oh, I always keep my best china in my chambers.

LADY LANDSWORTH: This looks like a gentleman's lodgings.

MRS FIDGET: 'Tis so, but he's very rarely in 'em; he lay abroad last night, and sent word he should not be home till twelve this night. I have a sad hand with him; here's his man at home, if any of your misses should sent to him; he has forty ladies, I think, after him. I must give him warning, my house will be scandalous else; though 'tis a good natured wretch, and can look as demure, I warrant, when a body chides him as any saint; nay, to some he'll carry himself like one too.

LADY LANDSWORTH: [*aside to* BETTY] Oh horrid, let us be gone, my ears are blasted!

BETTY: I could have told you as much, but durst not; you seemed to be well assured.

LADY LANDSWORTH: Dissembling wretch! Yet I will see him once again, then in my own freedom be safe, innocent, and far from this bewitching town, pass my days serenely; nor think of false mankind, nor trust; and therefore be deceived no more. [*to* JACK] Well, then there's no probability of seeing your hopeful master today.

JACK: Yes, yes, madam, I can find him in a minute, when the summons is to a fair lady.

LADY LANDSWORTH: That's well, thou art a diligent servant.

JACK: Aye, madam, though I say it, I am fit to be e'er a gentleman's pimp in England, and that's a bold word, now.

LADY LANDSWORTH: Excellent office; pray Mr Pimp, then do me the favour to tell your master, I'll be here at five o'clock, to look on some china.

JACK: It shall be done, madam.

MRS FIDGET: If he forgets, fear not madam, I'll remember.

LADY LANDSWORTH: No doubt on't, you have a noble vocation too, I suppose, though it has but a coarse name; come Betty, farewell, at night I'll choose some china.

[*Exit* LADY LANDSWORTH]

MRS FIDGET: You are very welcome, madam.

JACK: What think ye now, Madam Fidget?

MRS FIDGET: Faith, I know not what to think, her looks were cold and scornful.

JACK: Foh, foh, she's as wanton and warm as e'er a one of your daughters, after a zealous fit of devotion.

MRS FIDGET: Impudence! How dare you mention my daughters so irreverently.

JACK: Nay, no harm; come let's in, and take a glass to clear our understanding, and ripen our plot.

MRS FIDGET: You are an unlucky dog, I see it in your face, and will never bring it to anything.

JACK: Thou are old enough to be a prophetess, only truth and you were at mortal odds, ever since you eat chalk and tobacco pipes.

MRS FIDGET: Thou art a rogue, but sack shall atone.

JACK: Come then.   [*Exeunt*]

SCENE TWO

Scene changes to Mrs Rich's house

Enter MRS RICH, LADY LA BASSETT *and* MRS TRICKWELL

MRS RICH: Here, fellows, stand at all your several posts, and let the world know I am at home: I will appear in state.

MRS TRICKWELL: Why does not your ladyship establish your visiting-days?

MRS RICH: I have Mrs Trickwell, and the rude town takes no notice of 'em; would you believe it, I have sat ye five, six hours, and not a soul, but an ill-bred Citizen's wife, whose unconscionable visit lasted the whole time, and her whole discourse, let me die, of the awkward brutes, her children: o' my soul they were begot by her husband, the things were so ungenteel.

MRS TRICKWELL: Ha, ha, ha, ha, what a prodigious deal of wit your ladyship has.

MRS RICH: So amongst ourselves, I think too; yet would you believe that ill-mannered oaf, my husband's brother, had the confidence to tell me the envious world said I was a fool, my Lady Basset, a fool, would you believe it; I say, that parts, and sheer wit, could be so maligned.

LADY LA BASSET: 'Tis a censorious world. – [*aside*] I begin to hate her, though I win her money, now she's likely to get Sir John from me.

Enter LUCINDA.

LUCINDA: Oh ma'am, your la'ship's humble servant.

MRS RICH: So, that's pretty well; give yourself airs, child, when I admit ye into my company: humph! pluck up your head:

what! no motion with your fan: ah, 'tis awkward, but sure, by my example, she'll learn.

MRS TRICKWELL: [*aside*] To be ridiculous. – Mind your aunt, miss, if you'd be the emblem of perfection.

MRS RICH: Fie, fie, Mrs Trickwell, you flatter me.

LUCINDA: Oh la, I can't make my fan do like my aunt's.

MRS RICH: Oh my stars! She'll make a horrid person of quality: but prithee, niece, how dost thou know this Lord loves thee, hey.

LUCINDA: Oh ma'am, he has told me so, and my governess says 'tis unmannerly not to believe a Lord; besides, he makes verses on me.

MRS RICH: Verses, oh my stars! What a theme he has chose; let's see 'em.

LUCINDA: Here, aunt, they be pure verses; there's a hugeous[35] deal of love in 'em.

MRS RICH: [*reads*]
> I love you, charming fair one, more
> Than ever mortal loved before,
> And though, to my surprising joy,
> The little, wanton, beardless boy
> Had heard my prayers, and made you feel
> The amorous sharpness of his steel;
> Confusion seize me, if my heart,
> Don't with a mightier passion smart.

LADY LA BASSET: [*aside*] What do I hear! – And have you the impudence to say this poetry was designed for you!

LUCINDA: Ma'am! –

MRS RICH: Monkey, the girl has stolen 'em out of my cabinet.

LUCINDA: Aunt –

MRS RICH: Hold your peace, be gone, and let me never see that young bewitching face again.

LADY LA BASSET: I can hold no longer, the verses belong to me.

LUCINDA: The verses belong to you! That's furiously imposs-ible, as my aunt says; how should my Lord know you, to make verses of you; you may look high indeed, but not so high as a Lord, sure.

MRS RICH: By my stars that's well enough; have I not bid ye go, ye little impertinence; there must be some mistake.

[35] *hugeous*: huge

LUCINDA: There must so, ma'am, I warrant your lover has begged 'em of my Lord, and given 'em you.

MRS RICH: Unlucky creature, will ye go?

LUCINDA: Yes. I'll find my dear Lord, and ask him. Not that I care for the verses, so I have the man.   [*Exit*]

MRS RICH: What a confusion I am in; if I break with Lady Basset, she may expose my foibles to the whole town; and to brook a rival –   [*walks disturbed*]

MRS TRICKWELL: Observe how Mrs Rich is disturbed; here we shall lose a bubble for your foolish love affair.

LADY LA BASSET: Confound her! Have I kept Sir John, and run all the risks in the universe to maintain his port, and shall he dare address without my leave.

MRS TRICKWELL: 'Twas ever so, Lady Basset; we little ones dote upon the handsome footman first; make a hard shift to equip him, then some topping[36] dame swoops the dressed-up fellow, and he forgets his original.

LADY LA BASSET: I'll lower his top-sail! And make him know he's mine, and only mine.

MRS RICH: Is it any happy thing we know, my Lady! That has the honour to be yours, and only yours.

LADY LA BASSET: Yes verily, a thing you are fond of, and to convince ye how vain all your hopes are, know he sacrifices all his fools to me! Here's a list of 'em, chaw upon't and farewell!
                    [*Exit*]

MRS RICH: Mondieu! She has won three hundred pound of my money, and now she picks a quarrel with me. Civil I protest.

MRS TRICKWELL: Ungrateful wretch! Should I forsake my friend!

MRS RICH: Never whilst they have three hundred pound left! 'Tis against the rule of prudence.

MRS TRICKWELL: Alas madam, what d'ye mean?

MRS RICH: Your pardon Mrs Trickwell! I mean nothing; I am angry with the whole world, will indulge my ill-nature, and never bless 'em with a smile again.

MRS TRICKWELL: I thought your ladyship would have allowed your lover to have been beloved.

---

[36]*topping*: arrogant

MRS RICH: But not to love, 'there's the distinction. To increase my spleen, let's see what this Fury has left!

[*reads*] *A list of the fools that dote on my proper person.* So.

Dorimene the back-biter, at the gilt post in Twatling Square; very well.

The rich amorous banker's widow, removed from behind the Exchange, at the Citizens' Folly, into Covent Garden. Oh! How I hate myself, for having loved him.

Miranda the jilt in Scotland Yard. Arabella the affected, in Pride Lane, at the Dressing-Box. The Lady Hazard, under the doctors care in Covent Garden, at the Magdalene. – He's a monster.

The Fat Marchioness, with her shining face, near the Red House in Plaster Street. – Villain, I'll see him no more. Betty.

BETTY: Madam.

MRS RICH: 'Tis resolved on: I'll see Sir John no more.

BETTY: I believe I hear him.

MRS RICH: Whither do you go?

BETTY: I'm going to meet him, madam, to tell him you'll see him no more.

MRS RICH: No, no, Betty, let him come in, I will confound him, and see with what impudence he'll justify this list.

BETTY: Here he is, madam.

Enter SIR JOHN

SIR JOHN: Ah! Are you there, madam? You cannot imagine my impatience till I see you?

MRS RICH: From what quarter of the town came you, sir? From Twatling Square? Or Covent Garden? Or is it the rich amorous banker you left last?

SIR JOHN: I know not what you mean, madam!

MRS RICH: Not what I mean, perfidious man?

SIR JOHN: Upon my honour, madam, I do not understand you.

MRS RICH: See the obliging list of your fools sir.

SIR JOHN: Ha, ha, ha, and has this discomposed your la'ship; only a frolic at my Lady Jeerwell's: we were all set to abuse our friends; a lady put down her list, and writ me the leading coxcomb, at which we laughed for half an hour. I never knew your ladyship so out in the practice of quality in my whole life: why the wit of the age lies in abuses. I warrant ye, there's my

Lady Tossbum did a thousand ridiculous things, and at last cried for very vexation, that none of the scribblers would put her in rhyme doggerel.

MRS RICH: I fear I'm in the wrong, Mrs Trickwell.

MRS TRICKWELL: I fear so too; Sir John is nice, at these things extremely nice.

MRS RICH: Aye, but the verses, Mrs Trickwell.

MRS TRICKWELL: The verses, Sir John, the verses.

SIR JOHN: Why, that was the very adventure I was coming to laugh with your ladyship about: I must confess I was indiscreet enough to communicate; my heart and tongue being full of my passion, I went, madam, to the Chocolate House, where I met five or six wits; yes, madam, five or six; and let not that astonish you, for we live in a very fertile age for wits.

MRS RICH: And what then, sir?

SIR JOHN: What then, madam? Why, they told me, how that my Lord Fourbind had given these verses to a Citizen's young daughter; that Mr Flutter had sent them to a she-friend of his; that Sir Richard Welbred had obtained favours from his mistress by these verses, ha, ha, ha, ha. Is not this diverting, madam?

MRS RICH: So, I suppose, you are extremely vain, and pleased to see your works thus universal.

MRS TRICKWELL: As we are, madam, we leaders of the town, and fronters of the boxes, when we find a fashion begun by us, awkwardly aimed at by all the little pretenders to dress.

SIR JOHN: When, alas, borrowed wit, like borrowed clothes, fits none but the owners: to you, and you alone, the song is à propos;

> My heart is only sensible of so much fire,
> Your eyes have only power thus to inspire.

MRS TRICKWELL: How full of tenderness is all Sir John says. – [*aside*] – I shall deserve the five hundred pounds, Sir John.

MRS RICH: I grant his expressions are full of douceurs;[37] but then he wants sincerity and truth, Mrs Trickwell.

MRS TRICKWELL: Truth, in a compliment, or courtier, oh fie madam! 'Tis against the nature of the thing.

---

[37] *douceurs*: sweeteners

MRS RICH: Why, De la Bette, how charmingly contrary is this
to my City education: but canst thou believe Sir John's in love
with aught but that dear shadow of his, which he's caressing so
passionately in the glass?

BETTY: I dare swear that's his idol; but your ladyship will not
hear me.

MRS RICH: Yes Betty, I shall take a time, for I am vexed, but scorn
to show it.

BETTY: Madam —

MRS RICH: Peace, see, and admit 'em.   [*Exit* BETTY]

SIR JOHN: [*setting his wig in the glass*] Pox of this ill-favoured
curl, how many hairs it exceeds his fellows; this Monsieur
Cheurneux is a booby, damn me.

MRS RICH: How concerned Sir John is, in his justification,
madam.

MRS TRICKWELL: [*aside*] This fool will lose his opportunity, and
I my money: the glass robs us of your conversation, Sir John.

SIR JOHN: No, 'tis the lady robs me of myself; I am perpetually
studying new airs only to please her.

   Enter BETTY

BETTY: Madam, Mrs Clerimont, and a world of company to
wait on you.

MRS RICH: Oh my stars, and are the Indian curtains drawn, the
wax candles ready, the keys with the gold strings in the cabinet
doors.

   Enter FOOTMAN

BETTY: Yes, madam, all is in order.

MRS RICH: Why, Tam, Ralph, Waitwell.

BETTY: [*aside*] So, the fit of vanity returns. — They are, Madam,
where you commanded 'em.

MRS RICH: Oh heavens! Now Sir John should be caught saying
fine things to me, and he's practising grimaces in the glass.

MRS TRICKWELL: Sir John, here's visitors to the lady.

SIR JOHN: Ha! Where? Be near me Chris, we will receive 'em.

MRS RICH: Shall I be laughing, or in a passion, or how, dear Mrs
Trickwell; quick, quick, your instructions: some say I become a
passion rarely.

MRS TRICKWELL: In no passion, I beseech you, madam, but that
of joy to see your friends: look they are here.

MRS RICH: Well, I'll be advised; but my City neighbours said I
chid my maids with such a grace, they'd have given all the world
to have done like me.

   Enter BELVOIR, ELDER CLERIMONT, MRS CLERIMONT
    and TOBY

ELDER CLERIMONT: A neat place this, Toby; but our house
i'th' country was nigh as handsome, till the hounds, and my
hunts-folk tore it about.

TOBY: Aye master, but ye had not near so much earthen ware,
that ye had not, and our Mopsa would make rare work wi'it;
'udsnigs she would.

MRS CLERIMONT: Why, Mr Belvoir, I am baulked in my design
of my visit; I intended to have brought the younger Clerimont,
and the Lady Landsworth, to an interview; and his man has
whisked him away just as we came out of the coach.

BELVOIR: We must on now, there's no retreating; they look as
if they had been setting themselves this hour.

MRS CLERIMONT: I have a sudden whim, prithee assist.

BELVOIR: What is't?

MRS CLERIMONT: I'll make my lubberly cousin pass upon that
fantastic creature, for a beau in disguise.

BELVOIR: That's an odd fancy indeed, surely 'tis impossible.

MRS RICH: Sir John! Is this the mode of the wits, to come into
one's house, and find all the discourse among themselves.

SIR JOHN: I am in a maze, madam! Let us accost 'em.

MRS RICH: If you please give me leave Sir John, what honours
are these ye heap upon me, ma'am; to receive a visit from the
charming Mrs Clerimont!

MRS CLERIMONT: Charms and perfections lose their significa-
tion, when applied to any, where Mrs Rich is by.

MRS RICH: Oh madam –

ELDER CLERIMONT: Aye, Toby, here's words; I brought thee in
to learn a little.

TOBY: 'Udsnigs, 'tis rare, master.

SIR JOHN: Mr Belvoir, I cast me at your feet.

BELVOIR: Sir John, I kiss your hands.

SIR JOHN: [*to* CLERIMONT] Sir, I am yours.

TOBY: Nounce, what's he a-going to do, unbuckle master's
shoe?

ELDER CLERIMONT: What a plague; have run your mop in my face, and e'en choked me with your powder.

SIR JOHN: Ah hey! The meaning of this, my dear Belvoir?

BELVOIR: An uncommon fancy, Sir John, you cannot find out, I perceive.

SIR JOHN: Poison me, 'twas the oddest reception! For Pluto's sake, what is he?

TOBY: What is he? Why he is my master, 'udsnigs! Dan't provoke en, he'll have a game at fifty cuffs wi' ye, as well as e'er a man in vorty mile on him.

ELDER CLERIMONT: Let'n alone Toby, 'tis another o'th' libken souls, a high wind, or a shower frights into fits of the mother: I despise en.

MRS CLERIMONT: Let me beg your private ear; that man is the greatest nicest beau in Christendom.

MRS RICH: Ye amaze me madam.

MRS CLERIMONT: Very true upon my word. That fellow there, that looks so like a John-a-Nokes,[38] is the jemmest[39] valet; a countess has been in love with him.

MRS RICH: Oh my stars, can I believe you?

MRS CLERIMONT: You may, no creature knows it but myself, I beg ye keep it a secret, especially from Sir John, or murder will ensue.

MRS RICH: I engage, or I love a secret extremely, but what could be the occasion?

MRS CLERIMONT: A lady affronted him, and he swore never to address again, but in this strange disguise; because his mistress chose his rival only for having his wig better powdered, he'll not alter this behaviour, nor dress, till some other lady makes him amends. He's my relation, I wonder you can't perceive some airs of greatness through those clouds.

MRS RICH: Not I, I protest, but the more naturally he does it, he shows his parts the more.

MRS CLERIMONT: He calls his gentleman Toby. Could you think one bred a page had power to put on such a shuffling gait?[40]

MRS RICH: 'Tis a diverting whimsy now one knows it, he, he, he!

[38]*John-a-Nokes*: simpleton   [39]*jemmest*: smartest   [40]*gait*: walk

SIR JOHN: Won't ye give me leave to laugh with ye, ladies, at those strange figures? I beg it of ye, for I am ready to burst.

MRS RICH: It may be dangerous, Sir John, and I advise you to keep your countenance. How pretty 'tis to know a thing the rest of the company does not?

ELDER CLERIMONT: Come coz, what must we do next, we ha' stared about us long enough, madam. Ha' ye ne'er a smoking room and a cup of hearty March, ha —

TOBY: I' faykings, had master and I been at e'er a gentleman's house i'th' country, by this time we had been half-seas-over,[41] 'udsnigs.

MRS RICH: Rarely performed I vow.

MRS CLERIMONT: Now must I keep up the humour, and pretend to direct him. Fie cousin, talk of drinking before ladies, you should entertain them with fine conversation and songs.

ELDER CLERIMONT: I dan't pass, and I do gi' ye a song; come, a hunting song.

SIR JOHN: Ridiculous.

MRS RICH: Better and better, by my stars.

SIR JOHN: [*to* MRS TRICKWELL] She seems pleased.

MRS TRICKWELL: I am in the dark.

MRS RICH: Excellent.

SIR JOHN: Excellent! Abominable.

MRS CLERIMONT: Now if you please, madam, we'll pay a visit to my Lady Landsworth; my cousin said he would return.

MRS RICH: With all my heart, I believe she's not at home, but the opportunity will show my apartments.

SIR JOHN: Madam, my hand.

MRS RICH: Your pardon Sir John, this gentleman's a stranger.

SIR JOHN: Preferred to me!

ELDER CLERIMONT: Stand by, muskcat, you see the gentlewoman likes ye not.

TOBY: Well done, master, egad, he'll put by a hundred such Limberham's Beaux as you, egad, he will cram 'em in a mouse hole, i' faykings.

MRS CLERIMONT: Ah poor Sir John, e'en take that tattered frigate and be content.

---

[41]*half-seas-over*: almost drunk

MRS TRICKWELL: Let's follow and find out the meaning.

SIR JOHN: Ye gods, and goddesses; hell, devils and furies, I'll be revenged.

TOBY: Ha, ha, ah, what strange oaths he has?

SCENE THREE

Scene changes to Younger Clerimont's lodgings

Enter CLERIMONT *and* JACK

CLERIMONT: Where is she! How my desires are changed! Triumphant love prevails, a thousand fires shot from those fair eyes have warmed me; a thousand arguments pleading all for pleasure lead me on, the lord within plants and heaves my bosom, whilst circling tides roll round apace, and give tumultuous joys.

JACK: Aye, marry, sir, now you look and breathe another man, good fortune is your slave, she always waits upon the bold.

CLERIMONT: And what know I but the coy dame, who hides her face at the least word awry, and blushes to be gazed on, has in her heart looser fires than my gay mistress. How many an honest wretch that asked would swear his arms enfolded a Lucrece, yet truly hugs in the dissembled saint, a vile jilt?

JACK: Right, sir, right; oh I could burn my cap for joy to see you thus.

CLERIMONT: She's coming, and seems in busy talk, let us not disturb her.

Enter LADY LANDSWORTH *and* BETTY

BETTY: As soon as ever my lady was engaged, I fled to overtake ye, madam.

LADY LANDSWORTH: 'Twas kindly done. Yonder he stands, methinks I hate him, now he has lost that modest sweetness which caught my soul, his looks are wild and lewd, and all I ever feared in men appears in that deceitful face: I would I were away.

BETTY: Nay, madam, make this last trial, since you have gone so far.

CLERIMONT: May I yet approach.

LADY LANDSWORTH: You may, I do remember when we

parted last, 'twas on odd terms, nature seemed reversed, you fled and I pursued in vain, I practised all my charms, and tried my utmost art in vain, your virtue like the mountain snow, the nearer I advanced congealed the more, and in the bloom of youth, rigid and cold as frozen age, you awed me with severity. Are ye still thus resolved.

CLERIMONT: Oh no, I am altered quite, my very soul's on fire, do not my eyes speak for me? I languish, burn and die.

LADY LANDSWORTH: Then we have conquered, and like libertines we'll rove, tire every pleasure, tread rounds of joy, the insipid world shall wonder at, but never know to taste.

JACK: Nay, we shall live a delicious life that's certain, ha my dear damsel.

BETTY: Peace, and mind your betters.

CLERIMONT: What music's in that voice, it dances through my ears, and puts my heart in tune: not painted cherubs, not the first dawn of cheerful day, or opening spring is half so pleasing. Oh thou art rapture all, and all divine, down at thy loved sight each sense drinks deep draughts of joy.

LADY LANDSWORTH: Throw off these mourning weeds, and let me dress thee extravagant as my desires, like a queen's favourite, for I would be profuse.

JACK: Lard, lard, how fine we shall be.

CLERIMONT: If there must be profusion, let it be in love; there lay out all thy stock; let days and nights and years serve only to count the acts of love.

LADY LANDSWORTH: Yes, and teach us to deceive my keeper, his purse must help our riots, his credulity supply our mirth.

CLERIMONT: Ah, why hast dashed my rising ecstasies with the detested thought that thou art shared, but in thy arms I'll lose the goading torment; in those blissful moments I'm sure thou art only mine, my life, my all.　　　　　　　　*[embraces her]*

LADY LANDSWORTH: Stand off, thou monster, viler, worse than man, oh let thy contagious breath infect at distance. I will remove thee from my sight, and from my soul, as far as thou art gone from honour, truth and honest.

JACK: Here's a turn ye gods, why what's the matter now?

CLERIMONT: Madam —

LADY LANDSWORTH: Speak not, nor dare to stay me, for I'll

leave thee like thy good genius in thy distressful hours, never to return. Oh I could curse myself, my follies, to believe there was virtue in thy sex, thou vile dissembler; may it return upon thee; dissembled by thy joys; dissembled by thy friends; above all may thy mistress prove the abstract of dissimulation.

CLERIMONT: Hear me but speak.

LADY LANDSWORTH: No, haste thee to some mart of luxury and shame, preach there, but defile my ears no more; away, my friends away.

Let's fly that wretch, fly him and all mankind:
Now for the cursed pursuer leave a track behind.

[*Exeunt* LAND LANDSWORTH *and* BETTY]

CLERIMONT: What's the meaning of all this?

JACK: Mad, sir, raving mad.

CLERIMONT: Can she be honest?

JACK: Impossible, had she the roguish leer, the tip, the wink, the everything.

CLERIMONT: Peace rascal, she is, and not the world shall hide her from me.

JACK: Now must we go upon knight-errantry; may heaven be praised, we are as poor as knight-errants already.

CLERIMONT:
Fly, search, inquire,
She cannot, must not long remain unknown,
She'll be discovered by her charms alone,
I'll find, I'll claim, I'll seize her for my own,
Breathe at her feet my vows, nor thence remove,
Till I am blessed with her returning love.

Act Five

SCENE ONE

Enter YOUNGER CLERIMONT, MRS FIDGET *and* JACK

CLERIMONT: Sure 'twas all a dream, I neither saw nor liked, nor loved; it was a dream, the gaudy vision's vanished, and I am waked again to my calamities; or grant it real, what had I to do with love? Love's the gay banquet of luxurious hours, he shakes his golden wings, and flies detested poverty, to downy couches; under gilded roofs he flies, there lays his wanton head, there revels in the fair one's eyes.

JACK: Sir, sir.

CLERIMONT: When the poor join they hardly taste a night of peace: strife traces Hymen's steps so close, the haggard thrusts between at bed, at board, and drives the gentle god away. Oh! My distracted thoughts; why do ye follow me? Is misery denied the privilege to be alone?

MRS FIDGET: Ah, sir, 'tis that unlucky dog your man has done this.

JACK: Hist!

MRS FIDGET: Nay, it shall out.

CLERIMONT: What has he done? Speak!

MRS FIDGET: Why, sir –

JACK: Peace, I say, ye ungrateful cockatrice; now will not all the sack I have rammed down that unconscionable throat keep this poor secret in, though upon my word, I meant it for the best: believe that, I beseech you, sir?

CLERIMONT: What's the matter? What have ye said?

MRS FIDGET: Aye, said, there ye have hit it: he has said enough, by my troth.

JACK: I am sure you always say too much.

MRS FIDGET: Say ye so, sirrah, know then, sir, that hopeful rogue gave ye such a character to the young gentlewoman, 'twould have frighted the devil.

JACK: And what said you, Mrs Delilah?

MRS FIDGET: Even, the same, by thy instigation, thou tempter.

JACK: Keep that name to yourself, it belongs to you, woman: I thought, sir, she loved nothing but a rake, a madman. I did all for the best, indeed I did, sir.

CLERIMONT: No matter; 'tis the malice of my Fate, which would have found an instrument, hadst thou been silent.

MRS FIDGET: Come, hang melancholy, and cast away care; my mind gives me, this damsel will wheel about again: I never yet knew man or woman weary of an intrigue, when 'twas gone no further than yours has done.

JACK: Right: there ye are in the right, i'faith, landlady.

MRS FIDGET: Well, sauce, you'll never leave your impudence. Landlady; blockhead!

JACK: That ye, madam.

   Enter BELVOIR

BELVOIR: Still with folded arms and looks of sorrow. I come to cheer thee, my friend; to make thee laugh, to give thee lasting joy.

CLERIMONT: Impossible!

BELVOIR: Thy brother is fallen in love with the fantastical widow Rich; her wealth and beauty has charmed him: ye know that he is possessed of a great estate. He never had management enough to be master of money, and hearing the widow has so much he is distracted for't; whilst she takes him for a beau in masquerade, is wonderfully pleased; and, I believe, will be a match.

CLERIMONT: And what's all this to me?

BELVOIR: Oh! Much to your advantage, for he has promised Mrs Clerimont, if she can bring this marriage to pass, he will resign that part of the estate to you, your father in his lifetime had designed ye.

CLERIMONT: There thou speak'st comfort that suits my wishes, for I would fain travel, but want the means.

BELVOIR: Travel!

CLERIMONT: My friend, 'tis not wealth can make me happy now.

JACK: Ah, sir, but wealth's a good stroke. I see providence has not quite forgot us.

BELVOIR: Whatever you have resolved, I beg ye to go this moment with me to Mrs Clerimont's: a busy minute now is worth a lazy year.

CLERIMONT: Do even what you please with me.

BELVOIR: Come on then.

MRS FIDGET: Good luck attend ye.   [*Exeunt*]

SCENE TWO

Mrs Rich's house

Enter MRS RICH *and two* FOOTMEN

MRS RICH: I design a ball tonight, sots, and would have, if possible, you rascals clean; and you, d'ye hear –

Enter LADY LA BASSET *and* VERMIN

LADY LA BASSET: I'll fright this little pretender to quality, till she either quits Sir John, or buys him of me at a good round rate; he has made many a penny of me, now 'tis time to retaliate. Madam, send off your footmen; I would speak with ye alone.

MRS RICH: Madam!

LADY LA BASSET: Begone, scoundrels, or I shall drive ye hence.

MRS RICH: Fellows, be near me, I know not what her design is.

LADY LA BASSET: My design is honourable.

MRS RICH: Heavens! What can she mean?

LADY LA BASSET: Base coward, are ye afraid?

MRS RICH: Afraid, madam: I! I –

LADY LA BASSET: Come, no dallying; you have robbed me of Sir John: I demand satisfaction.

MRS RICH: Oh my stars! This is extravagant to the last degree. Alas, madam, what satisfaction can a lady give to a lady.

LADY LA BASSET: I'd have thee fight. Dare you set up for quality, and dare not fight, pitiful Citizen: 'tis for thy honour; 'tis modish too, extremely French, and agreeable to thy own phrase. I'll have thee fight, I say.

MRS RICH: What need I, when I have conquered already: can I help the power of my eyes, or Sir John's sensibility? My stars, this is prodigious! What weapon must we use in this unusual combat, hey, madam?

LADY LA BASSET: D'ye make a jest on't. Sword and pistol, madam.

MRS RICH: Oh, heavens! I swoon at the sight of either.

LADY LA BASSET: Thou art the offspring of an alderman, I of quality: I can fight, ride, play; equal the men in any virtue or vice. Thou little creature, yield, or sa, sa – thus for Sir John: sa, sa.

MRS RICH: The woman's mad: will ye come in my house and murder me?

LADY LA BASSET: Look, is this a jest? [*draws a pistol*]

MRS RICH: Murder! Murder! Jack! Jeffery! George! Help! Help!

Enter MR RICH

MR RICH: Hey day! What's the house turned into a perfect Bedlam, learning to fence, Madam Whimsical?

MRS RICH: Oh, brother, save me from that furious woman, and I'll submit, for the future, to your conduct.

LADY LA BASSET: [*aside*] Curse on him; this is a sensible fellow, and my design's lost.

MR RICH: And what are you, a Lady Errant, and this the squire of the body: he looks as if he had lived upon adventures indeed.

LADY LA BASSET: No matter what I am. I am mad.

MR RICH: I believe so.

MRS RICH: I shan't recover the fright this twelve month.

LADY LA BASSET: She would be a woman of quality, and dares not fight: by the honour of my ancestors, I'll go find out Sir John, and if he does not change his resolution, he and I shall dispute it. Come along, Vermin.

[*Exeunt* LADY LA BASSET *and* VERMIN]

MR RICH: Ha, ha, that would be a pretty combat, in troth; he dares not fight a man: this woman will be an excellent match for him. Dost thou yet see thy folly, thy own, and thy instructor's folly: these things teach thee to appear like the truly great. Alas, mistaken wretch, they are as far from noble natures, as light from darkness.

MRS RICH: I do begin to find my error, and am mending my conversation; yet think not, though ye have humbled me, you shall e'er bring me back to the City again. No, I have still spirit enough to defy the City, and all its works. By my stars, I'll never endure a greasy City feast; a set custard is my aversion of all aversions, as Olivia has it.

MR RICH: 'Tis impossible to turn the current of a woman's will, though it perpetually runs the wrong way.

Enter MRS BETTY

BETTY: Oh, madam, such a piece of treachery, such perfidious-ness have I discovered.

MRS RICH: In whom? My stars, this is a day of wonders!

BETTY: Even Sir John, going from your ladyship in a huff, because you smiled upon the worthy gentleman in disguise, met your niece; she flew upon him with a violent exclamation, 'My Lord Fourbind, yours entirely.' He answered in a passionate tone, '*ah mon cher*, I die for ye'.

MR RICH: My daughter!

BETTY: Yes, your daughter; and together they whisked cross the gallery, to miss's apartment: I left 'em there, and came to inform your ladyship.

MRS RICH: 'Tis all confusion and amazement!

MR RICH: I am distracted! My daughter: I'll kick him, burn his flaxen wig, dirty his white coat, knock out his butter teeth[42], wring off his nose, and spoil him for being a beau for ever.

MRS RICH: Whilst I conceal myself in one of the closets, if this be true, Betty, I have such a revenge shall make the town ring on't.

BETTY: Do, Madam. – [*aside to* MR RICH] – Now, sir, now's the time to clear the house of the locusts, these swarm of fools.

MR RICH: Set all thy wits at work, my good girl. Come show me this happy couple, I shall spoil their mirth egad.   [*Exeunt*]

Enter SIR JOHN, LUCINDA, CHRIS, *and* GOVERNESS

SIR JOHN: Beyond my wish! Mrs Rich's niece, the world shall applaud my revenge: but, my dear, are you sure none of the family will interrupt us.

LUCINDA: No, no, they mew me here eternally with that old woman; my aunt hates a younger face than her own should appear where she is: I am not such a child but I can find that. Come hasten, governess, pack up all my jewels; we'll steal out at the back door, bid adieu to my sweet aunt, till my dear Lord and I visit her in a coach-and-six.

[42]*butter teeth*: front teeth

SIR JOHN: That's my cherubim, help Chris, help, I long to be gone.

CHRIS: Mr Lord, we'll ha' down in a twinkling.

LUCINDA: But look you my Lord, I must tell you my mind in two or three words before we go, what you must trust to. Do you see I am not furiously in love; as my aunt says, I run away only for more pleasure, more liberty, etc. I will go every day to the play, or else to the Park; and every time I go to the park, to the lodge, to Chelsea: in fine, where I please, or as I run away with you, I'll run away from you, sue for my own fortune again, and live as I please: what I have heard how ladies with fortunes do.

SIR JOHN: [*aside*] A young gypsy this, who'd have thought it had been in her. *Mon cher amie*, you shall have your will.

LUCINDA: That you must expect, my dear Lord, for had I loved obedience I had still obeyed my father: and she that begins with her father generally makes an end with her husband; but that's furiously modish, and therefore so much the better. Quick, quick, good governess, and then a hey for disobedience.

Enter MR RICH *and* BETTY

MR RICH: And then a hey for disobedience, who is this, my daughter, with her 'a hey for disobedience'?

LUCINDA: Oh Gemini, my father! What shall I do now! Well, I'll e'en turn sides, take my father's part, if he's uppermost, and rail at my Lord furiously.

MR RICH: Art thou the flaring fop my hopeful sister's fond on, descended from thy duchess's bed-chamber, to steal my daughter?

SIR JOHN: I am a gentleman, sir, and expect to be used like one.

MR RICH: 'Tis false, thou art not, I have traced thy original, and found thou art none.

LUCINDA: Oh la! Not a gentleman, why he swore to me he was a Lord, out upon him.

SIR JOHN: Well said miss, I find we may e'en be marching, for any friends we have here. Thou unpolished thing, I answer thy affront, with my mien, my dress, my air, all show the gentleman, and give the lie to thy ill mannered malice.

MR RICH: Defy me, thou thing equipped! Canst thou justify the worst of thefts, stealing my child? Draw.

SIR JOHN: Your pardon, sir, not before the lady, I may discompose her, perhaps the sight of a sword may fright her into a fit.

LUCINDA: Oh la, don't let me hinder ye.

MR RICH: Art thou not a fool?

SIR JOHN: A fool, *à la mode*, sir.

MR RICH: A coward.

SIR JOHN: I am a beau, sir.

MR RICH: All sound and no sense.

SIR JOHN: I sing tolerably well. 'For who would in a cellar dine, when he may go to Lockets.'

MR RICH: Thou trifling coxcomb, all wig and no brains, begone this very instant, or I'll lead thee thus by the nose, I'll lead thee to a she-fop of thy acquaintance, coxcomb, I will, therefore make use of thy heels.

SIR JOHN: Egad, this is very uncivil.

MR RICH: I meant it so.

SIR JOHN: I'll lampoon thee, till your friends shall fly ye, your neighbours despise ye, and the world laugh at ye.

MR RICH: I believe your wit's as dangerous as your courage, begone, insect.

LUCINDA: Pretend to be a Lord, and baulk a young woman's expectations!

BETTY: Ah poor Sir John, ha, ha.

SIR JOHN: Has she been a spectator, I shall be jeered to death. I will study a revenge shall make you tremble, I will, thou barbarous Cit.

MR RICH: Go set your periwig to rights fop, ha, ha.

SIR JOHN: Curses, curses, ah I shall choke. [*Exit* SIR JOHN]

MR RICH: Farewell fool; you, madam, I shall find a time to discourse with; dear Mrs Betty, take her into your care, whilst I turn this old limb of iniquity out of doors; here you had a mind to run away, now I desire you to walk about your business. Begone thou unnecessary evil.

LUCINDA: Let her go, I say, she seduced me I'm sure.

GOVERNESS: Oh, fie, fie, miss.

MR RICH: Begone, 'twas her canting deceived me; what care we ought to take whom we set over our children.

　　　　Enter MRS RICH

MR RICH: So Madam, are you satisfied?

MRS RICH: Rage, spite, shame and resentment at once torment me, so base a coward, my stars, I shall go mad.

MR RICH: Dear sister, let your stars alone, and learn to shun folly, wheresoe'er you find it.

MRS RICH: Then I must shun you, myself and all the world. You have a set and formal folly, I a vain and airy folly, but he the basest, most betraying folly.

MR RICH: Then redeem your judgment, and stop censorious mouths, by accepting Mrs Clerimont's kinsman, whom your woman tells me has a plentiful estate, this will turn the laughter of the town upon Sir John, and leave you in happy circumstances.

MRS RICH: I will do something, something to plague that fellow.

BETTY: Here comes the lady, I believe to plead in her friend's behalf.

Enter LADY LANDSWORTH *and* MRS CLERIMONT

MRS CLERIMONT: Ah, madam, such misfortune.

MRS RICH: The whole deceitful world, by my stars, I think is full of nothing else.

MRS CLERIMONT: But this, madam, your bright eyes create.

MRS RICH: I – my eyes, that's pleasant.

MRS CLERIMONT: The strictness of his vow racks him, for he knows a lady thus accomplished can never like him as he appears.

LADY LANDSWORTH: Indeed I pity him.

MR RICH: Pray ladies, what's the case?

MRS CLERIMONT: Alas! Sir, a cousin of mine who wants not the goods of fortune; but lies under an obligation to seem the greatest clown in the universe, till fate has made his reparation for the affront he received, when all his study was dress and conversation.

MRS RICH: And has he a good estate?

MRS CLERIMONT: Four thousand a year I assure ye.

MR RICH: Gadzooks, what matter is it wherever he is dressed, as ye call it, again or no.

MRS RICH: Yes, yes, that is material upon my word, Mr Rich.

MRS CLERIMONT: Would you content to marry him, for so far his oath extends; believe me, madam, he'd soon break forth to your amazement.

MRS RICH: I profess ladies, you give me such an air of blushing, when I reflect on what ye are tempting me to.

MRS CLERIMONT: I profess, ma'am, 'tis a very becoming air.

MRS RICH: My stars! 'twill sound so odd.

MRS CLERIMONT: 'Twill surprise the town so prettily.

MR RICH: Zooks, 'tis the best thing to piece up your fantastical character; 'twill surprise the world indeed to see you do a wise thing.

MRS RICH: Speak not you, sir, for I yield only to the ladies. Well, where is the gentleman?

MRS CLERIMONT: Languishing within, madam; condemned to silence, lest his rough-hewn expressions should offend.

MRS RICH: De la Bette, a pen and ink, perhaps I may expose the knight, and satisfy your friend. Your pardon for some moments; come with me niece.

LUCINDA: Yes, madam, pray let us be revenged on this sham Lord, you can't think what a liar he is.

MRS RICH: Your servant.

MRS CLERIMONT: Yours. [*Exeunt* MRS RICH *and* LUCINDA]

LADY LANDSWORTH: Follow dear De la Bette, as thy lady has it, and now show thy masterpiece.

BETTY: I lay my life 'tis done, I see it in her eyes.

MR RICH: In hopes on't, I'll get a parson. This widow married, my affairs are prosperous, and my daughter and her fortune returned to me.

MRS CLERIMONT: Hasten, good sir, for this fair lady and I have a little business of our own.

MR RICH: More weddings, I hope, then we'll have dancing in abudance; come honest *de la Bette*, I promise thee a new portion to thy new name.

BETTY: I'll endeavour to deserve it, sir.

[*Exeunt* MR RICH *and* BETTY]

MRS CLERIMONT: My charming cousin, have not I found a pretty employment, to turn general match-maker? But for the younger Clerimont, I own I could do anything.

LADY LANDSWORTH: I should dissemble worse than I thought

he did, not to say I'm pleased to find his character what I so heartily wished it.

MRS CLERIMONT: To convince ye throughly, I have sent for his landlady, whose odd account of him must proceed from folly, or malice: oh here she comes!

Enter MRS FIDGET

MRS CLERIMONT: Your servant, madam, 'twas not for goods, as I pretended I gave you this trouble, but to ask after the deportment of my relation, Mr Clerimont, your lodger.

LADY LANDSWORTH: The wild, mad spark, that scarce ever lies at home: you know me, madam, I suppose?

MRS FIDGET: Yes, yes, madam, in verity I must beg your pardon, I did belie the gentleman, abominably belie him.

LADY LANDSWORTH: What provoked you to it?

MRS FIDGET: Truly, Ian contrived it, thinking it would please your ladyship.

LADY LANDSWORTH: Ian, pray who is Ian?

MRS FIDGET: My friend and his footman.

MRS CLERIMONT: My cousin, I am sure was always accounted a very modest, sober gentleman.

MRS FIDGET: Modest! 'Udsflesh, he has not his peer in the whole town; by my faykings, he's a little too modest, that's his fault.

MRS CLERIMONT: I dare affirm he's truly noble, not in these straights of fortune would he quit his honour to be great, or his integrity to be rich.

MRS FIDGET: Or his religion to be thought a wit.

LADY LANDSWORTH: Enough, ladies, I am fully satisfied; only to his love, if I have made any impression.

MRS CLERIMONT: That this moment you yourself shall be judge of; he's coming. If you please to retire you shall overhear me sound his inclinations.

MRS FIDGET: Aye, there he is, heaven bless him, he's a sweet young man.

LADY LANDSWORTH:

Come with me, Mrs Fidget. Now Clerimont,
If thy heart does with generous passion burn,
Then I with joy will love for love return.

[*Exeunt* LADY LANDSWORTH *and* MRS FIDGET]
Enter the YOUNGER CLERIMONT, BELVOIR *and* JACK

BELVOIR: I have brought him, madam, but I am ashamed to say with what reluctancy, he flies even you, you the fair contriver of his auspicious fortunes.

CLERIMONT: I am sure, I am ashamed to see you take such pains about a thing not worth your care.

MRS CLERIMONT: When the good suffer, the virtuous part of humankind are all concerned. When we suffer by our fate, and not our faults, heaven always makes the trial short, and shows an easy way for our deliverance.

CLERIMONT: In vain you soothe me with your friendship; did you fully know me, you would know, there scarce is left a room for hope.

MRS CLERIMONT: Suppose there is a lady in love with you, surrounded thus as you are with your misfortunes; suppose her chaste, and rich, and fair, who though her eyes never yet encountered yours, by my description, dotes upon a character so singular and different from your wild sex.

CLERIMONT: Were she as fair as woman would be thought; as virtuous as they were of old, e'er 'twas fashionable to be false; had she wealth would satisfy the vain, the miser, the ambitious; so far am I from once consenting to what your kindness has proposed, I would not to rid me of half my sorrow, so much as see her.

BELVOIR: Ah, my friend! This must be some prepossession; you already are in love.

CLERIMONT: It is enough to say I am a fool, must search the world and know it better, e'er I pretend to speak my thoughts. If, madam, from my brother ye can procure my father's first design, I shall own myself eternally obliged, and trouble ye no more.

MRS CLERIMONT: I sigh to say it is not in my power, since you refuse the advantageous offers of the lady's love.

CLERIMONT: Then all I beg, is that ye would enquire for me no more. There is no warding the blows of Fate; the wretch that's doomed unfortunate, no arm of power can save.

BELVOIR: But you look through despair: believe me, friend, 'tis a false glass. Fortune has a fairer face to show you.

MRS CLERIMONT: That pleasing task be mine. Madam, you hear the gentleman is obstinate, but now, sir, if you are not charmed with this appearance, you have a relish different from the universal world.

Re-enter LADY LANDSWORTH *and* MRS FIDGET

CLERIMONT: Ha! 'Tis she! 'Tis she! Here let me fix, thus let me clasp my bliss, thus forever, secure my only valued treasure!

JACK: Aye, 'tis she, 'tis she, egad, and my landlady too!

MRS FIDGET: Yes, manners, your landlady too.

LADY LANDSWORTH: And dare you venture upon me, after the alderman, the colonel, and the senator?

CLERIMONT: My eyes should have contradicted all other senses; sweet innocence is writ in that dear face, and virtue in her brightest characters.

MRS CLERIMONT: Virtuous and great, the charming widow of Sir John Landsworth: her husband formerly, I believe you have seen. What could you ask of Fate more, than to love and be beloved by her?

CLERIMONT: And have I been repining, when the bounteous heavens were pouring such lavish blessing down? Oh! My ravished soul! My first, my only dear!

LADY LANDSWORTH: 'Tis wondrous pretty, when love's soft passion first invades our breath, it brings a thousand charms, a thousand joys, unknown before; but ah! Too often in your sex, rolling time, or some newer face, puts out the kindly flame, and the forsaken fair is left to live, and languish on the kind words which she will hear no more. What can secure me from such a fate? Not even your present thoughts, for they may change.

CLERIMONT: Never, my charmer, never! To look on thee secures a heart like mine from roving: to hear thee talk, will fix me for ever in the chains of love. But, oh! To have thee all; there words cannot aim, there breath is lost in ecstasy.

MRS CLERIMONT: Here's a world of fine things; though I am a little of the lady's mind, 'twill scarce hold out seven years.

BELVOIR: So, there's two in perfect happiness. I hope, madam, you that were so compassionate to others, will not yourself be cruel, but reward my constant vows, nor let me longer sigh in vain.

MRS CLERIMONT: Mr Belvoir, I have allowed you too long a favoured lover in honour to go back; we are as good as married already.

BELVOIR: No, my dear angel, the greatest sweet's to come!

MRS CLERIMONT: Aye, and the sour too, that's the worst on't.
Look, here's another happy couple.

> *Enter* ELDER CLERIMONT, MRS RICH, MR RICH, LUCINDA
> BETTY *and* TOBY

MRS RICH: Well, ladies, what d'ye think I have been doing since
I went out? By my stars! a world of business; and that's a thing I
hate, writ a billet-doux to the beau in appearance; married the
beau in a disguise; given occasion for forty stories, and fifty
lampoons, ha, ha, ha! I have done it all in a humour, by my
stars!

MRS CLERIMONT: E'en carry it on, madam; never have a grave
fit and repent, I say.

ELDER CLERIMONT: Yes, faith, I'm sped, and all o'th'sudden;
she's handsomer trath than our sh'riff's daughter. How they'll
stare, Toby, when she shows her paces through our alley, to the
great pew. Brother Charles, how came you here? Well, I've gi'n
the writings into cousin's hands: 'udslids, does that pretty lady
belong to you? Why this is a rare place for handsome women,
by my troth.

MRS RICH: Come, sir, the transformation has been comical
enough, but now I beg you to reassume your former mien and
dress, and let me make as great a sacrifice to you, as the lady
made of you.

MRS CLERIMONT: Oh, dear Belvoir, say something to keep in
my laugh, or I'm undone.

BELVOIR: I dare not lift up my eyes, nor scarce open my lips to
let my words out.

MR RICH: I confess, my gravity is put to the test now.

MRS RICH: Come Mr Clerimont, will ye hasten; pray dress
immediately because I expect Sir John this moment.

ELDER CLERIMONT: Yes, 'facks, I'll dress, as soon as I can get
my clothes made; and since I'm wed, I'll bestow more money
than I thought, by five pound.

MRS RICH: Nay, now the humour's tiresome, here's only
friends.

BETTY: Oh, madam, I shall break my lace.

CLERIMONT: What's the meaning of all this?

LADY LANDSWORTH: The tittering damsel behind ye can tell.

MRS RICH: Come, I would not for a thousand pound Sir John should find you thus; this is carrying the jest too far. Speak to him madam.

MRS CLERIMONT: Indeed, madam, I fear it must go a little farther; for, to tell ye the plain truth, he has the estate I mentioned, and is my relation; but for the accomplishments you expect, they are yet to learn, upon my word.

MRS RICH: How! I'm undone! What, no conversation, no judgment in dress, no mien, no airs!

ELDER CLERIMONT: Prithee, coz, what is that same airs, d'ye see? I'd willingly please her, now I have her, d'ye see.

MRS CLERIMONT: Airs: why, 'tis a foolish word, used by those that do understand it, and those that do not; 'tis what's pretty, when nature gives it; and what, when affected, spoils all that nature gives beside.

MRS RICH: Oh! I shall go mad. Is that an object fit to please a woman nice as I am?

MR RICH: Come, sister, a long periwig, an à la mode steenkirk,[43] etc. has made a worse face a perfect beau e'er now: consider, he has some thousands a year.

ELDER CLERIMONT: Aye, marry have I; Nay, 'udslid, I have a title too; I value no more, d'ye see, killing a man, than I do killing a mouse; for I'd take up my patent, be a lord, and be tried by my peers.

BELVOIR: Thy peers! Where wouldst find 'em?

MRS RICH: Oh, my cursed stars! First a citizen's, and then a country squire's wife. Ah! I shall never endure him, that's certain.

ELDER CLERIMONT: Midhap so, and midhap ye may; I shan't cross ye mich. All the hunting season I'll be in the country: and you shall hunt pleasures here in town. G'e me a little of your money to pay my debt, and I won't trouble you, d'ye see.

LADY LANDSWORTH: Well said, Mr Bridegroom: come, madam, few beaux would be more complaisant.

BETTY: Madam, Sir John –

MRS RICH: Mountains cover my shame! What shall I say now?

[43] *à la mode steenkirk*: fashionable cravat

LADY LANDSWORTH: Say! Laugh at him, as all the world ought.

MRS CLERIMONT: Believe me, madam, ye have made the better choice.

MR RICH: A thousand times.

Enter SIR JOHN *and* MRS TRICKWELL

MRS TRICKWELL: You bring me here to see you triumph, I can never believe it; you have some trick put upon you, Sir John.

SIR JOHN: Have I not her own note, that spite of her jealousies, and her brother's tyranny, she will this day be married.

MRS TRICKWELL: She does not say to you. Ha! What a world of company is here?

SIR JOHN: The brother, and the young gypsy his daughter: I'll be gone.

BELVOIR: Nay, no retreating, Sir John, you must, at least, wish the lady joy.

MRS RICH: Pshaw, my design's broke, my plot's spoiled, can I triumph at his defeat, and show that awkward figure?

SIR JOHN: Madam, your summons brought me hither, I hoped to joys.

MRS RICH: I hate you, and all mankind.

LUCINDA: So do I; ye sham Lord, ye brag, ye bounce ye –

BELVOIR: Enough, good miss. Sir John, I perceive you must search for new gallantries; here the ladies are provided for, except this little one, who seems to have no inclination.

SIR JOHN: Pox take ye all; they were fond, I'm sure.

MR RICH: Come, ye young coquette, your education shall be altered, I assure ye, 'tis e'en high time.

MRS TRICKWELL: Well, I believe my booty with yonder fantastical lady is at an end, so I'll steal off unobserved.

[*Exit* MRS TRICKWELL]

Enter LADY LA BASSET

LADY LA BASSET: Where is this villain, this false ungrateful villain?

SIR JOHN: So; another outcry?

LADY LA BASSET: Yes, traitor, and a just one: know all, this was but a servant in Sir John Roverhead's family; I dressed him in these borrowed honours, knowing Sir John never came to town. I taught him the modes and manners here, and he has rewarded me with inconstancy.

SIR JOHN: Hold, hold; not so fast. How came you to be the Honourable, the Lady Basset: I think 'twas I dubbed ye. As I take it, ye were but the cast mistress of Sir Francis Basset, when I found ye.

MR RICH: See, sister, how the quality you were fond of, expose one another.

MRS CLERIMONT: And seeing this, be reconciled to your new spouse, who is of a noble family, and I promise to introduce ye to persons of merit and honour.

LADY LANDSWORTH: We shall all be fond of ye, for, of yourself, you are charming and sensible: 'tis only these wretches have rendered ye ridiculous.

MR RICH: Come, give him your hand, 'tis a gentle punishment for so much vanity.

MRS RICH: Well, since my malicious stars have thus decreed it; but, d'ye hear, I expect to have your estate in my power, and that same title you talk of looked into.

ELDER CLERIMONT: I' faykings and so you shall; but must not I have your fine person in my power too? Ha!

MRS RICH: Has the thing sense enough to be in love?

CLERIMONT: Now, I hope, all's well, and I have prevailed with my landlady to give ye a song.

LADY LANDSWORTH: Do, good Mrs Fidget.

MRS FIDGET: Anything to divert ye.

TOBY: And adod, after that, I'll give 'em a donce.

BELVOIR: Well said, honest Toby.

MRS RICH: Sir John, will ye participate in our diversion, or employ your time in reconciling yourself to this enraged lady.

SIR JOHN: Shame, disappointment and disreputation light upon you all; would all the whole sex were upon Salisbury Plain, and their rigging on fire about their ears.

[*Exit* SIR JOHN]

MRS CLERIMONT: And that's the dreadful curse of a defeated beau. Follow, madam, and put him in a better humour.

LADY LA BASSET: Hang him, as I would myself, you, and all the world. [*Exit*]

BETTY: A fair riddance.

CLERIMONT: Now the song, and then the dance.

MR RICH: Now, sister, and daughter, to you I chiefly speak, let this day's adventure make ye forever cautious of your conversation; you see how near these pretenders to quality had brought you to ruin: the truly great of a quite different character.

The glory of the world our British nobles are,
The ladies too renowned, and chaste and fair:
But to our City, Augusta's sons,
The conquering wealth of both the Indias runs;
Though less in name, of greater power by far,
Honours alone, but empty 'scutcheons are;
Mixed with their coin, the title sweetly sounds,
No such allay as twenty thousand pounds.

The Basset Table

by

SUSANNA CENTLIVRE

1705

DRAMATIS PERSONAE

WOMEN

LADY REVELLER,	a coquettish widow that keeps a basset table.
LADY LUCY,	her cousin, a religious sober lady.
VALERIA,	a philosophical girl, daughter to Sir Richard Plainman, in love with Ensign Lovely.
MRS SAGO,	a drugster's wife, a gaming profuse woman, great with my Lady Reveller, in love with Sir James Courtly.
ALPIEW,	woman to Lady Reveller.

MEN

LORD WORTHY,	a hater of gaming, in love with Lady Reveller.
SIR JAMES COURTLY,	an airy gentleman, given to gaming.
LOVELY,	an Ensign, in love with Valeria.
SIR RICHARD PLAIN- MAN,	formerly a Citizen, but now lives in Covent Garden, a great lover of a soldier and an inveterate enemy to the French.
CAPTAIN HENRY FIRE- BRAND,	a sea officer, designed by Sir Richard to marry Valeria.
MR SAGO,	a drugster in the City, very fond of his wife.
BUCKLE,	footman to Lord Worthy.

LADIES & GENTLEMEN OF THE BASSET TABLE, FOOTMEN, CHAIRMEN, ETC.

SETTING	Lady Reveller's lodgings in Covent Garden, four o'clock in the morning.

Act One

SCENE ONE

A large hall, a PORTER *with a staff, several chairs waiting, and* FOOTMEN *asleep, with torches and flambeaux standing about the room.*

FIRST FOOTMAN: Certainly they'll play all night, this is a cursed life.

PORTER: How long have you lived with your lady?

FIRST FOOTMAN: A month. Too long by thirty days. If this be her way of living, I shall be dead before the year's out; she games all night, and sleeps all day.

PORTER: Then you sleep too, what's the matter.

FIRST FOOTMAN: I deny that; for while she sleeps I'm employed in howd'ye-dos, from one end of the town to the other.

PORTER: But you rest while she's gaming. What would you do if you led my life? This is my lady's constant practice.

FIRST FOOTMAN: Your lady keeps a Basset Table, much good may do you with your service. – Hark, they are broke up.

SECOND FOOTMAN: [*offstage*] Ha, hie my Lady Gamewell's chair ready there. Mr Sonica's servants.

FIRST FOOTMAN: Where the devil's my flambeaux?

SECOND FOOTMAN: So – hey – Robin, get the chair ready, my Lady's coming; stay, stay, let me light my flambeaux.

THIRD FOOTMAN: [*yawning*] Hey, hoa, what han't they done play yet?

PORTER: They are coming down, but your lady is gone half an hour ago.

THIRD FOOTMAN: The devil she is! Why did not you call me.

PORTER: I did not see you.

THIRD FOOTMAN: Was you blind – she has lost her money,

that's certain – she never flinches upon a winning hand – her plate and jewels walk tomorrow to replenish her pocket – a pox of gaming, I say.   [*Exit*]

SECOND FOOTMAN: Mr Lascall's man –

FOURTH FOOTMAN: Here. – So – ho, who has stole my flambeaux?

SECOND FOOTMAN: My Lady Umbray's coach there –

FIRST FOOTMAN: Hey! Will, pull up there.   [*Exeunt omnes*]

    Enter LADY REVELLER *and* ALPIEW,[1] *her woman*

LADY REVELLER: My Lady Raffle is horridly out of humour at her ill fortune, she lost £300.

ALPIEW: She has generally ill luck, yet her inclination for play is as strong as ever. – Did your Ladyship win or lose, madam?

LADY REVELLER: I won about 50 pieces. – Prithee, what shall we do, Alpiew? 'Tis a fine morning, 'tis pity to go to bed.

ALPIEW: What does your Ladyship think of a walk in the Park? The Park is pleasant in a morning, the air is so very sweet.

LADY REVELLER: I don't think so – the sweetness of the Park is at eleven when the beau-monde make their tour there; 'tis an unpolished curiosity to walk when only birds can see one.

ALPIEW: Bless me, madam! Your uncle. – Now for a sermon of two hours.

    Enter SIR RICHARD PLAINMAN, *in a night-gown, as from bed*

SIR RICHARD: So, niece! I find you're resolved to keep on your course of life: I must be waked at four, with 'Coach, Coach', 'Chair, Chair'. Give over, for shame, and marry, marry, niece.

LADY REVELLER: [*aside*] Now would I forfeit the heart of my next admirer, to know the cause of this reproach. – Pray, uncle, explain yourself; for I protest I can't guess what crime I have unhappily committed to merit this advice.

SIR RICHARD: How can you look me in the face, and ask me that question? Can you who keeps a Basset Table, a public gaming-house, be insensible of the shame on't? I have often told you how much the vast concourse of people which day and night make my house their rendezvous incommode my health. Your apartment is a parade of men of all ranks, from the duke

---

[1] *alpiew*: a basset term for a mark on a card indicating a double stake.

to the fiddler, and your vanity thinks they all pay devoir to your beauty — but you mistake: everyone has his several ends in meeting here, from the lord to the sharper, each their separate interests to pursue. Some fools there may be, for there's seldom a crowd without.

LADY REVELLER: Malice! Some fools? I can't bear it.

ALPIEW: Nay, 'tis very affronting, truly, madam.

LADY REVELLER: Aye, is it not, Alpiew? Yet now I think on't, 'tis the defect of age to rail at the pleasures of youth, therefore I shall not disorder my face with a frown about it. Ha, ha! I hope, uncle, you'll take peculiar care of my cousin Valeria, in disposing of her according to the breeding you have given her.

SIR RICHARD: The breeding I have given her! I would not have her have your breeding, mistress, for all the wealth of England's bank.[2] No, I bred my girl in the country, a stranger to the vices of this town, and am resolved to marry her to a man of honour, probity, and courage.

LADY REVELLER: What, the sea-captain, uncle? Faugh! I hate the smell of pitch and tar, one that can entertain one with nothing but fire and smoke, 'larboard and starboard', and t'other bowl of punch; ha, ha, ha.

ALPIEW: And for every fault that she commits, he'll condemn her to the Bilboes![3] Ha! Ha!

LADY REVELLER: I fancy my cousin's philosophy and that captain's courageous bluster will make angelic harmony.

SIR RICHARD: Yes, madam; sweeter harmony that your 'Sept & Leva'[4] fops, rakes, and gamesters. Give me the man that serves my country, that preserves both my estate and life. — Oh, the glorious name of soldiers. If I were young, I'd go myself in person, but as it is —

ALPIEW: You'll send your daughter.

SIR RICHARD: Yes, minx, and a good dowry with her, as a reward for virtue, like the captain's.

ALPIEW: But, suppose, sir, Mrs Valeria should not like him?

SIR RICHARD: I'll suppose no such thing, mistress, she shall like him.

[2]Bank of England founded 1694
[3]*bilboes*: ship's dungeons   [4]*Sept & Leva*: Call in the game of basset

LADY REVELLER: Why, there 'tis now! Indeed, uncle, you're
  too positive.

SIR RICHARD: And you too impertinent. Therefore I resolve
  you shall quit my house. You shan't keep your revels under
  the roof where I am.

ALPIEW: I'd have you to know, sir, my Lady keeps no revels
  beneath her quality.

SIR RICHARD: Hold your tongue Mrs Pert, or I shall display
  your quality in its proper colours.

ALPIEW: I don't care. Say your worst of me and spare not,
  but for my Lady – my Lady's a widow, and widows are
  accountable to none for their actions. Well, I shall have a
  husband one of these days, and be a widow too, I hope.

SIR RICHARD: Not unlikely, for the man will hang himself
  the next day, I warrant him.

ALPIEW: And if any uncle pretends to control my actions –

SIR RICHARD: He'd lose his labour, I'm certain –

ALPIEW: I'd treat him –

SIR RICHARD: Don't provoke me, hussy, don't.

LADY REVELLER: Be gone, and wait in the next room.

                                            [*Exit* ALPIEW]

SIR RICHARD: The insolence of a servant is a great honour to
  the lady, no doubt, but I shall find a way to humble you
  both.

LADY REVELLER: Lookye, uncle, do what you can, I'm resolved to follow my own instructions.

SIR RICHARD: Which infallibly carry you to noise, nonsense,
  foppery and ruin. But no matter. You shall go out of my
  doors, I'll promise you. My house shall no longer bear the
  scandalous name of a Basset-Table; husbands shall no more
  have cause to date their ruin from my door, nor cry, 'There,
  there my wife gamed my estate away.' Nor children curse my
  posterity for their parents knowing my house.

LADY REVELLER: No more threatening, good uncle. Act as
  you please, but don't scold, or I shall be obliged to call
  Alpiew again.

SIR RICHARD: Very well, very well! See what will come on't
  – the world will censure those that game, and in my conscience, I believe not without cause.

> For she whose shame no good advice can wake,
>> When money's wanting will her virtue stake. [*Exit*]

LADY REVELLER: Advice! Ha! Ha! Ridiculous advice!

Enter LADY LUCY

LADY REVELLER: [*aside*] No sooner rid of one mischief but another follows. I forsee this to be a day of mortifications. Alpiew!

ALPIEW: Madam.

LADY REVELLER: My uncle's gone, you may come in! Ha! Ha! Ha!

LADY LUCY: Fie, cousin, does it become you to laugh at those that give you counsel for your good?

LADY REVELLER: For my good! Oh, mon coeur! Now cannot I divine what 'tis that I do more than the rest of the world to deserve this blame.

ALPIEW: Nor I, for the soul of me.

LADY LUCY: Should all the rest of the world follow your Ladyship's example the order of nature would be inverted, and every good designed by heaven become a curse; health and plenty no longer would be known among us. You cross the purpose of the day and night. You wake when you should sleep, and make all who have any dependance on you wake while you repose.

LADY REVELLER: Bless me! May not any person sleep when they please?

LADY LUCY: No. There are certain hours that good manners, modesty, and health require our care. For example, disorderly hours are neither healthful nor modest. And 'tis not civil to make company wait dinner for your dressing.

LADY REVELLER: Why, does anybody dine before four o'clock in London? For my part, I think it an ill-bred custom to make my appetite pendulum to the twelfth hour.

ALPIEW: Besides, 'tis out of fashion to dine by daylight; and so I told Sir Richard yesterday, madam.

LADY LUCY: No doubt but you did, Mrs Alpiew. And then you entertain such a train of people cousin, that my Lady Reveller is as noted as a public dining-room, where every fool with money finds a welcome.

LADY REVELLER: Would you have me shut my doors against

my friends? [*aside*] Now she is jealous of Sir James Courtly. Besides, is it possible to pass the evenings without diversions?

ALPIEW: No, certainly –

LADY LUCY: I think the playhouse the much more innocent and commendable diversion.

LADY REVELLER: To be seen there every night, in my opinion, is more destructive to the reputation.

LADY LUCY: Well, I had rather be noted every night in the front box, than by my absence once be suspected of gaming. One ruins my estate and character, the other diverts my temper, and improves my mind. Then you have such a number of lovers . . .

LADY REVELLER: Oh, Cupid! Is it a crime to have a number of lovers? If it be, 'tis the pleasantest crime in the world. A crime that falls not every day to every woman's lot.

LADY LUCY: I dare be positive every woman does not wish it.

LADY REVELLER: Because wishes have no effect, cousin, ha! Ha!

LADY LUCY: Methinks my Lord Worthy's assiduity might have banished the admiring crowd by this time.

LADY REVELLER: Banished 'em! Oh, mon coeur! What pleasure is there in one lover? 'Tis like being seen always in one suit of clothes. A woman with one admirer will ne'er be a reigning toast.

LADY LUCY: I am sure those that encourage more will never have the character of a reigning virtue.

LADY REVELLER: I slight the malicious censure of the town, yet defy it to asperse my virtue. Nature has given me a face, a shape, a mien, an air for dress, and wit and humour to subdue. And shall I lose my conquest for a name?

ALPIEW: Nay, and among the unfashionable sort of people too, madam, for persons of breeding and quality will allow that gallantry and virtue are not inseparable.

LADY LUCY: But coquetry and reputation are. And there is no difference in the eye of the world between having really committed the fault, and lying under the scandal. For my own part, I would take as much care to preserve my fame, as would you your virtue.

LADY REVELLER: A little pains will serve you for that,

cousin, for I never once heard you named. A mortification would break my heart, ha! ha!

LADY LUCY: 'Tis better never to be named than to be ill spoke of. But your reflections shall not disorder my temper. I could wish indeed, to convince you of your error because you share my blood, but since I see the vanity of the attempt, I shall desist.

LADY REVELLER: I humbly thank your Ladyship.

ALPIEW: Oh! Madam, here's my Lord Worthy, Sir James Courtly, and Ensign Lovely coming down. Will your Ladyship see them?

LADY REVELLER: [*aside*] Now have I strong inclination to engage Sir James to discompose her gravity, for if I have any skill in glances, she loves him. But then, my Lord Worthy is so peevish since our late quarrel that I'm afraid to engage the knight in a duel. Besides, my absence, I know, will tease him more; therefore upon consideration I'll retire. – Cousin Lucy, good morrow. I'll leave you to better company. There's a person at hand may prevent your six o'clock prayers. [*Exit*]

LADY LUCY: Ha! Sir James Courtly – I must own I think him agreeable, but am sorry she believes I do. I'll not be seen, for if what I scarce know myself be grown so visible to her, perhaps he, too, may discover it, and then I am lost.

> While in the breast our secrets close remain
>
> Tis out of Fortune's power to give us pain. [*Exit*]

Enter LORD WORTHY, SIR JAMES, *and* ENSIGN LOVELY

SIR JAMES: Ha! Was not that Lady Lucy?

ENSIGN LOVELY: It was. Ah, Sir James, I find your heart is out of order about that lady, and my Lord Worthy languishes for Lady Reveller.

SIR JAMES: And thou art sick for Valeria, Sir Richard's daughter. A poor distressed company of us.

ENSIGN LOVELY: 'Tis true, that little she-philosopher has made me do penance more heartily than ever my sins did. I deserve her by mere dint of patience. I have stood whole hours to hear her assert that fire cannot burn, nor water drown, nor pain afflict, and forty ridiculous systems –

SIR JAMES: And all her experiments on frogs, fish, and flies, ha, ha, without the least contradiction.

ENSIGN LOVELY: Contradiction, no, no! I allowed all she said with 'undoubtedly, madam', – and 'I am of your mind, madam, it must be so' – 'natural causes,' etcetera.

SIR JAMES: Ha, ha, ha! I think it is a supernatural cause which enables thee to go through this fatigue. If it were not to raise thy fortune I should think thee mad to pursue her. But go on and prosper. Nothing in my power shall be wanting to assist you. My Lord Worthy, your Lordship is as melancholy as a losing gamester.

LORD WORTHY: Faith, gentlemen, I'm out of humour, but I don't know at what.

SIR JAMES: Why then I can tell you: for the very same reason that made your Lordship stay here to be spectator of the very diversion you hate, gaming, the same cause makes you uneasy in all company, my Lady Reveller.

LORD WORTHY: Thou hast hit it, Sir James. I confess I love her person, but hate her humours, and her way of living. I have some reasons to believe I'm not indifferent to her, yet I despair of fixing her. Her vanity has got so much the mistress of her resolution; and yet her passion for gain surmounts her pride and lays her reputation open to the world. Every fool that has ready money shall dare to boast himself her very humble servant, s'death, when I could cut the rascal's throat.

SIR JAMES: Your Lordship is even with her one way, for you are as testy as she's vain, and as fond of an opportunity to quarrel with her as she of a gaming acquaintance. My opinion is, my Lord, she'll ne'er be won your way.

> To gain all women there's a certain rule:
> If wit should fail to please, then act the fool;
> And where you find simplicity not take,
> Throw off disguises, and profess the rake;
> Observe which way their strongest humours run,
> They're by their own loved cant the surest way undone.

LORD WORTHY: Thou'rt of a happy temper, Sir James. I wish I could be so too; but since I can't add to your diversion, I'll take my leave. Good morrow, gentlemen.   [*Exit*]

SIR JAMES: This it is to have more love than reason about one. You and I, Lovely, will go on with discretion, and yet I fear it's in Lady Lucy's power to banish it.

ENSIGN LOVELY: I find Mrs Sago, the drugster's wife's interest begins to shake, Sir James.

SIR JAMES: And I fear her love for play begins to shake her husband's bags too. Faith, I am weary of that intrigue, lest I should be suspected to have a hand in his ruin.

ENSIGN LOVELY: She did lose much tonight, I believe. Prithee, Sir James, what kind of a tempered woman is she? Has she wit?

SIR JAMES: That she has. A large portion, and as much cunning, or she could never have managed the old fellow so nicely. She has a vast passion for my Lady Reveller, and endeavours to mimic her in everything. Not a suit of clothes, or a top-knot, that is not exactly the same with hers. Then her plots and contrivances to supply these expenses put her continually upon the rack. Yet to give her her due, she has a fertile brain that way. But come, shall we go home and sleep two or three hours. At dinner I'll introduce you to Captain Hearty, the sea-officer, your rival that is to be. He's just come to town.

ENSIGN LOVELY: A powerful rival, I fear, for Sir Richard resolves to marry him to his daughter. All my hopes lie in her arguments, and you know philosophers are very positive. And if this captain does but happen to contradict one whimsical notion, the poles will as soon join as they couple, and rather than yield she would go to the Indies in search of Dampier's[5] ants.

SIR JAMES:
>   Nay, she is no woman if she obeys,
>   Women, like tides, with passions ebb and flow,
>   And like them too, their source no man can know.
>   To watch their motions, is the safest guide;
>   Who hits their honour, sails with wind and tide. [*Exeunt*]

[5]Dampier was a Buccaneer who discovered parts of Australia in 1697 and returned with various specimens of flora and fauna.

Act Two

SCENE ONE

Enter BUCKLE, *meeting* MRS ALPIEW

ALPIEW: Good morrow.

BUCKLE: Good morrow.

ALPIEW: 'Good morrow', 'good morrow', is that all your business here? What means that affected look, as if you longed to be examined what's the matter.

BUCKLE: The capriccios of love, mademoiselle; the capriccios of love.

ALPIEW: Why! Are you in love?

BUCKLE: I – in love! No! The devil take me, if ever I shall be infected with that madness! 'Tis enough for one in a family to fall under the whimsical circumstance of that distemper. My Lord has a sufficient portion for both. Here – here – here's a letter for your Lady. I believe the contents are not so full of stars and darts and flames as they used to be.

ALPIEW: My Lady will not concern herself with your Lord, nor his letters neither, I can assure you that.

BUCKLE: So much the better. I'll tell him what you say. – Have you no more?

ALPIEW: Tell him it is not my fault. I have done as much for his service as lay in my power, till I put her in so great a passion that 'tis impossible to appease her.

BUCKLE: Very good. My Lord is upon the square, I promise ye, as much enraged as her Ladyship, to the full. Well, Mrs Alpiew, to the longest day of his life, he swears never to forget yesterday's adventure, that has given him perfect, perfect liberty.

ALPIEW: I believe so. – What was it, pray?

BUCKLE: I'll tell you. 'Twas matter of consequence, I assure you, I've known lovers part for less trifle by half.

ALPIEW: No digressions, but to the point, what was it?

BUCKLE: This – my Lord, was at the fair with your Lady.

ALPIEW: What of that?

BUCKLE: In a raffling-shop[6] she saw a young gentleman, which she said was very handsome. At the same time, my Lord praised a young lady. She redoubles her commendations of the beau. He enlarges on the beauty of the belle. Their discourse grew warm on the subject. They pause. She begins again with the perfections of the gentleman. He ends with the same of the lady. Thus they pursued their arguments, still finding such mighty charms in their new favourite, till they found one another so ugly – so ugly – that they parted with full resolution never to meet again.

ALPIEW: Ha, ha, ha, pleasant! Well, if you have no more to tell me, adieu.

BUCKLE: Stay a moment. I see my Lord coming. I thought he'd follow me. Oh! Lovers' resolutions.

Enter LORD WORTHY

LORD WORTHY: [*to* BUCKLE] So, have you seen my Lady Reveller?

ALPIEW: My Lord –

LORD WORTHY: Ha! Mrs Alpiew.

BUCKLE: Here's your Lordship's letter.

[*gives him his own letter*]

LORD WORTHY: An answer! She has done me very much honour.

ALPIEW: My Lord, I am commanded –

LORD WORTHY: Hold a little, dear Mrs Alpiew.

[*All this while he is still opening the letter, thinking it from the Lady*]

BUCKLE: My Lord, she would not –

LORD WORTHY: Be quiet, I say.

ALPIEW: I am very sorry.

LORD WORTHY: But a moment. Why this is my own letter.

BUCKLE: Yes, my Lord.

LORD WORTHY: Yes, my Lord, What, she'd not receive it then?

BUCKLE: No, my Lord.

[6]*raffling-shop*: betting shop (on dice and cards)

LORD WORTHY: How durst you stay so long.

ALPIEW: I beg your Lordship not to harbour an ill opinion of me. I opposed her anger with my utmost skill, praised all your actions, all your parts, but all in vain.

LORD WORTHY: Enough, enough, madam. She has taken the best method in the world. Well, then we are ne'er to meet again.

ALPIEW: I know not that, my Lord . . .

LORD WORTHY: I rejoice at it, by my life I do. She has only prevented me. I came on purpose to break with her —

BUCKLE: [*aside*] Yes, so 'twas a sign, by the pleasure you discovered in thinking she had writ to you.

LORD WORTHY: I suppose she has entertained you with the cause of this.

ALPIEW: No, my Lord, never mentioned a syllable, only said, she had forever done with you, and charged me, as I valued her favour, to receive no message nor letter from you.

LORD WORTHY: May I become the veriest wretch alive, and all the ills imaginable fall upon my head, if I speak to her more, nay, ever think of her but with scorn. Where is she now?

ALPIEW: In her dressing room.

LORD WORTHY: There let her be. I am weary of her fantastic humours, affected airs, and unaccountable passions.

BUCKLE: [*aside*] For half an hour.

LORD WORTHY: Do you know what she's doing?

ALPIEW: I believe, my Lord, trying on a mantua,[7] I left her with Mrs Pleatwell, and that used to hold her a great while, for the woman is saucily familiar with all the quality, and tells her all the scandal.

LORD WORTHY: And conveys letters upon occasion; 'tis tacked to their profession. But, my Lady Reveller may do what she pleases, I am no more her slave, upon my word. I have broke my chain. She has not been out then since she rose?

ALPIEW: No, my Lord.

LORD WORTHY: Nay, if she has, or has not, 'tis the same thing to me. She may go to the end of the world, if she will, I shan't take any pains to follow her. Whose footman was that I met?

ALPIEW: I know not, my Lord, we have so many come with howd'ye's, I ne'er mind them.

[7]*mantua*: gown

LORD WORTHY: You are uneasy, child. Come, I'll not detain you. I have no curiosity. I protest I'm satisfied if she's so. I assure ye, let her despise me, let her hate me, 'tis all one. Adieu.

[*going*]

ALPIEW: My Lord, your servant.

LORD WORTHY: Mrs Alpiew, let me bet one favour of you; [*turns back*] not to say I was here.

ALPIEW: I'll do just as you please, my Lord.

LORD WORTHY: Do that then, and you'll oblige me. [*is going, and comes back often*]

ALPIEW: I will.

LORD WORTHY: Don't forget.

ALPIEW: Your Lordship may depend upon me.

LORD WORTHY: Hold! Now I think on't. Pray tell her you did see me. Do you hear?

ALPIEW: With all my heart.

LORD WORTHY: Tell her how indifferent she is to me in every respect.

ALPIEW: I shan't fail.

LORD WORTHY: Tell her everything just as I expressed it to you.

ALPIEW: I will.

LORD WORTHY: Adieu.

ALPIEW: Your servant.

LORD WORTHY: Now I think on't, Mrs Alpiew, I have a great mind she should know my sentiments from my own mouth.

ALPIEW: Nay, my Lord, I can't promise you that.

LORD WORTHY: Why?

ALPIEW: Because she has expressly forbid your admittance.

LORD WORTHY: I'd speak but one word with her.

ALPIEW: Impossible.

LORD WORTHY: Pugh, prithee let me see her.

BUCKLE: So, now all this mighty rage ends in a begging submission.

LORD WORTHY: Only tell her I'm here.

ALPIEW: Why should you desire me to meet her anger, my Lord.

LORD WORTHY: Come, you shall oblige me once.

[*puts a ring upon her finger*]

ALPIEW: Oh dear, my Lord, you have such a command over your servant, I can refuse nothing.   [*Exit*]

LORD WORTHY: Have you been at the goldsmith's about the bills, for I am fixed on travelling.

BUCKLE: Your Lordship's so disturbed, you have forgot you countermanded me, and sent me hither.

LORD WORTHY: True.

Enter MRS ALPIEW

ALPIEW: Just as I told your Lordship, she fell in a most violent passion at the bare mention of your name: 'Tell him,' said she, in an heroic strain, 'I'll never see him more and command him to quit that room, for I'm coming thither.'

LORD WORTHY: Tyrant, curse on my folly, she knows her power. Well, I hope I may walk in the gallery. I would speak with her uncle.

ALPIEW: To be sure, my Lord.   [*Exit* LORD WORTHY]

Enter LADY REVELLER

LADY REVELLER: Well, I'll swear, Alpiew, you have given me the vapours for all day.

ALPIEW: Ah! Madam, if you had seen him, you must have had compassion. I would not have such a heart of adamant for the world. Poor Lord, sure you have the strangest power over him.

LADY REVELLER: Silly – one often fancies one has power when one has none at all. I'll tell thee, Alpiew, he vexed me strangely before this grand quarrel. I was at piquet with my Lady Lovewit four nights ago and bid him read me a new copy of verses, because, you know, he never plays, and I did not well know what to do with him. He had scarce begun when I, being eager at a piquet, he rose up and said he believed I loved the music of my own voice crying 'nine and twenty', 'threescore', better than the sweetest poetry in the universe, and abruptly left us.

ALPIEW: A great crime, indeed, not to read. When people are at a game they are obliged to talk all the while.

LADY REVELLER: Crime. Yes, indeed was it, for my Lady loves poetry better than play, and perhaps before the poem had been done, had lost her money to me. But I wonder, Alpiew, by what art 'tis you engage me in this discourse. Why should I talk of a man that's utterly my aversion? Have you heard from Mrs Sago this morning?

ALPIEW: Certainly, madam, she never fails. She has sent your Ladyship the finest cargo, made up of chocolate, tea,

Montifiasco wine, and fifty rarities beside, with something to remember me, good creature, that she never forgets. Well, indeed, madam, she is the best-natured woman in the world. It grieves me to think what sums she loses at play.

LADY REVELLER: Oh, fie, she must! A citizen's wife is not to be endured amongst quality. Had she not money, 'twere impossible to receive her.

ALPIEW: Nay, indeed, I must say that of your women of quality, if there is but money enough, you stand not upon birth or reputation, in either sex. If you did, so many sharpers of Covent Gardens, and mistresses of St James's, would not be daily admitted.

LADY REVELLER: Peace, Impertinence! You take strange freedoms.

Enter VALERIA *running*

LADY REVELLER: [*stopping her*] Why in such haste, cousin Valeria?

VALERIA: Oh! Dear cousin, don't stop me, I shall lose the finest insect for dissection, a huge flesh-fly, which Mr Lovely sent me just now, and opening the box to try the experiment, away it flew.

LADY REVELLER: I am glad the poor fly escaped. Will you never be weary of these whimsies?

VALERIA: Whimsies! Natural philosophy a whimsy! Oh! The unlearned world!

LADY REVELLER: Ridiculous learning!

ALPIEW: Ridiculous indeed, for women. Philosophy suits our sex as jack-boots would do.

VALERIA: Custom would bring them as much in fashion as furbelows, and practice would make us as valiant as e'er a hero of them all. The resolution is in the mind. Nothing can enslave that.

LADY REVELLER: My stars! This girl will be mad, that's certain.

VALERIA: Mad! So Nero banished philosophers from Rome, and the first discoverer of the Antipodes was condemned as a heretic.

LADY REVELLER: In my conscience, Alpiew, this pretty creature's spoiled. Well, cousin, might I advise, you should bestow your fortune in founding a college for the study of philosophy, where none but women should be admitted; and to immortalise your name, they should be called Valerians. Ha, ha, ha!

VALERIA: What you make a jest of I'd execute were fortune in my power.

ALPIEW: All men would not be excluded ... The handsome Ensign, madam.

LADY REVELLER: In love! Nay, there's no philosophy against love. Solon[8] for that.

VALERIA: 'Pshaw, no more of this trifling subject. Cousin, will you believe there's anything without gall.

LADY REVELLER: I am satisfied I have none, when I lose at play, or see a Lady addressed when I am by. And 'tis equal to me, whether the rest of the creation have or not.

VALERIA: Well, but I'll convince you then. I have dissected my dove, and positively I think the vulgar notion true, for I could find none.

LADY REVELLER: Oh, barbarous! Killed your pretty dove.

VALERIA: Killed it! Why, what did you imagine I bred it up for? Can animals, insects, or reptiles, be put to a nobler use than to improve our knowledge? Cousin, I'll give you this jewel for your Italian greyhound.

LADY REVELLER: What to cut to pieces? Oh, horrid! He had need be a soldier that ventures on you. For my part, I should dream of nothing but incision, dissection, and amputation, and always fancy the knife at my throat.

    Enter SERVANT

SERVANT: Madam, here's Sir Richard, and a ...

VALERIA: A ... What? Is it an accident, a substance, a material being, or a being of reason?

SERVANT: I don't know what you call a material being. It is a man.

VALERIA: 'Pshaw, a man, that's nothing.

LADY REVELLER: She'll prove by and by, out of Descartes that we are all machines.

    Enter SIR RICHARD *and* CAPTAIN FIREBRAND

ALPIEW: Oh, madam, do you see who observes you? My Lord walking in the gallery, and every minute gives a peep.

[8]*Solon:* Roman philosopher

LADY REVELLER: Does he so! I'll fit him for eavesdropping.

SIR RICHARD: Sir, I like the relation you have given me of your Naval expedition. Your discourse speaks you a man fit for the sea.

CAPTAIN FIREBRAND: You had it without a flourish, Sir Richard. My word is this: I hate the French, love a handsome woman, and a bowl of punch.

VALERIA: Very blunt.

SIR RICHARD: This is my daughter, Captain, a girl of sober education. She understands nothing of gaming, parks, or plays.

ALPIEW: [*aside*] But wanting these diversions, she has supplied the vacancy with greater follies.

CAPTAIN FIREBRAND: [*salutes her*] A tight little frigate. [*aside*] 'Faith, I think she looks like a fresh man sea-sick. – But here's a gallant vessel, with all her streamers out, top and top-gallant. [*salutes* LADY REVELLER] With your leave, madam. Who is that lady, Sir Richard?

SIR RICHARD: 'Tis a niece of mine, Captain – though I am sorry she is so. She values nothing that does not spend their days at their glass, and their nights at Basset, such who ne'er did good to their Prince, nor country, except their tailor, peruke-maker, and perfumer.

LADY REVELLER: Fie, fie, sir, believe him not. I have a passion, an extreme passion for a hero, especially if he belongs to the sea. Methinks he has an air so fierce, so piercing, his very looks commands respect from his own sex, and all the hearts of ours.

SIR RICHARD: The devil! Now, rather than let another female have a man to herself, she'll make the first advances.

CAPTAIN FIREBRAND: Aye, madam, we are preferred by you fine ladies, sometimes before the sprucer sparks. There's a conveniency in't; a fair wind, and we hale out, and leave you liberty and money, two things the most acceptable to a wife in nature.

LADY REVELLER: Oh! Aye, it's so pretty to have one's husband gone nine months of the twelve. And then to bring one home fine china, fine lace, fine muslin, and fine Indian birds, and a thousand curiosities.

SIR RICHARD: No, no. Nine is a little too long. Six would do better for one of your condition, mistress.

CAPTAIN FIREBRAND: Well, madam, what think you of a cruising voyage towards the Cape of Matrimony. Your father designs me for the pilot. If you'll agree to it, we'll hoist sail immediately.

VALERIA: I agree to anything dictated by good sense, and comprehended within the borders of elocution. The converse I hold with your own sex is only to improve and cultivate the notions of my mind.

SIR RICHARD: [*aside*] What the devil is she going upon now?

VALERIA: I presume you are a mariner, sir —

CAPTAIN FIREBRAND: I have the honour to bear the Queen's commission, madam.

VALERIA: Pray speak properly, positively, laconically, and naturally.

CAPTAIN FIREBRAND: Laconically! Why, why, what is your daughter, Sir Richard?

SIR RICHARD: May I be reduced to wooden shoes if I can tell you. The devil! Had I lived near a college, the haunts of some pedant might have brought this curse upon me, but to have got to my estate in the City, and to have a daughter run mad after philosophy, I'll ne'er suffer it in the rage I am in. I'll throw all the books and mathematical instruments out of the window!

LADY REVELLER: I dare say, uncle, you have shook hands with philosophy, for I'm sure you have banished patience! Ha, ha, ha!

SIR RICHARD: And you, discretion. By all my hatred for the French, they'll drive me mad. Captain, I'll expect you in the next room, and you Mrs Laconic, with your philosophy at your tail.   [*Exit*]

LADY REVELLER: Shan't I come too, uncle! Ha, ha!

CAPTAIN FIREBRAND: By Neptune, this is a find of whimsical family! Well, madam, what was you going to say so positively and properly, and so forth?

VALERIA: I would have asked you, sir, if ever you had the curiosity to inspect a mermaid, or if you are convinced there is a world in every star? We, by our telescopes, find seas, groves, and plains, and all that, but what they are peopled with, there's the query.

CAPTAIN FIREBRAND: Let your next contrivance be how to get thither, and then you'll know a world in every star. Ha, ha! She's fitter for Moorfields[9] than matrimony. Pray, madam, are you always infected, full of change, with this distemper?

VALERIA: How has my reason erred, to hold converse with an irrational being. Dear, dear philosophy, what immense pleasures dwell in thee!

   Enter SERVANT

SERVANT: Madam, John has got the fish you sent him in search of.

VALERIA: Is is alive?

SERVANT: Yes, madam.

VALERIA: Your servant! Your servant! I would not lose the experiment for anything, but the tour of the new world. [*Exit*]

CAPTAIN FIREBRAND: Ha, ha, ha! Is your Ladyship troubled with these vagaries[10] too? Is the whole house possessed?

LADY REVELLER: Not I, Captain, the speculative faculty is not my talent. I am for the practice, can listen all day to hear you talk of fire, substantial fire, rear and front, and line of battle, admire a seaman, hate the French – love a bowl of punch. Oh! Nothing so agreeable as your conversation, nothing so jaunty as a sea-captain.

ALPIEW: [*aside*] So, This engages him to play, if he has either manners or money.

CAPTAIN FIREBRAND: Aye. Give me the woman that can hold me tack in my own dialect. [*aside*] She's mad too, I suppose, but I'll humour her a little. – Oh, madam, not a fair wind, nor a rich prize, nor conquest o'er my enemies can please like you. Accept my heart without capitulation. 'Tis yours, a prisoner at discretion.   [*kisses her hand*]

   Enter LORD WORTHY

LORD WORTHY: Hold, sir, you must there contend with me. The victory is not so easy as you imagine.

LADY REVELLER: Oh, fie, my Lord, you won't fight for one you hate and despise? I may trust you with the Captain. Ha, ha, ha!
                                    [*Exit*]

CAPTAIN FIREBRAND: [*aside*] This must be her lover, and he is

---

[9]*Moorfields*: Fair, with eccentrics, prophets and preachers *and* a lunatic asylum
[10]*vagaries*: caprices

mad another way. This is the most unaccountable family I ever met with. Look ye, sir, what you mean by contending, I know not, but I must tell you, I don't think any woman I have seen since I came ashore worth fighting for. The philosophical gimcrack I don't value of a cockle-shell. And am too well acquainted with the danger of rocks and quick-sands to steer into t'other's harbour.

LORD WORTHY: [*aside*] He has discovered her already. I, only I, am blind.

CAPTAIN FIREBRAND: But, sir, if you have a mind to a breathing, here, tread upon my toe, or speak but one word in favour of the French, or against the courage of our fleet, and my sword will start of itself to do its master and my country justice.

LORD WORTHY: How ridiculous do I make myself. Pardon me, sir, you are in the right. I confess I scarce knew what I did.

CAPTAIN FIREBRAND: I thought so. Poor gentleman, I pity him. This is the effect of love on shore. When do we hear of a tar in these fits, longer than the first fresh gale? Well, I'll into Sir Richard, eat with him, drink with him, but to match into his generation, I'd as soon marry one of his daughter's mermaids.

[*Exit*]

LORD WORTHY: Was ever man so stupid as myself? But I will rouse from this lethargic dream, and seek elsewhere what is deny'd at home. Absence may restore my liberty.

Enter MR SAGO

MR SAGO: Pray, my Lord, did you see my Keecky?

LORD WORTHY: Keecky, what's that?

MR SAGO: My wife, you must know. I call her Keecky, ha, ha!

LORD WORTHY: Not I, indeed . . .

MR SAGO: Nay, pray my Lord ben't angry. I only want to tell her what a present of fine wine is sent her just now, and ha, ha, ha, ha, what makes me laugh is that no soul can tell from whence it comes!

LORD WORTHY: Your wife knows, no doubt.

MR SAGO: No more than myself, my Lord. We have often wine and sweetmeats, nay, whole pieces of silk, and the deuce take me if she could devise from whence. Nay, sometimes she has been for sending them back again, but I cried, 'who's a fool then'.

LORD WORTHY: I'm sure thou art one in perfection, and to me insupportable.

MR SAGO: My Lord, I know your Lordship has the privilege of this house, pray do me the kindness, if you find my wife, to send her out to me. [*Exit,* LORD WORTHY] I ne'er saw so much of this Lord's humour before. He is very surly, methinks. Adod, there are some lords of my wife's acquaintance as civil and familiar with me as I am with my journeyman. Oh! here she comes.

   Enter MRS SAGO *and* ALPIEW

MRS SAGO: Oh, Puddy, see what my Lady Reveller has presented me withal.

MR SAGO: Hey, Keecky, why sure you rise, as the saying is, for at home there's four hampers of wine sent ye.

MRS SAGO: From whence, dear Puddy?

MR SAGO: Hay, there's the jest, neither you nor I know. I offered the rogue that brought it a guinea to tell from whence it came, and he swore he durst not.

MRS SAGO: [*aside*] No, if he had, I'd never have employed him again.

MR SAGO: So I gave him half a crown, and let him go.

MRS SAGO: It comes very opportunely; pray, Puddy, send a couple of the hampers to my Lady Reveller's, as a small acknowledgement for the rich present she has made me.

MR SAGO: With all my heart, my jewel, my precious.

MRS SAGO: Puddy, I am strangely obliged to Mrs Alpiew; do, Puddy, do, dear Puddy.

MR SAGO: What?

MRS SAGO: Will ye, then? Do, dear Puddy, do, lend me a guinea to give her, do.   [*hanging upon him in a wheedling tone*]

MR SAGO: 'Pshaw, you are always wanting guineas. I'll send her half a pound of tea, Keecky.

MRS SAGO: Tea – pshaw – she drinks ladies tea. Do, dear Puddy, do. Can you deny Keecky, now?

MR SAGO?   Well, well, there.   [*gives it to her*]

MRS SAGO: Mrs Alpiew, will you please to lay the silk by for me, till I send for it, and accept of that?

ALPIEW: Your servant, madam. I'll be careful of it.

MRS SAGO: Thank ye. [*aside to* ALPIEW] Borrow as much as you can on't, dear Alpiew.

ALPIEW: [*aside to* MRS SAGO] I warrant you, madam. [*Exit*]

MRS SAGO: I must raise a sum for basset against night.

MR SAGO: Prithee, Keecky, what kind of humoured man is Lord Worthy? I did but ask him if he saw thee, and I thought he would have snapped my nose off.

MRS SAGO: Oh, a mere woman, full of spleen and vapours, he and I never agree.

MR SAGO: Adod, I thought so. I guessed he was none of thy admirers, ha, ha, ha! Why, there's my Lord Courtall, and my Lord Horncit, bow down to the ground to me where ever they meet me.

Enter ALPIEW

ALPIEW: [*to* MRS SAGO] Madam, madam, the goldsmith has sent in the plate.

MRS SAGO: [*to* ALPIEW] Very well, take it along with the silk.

ALPIEW: [*to* MRS SAGO] Here's the jeweller, madam, with the diamond ring, but he don't seem willing to leave it without money. [*Exit*]

MRS SAGO: [*aside*] Humph! I have a sudden thought. Bid him stay, and bring me the ring. Now for the art of wheedling.

MR SAGO: What are you whispering about? Ha! Precious!

MRS SAGO: Mrs Alpiew says a friend of hers has a diamond ring to sell, a great pennyworth, and I know you love a bargain, Puddy.

Enter ALPIEW, *and gives her the ring*

MR SAGO: 'Pshaw, I don't care for rings. It may be a bargain, and it may not; and I can't spare money. I have paid for a lot this morning. Consider, trade must go forward, lambkin.

ALPIEW: See how it sparkles.

MRS SAGO: Nay, Puddy, if it be not worth your money, I don't desire you to buy it; but don't it become my finger, Puddy, Puddy? See now.

MR SAGO: Ah! That hand, that hand it was which first got hold of my heart. Well, what's the price of it? Ha! I am ravished to see it upon Keecky's finger.

MRS SAGO: [*to* ALPIEW] What did he say the price of it was?

ALPIEW: [*to* MRS SAGO] Two hundred guineas, madam.

MRS SAGO: Threescore pounds, dear Pudd. [*aside*] The devil's in't if he won't give that.

MR SAGO: Threescore pounds! Why, 'tis worth a hundred, child, richly. 'Tis stole . . . 'tis stole!

ALPIEW: Stole! I'd have you to know the owner is my relation, and has been as great a merchant as any in London, but has had the misfortune to have his ships fall into the hands of the French, or he'd not have parted with it at such a rate. It cost him two hundred guineas.

MRS SAGO: I believe as much. Indeed it is very fine.

MR SAGO: So it is, Keecky, and that dear little finger shall have it too. Let me bite it a little tiny bit.   [*bites her finger*]

MRS SAGO: Oh! Dear Pudd, you hurt me.

MR SAGO: Here – I han't so much money about me, but there's a bill, lambkin. There now, you'll buss poor Puddy now, won't you?

MRS SAGO: Buss him. Yes, that I will, again and again and again, dear Pudd.   [*flies about his neck*]

MR SAGO: You'll go home with Puddy now to dinner, won't you?

MRS SAGO: Yes – a – dear Puddy, if you desire it, I will.

MR SAGO: But what?

MRS SAGO: But I promised my Lady Reveller to dine with her, deary. Do, let me, Pud. I'll dine with you tomorrow day.

ALPIEW: Nay, I'm sure my Lady won't eat a bit, if she don't stay.

MR SAGO: Well, they are all so fond of my wife, my Keecky. Show me thy little finger. Oh dear little finger, my Keecky.
          [*Exit*]

MRS SAGO: My own Pudd. [*to* ALPIEW] Here, Alpiew, give him his ring again. I have my end. Tell him 'tis too dear.

ALPIEW: But what will you say when Mr Sago misses it?

MRS SAGO: I'll say . . . that it was too big for my finger, and I lost it. 'Tis but a crying bout and the good man melts into pity.

MRS SAGO:

> I th'married state, this only bliss we find,
> An easy husband to our wishes kind.
> I've gaind my point, replenishd purse once more,
> Oh! Cast me, Fortune, on the winning shore.
> Now let me gain what I have lost before.   [*Exit*]

Act Three

SCENE ONE

The scene opens, and discovers VALERIA *with books upon a table, a microscope, putting a fish upon it, several animals lying by.*

VALERIA: 'Pshaw! Thou fluttering thing. So, now I've fixed it.
  Enter ALPIEW

ALPIEW: Madam, here's Mr Lovely. I have introduced him as one of my Lady's visitors, and brought him down the back-stairs.

VALERIA: I'm obliged to you, he comes opportunely.
  Enter LOVELY

VALERIA: Oh Mr Lovely! Come, come here, look through this glass, and see how the blood circulates in the tail of this fish.

ENSIGN LOVELY: Wonderful! But it circulates prettier in this fair neck.

VALERIA: 'Pshaw, be quiet. I'll show you a curiosity, the greatest that ever nature made. [*opens a box*] In opening a dog the other day, I found this worm.

ENSIGN LOVELY: Prodigious! 'Tis the joint worm, which the learned talk of so much.

VALERIA: Aye. The Lumbricus Laetus, or Faescia, as Hippocrates calls it, or vulgarly in English, the tape-worm. Thadaeus tells us of one of these worms found in a human body, two hundred feet long, without head or tail.

ENSIGN LOVELY: [*aside*] I wish they be not got into thy brain. Oh, you charm me with these discoveries.

VALERIA: Here's another sort of worm called Lumbricus Teres Intestinalis.

ENSIGN LOVELY: I think the first you showed me the greatest curiosity.

VALERIA: 'Tis very odd, really, that there should be every inch a joint, and every joint a mouth. Oh, the profound secrets of Nature!

ENSIGN LOVELY: 'Tis strangely surprising. But now let me be heard, for mine's the voice of Nature too. Methinks you neglect yourself, the most perfect piece of all her works.

VALERIA: Why, what fault do you find in me?

ENSIGN LOVELY: You have not love enough. That fire would consume and banish all studies but its own. Your eyes would sparkle and spread I know not what, of lively and touching, o'er the whole face. This hand when pressed by him you love would tremble to your heart.

VALERIA: Why so it does. Have I not told you twenty times I love you, for I hate disguise? Your temper being adapted to mine gave my soul the first impression. You know my father's positive, but do not believe he shall force me to anything that does not love philosophy.

ENSIGN LOVELY: But that sea-captain, Valeria.

VALERIA: If he was a whale he might give you pain, for I should long to dissect him. But as he is a man, you have no reason to fear him.

ENSIGN LOVELY: Consent then to fly with me.

VALERIA: What, and leave my microscope and all my things for my father to break in pieces?

SIR RICHARD:[offstage] Valeria, Valeria.

VALERIA: Oh heavens! He is coming up the back-stairs. What shall we do?

ENSIGN LOVELY: Humph! Ha, can't you put me in that closet there?

VALERIA: Oh no, I han't the key.

ENSIGN LOVELY: I'll run down the great stairs, let who will see me.   [going]

VALERIA: Oh no, no, no, no, not for your life. Here, here, get under this tub. [Throws out some fish in haste and turns the tub over him.] Sir, I'm here.

     Enter SIR RICHARD

SIR RICHARD: What, at your whims and whirligigs, ye baggage! I'll out at window with them.

                                                [throwing away the things]

VALERIA: Oh! Dear father, save my Lumbricus Laetus.

SIR RICHARD: I'll lamprey and latum you! What's that I wonder? Ha! Where the devil got you names that your father don't understand? Ha! [*treads upon them*]

VALERIA: Oh, my poor worm! Now you have destroyed a thing like that, for ought I know, England can't produce again.

SIR RICHARD: What is it good for? Answer me that. What's this tub here for? Ha? [*kicks it*]

VALERIA: What shall I do now? It is a . . . 'tis a . . . Oh dear sir! Don't touch the tub, for there's a bear's young cub that I have bought for dissection, but I dare not touch it till the keeper comes.

SIR RICHARD: I'll cub you, and keeper you, with a vengeance to you. Is my money laid out in bears' cubs? I'll drive out your cub —

[*Opens the door, stands at a distance off, and with his cane lifts up the tub.* LOVELY *rises.*]

ENSIGN LOVELY: Oh the devil! Discovered! Your servant, sir.
[*Exit*]

SIR RICHARD: Oh! Your servant. Sir. What, is this your bear's cub? Ha, mistress! His tailor has licked him into shape, I find. What did this man do here? Ha, hussy? I doubt you have been studying natural philosophy with a vengeance.

VALERIA: Indeed, sir, he only brought me a strange fish, and hearing your voice, I was afraid you would be angry, and so that made me hide him.

SIR RICHARD: A fish! 'Tis the flesh I fear. I'll have you married tonight. I believe this fellow was the beggarly ensign who never marched farther than from Whitehall to the Tower, who wants your portion to make him a brigadier without ever seeing a battle. Hussy! Ha! Though your philosophical cant, with a murrain[11] to you, has put the Captain out of conceit, I have a husband still for you. Come along, come along, I'll send the servants to clear this room of your baubles. [*pulls her off*] I will so.

VALERIA: But the servants won't, old gentleman, that's my comfort still. [*Exit*]

[11]*murrain*: plague

Re-enter LOVELY

ENSIGN LOVELY: I'm glad they are gone, for the deuce take me if I could hit the way out.

Enter SIR JAMES

SIR JAMES: Ha! Ensign! Luckily met. I have been labouring for you, and I hope done you a piece of service. Why, you look surprised.

ENSIGN LOVELY: Surprised! So would you, Sir James, if you had been whelmed under a tub without room to breathe.

SIR JAMES: Under a tub! Ha, ha, ha!

ENSIGN LOVELY: 'Twas the only piece of shelter.

SIR JAMES: Come, come, I have a better prospect. The Captain is a very honest fellow, and thinks if you can bear with the girl, you deserve her fortune. [*gives a paper*] Here's your part. He'll give you your cue. He stays at his lodgings for you.

ENSIGN LOVELY: What's the design?

SIR JAMES: That will tell you. Quick, dispatch.

ENSIGN LOVELY: Well, Sir James, I know you have a prolific brain, and will rely on your contrivances, and if it succeeds, the Captain shall have a bowl of punch large enough to set his ship afloat.   [*Exit*]

Enter LADY REVELLER, LADY LUCY *and* MRS SAGO

SIR JAMES: The tea-table broke up already! I fear there has been but small recruits of scandal today.

MRS SAGO: Well, I'll swear I think the Captain's a pleasant fellow.

SIR JAMES: [*aside*] That's because he made his court to her.

LADY REVELLER: Oh, I nauseate those amphibious creatures.

SIR JAMES: [*aside*] Umph, she was not addressed to.

LADY LUCY: He seems neither to want sense, honour, nor true courage, and methinks there is a beauty in his plain delivery.

SIR JAMES: [*aside*] There spoke sincerity without affectation.

LADY REVELLER: How shall we pass the afternoon?

SIR JAMES: Aye, ladies, how shall we?

LADY REVELLER: You here! I thought you had listed yourself volunteer under the Captain, to board some prize, you whispered so often, and sneaked out one after another.

SIR JAMES: Who would give oneself the pains to cruise abroad, where all one values is at home?

LADY REVELLER: To whom is this directed? Or will you monopolise and engross us all?

SIR JAMES: No. Though you would wake desire in every beholder, I resign you to my worthy friend.

LADY LUCY: And the rest of the company have no pretence to you.

MRS SAGO: [*aside*] That's more than she knows.

SIR JAMES: Beauty like yours would give all mankind pretence.

MRS SAGO: [*in an uneasy air*] So, not a word to me. Are these his vows?

LADY LUCY: [*aside*] There's one upon the tease already.

LADY REVELLER: Why, you are in disorder, my dear. You look as if you have lost a trant leva! What have you said to her, Sir James?

SIR JAMES: I said, madam! I hope I never say anything to offend the ladies. [*aside*] The devil's in these married women. They can't conceal their own intrigues, though they swear us to secrecy.

LADY LUCY: You mistake, cousin. 'Tis his saying nothing to her that has put her upon the fret.

LADY REVELLER: Ah! Your observations are always malicious.

MRS SAGO: I despise them, dear Lady Reveller. Let's in to piquet. I suppose Lady Lucy would be pleased with Sir James alone to finish her remarks.

LADY LUCY: Nay, if you remove the cause, the discourse ceases.

SIR JAMES: [*going up to her, aside to her*] This you draw upon yourself. You will discover it.

LADY LUCY: [*to him*] Yes, your falsehood.

LADY REVELLER: Come, my dear Sir James, will you make one at a pool?

SIR JAMES: Pardon me, madam, I'm to be at White's[12] in half an hour, anon at the basset table. I'm yours.

MRS SAGO: No, no, he can't leave her.

LADY LUCY: They play gold, Sir James.

SIR JAMES: [*going up to* LADY LUCY] Madam, were your heart the stake I'd renounce all engagements to win that, or retrieve my own.

LADY LUCY: I must like the counter-stake very well e'er I play so high.

[12]*White's*: fashionable gaming house in St James Street

MRS SAGO: [*breaking from* LADY REVELLER'S *hand, pulling* SIR JAMES *by the sleeve*] Sir James, hark ye, one word with you.

LADY LUCY: Ha, ha, I knew she could not stir. I'll remove your constraint, but with my wonted freedom will tell you plainly; your husband's shop would better become you than gaming and gallants. Oh, shame to virtue, that women should copy men in their most reigning vices!

> Of virtue's wholesome rules unjustly we complain,
> When search of pleasures give us greater pain,
> How slightly we our reputation guard,
> Which lost but once can never be repaired. [*Exit*]

LADY REVELLER: Farewell sentences.

Enter ALPIEW

ALPIEW: Madam. [*whispers to her Lady*]

MRS SAGO: So then, you persuade me 'twas the care of my fame.

SIR JAMES: Nothing else, I protest, my dear little rogue. I have as much love as you, but I have more conduct.

MRS SAGO: Well, you know forgive you your faults.

SIR JAMES: [*aside*] Now to what purpose have I lied myself into her good graces, when I would be glad to be rid of her?

LADY REVELLER: Booted and spurred say you! Pray send him up, Sir James. I suppose trusty Buckle is come with some diverting embassy from your friend.

Enter BUCKLE *in a riding-dress*

LADY REVELLER: Mr Buckle, why in this equipage?

BUCKLE: Ah! Madam . . .

LADY REVELLER: Out with it.

BUCKLE: Farewell, friends, parents, and my country, thou, dear play-house, and sweet park. Farewell!

LADY REVELLER: Farewell? Why, whither are you going.

BUCKLE: My Lord and I am going where they never knew deceit.

SIR JAMES: That land is invisible, Buckle.

LADY REVELLER: Ha, ha, ha!

SIR JAMES: Were my Lord of my mind, your Ladyship should not have had so large a theme for your mirth. Your servant, ladies. [*Exit*]

LADY REVELLER: Well, but what's your business?

BUCKLE: My Lord charged me in his name to take his ever-lasting leave of your Ladyship.

LADY REVELLER: Why, where is he going, pray?

BUCKLE: In search of a country where there is no women.

MRS SAGO: Oh dear! Why, what have the women done to him, pray?

BUCKLE: Done to him, madam! He says they are all proud, perfidious, vain, inconstant conquettes in England.

MRS SAGO: Oh! He'll find they are everywhere the same.

LADY REVELLER: And this is the cause of his whimsical pilgrimage? Ha, ha!

BUCKLE: And this proceeds from your ill-usage, madam. When he left your house, he flung himself into his coach with such a force, that he broke all the windows, as they say. For my part I was not there. When he came home, he beat all his servants round to be revenged.

ALPIEW: Was you there, Buckle?

BUCKLE: No, I thank my stars, when I arrived, the expedition was over. In haste he mounted his chamber, flung himself upon his bed, burst out into a violent passion. 'Oh, that ever I should suffer myself to be imposed upon', said he, 'by this coquettish beauty!'

LADY REVELLER: Meaning me, Buckle. Ha, ha!

BUCKLE: Stay till I have finished the piece, madam, and your Ladyship shall judge. 'She's as fickle as she's fair. She does not use more art to gain a lover', said he, 'than to deceive him when he is fixed! . . . Humph!'   [*leering at her*]

LADY REVELLER: Pleasant! And does he call this taking leave?

MRS SAGO: A comical adieu.

BUCKLE: Oh! madam, I'm not come to the tragical part of it yet. Starting from his bed . . .

LADY REVELLER: I thought it had been all farce. If there be anything heroic in't, I'll set my face and look grave.

BUCKLE: My relation will require it, madam, for I am ready to weep at the repetition. Had you but seen how often he traversed the room, [*acting it*] heard how often he stamped, what distorted paces he made, casting up his eyes thus, biting his thumbs thus.

LADY REVELLER: Ha, ha, ha! You'll make an admirable actor! Shall I speak to the patentees[13] for you?

MRS SAGO: But pray how did this end?

BUCKLE: At last, madam, quite spent with rage, he sunk down upon his elbow, and his head fell upon his arm.

LADY REVELLER: What, did he faint away?

BUCKLE: Oh, no.

MRS SAGO: He did not die?

BUCKLE: No, but he fell asleep.

LADY REVELLER: Oh brave Prince Prettiman![14]

ALL: Ha, ha, ha!

BUCKLE: After three hours' nap, he waked, and calling hastily, 'My dear Buckle,' said he, 'let's go to the end of the world, and try to find a place where the sun shines not here and there at one time, for 'tis not fit that it should at once look upon two persons whose sentiments are so different. She no longer regards my pain, ungrateful, false, inhuman, barbarous woman.'

LADY REVELLER: Foolish, fond, believing, easy man. There's my answer. Come, shall we to piquet, my dear?

BUCKLE: Hold, hold, madam. I han't half done . . .

MRS SAGO: Oh! Pray my Lady Reveller, let's have it out, 'tis very diverting . . .

BUCKLE: He called me in a feeble voice, 'Buckle,' said he, 'bring me my little scrutore,[15] for I will write to Lady Reveller before I part from this place, never to behold her more.' What, don't you cry, madam?

LADY REVELLER: Cry . . . No, no; go on, go on.

BUCKLE: 'Tis done, madam, and there's the letter.

[*gives her the letter*]

LADY REVELLER: So this completes the narration. [*reads*]
   Madam, since I cannot live in a place where there is a possibility of seeing you without admiring, I resolve to fly; I am going to Flanders. Since you are false, I have no business here. I need not describe the pain I feel, you are but too well acquainted with that. Therefore I'll chase Death rather than return. Adieu.

[13]*patentees*: theatre licence-holders
[14]*Prince Prettiman*: character in heroic play
[15]*scrutore*: writing desk

BUCKLE: Can any man in the world write more tenderly, madam? Does he not say 'tis impossible to love you, and go for Flanders? And that he would rather hear of your death than return . . .

LADY REVELLER: Excellent. Ha, ha!

BUCKLE: What, do you laugh?

MRS SAGO: Who can forbear?

BUCKLE: I think you ought to die with grief. I warrant Heaven will punish you all.   [*going*]

ALPIEW: But hark ye, Buckle, where are you going now?

BUCKLE: To tell my Lord in what manner your Lady received his letter. Farewell. Now for Flanders.

ALPIEW: A fair wind and a good voyage to you.

As he goes out, enter LORD WORTHY

BUCKLE: My Lord here! So, now may I have my head broke for my long harangue, if it comes out.

LADY REVELLER: Oh, miraculous! My Lord! You have not finished your campaign already, have you? Ha, ha, ha! Or has the French made peace at hearing of your Lordship's intended bravery, and left you no enemies to combat?

LORD WORTHY: My worst of foes are here, here, within my breast: your image, madam.

LADY REVELLER: Oh dear, my Lord, no more of that theme, for Buckle has given us a surfeit on't already, even from your breaking the glasses of your coach, to your falling fast asleep! Ha, ha, ha!

LORD WORTHY: The glasses of my coach! What do you mean, Madam! Oh, Hell!   [*biting his thumb*]

BUCKLE: Ruined quite. Madam, for heaven's sake, what does your Ladyship mean? I lied in every syllable I told you, madam.

LADY REVELLER: Nay, if your Lordship has a mind to act it over again, we will oblige you for once. Alpiew, set chairs. Come, dear Sago, sit down and let the play begin. Buckle knows his part, and upon necessity could act yours too, my Lord.

LORD WORTHY: [*aside*] What has this dog been doing? When he was only to deliver my letter, to give her new subject for mirth. Death, methinks I hate her. Oh that I could hold that mind. [*to* BUCKLE] What makes you in this equipage? Ha, Sirrah?

BUCKLE: My Lord, I, I, I, I . . .

LORD WORTHY: Peace, villain . . .   [*strikes him*]

LADY REVELLER: Hey, This is changing the scene.

BUCKLE: [*aside*] Who the devil would rack his brains for these people of quality, who like nobody's wit but their own?

MRS SAGO: If the beating were invention before, thou hast it now in reality. If wars begin, I'll retire. They may agree better alone perhaps.   [*Exit*]

LADY REVELLER: Where did you learn this rudeness, my Lord, to strike your servant before me?

LORD WORTHY: When you have deprived a man of his reason, how can you blame his conduct?

BUCKLE: [*aside*] Reason? Egad, there's not three drams of reason between you both, as my cheek can testify.

LADY REVELLER: The affront was meant to me. Nor will I endure these passions. I thought I had forbid your visits.

LORD WORTHY: I thought I had resolved against them too.

ALPIEW: [*aside*] But resolutions are of small force of either side.

LORD WORTHY: Grant me but this one request, and I'll remove this hated object.

LADY REVELLER: Upon condition 'tis the last.

LORD WORTHY: It shall. I think it shall at least. Is there a happy man for whom I am despised?

LADY REVELLER: I thought 'twas some such ridiculous question. I'm of the Low-church, my Lord, consequently hate confessors! Ha, ha, ha!

BUCKLE: [*aside*] And penance, too, I dare swear.

LORD WORTHY: And everything but play.

LADY REVELLER: Dare you, the subject of my power, you, that petition love, arraign my pleasures? Now I'm fixed, and will never see you more.

BUCKLE: Now would anybody swear she's in earnest.

LORD WORTHY: I cannot bear that curse. See me at your feet again. [*kneels*] Oh you have tortured me enough, take pity now, dear tyrant, and let my sufferings end.

LADY REVELLER: [*aside*] I must not be friends with him, for then I shall have him at my elbow all night, and spoil my luck at the basset table. [*to him*] Either cringing or correcting; always in extremes. I am weary of this fatigue.

He that would gain my heart, must learn the way
Not to control, but readily obey;
For he that once pretends my faults to see,
That moment makes himself all faults to me.　　　[*Exit*]

BUCKLE: [*aside*] There's the inside of a woman.

LORD WORTHY: Gone. Now, curses on me for a fool, the worst of fools, a woman's fool

Whose only pleasure is to feed her pride.
Fond of herself, she cares for none beside.
So true coquets their numerous charms display
And strive to conquer, purpose to betray.　　　[*Exeunt*]

Act Four

SCENE ONE

Enter LORD WORTHY *and* SIR JAMES

SIR JAMES: Well, my Lord, I have left my cards in the hand of a friend to hear what you have to say to me. Love I'm sure is the text, therefore divide and subdivide as quick as you can.

LORD WORTHY: Could'st thou infuse into me thy temper, Sir James, I should have thy reason too, but I am born to love this fickle, faithless fair. What have I not essayed to raze her from my breast? But all in vain! I must have her, or I must not live.

SIR JAMES: Nay, if you are so far gone my Lord, your distemper requires an able physician. What thinks you of Lovely's bringing a file of musketeers and carry her away, vi and armis?[16]

LORD WORTHY: That way might give her person to my arms, but where's the heart?

SIR JAMES: A trifle in competition with her body.

LORD WORTHY: The heart's the gem that I prefer.

SIR JAMES: Say you so, my Lord? I'll engage three parts of Europe will make that exchange with you. Ha, ha, ha!

LORD WORTHY: That maxim wou'd hold with me perhaps in all but her. There I must have both or none. Therefore instruct me, friend, thou who negligent in love, keeps always on the level with the fair, what method shall I take to sound her soul's design? For though her carriage puts me on the rack when I behold that train of fools about her, yet my heart will plead in her excuse, and calm my anger spite of all efforts.

SIR JAMES: Humph? I have a plot, my Lord, if you will comply with it.

LORD WORTHY: Nothing of force.

[16]*vi and armis*: by force and by arms

SIR JAMES: Whate'er it be you shall be witness of it, 'twill either quench your flame, or kindle hers. I only will appear the guilty. But here's company, I'll tell you all within.

Enter CAPTAIN FIREBRAND *and* LOVELY, *dressed like a tar*

LORD WORTHY: I'll expect you. [*Exit*]

SIR JAMES: Ha, Captain, how sits the wind between you and your mistress? Ha?

CAPTAIN FIREBRAND: North and by South. But here's one sail full East, and without some unexpected tornado from the old man's coast he makes his port I warrant ye.

ENSIGN LOVELY: I wish I were at anchor once.

SIR JAMES: Why, thou art as errant a tar, as if thou had'st made an East-India voyage, ha, ha!

ENSIGN LOVELY: Aye, am I not, Sir James? But egad I hope the old fellow understands nothing of navigation. If he does, I shall be at a loss for the terms.

SIR JAMES: Oh! No matter for terms: look big, and bluster for your country. Describe the Vigo business, public news will furnish you with that, and I'll engage the success.

CAPTAIN FIREBRAND: Aye, aye, let me alone, I'll bear up with Sir Richard, and thou shalt board his pinnace[17] with consent, ne'er fear. Ho, here he comes full sail.

Enter SIR RICHARD

CAPTAIN FIREBRAND: I'm glad to see you. This is my kinsman which I told you of; as soon as he landed I brought him to kiss your hands.

SIR RICHARD: I honour you, you are welcome.

ENSIGN LOVELY: I thank you, sir. I'm not for compliments, 'tis a land language, I understand it not. Courage, honesty, and plain-dealing truth is the learning of our element; if you like that I am for ye.

SIR JAMES: [*aside*] The rogue does it to a miracle.

CAPTAIN FIREBRAND: [*aside*] He's an improving spark, I find, ha, ha!

SIR RICHARD: Like it, sir? Why 'tis the only thing I do like; hang compliments and court breeding, it serves only to make men a prey to one another, to encourage cowardice and ruin

---

[17]*pinnace*: ship

trade. No, sir, give me the man that dares meet death and dinner with the same appetite, one who rather than let in Popery would let out his blood. To maintain such men I'd pay double custom. Nay, all my gain should go for their support.

SIR JAMES: The best well-wisher to his country of an Englishman I ever heard.

ENSIGN LOVELY: Oh! Sir Richard, I wish the nation were all of your mind. 'Twould give the soldiers and the sailors life. Captain launch off a roundelay[18] or two.

CAPTAIN FIREBRAND: And make us fight with heart and hand. My kinsman, I'll assure, fits your principle to a hair; he hates the French so much, he ne'er fails to give them a broadside where'er he meets them, and has brought in more privateers this War than half the captains in the Navy. He was the first man that boarded the French fleet at Vigo, and in Gibralter business. The Gazetteer will inform you of the name of Captain Match.

SIR JAMES: Is this that Captain Match?

ENSIGN LOVELY: For want of a better, sir.

SIR JAMES: Sir, I shall be proud of being known to you.

SIR RICHARD: And I of being related to you, sir. I have a daughter young and handsome, and I'll give her a portion shall make thee an admiral, boy, for a soul like thine is only fit to command a Navy. What say'st thou? Art thou for a wife?

SIR JAMES: [aside] So, 'tis done, ha, ha, ha!

CAPTAIN FIREBRAND: A prosperous gale, i' faith.

ENSIGN LOVELY: I don't know, Sir Richard, mayhap a woman may not like me. I am rough and storm-like in my temper, unacquainted with the effeminacy of courts. I was born upon the sea, and since I can remember, never lived two months on shore. If I marry, my wife must go aboard, I promise you that.

SIR RICHARD: Aboard man? Why she shall go to the Indies with thee. Oh! Such a son-in-law! How shall I be blessed in my posterity? Now do I foresee the greatness of my grandchildren. The sons of this man shall, in the ages to come, make France a tributary nation.

ENSIGN LOVELY: Once in an engagement, sir, as I was giving

---

[18]*roundelay*: song

orders to my men, comes a ball and took off a fellow's head, and struck it full in my teeth. I whipp'd it up, clasped it into a gun, and shot it at the enemy again.

SIR RICHARD: Without the least concern!

ENSIGN LOVELY: Concern, sir! Ha, ha, ha! If it had been my own head I would have done the like.

SIR RICHARD: Prodigious effect of courage! Captain, I'll fetch my girl and be here again in an instant. What an honour will it be to have such a son. [*Exit*]

CAPTAIN FIREBRAND: Ha, ha, ha, ha! You outdo your master.

SIR JAMES: Ha, ha, ha, ha! The old knight's transported.

ENSIGN LOVELY: I wish it was over. I'm all in a sweat. Here he comes again.

Enter SIR RICHARD *and* VALERIA

SIR RICHARD: I'll hear none of your excuses. Captain, your hand. There take her, and these gentlemen shall be witnesses, if they please, to this paper, wherein I give her my whole estate when I die, and twenty thousand pounds down upon the nail. I care not whether my boy be worth a groat, get me but grandsons and I'm rich enough.

CAPTAIN FIREBRAND: Generously said, i' faith. Much good may do him with her.

SIR JAMES: I wish you joy, Captain, and you, madam.

VALERIA: That's impossible. Can I have joy in a species so very different from my own? Oh, my dear Lovely! We were only formed for one another, thy dear enquiring soul is more to me than all these useless lumps of animated clay. Duty compels my hand, but my heart is subject only to my mind; the strength of that they cannot conquer. No, with the resolution of the great unparalleled Epictetus, I here protest my will shall ne'er assent to any but my Lovely.

SIR RICHARD: Aye, you and your will may philosophise as long as you please, mistress, but your body shall be taught another doctrine. It shall so. Your mind and your soul quotha! Why, what a pox has my estate to do with them? Ha! 'Tis the flesh, housewife, that must raise heirs, and supporters of my name, and since I knew the getting of the estate, 'tis fit I should dispose of it. And therefore no more excuses. This is your husband. Do you see? Take my word for it.

VALERIA:
> The outward empty form of marriage take,
> But all beyond I keep for Lovely's sake.
> Thus on the ground for ever fix my eyes,
> All sights but Lovely shall their balls despise.

SIR RICHARD: Come, Captain, my chaplain is within. He shall do the business this minute. [*aside*] If I don't use the authority of a father this baggage will make me lose such a son-in-law that the City's wealth can't purchase me his fellow.

ENSIGN LOVELY:
> Thanks dear invention for this timely aid;
> The bait's gone down, he's by himself betrayed.
> Thus still were arts both true and honest fail,
> Deceitful wit and policy prevail.

VALERIA: To death, or anything. 'Tis all alike to me.

> [*Exit* VALERIA *and* LOVELY]

SIR RICHARD: Get you in I say. Hussy, get you in. In my conscience, my niece has spoiled her already, but I'll have her married this moment. Captain, you have bound me ever to you by this match. Command me and my house forever. But shall I not have your company, gentlemen, to be witnesses of this knot, this joyful knot?

CAPTAIN FIREBRAND: Yes, faith, Sir Richard, I have too much respect for my kinsman to leave him till I see him safe in harbour. I'll wait on you presently.

SIR JAMES: I am engaged in the next room at play. I beg your pardon, Sir Richard, for an hour. I'll bring the whole company to congratulate the bride and bridegroom.

SIR RICHARD: Bride and bridegroom! Congratulate me, man! Methinks I already see my race recorded amongst the foremost heroes of my nation. Boys, all boys, and all sailors.
> They shall the pride of France and Spain pull down,
> And add their Indies to our English Crown. [*Exit*]

SIR JAMES: Ha, ha, ha! Never was man so bigoted before. How will this end when he discovers the cheat? Ha, ha! Won't you make one with the ladies, Captain?

CAPTAIN FIREBRAND: I don't care if I do venture a piece or two. I'll but dispatch a little business and meet you at the table, Sir James.

Enter LADY LUCY

SIR JAMES: Ha, Lady Lucy! Is your Ladyship reconciled to basset yet? Will you give me leave to lose this purse to you, madam?

LADY LUCY: I thank fortune, I neither wish, nor need it, Sir James. I presume the next room is furnished with avarice enough to serve you in that affair if it is a burthen to you, or Mrs Sago's ill luck may give you an opportunity of returning some of the obligations you lie under.

SIR JAMES: Your sex, madam, extorts a duty from ours, and a well-bred man can no more refuse his money to a lady than a sword to a friend.

LADY LUCY: That superfluity of good manners, Sir James, would do better converted into charity. This town abounds with objects. Would it not leave a more glorious fame behind you to be the founder of some pious work, when all the poor, at mention of your name, shall bless your memory, than that posterity should say you wasted your estate on cards and women.

SIR JAMES: [*aside*] Humph! 'Tis a pity she were not a man, she preaches so emphatically. Faith, madam, you have a very good notion, but something too early. When I am old I may put your principles in practice, but youth for pleasure was design'd.

LADY LUCY: The truest pleasure must consist in doing good, which cannot be in gaming.

SIR JAMES: Everything is good in its kind, madam. Cards are harmless bits of paper, dice insipid bones, and women made for men.

LADY LUCY: Right, Sir James. But all these things may be perverted. Cards are harmless bits of paper in themselves, yet through them what mischiefs have been done? What orphans wronged? What tradesmen ruined? What coaches and equipage dismissed for them.

SIR JAMES: But then, how many coaches and equipages have they set up, madam?

LADY LUCY: Is it the more honourable for that? How many misses[19] keep coaches too? Which arrogance in my opinion only makes them more eminently scandalous . . .

[19] *misses*: prostitutes

SIR JAMES: Oh! Those are such as have a mind to be damned in this state, madam. But I hope your Ladyship don't rank them amongst us gamesters.

LADY LUCY: They are inseparable, Sir James. Madam's grandeur must be upheld, though the baker and butcher shut up shop.

SIR JAMES: Oh! Your Ladyship wrongs us middling gentlemen there. To ruin tradesmen is the quality's prerogative only, and none beneath a Lord can pretend to do't with an honourable air. Ha, ha!

LADY LUCY: Their example always the meaner sort. I grieve to think that Fortune should exalt such vain, such vicious souls, whilst virtue's clothed in rags.

SIR JAMES: Ah! Faith, she'd make but a scurvy figure at Court, madam. The statesmen and politicians would suppress her quickly. But whilst she remains in your breast she's safe and makes as all in love with that fair covering.

LADY LUCY: Oh! Fie, fie Sir James, you could not love one that hates your chief diversion.

SIR JAMES: I should hate it too, madam, on some terms that I could name.

LADY LUCY: What would make that conversion, pray?

SIR JAMES: Your heart.

LADY LUCY: I could pay that price. [*aside*] But dare not venture upon one so wild. First let me see the fruit, e'er I take a lease of the garden, Sir James.

SIR JAMES: Oh! Madam, the best way is to secure the ground, and then you may manure and cultivate it as you please.

LADY LUCY: That's a certain trouble, and uncertain profit, and in this affair I prefer the theory before the practice. But I detain you from the table, Sir James. You are wanted to tally. Your servant. [*Exit*]

SIR JAMES: Nay, if you leave me, madam, the devil will tempt me. She's gone, and now I can't shake off the thought of seven wins, eight loses, for the blood of me, and all this grave advice of hers is lost. Faith, though I do love her above the rest of her sex, she's an exact model of what all women ought to be. And yet your merry little coquettish tits[20] are very diverting. Well,

---

[20]*tits*: girls

now for basset. Let me see what money have I about me. Humph! About a hundred guineas half of which will set the ladies to cheating false parolies²¹ in abundance.

Each trifling toy would tempt in times of old,
Now nothing melts a woman's heart like gold.
Some bargains drive others more nice than they,
Who'd have you think they scorn to kiss for pay;
To purchase them you must lose deep at play.
With several women, several ways prevail
But gold's a certain way that cannot fail.   [*Exit*]

SCENE TWO

LADY REVELLER, MRS SAGO *and several gentlemen and ladies round a table at basset.*

> *Enter* SIR JAMES

LADY REVELLER: Oh! Sir James, are you come? We want you to tally for us.

SIR JAMES: What luck, ladies?

LADY REVELLER: I have only won a sept and leva.

MRS SAGO: And I have lost a trante and leva. My ill fortune has not forsook me yet I see.

SIR JAMES: I go a guinea upon that card.

LADY REVELLER: You lose that card.

MRS SAGO: I raise Sir James' card double.

BANKER: Seven wins, and five loses. You have lost it, madam.

MRS SAGO: Again? Sure never was woman so unlucky . . .

BANKER: Knave wins, and ten loses. You have won, Sir James.

LADY REVELLER: Clean cards here.

MRS SAGO: Burn this book, 't has an unlucky air. [*tears them*] Bring some more books.

> *Enter* CAPTAIN FIREBRAND

LADY REVELLER: Oh! Captain, here set a chair. Come, Captain, you shall sit by me. [*aside*] Now if we can but strip this tar.

CAPTAIN FIREBRAND: With all my heart, madam. Come, what do you play gold? That's something high though. Well, guinea upon this honest knave of clubs.

---

²¹*parolies*: basset calls

LADY REVELLER: You lose it for a guinea more.

CAPTAIN FIREBRAND: Done, madam.

BANKER: The five wins, and the knave loses.

LADY REVELLER: You have lost it, Captain.

SIR JAMES: The knave wins for two guineas more, madam.

LADY REVELLER: Done, Sir James.

BANKER: Six wins. Knave loses.

SIR JAMES: Oh! The devil, I face, I had rather have lost all.

BANKER: Nine wins. Queen loses. You have won.

MRS SAGO: I'll make a paroli. I mase as much more. Your card loses, Sir James, for two guineas. Yours, Captain, loses for a guinea more.

BANKER: Four wins. Nine loses. You have lost, madam.

MRS SAGO: Oh! I could tear my flesh, as I tear these cards. Confusion! I can never win above a wretched paroli, for if I push to sept and leva, 'tis gone.   [*walks about disorderly*]

BANKER: Ace wins. Knave loses.

CAPTAIN FIREBRAND: Sink the knave, I'll set no more on't.

LADY REVELLER: Face again. What's the meaning of this ill luck tonight? Bring me a book of hearts, I'll try if they are more successful. That on the Queen. Yours and your card loses.

MRS SAGO: Bring me a fresh book. Bring me another book. Bring me all diamonds.
   [*Looks upon them one by one, then throws them over her shoulder.*]

LADY REVELLER: [*aside*] That can never be lucky. The name of jewels don't become a citizen's wife.

BANKER: King wins. The trey loses.

SIR JAMES: You have great luck tonight, Mr Sharper.

MR SHARPER: So I have, Sir James. I have won soneca every time.

LADY REVELLER: [*aside*] But if he has got the knack of winning thus, he shall sharp no more here I promise him.

MRS SAGO: I mase that.

LADY REVELLER: Sir James, pray will you tally.

SIR JAMES: With all my heart, madam.
                               [*takes the cards and shuffles them*]

MRS SAGO: Pray give me the cards, sir.

[*Takes them, and shuffles them, and gives them to him again.*]

CAPTAIN FIREBRAND: I set that.

LADY REVELLER: I set five guineas upon this card, Sir James.

SIR JAMES: Done, madam. Five wins, Six loses.

MRS SAGO: I set that.

SIR JAMES: Five don't go, and seven loses.

CAPTAIN FIREBRAND: I mase double.

LADY REVELLER: I mase that.

SIR JAMES: Three wins. Six loses.

MRS SAGO: I mase, I mase double, and that. Oh ye malicious stars! Again!

SIR JAMES: Eight wins. Seven loses.

CAPTAIN FIREBRAND: So, this trante and leva makes some amends. Adsbud, I hate cheating. What's that false cock made for now. Ha, madam.

LADY REVELLER: Nay, Mrs Sago, if you begin to play foul.

MRS SAGO: Rude brute, to take notice of the sleight of hand in our sex. I protest he wrongs me, madam, there's the dernier stake, and I'll set it all. Now Fortune favour me, or this moment is my last.

LADY REVELLER: There's the last of fifty pounds. What's the meaning of this?

SIR JAMES: Now for my plot. Her stock is low, I perceive.
    [*Slips a purse of gold into the furbelows of Lady Reveller's apron.*]

LADY REVELLER: I never had such ill luck. I must fetch more money. [*Discovers a purse in the furbelows of her apron.*] Ha, from whence came this? This is the genteelest piece of gallantry; the action is Sir Harry's, I see by his eyes.

SIR JAMES: Nine wins. Six loses.

MRS SAGO: I am ruined and undone for ever. Oh, oh, oh, to lose every card. Oh, oh, oh!   [*bursts out crying*]

CAPTAIN FIREBRAND: So, there's one vessel sprung a leak, and I am almost ashore. If I go on at this rate, I shall make but a lame voyage on't I doubt.

SIR JAMES: Deuce wins. King loses.

CAPTAIN FIREBRAND: I mase again. I mase double, I mase again. Now the devil blow my head off if ever I saw cards run so. Damn 'em.   [*tears the cards and stamps on them*]

SIR JAMES: Fie, Captain, this concern among the ladies is indecent.

CAPTAIN FIREBRAND: Damn the ladies. Mayn't I swear, or tear my cards, if I please. I'm sure I have paid for them. Pray count the cards. I believe there's a false tally.

SIR JAMES: No, they are right, sir.   [SIR JAMES *counts them*]

MRS SAGO: Not to turn one card! Oh, oh, oh!
[*stamps up and down*]

LADY REVELLER: Madam, if you play no longer, pray don't disturb those that do. Come, courage, Captain, Sir James' gold was very lucky. [*aside*] Who could endure these men, did they not lose their money?

CAPTAIN FIREBRAND: Bring another book here. That upon ten, and I mase that.   [*put down a card and turns another*]

SIR JAMES: King faced. Eight wins. Ten loses.

CAPTAIN FIREBRAND: Fire and gunpowder.   [*Exit*]

LADY REVELLER: Ha, ha, ha! What, is the Captain vanished in his own smoke? Come, I bet it with you, Mr Sharper. Your card loses.

Re-enter CAPTAIN FIREBRAND, *pulling in a* STRANGER, *which he had fetched out of the street.*

CAPTAIN FIREBRAND: Sir, do you think it possible to lose a trante and leva, a quinze-leva, and a sept leva, and never turn once.

STRANGER: No, sure, 'tis impossible.

CAPTAIN FIREBRAND: 'Ounds you lie. I did sir.
[*laying his hand on his sword*]

ALL THE WOMEN: Ah, ha! Ah, ha!   [*shriek and run off*]

CAPTAIN FIREBRAND: What the devil had I to do among these land-rats? Zounds, to lose forty pound for nothing, not so much as a wench for it. Ladies, quotha! A man had as good be acquainted with pick-pockets.   [*Exit*]

SIR JAMES: Ha, ha, ha! The Captain has frightened the women out of their wits. Now to keep my promise with my Lord, though the thing has but an ill face, no matter.

They join together to enslave us men,
And why not we to conquer them again.   [*Exit*]

Act Five

SCENE ONE

Enter SIR JAMES *from one side, and* LADY REVELLER *from the other*

LADY REVELLER: Sir James, what have you done with the rude porpoise?

SIR JAMES: He is gone to your uncle's apartment, madam, I suppose. I was in pain till I knew how your Ladyship did after your fright.

LADY REVELLER: Really, Sir James, the fellow has put me into the spleen by his ill manners. Oh, my stars! That there should be such an unpolished piece of humanity to be in that disorder for losing his money to us women. I was apprehensive he would have beat me, ha, ha!

SIR JAMES: Ha, ha! Your ladyship must impute his ill-breeding to the want of conversation with your sex. But he is a man of honour with his own, I assure you.

LADY REVELLER: I hate out-of-fashioned honour. But where's the company, Sir James? Shan't we play again?

SIR JAMES: All dispersed, madam.

LADY REVELLER: Come, you and I will go to piquet then?

SIR JAMES: Oh, I'm tired with cards, madam. Can't you think of some other diversion to pass a cheerful hour? I could tell you one, if you'd give me leave.

LADY REVELLER: Of your own invention? Then it must be a pleasant one.

SIR JAMES: Oh, the pleasantest in the world.

LADY REVELLER: What is it, I pray?

SIR JAMES: Love, love, my dear charmer.   [*approaches her*]

LADY REVELLER: Oh, Cupid! How came that in your head?

SIR JAMES: Nay, 'tis in my heart, and except you pity me, the wound is mortal.

LADY REVELLER: Ha, ha, ha! Is Sir James got into Lord Worthy's club? You that could tell me I should not have so large a theme for my diversion were you in his place? Ha, ha, ha! What, and is the gay, the airy, the witty, inconstant Sir James overtaken? Ha, ha!

SIR JAMES: Very true, madam, you see there is no jesting with fire. Will you be kind? [*gets between her and the door*]

LADY REVELLER: Kind? What a dismal sound was there? I'm afraid your fever's high, Sir James, ha, ha!

SIR JAMES: If you think so, madam, 'tis time to apply cooling medicine. [*locks the door*]

LADY REVELLER: Ha, what insolence is this? The door locked! What do you mean, Sir James?

SIR JAMES: Oh, 'tis something indecent to name it, madam, but I intend to show you. [*lays hold on her*]

LADY REVELLER: Unhand me, villain, or I'll cry out . . .

SIR JAMES: Do, and make yourself the jest of servants, expose your reputation to their vile tongues, which, if you please, shall remain safe within my breast. But if with your own noise you blast it, here I bid defiance to all honour and secrecy, and the first man that enters, dies. [*struggles with her*]

LADY REVELLER: What shall I do? Instruct me Heaven. Monster! Is this your friendship to my Lord? And can you wrong the woman he adores?

SIR JAMES: Aye, but the woman does not care a souse for him. And therefore he has no right above me. I love you as much, and will possess.

LADY REVELLER: Oh! Hold! Kill me rather than destroy my honour. What devil has debauched your temper? Or, how has my carriage drawn this curse upon me? What have I done to give you cause to think you ever should succeed in this hated way? [*weeps*]

SIR JAMES: Why this question, madam? Can a lady that loves play so passionately as you do, that takes as much pains to draw men in to lose their money as a town miss to their destruction, that caresses all sorts of people for your interest, that divides your time between your toilet and basset table, can you, I say, boast of innate virtue? Fie, I am sure you must have guessed for what I played so deep. We never part with our money without

design, or writing fool upon our foreheads. Therefore no more
of this resistance, except you would have more money.

LADY REVELLER: Oh! Horrid!

SIR JAMES: There was fifty in that purse, madam. Here's fifty
more. Money shall be no dispute.   [*offers her money*]

LADY REVELLER: [*strikes it down*] Perish your money with
yourself, you villain. There, there, take your boasted favours
which I resolved before to have paid in specie. Basest of men, I'll
have your life for this affront. What ho! Within there!

SIR JAMES: Hush! 'Faith, you'll raise the house. [*lays hold on
her*] And 'tis in vain. You're mine. Nor will I quit this room 'till
I'm possessed.   [*struggles*]

LADY REVELLER: Raise the house! I'll raise the world in my
defence. Help, murder! Murder! Rape! Rape!

Enter LORD WORTHY *from another room with his sword
drawn.*

LORD WORTHY: Ha! Villain, unhand the lady, or this moment
is thy last.

SIR JAMES: Villain, back my Lord. Follow me.   [*Exit*]

LADY REVELLER: By the bright sun that shines, you shall not
go. No, you've saved my virtue, and I will preserve your life. Let
the vile wretch be punished by viler hands. Yours shall not be
profaned with blood so base, if I have any power . . .

LORD WORTHY: Shall the traitor live? Though your barbarous
usage does not merit this from me, yet, in the consideration that
I loved you once, I will chastise his insolence.

LADY REVELLER: Once? Oh! Say not once. Do you not love me
still? Oh! How pure your soul appears to me above that
dreadful wretch.   [*weeps*]

SIR JAMES: [*peeping in, aside*] It takes as I could wish.

LORD WORTHY: Yet how have I been slighted. Every fop
preferred to me! Now you discover what inconveniency your
gaming has brought you into. This from me would have been
unpardonable advice, now you have proved it at your own
expense.

LADY REVELLER: I have, and hate myself for all my folly. Oh!
Forgive me and, if still you think me worthy of your heart, I here
return you mine, and will this hour sign it with my hand.

SIR JAMES: [*aside*] How I applaud myself for this contrivance.

LORD WORTHY: Oh, the transporting joy. It is the only happiness I covet here.

Haste then my charmer, haste the longed-for bliss,
The happiest minute of my life is this.   [*Exit*]

SIR JAMES: Ha, ha, ha, ha! How am I censured now for doing this lady a piece of service, in forcing that upon her which only her vanity and pride restrained.

So blushing maids refuse the courted joy,
Though wishing eyes, and pressing hands comply;
Till by some stratagem the lover gains,
What she denied to all his amorous pains.

[*As* SIR JAMES *is going off, enter* LADY LUCY *meeting him*]

SIR JAMES: Ha, Lady Lucy! [*aside*] Having succeeded for my friend, who knows but this may be my lucky minute too? Madam, you come opportunely to hear.

[*takes her by the hand*]

LADY LUCY: Stand off, basest of men, I have heard too much. Could'st thou choose no house but this to act thy villainies in? And could'st thou offer vows to me, when thy heart, poisoned with vicious thoughts, harboured this design against my family!

SIR JAMES: Very fine, Faith, this is like to be my lucky minute with a witness. But madam . . .

LADY LUCY: Offer no excuse, 'tis height of impudence to look me in the face.

SIR JAMES: [*aside*] Egad! She loves me. Oh! Happy rogue! This concern can proceed from nothing else.

LADY LUCY: My heart, till now unused to passion, swells with this affront, would reproach thee, would reproach myself, for having harboured one favourable thought of thee.

SIR JAMES: Why did you, madam? [*aside*] Egad I owe more to her anger than ever I did to her morals.

LADY LUCY: Ha! What have I said?

SIR JAMES: The only kind word you ever uttered.

LADY LUCY: Yes, imposter. Know to thy confusion that I did love thee, and fancied I discovered some seeds of virtue amongst that heap of wickedness, but this last action has betrayed the fond mistake, and showed thou art all o'er fiend.

SIR JAMES: Give me leave, madam . . .

LADY LUCY: Think not this confession meant to advance thy impious love, but hear my final resolution.

SIR JAMES: Egad, I must hear it, I find, for there's no stopping her.

LADY LUCY: From this moment I'll never . . .

SIR JAMES: [*clapping his hand before her mouth*] Nay, nay, nay, after sentence, no criminal is allowed to plead, therefore I will be heard. Not guilty, not guilty, madam, but if I don't prove that this is all a stratagem, contrived, studied, designed, prosecuted, and put in execution to reclaim your cousin, and give my Lord possession – may you finish your curse, and I be doomed to everlasting absence. Egad I'm out of breath!

LADY LUCY: Oh! Could'st thou prove this?

SIR JAMES: I can, if by the proof you'll make me happy. My Lord shall convince you.

LADY LUCY: To him I will refer it, on this truth your hopes depend.

> In vain we strive our passions to conceal,
> Our very passions do our loves reveal
> When once the heart yields to the tyrant's sway,
> The eyes our tongue will soon the flame betray.   [*Exit*]

SIR JAMES: I was never out at a critical minute in my life.

Enter MR SAGO *and* TWO BAILIFFS *meeting* ALPIEW

MR SAGO: Hark ye, mistress, is my wife here?

ALPIEW: [*aside*] Truly, I shan't give myself the trouble of seeking her for him, now she has lost all her money. Your wife is a very indiscreet person, sir.

MR SAGO: I'm afraid I shall find it so to my cost.

BAILIFF ONE: Come, come, sir, we can't wait all day.

BAILIFF TWO: The actions are a thousand pounds. You shall have time to send for bail and what friends you please.

MR SAGO: A thousand pounds! [*Enter* MRS SAGO] Oh Lambkin! Have you spent me a thousand pounds?

MRS SAGO: Who, I Pudd? Oh! Undone for ever!

MR SAGO: Pudd me no Pudd. Do you owe Mr Taby the mercer two hundred pounds, ha?

MRS SAGO: I, I, I don't know the sum, dear Pudd, but, but, but, I do owe him something, but I believe he made me pay too dear.

MR SAGO: Oh! Thou wolfkin instead of lambkin, for thou hast devoured my substance! And dost thou owe Mr Dollar, the goldsmith, three hundred pounds? Dost thou? Ha, speak tigress.

MRS SAGO: Sure it can't be quite three hundred pounds.

[*sobbing*]

MR SAGO: Thou island crocodile, thou! And dost thou owe Ratsbane the vintner an hundred pounds? And were those hampers of wine which I received so joyfully, sent by thyself to thyself, ha?

MRS SAGO: Yes, indeed, Puddy, I, I beg your pardon. [*sobbing*]

MR SAGO: And why didst not thou tell me of them, thou rattlesnake, for they say they have sent a hundred times for their money, else I had not been arrested in my shop.

MRS SAGO: Be, be, be because I, I, I was afraid, dear Puddy.

[*crying*]

MR SAGO: But wert thou not afraid to ruin me though, dear Pudd? Ah! I need ask thee no more questions, thou serpent in petticoats. Did I dote upon thee for this? Here's a bill from Callico the linen draper, another from Setwell the jeweller, from Coupler a mantua-maker, and Pimpwell the milliner; a tribe of locusts enough to undo a lord mayor.

MRS SAGO: I hope not, truly, dear, deary. I'm sure that's all.

MR SAGO: All, with a pox. No, Mrs Jezebel, that's not all. There's two hundred pounds due to myself for tea, coffee, and chocolate, which my journeyman has confessed, since your roguery came out, that you have embezzled, hussy, you have. So, this comes of your keeping quality company. E'en let them keep you now, for I have done with you. You shall come no more within my doors, I promise you.

MRS SAGO: Oh! Kill me rather. I never did it with design to part with you, indeed, Puddy.   [*sobbing*]

MR SAGO: No, no, I believe not, whilst I was worth a groat. Oh!

Enter SIR JAMES

SIR JAMES: How! Mrs Sago in tears, and my honest friend in ruffians' hands! The meaning of this?

MR SAGO: Oh! Sir James, my hypocritical wife is as much a wife as any wife in the City. I'm arrested here in an action of a thousand pounds that she has taken up goods for and gamed away. Get out of my sight, get out of my sight, I say.

MRS SAGO: Indeed, and indeed, [*sobbing*] dear Puddy, but I cannot go. Here I will hang for ever on this neck.

[*flies about his neck*]

MR SAGO: Help, murder, murder! Why, why, what, will you collar me?

SIR JAMES: Right, woman. I must try to make up this breach. Oh! Mr Sago, you are unkind, 'tis pure love that thus transports your wife, and not such base designs as you complain of.

MR SAGO: Yes, yes, and she run me in debt out of pure love too, no doubt.

MRS SAGO: So it was, Pudd.

MR SAGO: What was it, ha, mistress, out of love to me that you have undone me? Thou, thou, thou, I don't know what to call thee bad enough.

MRS SAGO: You won't hear your Keecky out, dear Pudd; it was not out of love for play, but for lo-, lo-, love to you, dear Pudd. If you'll forgive me, I'll ne'er play again.

[*crying and sobbing all the while*]

SIR JAMES: Nay, now, sir, you must forgive her.

MR SAGO: What! Forgive her that would send me to gaol?

SIR JAMES: No, no, there's no danger of that. I'll bail you, Mr Sago, and try to compound these debts. You know me, Officers.

BAILIFF ONE: Very well, Sir James, your Worship's word is sufficient.

SIR JAMES: There's your fees then. Leave here your prisoner. I'll see him forthcoming.

BAILIFF TWO: With all our hearts. Your servant, sir.

[*Exit* BAILIFFS]

MR SAGO: Oh, thou wicked woman. How have I doted on those eyes! How often have I kneeled to kiss that hand! Ha, is not this true, Keecky?

MRS SAGO: Yes, deary. I, I, I, I do confess it.

MR SAGO: Did ever I refuse to grant whatever thou asked me?

MRS SAGO: No, never, Pudd . . .   [*weeps still*]

MR SAGO: Might'st not thou have eated gold, as the saying is, ha? Oh Keecky, Keecky!   [*ready to weep*]

SIR JAMES: Leave crying, and wheedle him, madam, wheedle him.

MRS SAGO: I do confess it. And can't you forgive your Keecky then, that you have been so tender of, that you so often confess your heart has jumped up to your mouth when you have heard my beauty praised.

MR SAGO: So it has, I profess, Sir James, I begin to melt. I do. I am a good-natured fool, that's the truth on't. But, if I should forgive you, what would you do to make me amends? For that fair face, if I turn you out of doors, will quickly be a cheaper drug than any in my shop.

SIR JAMES: And not maintain her half so well. Promise largely, madam.

MRS SAGO: I'll love you for ever, deary.

MR SAGO: But you'll jig to Covent Garden again.

MRS SAGO: No, indeed, I won't come within the air on't, but take up with City acquaintance, rail at the Court, and go twice a week with Mrs Outside to Pinmakers Hall.

MR SAGO: That would rejoice my heart.   [*ready to weep*]

SIR JAMES: See, if the good man is not ready to weep. Your last promise has conquered. Come, come buss and be friends, and end the matter. [*aside*] I'm glad the quarrel is made up, or I had had her upon my hands.

MRS SAGO: Pudd, don't you hear Sir James, Pudd?

MR SAGO: I can hold no longer. Yes, I do hear him. Come then to the arms of thy nown Pudd.   [*run into one another's arms*]

SIR JAMES: Now, all's well. And for your comfort, Lady Reveller is by this time married to my Lord Worthy, and there will be no more gaming, I assure you, in that house.

MR SAGO: Joys upon joys. Now if these debts were but accommodated, I should be happier than ever, I should indeed, Keecky.

SIR JAMES: Leave that to me, Mr Sago. I have won part of your wife's money, and will that way restore it you.

MR SAGO: I thank you, good Sir James, I believe you are the first gamester that ever refunded.

MRS SAGO: Generously done. Fortune has brought me off this time, and I'll never trust her more.

SIR JAMES: But see the bride and bridegroom.

Enter LORD WORTHY *and* LADY REVELLER, LADY LUCY, BUCKLE *and* ALPIEW

LADY LUCY: This match, which I have now been witness to, is what I long have wished. Your course of life must of necessity be changed.

LADY REVELLER: Ha, Sir James here! Oh, if you love me, my Lord, let us avoid that brute. You must not meet him.

SIR JAMES: Oh, there's no danger, madam. My Lord, I wish you joy with all my heart. We only quarrelled to make you friends, madam. Ha, ha, ha!

LADY REVELLER: What, am I tricked into a marriage then?

LORD WORTHY: Not against your will, I hope.

LADY REVELLER: No, I forgive you. Though had I been aware of it, it should have cost you a little more pains.

LORD WORTHY: I wish I could return thy plot, and make this Lady thine, Sir James.

SIR JAMES: Then I should be paid with interest, my Lord.

LADY LUCY: My fault is consideration you know, I must think a little longer on't.

SIR JAMES: And my whole study shall be to improve those thoughts to my own advantage.

MR SAGO;   I wish your Ladyship joy, and hope I shall keep my Keecky to myself now.

LADY LUCY: With all my heart, Mr Sago. She has had ill luck of late, which I am sorry for.

MRS SAGO: My Lord Worthy will confine your Ladyship from play as well as I, and my injunction will be more easy when I have your example.

BUCKLE: Nay, 'tis time to throw up the cards when the game's out.

   Enter SIR RICHARD, CAPTAIN FIREBRAND, LOVELY *and* VALERIA

CAPTAIN FIREBRAND: Well, Sir James, the danger's over. We have doubled the Cape, and my kinsman is sailing directly to the port.

SIR JAMES: A boon voyage.

SIR RICHARD: 'Tis done, and my heart is at ease. Did you ever see such a perverse baggage? Look in his face, I say, and thank your stars, for their best influences gave you this husband.

ENSIGN LOVELY: Will not Valeria look upon me? She used to be more kind when we have fished for eels in vinegar.

VALERIA: My Lovely, is it thee? And has natural sympathy forborn to inform my sense thus long? [*flies to him*]

SIR RICHARD: How! How! This, Lovely? What? Does it prove the Ensign I have so carefully avoided?

ENSIGN LOVELY: Yes, sir, the same. I hope you may be brought to like a land-soldier, as well as a seaman.

SIR RICHARD: And, Captain, have you done this?

CAPTAIN FIREBRAND: Yes, faith, she was too whimsical for our element. Her hard words might have conjured up a storm for ought I know. So I have set her ashore.

LADY REVELLER: What, my uncle deceived with his stock of wisdom? Ha, ha, ha!

BUCKLE: Here's such a coupling, Mrs Alpiew, han't you a month's mind?

ALPIEW: Not to you, I assure you.

BUCKLE: I was but in jest, child. Say nay, when you're asked.

SIR JAMES: That principal part of this plot was mine, Sir Richard.

SIR RICHARD: [*aside*] Would 'twas in my power to hang you for't.

SIR JAMES: And I have no reason to doubt you should repent it. He is a gentleman, tho' a younger brother. He loves your daughter, and she him, which has the best face of happiness in a married state. You like a man of honour, and he has as much as anyone, that I assure you, Sir Richard.

SIR RICHARD: Well, since what's past is past recall, I had as good be satisfied as not. Therefore take her, and bless ye together.

LORD WORTHY: So now each man's wish is crowned, but mine with double joy.

CAPTAIN FIREBRAND: Well said, Sir Richard, let's have a bowl of punch, and drink to the bridegroom's good voyage tonight. Steady, steady! Ha, ha!

MR SAGO: I'll take a glass with you, Captain. I reckon myself a bridegroom too.

BUCKLE: [*aside*] I doubt Keecky won't find him such.

MRS SAGO:
Well, poor Keecky's bound to good behaviour,
Or she had quite lost her Puddy's favour.

Shall I for this repine at Fortune? No,
I'm glad at heart that I'm forgiven so.
Some neighbours' wives have but too lately shown,
When spouse had left 'em, all their friends were flown.
Then all you wives that would avoid my fate,
Remain contented with your present state.

The Busybody

by

SUSANNA CENTLIVRE

1709

DRAMATIS PERSONAE

WOMEN

MIRANDA,	*an heiress worth thirty thousand pounds, really in love with Sir George Airy, but pretends to be so with her guardian, Sir Francis Gripe.*
ISABINDA,	*daughter to Sir Jealous Traffic, in love with Charles, but designed for a Spanish merchant by her father, and kept up from the sight of all men.*
PATCH,	*Isabinda's woman.*
SCENTWELL,	*Miranda's woman.*

MEN

MARPLOT,	*a sort of a silly fellow, cowardly, but very inquisitive to know everybody's business, generally spoils all he undertakes, but without design.*
SIR GEORGE AIRY,	*a gentleman of four thousand a year, in love with Miranda.*
SIR FRANCIS GRIPE,	*guardian to Miranda and Marplot, father to Charles, in love with Miranda.*
CHARLES,	*friend to Sir George, in love with Isabinda.*
SIR JEALOUS TRAFFICK,	*a merchant that had lived some time in Spain, a great admirer of Spanish customs, father to Isabinda.*
WHISPER,	*manservant to Charles.*

Act One

SCENE ONE

The Park

SIR GEORGE AIRY *meeting* CHARLES

CHARLES: Ha! Sir George Airy! A-birding thus early! What forbidden game roused you so soon? For no lawful occasion could invite a person of your figure abroad at such unfashionable hours.

SIR GEORGE: There are some men, Charles, whom Fortune has left free from inquietude, who are diligently studious to find out ways and means to make themselves uneasy.

CHARLES: Is it possible that anything in nature can ruffle the temper of a man whom the four seasons of the year compliment with as many thousand pounds; nay, and a father at rest with his ancestors?

SIR GEORGE: Why there 'tis now! A man that wants money thinks none can be unhappy that has it; but my affairs are in such a whimsical posture, that it will require a calculation of my nativity[1] to find if my gold will relieve me, or not.

CHARLES: Ha, ha, ha! Never consult the stars about that. Gold has a power beyond them; gold unlocks the midnight councils; gold outdoes the wind, becalms the ship, or fills her sails. Gold is omnipotent below: it makes whole armies fight or fly; it buys even souls, and bribes the wretches to betray their country. Then what can the business be, that gold won't serve thee in?

SIR GEORGE: Why, I'm in love.

CHARLES: In love! – Ha, ha, ha, ha! In love, ha, ha, ha, with what, prithee? A cherubim?

[1]*calculation of my nativity*: astrological chart

SIR GEORGE: No, with a woman.

CHARLES: A woman, good, ha, ha, ha! And gold not help thee?

SIR GEORGE: But suppose I'm in love with two —

CHARLES: Aye, if thou'rt in love with two hundred, gold will fetch 'em, I warrant thee, boy. But who are they! Who are they! Come.

SIR GEORGE: One is a lady whose face I never saw, but witty as an angel; the other beautiful as Venus —

CHARLES: And a fool —

SIR GEORGE: For aught I know, for I never spoke to her, but you can inform me. I am charmed for the wit of one, and die for the beauty of the other.

CHARLES: And pray which are in quest of now?

SIR GEORGE: I prefer the sensual pleasure; I'm for her I've seen, who is thy father's ward, Miranda.

CHARLES: Nay then I pity you; for the jew, my father, will no more part with her and 30,000 pounds, than he would with a guinea to keep me from starving.

SIR GEORGE: Now you see gold can't do everything, Charles.

CHARLES: Yes: for 'tis her gold that bars my father's gate against you.

SIR GEORGE: Why, if he is that avaricious wretch, how cam'st thou by such a liberal education?

CHARLES: Not a souse out of his pocket I assure you: I had an uncle who defrayed that charge, but for some little wildnesses of youth, though he made me his heir, left Dad my guardian 'till I came to years of discretion, which I presume the old gentleman will never think I am; and now he has got the estate into his clutches, it does me no more good that if it lay in Prester-John's[2] dominions.

SIR GEORGE: What, can'st thou find no strategem to redeem it?

CHARLES: I have made many essays to no purpose: though want, the mistress of invention still tempts me on, yet still the old fox is too cunning for me — I am upon my last project, which if it fails, then for my last refuge, a brown musket.

SIR GEORGE: What is't? Can I assist thee?

CHARLES: Not yet; when you can, I have confidence enough in you to ask it.

[2]*Prester-John*: the richest king in the world

SIR GEORGE: I am always ready. But what does he intend to do with Miranda? Is she to be sold in private? Or will he put her up by way of auction, at who bids most? If so, egad I'm for him: my gold, as you say, shall be subservient to my pleasure.

CHARLES: To deal ingenuously with you, Sir George, I know very little of her, or home: for since my uncle's death, and my return from travel, I have never been well with my father; he thinks my expenses too great, and I his allowance too little; he never sees me, but he quarrels; and to avoid that, I shun his house as much as possible. The report is, he intends to marry her himself.

SIR GEORGE: Can she consent to it?

CHARLES: Yes, faith, so they say; but I tell you I am wholly ignorant of the matter. Miranda and I are like two violent members of a contrary party: I can scarce allow her beauty, though all the world does; nor she me civility, for that contempt: I fancy she plays the mother-in-law already, and sets the old gentleman on to do mischief.

SIR GEORGE: Then I've your free consent to get her.

CHARLES: Aye, and my helping hand if occasion be.

SIR GEORGE: Pugh, yonder's a fool coming this way, let's avoid him.

CHARLES: What, Marplot? No, no, he's my instrument; there's a thousand conveniences in him; he'll lend me his money, when he has any, run of my errands, and be proud on't; in short, he'll pimp for me, lie for me, drink for me, do any thing but fight for me, and that I trust to my own arm for.

SIR GEORGE: Nay, then he's to be endured; I never knew his qualifications before.

Enter MARPLOT *with a patch across his face*.

MARPLOT: Dear Charles, yours – [*aside*] – Ha! Sir George Airy, the man in the world I have an ambition to be known to. – Give me thy hand dear boy –

CHARLES: A good assurance! But hark ye, how came your beautiful countenance clouded in the wrong place?

MARPLOT: I must confess 'tis a little mal-à-propos, but no matter for that; a word with you, Charles: prithee introduce me to Sir George – he is a man of wit, and I'd give ten guineas to –

CHARLES: When you have 'em you mean.

MARPLOT: Aye, when I have 'em; pugh, pox you cut the thread
of my discourse – I would give ten guineas, I say, to be ranked in
his acquaintance: well, 'tis a vast addition to a man's fortune,
according to the rout of the world, to be seen in the company
of leading men; for then we are all thought to be politicians,
or Whigs, or Jacks,[3] or high-flyers,[4] or low-flyers,[5] or Levellers[6] – and so forth; for you must know, we all herd in parties
now.

CHARLES: Then a fool for diversion is out of fashion, I find.

MARPLOT: Yes, without it be a mimicking fool, and they are
darlings everywhere; but prithee, introduce me.

CHARLES: Well, on condition you'll give us a true account how
you came by that mourning nose, I will.

MARPLOT: I'll do it.

CHARLES: Sir George, here's a gentleman has a passionate
desire to kiss your hand.

SIR GEORGE: Oh, I honour men of the sword, and I presume
this gentleman is lately come from Spain or Portugal[7] – by his
scars.

MARPLOT: No, really, Sir George, mine sprung from civil duty:
happening last night into the Groom-Porter's[8] – I had a strong
inclination to go ten guineas with a sort of a, sort of a – kind of a
milk-sop[9] as I thought. A pox of the dice he flung out, and my
pockets being empty, as Charles knows they often are, he
proved a surly North-Briton,[10] and broke my face for my
deficiency.

SIR GEORGE: Ha! Ha! And did not you draw?

MARPLOT: Draw, sir! Why I did but lay my hand upon my
sword, to make a swift retreat, and he roared out, 'Now the
de'il a ma sol, sir, gin ye touch yer steel, I'se whip mine through
yer wem.'

SIR GEORGE: Ha, ha, ha!

CHARLES: Ha, ha, ha! Safe was the word, so you walked off, I
suppose.

---

[3]*Jacks*: Jacobites   [4]*high-flyers*: high churchmen
[5]*low-flyers*: low churchmen   [6]*Levellers*: Agrarian reformers
[7]*Spain or Portugal*: the war of Spanish succession was taking place when the
play was written   [8]*Groom-Porter*: a gaming club
[9]*milk-sop*: an effeminate fellow   [10]*North-Briton*: Scot

MARPLOT: Yes: for I avoid fighting, purely to be serviceable to my friends, you know –

SIR GEORGE: Your friends are much obliged to you, sir; I hope you'll rank me in that number.

MARPLOT: Sir George, a bow from the side-box, or to be seen in your chariot, binds me ever yours.

SIR GEORGE: Trifles; you may command 'em when you please.

CHARLES: Provided he may command you –

MARPLOT: Me! why I live for no other purpose – Sir George, I have the honour to be caressed by most of the reigning toasts of the town; I'll tell them you are the finest gentleman –

SIR GEORGE: No, no prithee let me alone to tell the ladies – my parts – can you convey a letter upon occasion or deliver a message with an air of business, ha?

MARPLOT: With the assurance of a page, and the gravity of a statesman.

SIR GEORGE: You know Miranda!

MARPLOT: What, my sister ward? Why her guardian is mine, we are fellow sufferers. Ah! He is a covetous, cheating, fancifiewd curmudgeon; that Sir Francis Gripe is a damned old –

CHARLES: I suppose, friend, you forget that he is my father –

MARPLOT: I ask your pardon, Charles; but it is for your sake I hate him. Well, I say, the world is mistaken in him, his outside piety makes him every man's executioner; and his inside cunning makes him every heir's jailor. Egad, Charles, I'm half-persuaded that thou'rt some ward too, and never of his getting; for thou art as honest a debauchee as ever cuckolded man of quality.

SIR GEORGE: A pleasant fellow.

CHARLES: The dog is diverting sometimes, or there would be no enduring his impertinence. He is pressing to be employed and willing to execute, but some ill-fate generally attends all he undertakes, and he oftener spoils an intrigue than helps it –

MARPLOT: If I miscarry, 'tis none of my fault, I follow my instructions.

CHARLES: Yes; witness the merchant's wife.

MARPLOT: Pish, pox, that was an accident.

SIR GEORGE: What was it, prithee?

CHARLES: Why you must know, I had lent a certain merchant my hunting horses, and was to have met his wife in his absence:

sending him along with my groom to make the compliment, and to deliver a letter to the lady at the same time; what does he do, but gives the husband the letter and offers her the horses.

MARPLOT: I remember you was even with me, for you denied the letter to be yours, and swore I had a design upon her which my bones paid for.

CHARLES: Come, Sir George, let's walk round, if you are not engaged; for I have sent my man upon a little earnest business, and I have ordered him to bring me the answer into the Park.

MARPLOT: Business, and I do not know it! Egad, I'll watch him.

SIR GEORGE: I must beg your pardon, Charles, I am to meet your father.

CHARLES: My father!

SIR GEORGE: Aye, and about the oddest bargain perhaps you ever heard of; but I'll not impart till I know the success.

MARPLOT: [aside] What can his business be with Sir Francis? Now would I give all the world to know it? Why the devil should not one know every man's concern!

CHARLES: Prosperity to't whate'er it be. I have private affairs too; over a bottle we'll compare notes.

MARPLOT: [aside] Charles knows I love a glass as well as any man, I'll make one: shall it be tonight? And I long to know their secrets.

   Enter WHISPER

WHISPER: [to CHARLES] Sir, sir, Mrs Patch says Isabinda's Spanish father has quite spoiled the plot, and she can't meet you in the Park, but he infallibly will go out this afternoon, she says; but I must step again to know the hour.

MARPLOT: [aside] What did Whisper say now? I shall go stark mad, if I'm not let into the secret.

CHARLES: Cursed misfortune! Come along with me, my heart feels pleasure at her name. Sir George, yours; we'll meet at the old place the usual hour.

SIR GEORGE: Agreed. I think I see Sir Francis yonder.   [*Exit*]

CHARLES: Marplot, you must excuse me, I am engaged.   [*Exit*]

MARPLOT: Engaged! Egad I'll engage my life I'll know what your engagement is.   [*Exit*]

   Enter MIRANDA, *coming from a chair*

MIRANDA: Let the chair wait: my servant that dodged Sir George said he was in the Park.

Enter PATCH

MIRANDA: Ha! Miss Patch alone! Did not you tell me you had contrived a way to bring Isabinda to the Park?

PATCH: Oh, madam, your ladyship can't imagine what a wretched disappointment we have met with: just as I had fetched a suit of my clothes for a disguise, comes my old master into his closet, which is right against her chamber-door; this struck us into a terrible fright. – At length I put on a grave face, and asked him if he was at leisure for his chocolate, in hopes to draw him out of his hole; but he snapped my nose off, 'No I shall be busy here these two hours.' At which my poor mistress, seeing no way of escape, ordered me to wait on your ladyship with the sad relation.

MIRANDA: Unhappy Isabanda! Was ever anything so unaccountable as the humour of Sir Jealous Traffic?

PATCH: Oh, madam, it's his living so long in Spain; he vows he'll spend half his estate, but he'll be a Parliament-man, on purpose to bring in a Bill for women to wear veils, and the other odious Spanish customs – he swears it is the height of impudence to have a woman seen bare-faced, even at church, and scarce believes there's a true-begotten child in the City.

MIRANDA: Ha, ha, ha! How the old fool torments himself! Suppose he could introduce his rigid rules – does he think we could not match them in contrivance? No, no, let the tyrant man make what laws he will, if there's a woman under the government, I warrant she finds a way to break 'em. Is his mind set upon the Spaniard for his son-in-law still?

PATCH: Aye, and he expects him by the next fleet, which drives his daughter to melancholy and despair; but, madam, I find you retain the same gay, cheerful spirit you had, when I waited in your ladyship. – My lady is mighty good-humoured too; and I have found a way to make Sir Jealous believe I am wholly in his interest, when my real design is to serve her: he makes me her jailor, and I set her at liberty.

MIRANDA: I knew thy prolific brain would be of singular service to her, or I had not parted with thee to her father.

PATCH: But, madam, the report is, that you are going to marry your guardian.

MIRANDA: It is necessary such a report should be, Patch.

PATCH: But is it true madam?

MIRANDA: That's not absolutely necessary.

PATCH: I thought it was only the old strain, coaxing him still for your own, and railing at all the young fellows-about-town. In my mind, now, you are as ill-plagued with your guardian, madam, as my lady is with her father.

MIRANDA: No, I have liberty, wench; that she wants. What would she give now to be in this déshabillé[11] in the open air; nay more, in pursuit of the young fellow she likes; for that's my case, I assure you.

PATCH: As for that, madam, she's even with you; for though she can't come abroad, we have a way to bring him home in spite of old Argus.[12]

MIRANDA: Now, Patch, your opinion of my choice, for here he comes. -- Ha! My guardian with him: what can be the meaning of this? I'm sure Sir Francis can't know me in this dress – let's observe them.   [*they withdraw*]

     Enter SIR FRANCIS GRIPE *and* SIR GEORGE AIRY

SIR FRANCIS: Verily, Sir George, thou wilt repent throwing away thy money so; for I tell thee sincerely, Miranda, my charge, does not love a young fellow; they are all vicious, and seldom make good husbands; in sober sadness she cannot abide them.

MIRANDA: [*peeping*] In sober sadness you are mistaken – what can this mean?

SIR GEORGE: Look ye, Sir Francis, whether she can or cannot abide young fellows, is not the business: will you take the fifty guineas?

SIR FRANCIS: In good truth – I will not; for I knew thy father: he was a hearty wary man, and I cannot consent that his son should squander away what he saved to no purpose.

MIRANDA: [*peeping*] Now, in the name of wonder, what bargain can he be driving about me for fifty guineas?

PATCH: I wish it ben't for the first night's lodging, madam.

---

[11]*déshabillé*: state of undress   [12]*Argus*: god with many eyes

SIR GEORGE: Well, Sir Francis, since you are so conscientious for my father's sake, then permit me the favour gratis.

MIRANDA: [*peeping*] The favour! O' my life, I believe 'tis as you said, Patch.

SIR FRANCIS: No, verily, if thou dost not buy thy experience, thou wilt never be wise; therefore give me a hundred, and try Fortune.

SIR GEORGE: The scruples arose, I find from the scanty sum – let me see – a hundred guineas – [*takes them out of purse and chinks them*] – Ha! They have a very pretty sound, and a very pleasing look – but then, Miranda – but if she should be cruel –

MIRANDA: [*peeping*] As ten to one I shall –

SIR FRANCIS: Aye, do consider on't, he he, he, he.

SIR GEORGE: No, I'll do't.

PATCH: Do't! What, whether you will or no, madam!

SIR GEORGE: Come to the point, here's the gold, sum up the condition –

   [SIR FRANCIS *pulling out a paper*]

MIRANDA: [*peeping*] Aye, for heaven's sake do, for my expectation is on the rack.

SIR FRANCIS: Well, at your peril be it.

SIR GEORGE: Aye, aye, go on.

SIR FRANCIS: Imprimis,[13] you are to be admitted into my house, in order to move your suit to Miranda, for the space of ten minutes, without let or molestation, provided I remain in the same room.

SIR GEORGE: But out of earshot.

SIR FRANCIS: Well, well; I don't desire to hear what you say; ha, ha, ha; in consideration I am to have that purse and a hundred guineas.

SIR GEORGE: Take it –   [*gives him the purse*]

MIRANDA: [*peeping*] So, 'tis well 'tis no worse; I'll fit you both –

SIR GEORGE: And this agreement is to be performed today.

SIR FRANCIS: Aye, aye, the sooner the better. Poor fool, how Miranda and I shall laugh at him. – Well, Sir George, ha, ha, ha! Take the last sound of your guineas – [*chinks them*] ha, ha, ha!

                                                              [*Exit*]

---

[13] *Imprimis*: in the first place

MIRANDA: [*peeping*] Sure he does not know I am Miranda.

SIR GEORGE: A very extraordinary bargain I have made truly, if she should be really in love with this old cuff[14] now – pshaw, that's morally impossible – but then what hopes have I to succeed, I never spoke to her –

MIRANDA: [*peeping*] Say you so? Then I am safe.

SIR GEORGE: What though my tongue never spoke, my eyes said a thousand things, and my hopes flattered me her's answered 'em. If I'm lucky – if not, it is but a hundred guineas thrown away.

[MIRANDA *and* PATCH *come forward*.]

MIRANDA: Upon what, Sir George?

SIR GEORGE: Ha! My incognita[15] – upon a woman, madam.

MIRANDA: They are the worst things you can deal in, and damage the soonest; your very breath destroys 'em, and I fear you'll never see your return, Sir George, ha, ha.

SIR GEORGE: Were they more brittle than china, and dropped to pieces with a touch, every atom of her I have ventured at, if she is but mistress of my wit, balances ten times the sum – prithee let me see thy face.

MIRANDA: By no means; that may spoil your opinion of my sense –

SIR GEORGE: Rather confirm it, madam.

PATCH: So rob the lady of your gallantry, sir.

SIR GEORGE: No, child, a dish of chocolate in the morning never spoils my dinner; the other lady I design a set-meal; so there's no danger. –

MIRANDA: Matrimony! Ha, ha, ha! What crimes have you committed against the god of love that he should revenge 'em so severely to stamp husband upon your forehead?

SIR GEORGE: For my folly, in having so often met you here, without pursuing the laws of nature, and exercising her command – but I resolve, ere we part now, to know who you are, – where you live, and what kind of flesh and blood your face is. Therefore unmask, and don't put me to the trouble of doing it for you.

MIRANDA: My face is the same flesh and blood with my hand, Sir George, which if you'll be so rude to provoke –

[14]*cuff*: a miserly old fellow   [15]*incognita*: unknown woman

SIR GEORGE: You'll apply it to my cheek – the ladies' favours are always welcome; but I must have that cloud withdrawn. [*taking hold of her*] Remember you are in the Park, child, and what a terrible thing would it be to lose this pretty white hand?

MIRANDA: And how will it sound in the chocolate-house that Sir George Airy rudely pulled off a lady's mask, when he had given her his honour that he never would directly or indirectly endeavour to know her till she gave him leave?

PATCH: I wish we were safe out.

SIR GEORGE: But if that lady thinks fit to pursue and meet me at every turn, like some troubled spirit, shall I be blamed if I enquire into the reality? I would have nothing dissatisfied in a female shape.

MIRANDA: [*pauses*] What shall I do?

SIR GEORGE: Aye, prithee consider, for thou shalt find me very much at thy service.

PATCH: Suppose, sir, the lady should be in love with you.

SIR GEORGE: Oh! I'll return the obligation in a moment.

PATCH: And marry her?

SIR GEORGE: Ha, ha, ha! That's not the way to love her, child.

MIRANDA: If he discovers me, I shall die – which way shall I escape? – let me see. [*pauses*]

SIR GEORGE: Well, madam –

MIRANDA: I have it – Sir George, 'tis fit you should allow something; if you'll excuse my face, and turn your back (if you look upon me, I shall sink, even masked as I am) I will confess why I have engaged you so often, who I am, and where I live.

SIR GEORGE: Well, to show you I'm a man of honour, I accept the conditions. Let me but once know those, and the face won't be long a secret to me.

PATCH: What mean you, madam?

MIRANDA: To get off.

SIR GEORGE: 'Tis something indecent to turn one's back upon a lady; but you command, and I obey. [*turns his back*] Come, madam, begin –

MIRANDA: [*draws back a little while and speaks*] First then it was my unhappy lot to see you at Paris, at a ball upon a Birthday; your shape and air charmed my eyes; your wit and complaisance my soul; and from that fatal night I loved you. [*drawing back*]

> And when you left the place, grief seized me so,
> No rest my heart, no sleep my eyes could know,
> Last I resolved a hazardous point to try,
> And quit the place in search of liberty.   [*Exit*]

SIR GEORGE: Excellent – I hope she's handsome – Well, now, madam, to the other two things: your name, and where you live? – I am a gentleman, and this confession will not be lost upon me. – Nay, prithee don't weep, but go on – for I find my heart melts in thy behalf. – Speak quickly, or I shall turn about. – Not yet – Poor lady, she expects I should comfort her! And to do her justice, she has said enough to encourage me.

[*turns about*]

Ha! Gone! The devil. Jilted! Why what a tale has she invented of Paris, balls and birthdays. – Egad, I'd give ten guineas to know who the gipsy is – a curse on my folly – I deserve to lose her: What woman can forgive a man that turns his back!

> The bold and resolute in love and war,
> To conquer take the right and swiftest way:
> The boldest lover soonest gains the fair,
> As courage makes the rudest force obey.
> Take no denial, and the dames adore ye,
> Closely pursue them, and they fall before you.   [*Exit*]

Act Two

SCENE ONE

Sir Francis Gripe's House

Enter SIR FRANCIS GRIPE *and* MIRANDA

SIR FRANCIS: Ha, ha, ha, ha, ha!

MIRANDA: Ha, ha, ha, ha, ha, ha, ha! Oh I shall die with laughing. – The most romantic adventure. Ha, ha! What does the odious young fop mean? A hundred pieces to talk an hour with me! Ha, ha!

SIR FRANCIS: And I am to be by too; there's the jest: adod, if it had been in private, I should not have cared to trust the young dog.

MIRANDA: Indeed and indeed, but you might, guardie. – Now methinks there's nobody handsomer than you: so neat, so clean, so good-humoured and so loving –

SIR FRANCIS: Pretty rogue, pretty rogue; and so thou shalt find me, if thou dost prefer thy guardie before these caperers of the age; thou shalt outshine the Queen's box on an Opera night; thou shalt be the envy of the Ring (for I will carry thee to Hyde Park) and thy equipage shall surpass the – what d'ye call 'em – Ambassadors.

MIRANDA: Nay I am sure the discreet part of my sex will envy me more for the inside furniture, when you are in it, than my outside equipage.

SIR FRANCIS: A cunning baggage, i'faith thou art, and a wise one too: and to show thee thou hast not chose amiss, I'll this moment disinherit my son, and settle my whole estate upon thee.

MIRANDA: [*aside*] There's an old rogue now. – No guardie, I would not have your name be so black in the world. – You know my father's will runs, that I am not to possess my estate without your consent, till I'm five-and-twenty; you shall only abate the odd seven years, and make me mistress of my estate today, and I'll make you master of my person tomorrow.

SIR FRANCIS: Humph! That may not be safe. – No chargie, I'll settle it upon thee for pin-money; and that will be every bit as well, thou know'st.

MIRANDA: [*aside*] Unconscionable old wretch, bribe me with my own money – which way shall I get it out of his hands!

SIR FRANCIS: Well, what are thou thinking on, my girl, ha? How to banter Sir George?

MIRANDA: [*aside*] I must not pretend to banter; he knows my tongue too well. – No guardie, I have thought of a way will confound him more than all I could say if I should talk to him seven years.

SIR FRANCIS: How's that! Oh! I'm transported, I'm ravished, I'm mad –

MIRANDA: [*aside*] It would make you mad if you knew all. – I'll not answer him a word, but be dumb to all he says –

SIR FRANCIS: Dumb! Good. Ha, ha, ha! Excellent, ha, ha, ha! I think I have you now, Sir George. Dumb! He'll go distracted! – Well, she's the wittiest rogue. – Ha, ha? Dumb! I can but laugh, ha, ha! To think how damned mad he'll be when he finds he has given his money away for a dumb-show. Ha, ha, ha!

MIRANDA: Nay guardie, if he did but know my thoughts of him, it would make him ten times madder: ha, ha, ha!

SIR FRANCIS: Aye, so it would, chargie, to hold him in such derision, to scorn to answer him, to be dumb! Ha, ha, ha!

    Enter CHARLES

SIR FRANCIS: How now sirrah! Who let you in?

CHARLES: My necessity, sir.

SIR FRANCIS: Sir, your necessities are very impertinent, and ought to have sent before they entered.

CHARLES: Sir, I knew 'twas a word would gain admittance nowhere.

SIR FRANCIS: Then sirrah, how dursrt you rudely thrust that upon your father, which nobody else would admit?

CHARLES: Sure the name of a son is a sufficient plea. I ask this lady's pardon if I have intruded.

SIR FRANCIS: Aye, aye, ask her pardon and her blessing too, if you expect anything from me.

MIRANDA: I believe yours, Sir Francis, is a purse of guineas, would be more material. Your son may have business with you, I'll retire.

SIR FRANCIS: I guess his business, but I'll dispatch him; I expect the knight every minute: you'll be in readiness?

MIRANDA: Certainly! My expectation is more upon the wing than yours, old gentleman. [*Exit*]

SIR FRANCIS: Well, sir!

CHARLES: Nay, it is very ill, sir; my circumstances are, I'm sure.

SIR FRANCIS: And what's that to me, sir; your management should have made them better.

CHARLES: If you please to entrust me with the management of my estate, I shall endeavour it, sir.

SIR FRANCIS: What, to set upon a card, and buy a lady's favour at the price of a thousand pieces, to rig out an equipage for a wench, or by your carelessness enrich your steward to sign for sheriff, or put up for parliament-man?

CHARLES: I hope, I should not spend it this way. However, I ask only for what my uncle left me; yours you may dispose of as you please, sir.

SIR FRANCIS: That I shall, out of your reach, I assure you, sir. Adod these young fellows think old men get estates for nothing but them to squander away, in dicing, wenching, drinking, dressing, and so forth.

CHARLES: I think I was born a gentleman sir! I'm sure my uncle bred me like one.

SIR FRANCIS: From which you would infer, sir, that gaming, whoring, and the pox, are requisites to a gentleman.

CHARLES: [*aside*] Monstrous! When I would ask him only for a support, he falls into these unmannerly reproaches; I must, though against my will, employ invention, and by stratagem relieve myself.

SIR FRANCIS: Sirrah, what is it you mutter sirrah, ha? [*holds up his cane*] I say you shan't have a groat out of my hands till I please – and maybe I'll never please, and what's that to you?

CHARLES: Nay, to be robbed or to have one's throat cut, is not much –

SIR FRANCIS: What's that sirrah? Would ye rob me, or cut my throat, ye rogue?

CHARLES: Heaven forbid, sir, – I said no such thing.

SIR FRANCIS: Mercy on me! What a plague it is to have a son of one-and-twenty, who wants to elbow one out of one's life to edge himself into the estate!

Enter MARPLOT

MARPLOT: Egad, he's here – I was afraid I had lost him: his secret could not be with his father, his wants are public there – guardian – your servant Charles, I know by that sorrowful countenance of thine, the old man's fist is as close as his strong-box – but I'll help thee –

SIR FRANCIS: So: here's another extravagant coxcomb, that will spend his fortune before he comes to't; but he shall pay swinging interest, and so let the fool go on – Well, what! Does necessity bring you too sir?

MARPLOT: You have hit it, guardian – I want a hundred pounds.

SIR FRANCIS: For what?

MARPLOT: Pugh, for a hundred things: I can't for my life tell you for what.

CHARLES: Sir, I suppose I have received all the answer I am like to have.

MARPLOT: Oh, the devil, if he gets out before me, I shall lose him again.

SIR FRANCIS: Aye, sir, and you may be marching as soon as you please. – I must see a change in your temper ere you find one in mine.

MARPLOT: Pray, sir, dispatch me. The money, sir, I'm in mighty haste.

SIR FRANCIS: Fool, take this and go to the cashier; I shan't be long plagued with thee.   [*gives him a note*]

MARPLOT: Devil take the cashier, I shall certainly have Charles gone out before I come back again.   [*Exit*]

CHARLES: Well, sir, I take my leave – but remember, you expose an only son to all the miseries of wretched poverty, which too often lays the plan for scenes of mischief.

SIR FRANCIS: Stay, Charles, I have a sudden thought come into my head, may prove to thy advantage.

CHARLES: Ha, does he relent?

SIR FRANCIS: My lady Wrinkle, worth forty thousand pounds,

sets up for a handsome young husband; she praised thee t'other day; though the match-makers can get twenty guineas for a sight of her, I can introduce thee for nothing.

CHARLES: My lady Wrinkle, sir! Why she has but one eye.

SIR FRANCIS: Then she'll see but half your extravagance, sir.

CHARLES: Condemn me to such a piece of deformity! Toothless, dirty, wry-necked, hunch-backed hag.

SIR FRANCIS: Hunch-backed! So much the better, then she has a rest for her misfortunes; for thou wilt load her swingingly. Now I warrant you think, this is no offer of a father; forty thousand pounds is nothing with you.

CHARLES: Yes, sir, I think it too much; a young beautiful woman with half the money would be more agreeable. I thank you, sir; but you chose better for yourself, I find.

SIR FRANCIS: Out of my doors, you dog; you pretend to meddle with my marriage, sirrah!

CHARLES: Sir, I obey –

SIR FRANCIS: But me no buts – be gone, sir: dare to ask me for money again – refuse forty thousand pounds! Out of my doors, I say, without reply. [*Exit* CHARLES]

    Enter SERVANT

SERVANT: One Sir George Airy enquires for you, sir.

    Enter MARPLOT *running*

MARPLOT: Ha! Gone! Is Charles gone, guardian?

SIR FRANCIS: Yes, and I desire your wise worship to walk after him.

MARPLOT: Nay, egad, I shall run, I tell you but that. Ah! Pox of this cashier for detaining me so long; where the devil shall I find him now? I shall certainly lose this secret. [*Exit hastily*]

SIR FRANCIS: What, is the fellow distracted? – Desire Sir George to walk up – now for a trial of skill that will make me happy, and him a fool; Ha, ha, ha! In my mind he looks like an ass already.

    Enter SIR GEORGE

SIR FRANCIS: Well, Sir George, do ye hold in the same mind, or would you capitulate? Ha, ha, ha! look, here are the guineas. [*chinks them*] Ha, ha, ha!

SIR GEORGE: Not if they were twice the sum, Sir Francis: therefore be brief, call in the lady, and take your post – [*aside*] if she's a woman, and not seduced by witchcraft to this old rogue,

I'll make his heart ache; for if she has but one grain of inclination about her, I'll vary a thousand shapes but find it.

    Enter MIRANDA

SIR FRANCIS: Agreed – Miranda, there's Sir George, try your fortune.   [*takes out his watch*]

SIR GEORGE:
    So from the eastern chambers breaks the sun,
      Dispels the clouds, and gilds the vales below. [*salutes her*]

SIR FRANCIS: Hold sir, kissing was not in our agreement.

SIR GEORGE: Oh! That's by way of prologue: – prithee, old mammon,[16] to thy post.

SIR FRANCIS: Well, young Timon,[17] 'tis now four exactly; one hour, remember, is your utmost limit, not a minute more.

                        [*retires to the rear of the stage*]

SIR GEORGE: Madam, whether you'll excuse or blame my love, the author of this rash proceeding depends upon your pleasure, as also the life of your admirer! Your sparkling eyes speak a heart susceptible of love; your vivacity a soul too delicate to admit the embraces of decayed mortality.

MIRANDA: [*aside*] Oh! that I durst speak –

SIR GEORGE: Shake off this tyrant guardian's yoke, assume yourself, and dash his bold aspiring hopes; the deity of his desires, avarice; a heretic in love, and ought to be banished by the Queen of Beauty. See, madam, a faithful servant kneels and begs to be admitted in the number of your slaves.

    [MIRANDA *gives him her hand to raise him*]

SIR FRANCIS: I wish I could hear what he says now. [*running up*] Hold, hold, hold, no palming, that's contrary to articles –

SIR GEORGE: 'Sdeath, sir keep your distance, or I'll write another article in your guts.   [*lays his hand to his sword*]

SIR FRANCIS: [*going back*] A bloody minded fellow! –

SIR GEORGE: Not answer me! Perhaps she thinks my address too grave: I'll be more free – can you be so unconscionable, madam, to let me say all these fine things to you without one single compliment in return? View me well, am I not a proper handsome, fellow, ha? Can you prefer that old, dry withered sapless log of sixty-five, to the vigorous, gay, sprightly love of twenty-four? With snoring only he'll awake thee, but I with

---

[16] *mammon*: seeker of riches   [17] *Timon*: misanthrope

ravishing delight would make thy senses dance in consort with the joyful minutes. – Ha! Not yet? Sure she is dumb? – Thus wou'd I steal and touch thy beauteous hand, [*takes hold of her hand*] till by degrees, I reached thy snowy breasts, then ravish kisses thus. [*embraces her in the ecstacy*]

MIRANDA: [*struggles and flings from him*] [*aside*] Oh heavens! I shall not be able to contain myself.

SIR FRANCIS: [*running up with his watch in his hand*] Sure she did not speak to him – there's three-quarters of an hour gone, Sir George – adod, I don't like those close conferences –

SIR GEORGE: More interruptions – you will have it, sir.
[*lays his hand to his sword*]

SIR FRANCIS: [*aside, going back*] No, no, you shant have her neither.

SIR GEORGE: Dumb still – sure this old dog has enjoined her silence. I'll try another way. I must conclude, madam, that in compliance to your guardian's humour, you refuse to answer me. – Consider the injustice of his injunction. This single hour cost me an hundred pounds – and would you answer me, I could purchase the twenty-four so. However madam, you must give me leave to make the best interpretation I can for my money, and take the indication of your silence for the secret liking of my person; therefore, madam, I will instruct you how to keep your word inviolate to Sir Francis, and yet answer me to every question; as for example when I ask anything to which you would reply in the affirmative, gently nod your head: thus; and when in the negative: thus; [*shakes his head*] and in the doubtful: a tender sigh, thus. [*sighs*]

MIRANDA: [*aside*] How every action charms me – but I'll fit him for signs, I warrant him.

SIR FRANCIS: [*aside*] Ha, ha, ha, ha! Poor Sir George, Ha, ha, ha, ha!

SIR GEORGE: Was it by his desire that you are dumb, madam, to all that I can say?

MIRANDA: [*nods*]

SIR GEORGE: Very well! she's tractable, I find – and is it possible that you can love him!

MIRANDA: [*nods*]

SIR GEORGE: Miraculous! Pardon the bluntness of my questions, for my time is short; may I not hope to supplant him in you esteem?

MIRANDA: [*sighs*]

SIR GEORGE: Good, she answers me as I could wish. – You'll not consent to marry him then?

MIRANDA: [*sighs*]

SIR GEORGE: How! Doubtful in that – undone again – humph! But that may proceed from his power to keep her out of her estate 'till twenty-five; I'll try that – come madam, I cannot think you hesitate on this affair out of any motive but your fortune. Let him keep it 'till those few years are expired; make me happy with your person, let him enjoy your wealth –

MIRANDA: [*holds up her hands*]

SIR GEORGE: Why, what sign is that now? Nay, nay madam, except you observe my lesson, I can't understand your meaning –

SIR FRANCIS: What a vengeance are they talking by signs? 'Ad I may be fooled here; what do you mean, Sir George?

SIR GEORGE: To cut your throat, if you dare mutter another syllable.

SIR FRANCIS: Od! I wish he were fairly out of my house.

SIR GEORGE: Pray madam, will you answer me to the purpose?

MIRANDA: [*shakes her head and points to* SIR FRANCIS]

SIR GEORGE: What! Does she mean she won't answer me to the purpose, or is she afraid yon' old cuff should understand her signs? – Aye, it must be that; I perceive, madam, you are too apprehensive of the promise you have made to follow my rules; therefore I'll suppose your mind, and answer for you. – First, for myself, madam, that I am in love with you is an infallible truth. Now for you. [*turns to her side*] Indeed, Sir, and may I believe it? – [*in his own person, on one knee*] – as certainly, madam, as that 'tis daylight, or that I die if you persist in silence. – Bless me with the music of your voice, and raise my spirits to their proper heaven; thus low let me entreat; ere I'm obliged to quit this place, grant me some token of a favourable reception to keep my hopes alive. – [*arises hastily, turns to her side*] – Rise, sir, and since my guardian's presence will not allow me privilege of tongue, read that, and rest assured you are not indifferent to me. – [*offers her a letter*] Ha!

MIRANDA: [*strikes it down*]

SIR GEORGE: Ha! Right woman! But no matter, I'll go on.

SIR FRANCIS: Ha! What's that, a letter? – Ha, ha, ha! Thou art baulked.

MIRANDA: [*aside*] The best assurance I ever saw –

SIR GEORGE: Ha! A letter! Oh! Let me kiss it with the same raptures that I would do the dear hand that touched it. [*opens it*] Now for a quick fancy, and a long extempore – what's here? [*reads*] '*Dear Sir George, this virgin muse I consecrate to you, which when it has received the addition of your voice, 'twill charm me into a desire of liberty to love, which you, and only you can fix,*'

My angel! Oh you transport me! [*kisses the letter*] And see the power of your command; the god of love has set the verse already; the flowing numbers dance into a tune; and I'm inspired with a voice to sing it.

MIRANDA: [*aside*] I'm sure thou art inspired with impudence enough.

SIR GEORGE: [*sings*]

               Great love inspire him;
               Say I admire him.
               Give me the lover
               That can discover
               Secret devotion
               From silent motion;
               Then don't betray me,
               But hence convey me.

                      [*taking hold of* MIRANDA]

               With all my heart,
               This moment let's retire.

SIR FRANCIS: [*coming up hastily*] The hour is expired, sir, and you must take your leave. There my girl, there's the hundred pounds, which thou hast won; go, I'll be with you presently, Ha, ha, ha, ha!   [*Exit* MIRANDA]

SIR GEORGE: Ads-heart, madam, you won't leave me just in the nick, will you?

SIR FRANCIS: Ha, ha, ha! She has nicked you, Sir George, I think, ha, ha, ha! Have ye any more hundred pounds to throw away upon such courtship? Ha, ha, ha!

SIR GEORGE: He, he, he, he, a curse on your fleering jests – yes, however ill I succeeded, I'll venture the same wager, she does not value thee a spoonful of snuff. – Nay more, though you enjoined her silence to me, you'll never make her speak to the purpose with yourself.

SIR FRANCIS: Ha, ha, ha! Did not I tell thee thou wouldst repent thy money? Did not I say, she hated young fellows? Ha, ha, ha!

SIR GEORGE: And I'm positive she's not in love with Age.

SIR FRANCIS: Ha, ha! no matter for that, ha, ha! She's not taken with your youth, nor your rhetoric to boot, ha, ha!

SIR GEORGE: Whate'er her reasons are for disliking of me, I am certain she can be taken with nothing about thee.

SIR FRANCIS: Ha, ha, ha! How he swells with envy – poor man, poor man. – Ha, ha! I must beg your pardon, Sir George; Miranda will be impatient to have her share of mirth: verily we shall laugh at thee most egregiously;[18] ha, ha, ha!

SIR GEORGE: With all my heart, faith, – I shall laugh in my turn too. – For if you dare marry her, old Beelzebub, you will be cuckolded most egregiously: remember that and tremble –

> She that to age her beauteous self resigns,
> Shows witty management for close designs.
> Then if thou'rt graced with fair Miranda's bed,
> Actæon's[19] horns she means shall crown thy head.   [*Exit*]

SIR FRANCIS:

> Ha, ha, ha! he is mad.
> These fluttering fops imagine they can wind,
> Turn and decoy to love all womankind:
> But here's a proof of wisdom in my charge,
> Old men are constant, young men live at large;
> The frugal hand can bills at sight defray,
> When he that lavish is, has nought to pay.   [*Exit*]

---

[18]*egregiously*: outrageously   [19]*Actæon's horns*: cuckold's horns

SCENE TWO

Sir Jealous Traffick's house.

Enter SIR JEALOUS *and* ISABINDA *with* PATCH *following*

SIR JEALOUS: What, in the balcony again, notwithstanding my positive commands to the contrary! – Why don't you write a bill on your forehead, to show passengers there's something to be let –

ISABINDA: What harm can there be in a little fresh air, sir?

SIR JEALOUS: Is your constitution so hot, mistress, that it wants cooling, ha? Apply the virtuous Spanish rules, banish your taste, and thoughts of flesh, feed upon roots, and quench your thirst with water.

ISABINDA: That and a close room would certainly make me die of the vapours.

SIR JEALOUS: No, mistress, 'tis your high-fed, lusty, rambling, rampant ladies – that are troubled with the vapours: 'tis your ratafia,²⁰ persico,²¹ cinnamon, citron, and spirit of clary,²² cause such swi-mm-ing in the brain, that carries many a guinea²³ full tide to the doctor. But you are not to be bred this way; no galloping abroad, no receiving visits at home; for in our loose country, the women are as dangerous as the men.

PATCH: So I told her, sir; and that it was not decent to be seen in a balcony – but she threatened to slap my chaps,²⁴ and told me, I was her servant, not her governess.

SIR JEALOUS: Did she so? But I'll make her to know that you are her Duenna.²⁵ Oh! That incomparable custom of Spain! Why there's no depending upon old women in my country – for they are as wanton at eighty, as a girl of eighteen; and a man may as safely trust to Asgill's²⁶ translation as to his great grandmother's not marrying again.

ISABINDA: Or to the Spanish ladies' veils and duennas, for the safeguard of their honour.

---

²⁰*ratafia*: almond cordial   ²¹*persico*: peach cordial
²²*clary*: sage liqueur   ²³*guinea*: prostitute
²⁴*chaps*: cheeks   ²⁵*duenna*: a female chaperone
²⁶*Asgill's*: John Asgill in 1700 claimed that the rules of English law proved that the redeemed need not die.

SIR JEALOUS: Dare to ridicule the cautious conduct of that wise nation, and I'll have you locked up this fortnight without a peep-hole.

ISABINDA: If we had but the ghostly helps in England, which they have in Spain, I might deceive you if you did. – Sir, 'tis not the restraint, but the innate principles, secures the reputation and honour of our sex. – Let me tell you, sir, confinement sharpens the invention, as want of sight strengthens the other senses, and is often more pernicious than the recreation innocent liberty allows.

SIR JEALOUS: Say you so, mistress; who the devil taught you the art of reasoning? I assure you, they must have a greater faith than I pretend to, that can think any woman innocent who requires liberty. Therefore, Patch, to your charge I give her; lock her up 'till I come back from 'Change: I shall have some sauntering coxcomb, with nothing but a red coat and feather, think by leaping into her arms, to leap into my estate. – But I'll prevent them; she shall be only Babinetto's.

PATCH: Really, sir, I wish you would employ anybody else in this affair; I lead a life like a dog, with obeying your commands. Come, madam, will you please to be locked up?

ISABINDA: [aside] Aye, to enjoy more freedom that he is aware of. [Exit, with PATCH]

SIR JEALOUS: I believe this wench is very true to my interest; I am happy I met with her, if I can but keep my daughter from being blown upon till Signior Babinetto arrives; who shall marry her as soon as he comes, and carry her to Spain as soon as he has married her; she has a pregnant wit, and I'd no more have her an English wife than the grand signior's mistress. [Exit]

Enter WHISPER

WHISPER: So, I saw Sir Jealous go out; where shall I find Mrs Patch now?

Re-enter PATCH

PATCH: Oh, Mr Whisper! My lady saw you out at the window, and ordered me to bid you fly, and let your master know she's now alone.

WHISPER: Hush, speak softly; I go, I go: but hark ye, Mrs Patch, shall not you and I have a little confabulation, when my master and your lady are engaged?

PATCH: Aye, aye, farewell.   [*Exits, shutting the door*]
   Re-enter SIR JEALOUS TRAFFICK, *meeting* WHISPER

SIR JEALOUS: Sure whilst I was talking with Mr Tradewell, I
  heard my door clap. [*seeing* WHISPER] Ha! a man lurking
  about my house; who do you want there, sir?

WHISPER: Want – want, a pox! Sir Jealous! What must I say
  now?

SIR JEALOUS: Aye, want: have you a letter or message for
  anybody there? – O' my conscience this is some he-bawd –

WHISPER: Letter or message, sir?

SIR JEALOUS: Aye, letter or message, sir.

WHISPER: No, not I, sir.

SIR JEALOUS: Sirrah, sirrah, I'll have you set in the stocks, if
  you don't tell me your business immediately.

WHISPER: Nay, sir, my business – is not great matter of
  business neither; and yet 'tis business of consequence too.

SIR JEALOUS: Sirrah, don't trifle with me.

WHISPER: Trifle, sir! Have you found him, sir?

SIR JEALOUS: Found what, you rascal?

WHISPER: Why Trifle is the very lap-dog my lady lost, sir; I
  fancied I saw him run into this house. I'm glad you have him. –
  Sir, my lady will be overjoyed that I have found him.

SIR JEALOUS: Who is your lady, friend?

WHISPER: My Lady Lovepuppy, sir.

SIR JEALOUS: My Lady Lovepuppy! Then prithee carry thyself
  to her, for I know no other whelp that belongs to her; and let me
  catch you no more a-puppy-hunting about my doors, lest I have
  you pressed into the service, sirrah.

WHISPER: By no means, sir – your humble servant; I must
  watch whether he goes, or no, before I can tell my master.
                                 [*Exit*]

SIR JEALOUS: This fellow has the officious leer of a pimp; and I
  half suspect a design, but I'll be upon them before they think on
  me, I warrant 'em.   [*Exit*]

SCENE THREE

Charles's lodgings

Enter CHARLES *and* MARPLOT

CHARLES: Honest Marplot, I thank thee for this supply: I expect my lawyer with a thousand pounds I have ordered him to take up, and then you shall be repaid.

MARPLOT: Foh, foh, no more of that: here comes Sir George Airy. Cursedly out of humour at his disappointment: see how he looks! Ha, ha, ha!

Enter SIR GEORGE

SIR GEORGE: Ah, Charles, I am so humbled in my pretensions to plots upon women, that I believe I shall never have courage enough to attempt a chamber-maid – I'll tell thee.

CHARLES: Ha, ha! I'll spare you the relation, by telling you. – Impatient to know your business with my father, when I saw you enter I slipped back into the next room, where I overheard every syllable.

SIR GEORGE: That I said. – I'll be hanged if you heard her answer. – But prithee tell me, Charles, is she a fool?

CHARLES: I ne'er suspected her for one; but Marplot can inform you better, if you'll allow him a judge.

MARPLOT: A fool! I'll justify she has more wit than all the rest of her sex put together; why she'll rally me till I han't one word to say for myself.

CHARLES: A mighty proof of her wit truly –

MARPLOT: There must be some trick in't, Sir George; egad I'll find it out, if it cost me the sum you paid for't.

SIR GEORGE: Do, and command me –

MARPLOT: Enough, let me alone to trace a secret –

Enter WHISPER, *and speaks aside to his master.*

MARPLOT: The devil! Whisper here again! That fellow never speaks out. Is this the same, or a new secret? – Sir George, won't you ask Charles what news Whisper brings?

SIR GEORGE: Not I, sir; I suppose it does not relate to me.

MARPLOT: Lord, lord, how little curiosity some people have! Now my chief pleasure lies in knowing everybody's business.

SIR GEORGE: I fancy, Charles, thou hast some engagement

upon thy hands: I have a little business too. Marplot, if it fall in your way to bring me any intelligence from Miranda, you'll find me at the Thatched House at six —

MARPLOT: You do me much honour.

CHARLES: You guess right, Sir George, wish me success.

SIR GEORGE: Better than attended me. Adieu. [*Exit*]

CHARLES: Marplot, you must excuse me —

MARPLOT: Nay, nay, what need of any excuse amongst friends: I'll go with you.

CHARLES: Indeed you must not.

MARPLOT: No! Then I suppose 'tis a duel, and I will go to secure you.

CHARLES: Well, but it is no duel, consequently no danger: therefore prithee be answered.

MARPLOT: What, is't a mistress then? — Mum! — You know I can be silent upon occasion.

CHARLES: I wish you could be civil too: I tell you, you neither must nor shall go with me. Farewell. [*Exit*]

MARPLOT: Why then, — I must and will follow you. [*Exit*]

Act Three

SCENE ONE

Outside the house of Sir Jealous

Enter CHARLES

CHARLES: Well, here's the house which holds the lovely prize quiet and serene: here no noisy footmen throng to tell my world, that beauty dwells within; no ceremonious visit makes the lover wait; no rival to give my heart a pang: who would not scale the window at midnight without fear of the jealous father's pistol, rather than fill up the train of a coquette, where every minute he is jostled out of place? [*knocks softly*] Mrs Patch. Mrs Patch!

Enter PATCH

PATCH: Oh, are you come, sir? All's safe.

CHARLES: So, in, then. [*They exit*]

Enter MARPLOT

MARPLOT: There he goes: who the devil lives here? Except I can find out that, I am as far from knowing his business as ever; 'gad I'll watch, it may be a bawdy-house, and he may have his throat cut; if there should be any mischief, I can make oath he went in. Well Charles, in spite of your endeavour to keep me out of the secret, I may save your life for aught I know. At that corner I'll plant myself, there I shall see whoever goes in, or comes out. 'Gad, I love discoveries. [*Exit*]

SCENE TWO

Inside the house of Sir Jealous

Enter CHARLES, ISABINDA *and* PATCH

WHISPER: Patch, look out sharp; have a care of Dad.

PATCH: I warrant you.

ISABINDA: Well, sir, if I may judge your love by your courage, I ought to believe you sincere; for you venture into the lion's den, when you come to see me.

CHARLES: If you'd consent whilst the furious beast is abroad, I'd free you from the reach of his paws.

ISABINDA: That would be but to avoid one danger by running into another; like poor wretches who fly the burning ship, and meet their fate in the water. Come, come Charles, I fear if I consult my reason, confinement and plenty is better than liberty and starving. I know you'd make the frolic pleasing for a little time, by saying and doing a world of tender things; but when our small substance is exhausted, and a thousand requisites for life are wanting, love, who rarely dwells with poverty, would also fail us.

CHARLES: Faith, I fancy not; methinks my heart has laid up a stock will last for life; to back which, I have taken a thousand pounds upon my uncle's estate; that surely will support us till one of our fathers relent.

ISABINDA: There's no trusting to that, my friend; I doubt your father will carry his humour to the grave, and mine till he sees me settled in Spain.

CHARLES: And can ye then cruelly resolve to stay till that cursed Don arrives, and suffer that youth, beauty, fire, and wit to be sacrificed to the arms of a dull Spaniard, to be immured, and forbid the sight of anything that's human?

ISABINDA: No, when it comes to the extremity, and no stratagem can relieve us, thou shalt 'list for a soldier, and I'll carry thy knapsack after thee.

CHARLES: Bravely resolved; the world cannot be more savage than our parents, and Fortune generally assists the bold: therefore consent now. Why should we put it to a future hazard? Who knows when we shall have another opportunity?

ISABINDA: Oh, you have your ladder of ropes, I suppose, and the closet-window stands just where it did, and if you han't forgot to write in characters, Patch will find a way for our assignations. Thus much of the Spanish contrivance my father's severity has taught me, I thank him; though I hate the nation, I admire their management in these affairs.

Enter PATCH

PATCH: Oh, madam, I see my master coming up the street.

CHARLES: Oh, the devil, would I had my ladder now, I thought you had not expected him till night; why, why, why, why, what shall I do, madam?

ISABINDA: Oh! For Heaven's sake! don't go that way, you'll
meet him full in the teeth. Oh, unlucky moment! –

CHARLES: 'Adheart, can you shut me into no cupboard, ram me
into a chest, ha?

PATCH: Impossible, sir, he searches every hole in the house.

ISABINDA: Undone for ever! If he sees you, I shall never see you
more.

PATCH: I have thought on it: run to your chamber, madam;
and, sir, come you along with me, I'm certain you may easily get
down from the balcony.

CHARLES: My life, adieu – lead on guide.   [*Exit*]

ISABINDA: Heaven preserve him.   [*Exit*]

SCENE THREE

The street outside the house of Sir Jealous

Enter SIR JEALOUS, *with* MARPLOT *behind him.*

SIR JEALOUS: I don't know what's the matter, but I have a
strong suspicion all is not right within; that fellow's sauntering
about my door, and his tale of a puppy had the face of a lie
methought. By St Iägo, if I should find a man in the house, I'd
make mince-meat of him –

MARPLOT: Ah, poor Charles – Ha! Egad he is old – I fancy I
might bully him, and make Charles have an opinion of my
courage.

SIR JEALOUS: [*feeling for his key*] My own key shall let me in,
I'll give them no warning.

MARPLOT: [*going up to* SIR JEALOUS] What's that you say, sir?

SIR JEALOUS: [*turning quick upon him*] What's that to you, sir?

MARPLOT: Yes, 'tis to me, sir: for the gentleman you threaten is
a very honest gentleman. Look to't; for if he comes not as safe
out of your house as he went in, I have half a dozen
Myrmidons²⁷ hard by shall beat it about your ears.

SIR JEALOUS: Went in! What is he in then? Ah! a combination
to undo me – I'll Myrmidon you, ye dog you – thieves, thieves!
[*beats* MARPLOT *all the while he cries 'thieves'*]

MARPLOT: Murder, murder; I was not in your house, sir.

Enter SERVANT

²⁷*Myrmidons*: ruffians

SERVANT: What's the matter, sir?

SIR JEALOUS: The matter, rascal! Have you let a man into my house! But I'll flea him alive; follow me, I'll not leave a mouse-hole unsearched; if I find him, by St Iägo I'll equip him for the Opera.[28]

MARPLOT: A deuce of his cane, there's no trusting to age. – What shall I do to relieve Charles? Egad, I'll raise the neighbourhood – murder, murder –

[CHARLES *drops down upon him from the balcony*]

MARPLOT: Charles, faith I'm glad to see thee safe out with all my heart.

CHARLES: A pox of your bawling: how the devil came you here?

MARPLOT: Here! 'Gad, I have done you a piece of service; I told the old thunderbolt that the gentleman that was gone in, was –

CHARLES: Was it you that told him, sir? [*laying hold of him*] 'Sdeath, I could crush thee into atoms. [*Exit* CHARLES]

MARPLOT: What, will ye choke me for my kindness? – Will my enquiring soul never leave searching into other people's affairs till it gets squeezed out of my body? I dare not follow him now, for my blood, he's in such a passion – I'll to Miranda; if I can discover aught that may oblige Sir George, it may be a means to reconcile me again to Charles. [*Exit*]

Enter SIR JEALOUS *and* SERVANTS

SIR JEALOUS: Are you sure you have searched everywhere?

SERVANT: Yes, from the top of the house to the bottom.

SIR JEALOUS: Under the beds, and over the beds?

SERVANT: Yes, and in them too; but found nobody sir.

SIR JEALOUS: Why, what could this rogue mean?

Enter ISABINDA *and* PATCH

PATCH: [*aside to* ISABINDA] Take courage, madam, I saw him safe out.

ISABINDA: Bless me! what's the matter, sir?

SIR JEALOUS: You know best – pray where's the man that was here just now?

ISABINDA: What man, sir: I saw none!

PATCH: Nor I, by the trust you repose in me; do you think I would let a man come within these doors, when you are absent?

[28]castrate him

SIR JEALOUS: Ah, Patch, she may be too cunning for thy honesty: the very scout that he had set to give warning, discovered it to me – and threatened me with half a dozen Myrmidons. – But I think I mauled the villain. These afflictions you draw upon me, mistress!

ISABINDA: Pardon me, sir, 'tis your own ridiculous humour draws you into these vexations, and gives every fool pretence to banter you.

SIR JEALOUS: No, 'tis your idle conduct, your coquettish flirting into the balcony. – Oh with what joy shall I resign thee into the arms of Don Diego Babinetto!

ISABINDA: [*aside*] And with what industry shall I avoid him!

SIR JEALOUS: Certainly that rogue had a message from somebody or other; but being balked by my coming, popped that sham upon me. Come along ye sots, let's see if we can find the dog again. Patch, lock her up; d'ye hear?

PATCH: Yes, sir. – Aye, walk till your heels ache, you'll find nobody, I'll promise you.

ISABINDA: Who could that scout be which he talks of?

PATCH: Nay, I can't imagine, without it was Whisper.

ISABINDA: Well, dear Patch, let's employ all our thoughts how to escape this horrid Don Diego, my very heart sinks at his terrible name.

PATCH: Fear not, madam, Don Carlo shall be the man, or I'll lose the reputation of contrivine;²⁹ and then what's a chambermaid good for?

ISABINDA:
Say'st thou so, my girl? Then –
Let Dad be jealous, multiply his cares.
While love instructs me to avoid the snares;
I'll, spite of all his Spanish caution, show
How much for love a British maid can do.   [*Exit*]

SCENE FOUR

Sir Francis Gripe's house

Enter SIR FRANCIS *and* MIRANDA, *meeting*

MIRANDA: Well guardie, how did I perform the dumb scene?

²⁹*contrivine*: schemer

SIR FRANCIS: To admiration – thou dear little rogue, let me buss thee for it; nay, adod I will, chargie, so muzzle, and tuzzle, and hug thee, I will, i'faith, I will.

[hugging and kissing her]

MIRANDA: Nay guardie, don't be so lavish; who would ride post, when the journey lasts for life?

SIR FRANCIS: Ah wag, ah wag – I'll buss thee again, for that.

MIRANDA: *[aside]* Faugh! How he stinks of tobacco! What a delicate bedfellow I should have!

SIR FRANCIS: Oh I'm transported! When, when, my dear, wilt thou convince the world of thy happy day? When shall we marry, ha?

MIRANDA: There's nothing wanting but your consent, Sir Francis.

SIR FRANCIS: My consent! What does my charmer mean?

MIRANDA: Nay, 'tis only a whim, but I'll have everything according to form – therefore when you sign an authentic paper, drawn up by an able lawyer, that I have your leave to marry, the next day makes me yours, guardie.

SIR FRANCIS: Ha, ha, ha! A whim indeed! Why is it not demonstration I give my leave when I marry thee?

MIRANDA: Not for your reputation, guardie: the malicious world will be apt to say you tricked me into a marriage, and so take the merit from my choice. Now I will have the act my own, to let the idle fops see how much I prefer a man loaded with years and wisdom.

SIR FRANCIS: Humph! Prithee leave out years, chargie, I'm not so old, as thou shalt find: adod, I'm young, there's a caper for ye.   *[jumps]*

MIRANDA: Oh, never excuse it; why, I like you the better for being old. – But I shall suspect you don't love me, if you refuse me this formality.

SIR FRANCIS: Not love thee, chargie! Adod, I do love thee better than, than, than, better than – what shall I say? Egad, better than money; i'faith I do.

MIRANDA: *[aside]* That's false, I'm sure. – To prove it, do this then.

SIR FRANCIS: Well, I will do it, chargie, provided I bring a licence at the same time.

MIRANDA: Aye and a parson too, if you please. Ha, ha, ha! I
   can't help laughing to think how all the young coxcombs
   about town will be mortified when they hear of our
   marriage.

SIR FRANCIS: So they will, so they will; ha, ha, ha!

MIRANDA: Well, I fancy I shall be so happy with my guardie!

SIR FRANCIS: If wearing pearls and jewels, or eating gold, as
   the old saying is, can make thee happy, thou shalt be so, my
   sweetest, my lovely, my charming, my – verily, I know not
   what to call thee.

MIRANDA: You must know, guardie, that I am so eager to
   have this business concluded, that I have employed my
   woman's brother, who is a lawyer in the Temple, to settle
   matters just to your liking; you are to give your consent to
   my marriage, which is to yourself, you know; but mum, you
   must take no notice of that. So then I will, that is, with your
   leave, put my writings into his hands; then tomorrow we
   come slap upon them with a wedding that nobody thought
   on; by which you seize me and my estate, and I suppose,
   make a bonfire of your own act and deed.

SIR FRANCIS: Nay, but chargie, if –

MIRANDA: Nay, guardie, no ifs – have I refused three northern lords, two British Peers, and half-a-score knights, to have
   put in your ifs? –

SIR FRANCIS: So thou hast indeed, and I will trust to thy
   management. Od, I'm all of a fire.

MIRANDA: [*aside*] 'Tis a wonder the dry stubble does not
   blaze.

   Enter MARPLOT

SIR FRANCIS: How now, who sent for you, sir? What, is the
   hundred pound gone already?

MARPLOT: No, sir, I don't want money now.

SIR FRANCIS: No: that's a miracle! But there's one thing you
   want, I'm sure.

MARPLOT: Aye, what's that guardian?

SIR FRANCIS: Manners: what, had I no servants without?

MARPLOT: None that could do my business, guardian, which
   is at present with this lady.

MIRANDA: With me, Mr Marplot! What is it, I beseech you?

SIR FRANCIS: Aye, sir, what is it? Anything that relates to her may be delivered to me.

MARPLOT: I deny that.

MIRANDA: That's more than I do, sir.

MARPLOT: Indeed, madam! Why then to proceed. Fame says, that you and my most conscionable guardian here designed, contrived, plotted and agreed, to chouse a very civil, honest, honourable gentleman out of an hundred pound.

MIRANDA: That I contrived it!

MARPLOT: Aye you – you said never a word against it, so far you are guilty.

SIR FRANCIS: Pray tell that civil, honest, honourable gentleman, that if he has any more such sums to fool away, they shall be received like the last. Ha, ha, ha, ha! 'Choused',[30] quotha! But hark ye, let him know at the same time, that if he dared to report I tricked him of it, I shall recommend a lawyer to him shall show him a trick for twice as much. D'ye hear? Tell him that.

MARPLOT: So, and this is the way you use a gentleman and my friend?

MIRANDA: Is the wretch thy friend?

MARPLOT: The wretch! Look ye, madam, don't call names. Egad, I won't take it.

MIRANDA: Why, you won't beat me, will you? Ha, ha!

MARPLOT: I don't know whether I will or no.

SIR FRANCIS: Sir, I shall make a servant show you out at the window, if you are saucy.

MARPLOT: I am your most humble servant, guardian; I design to go out the same way I came in. I would only ask this lady, if she does not think in her soul Sir George Airy is not a fine gentleman?

MIRANDA: He dresses well.

SIR FRANCIS: Which is chiefly owing to his tailor and valet-de-chambre.

MARPLOT: The judicious part of the world allows him wit, courage, gallantry, and management; though I think he forfeited that character when he flung away a hundred pound upon your dumb ladyship.

[30]*choused*: cheated

SIR FRANCIS: Does that gall him? Ha, ha, ha!

MIRANDA: So, Sir George remaining in deep discontent, has sent you his trusty squire to utter his complaint: ha, ha, ha!

MARPLOT: Yes, madam; and you like a cruel, hard-hearted jew value it no more – than I would your ladyship, were I Sir George, you, you, you –

MIRANDA: Oh, don't call names, I know you love to be employed and I'll oblige you, and you shall carry him a message from me.

MARPLOT: According as I like it: what is it?

MIRANDA: Nay, a kind one you may be sure – first tell him, I have chose this gentleman to have and to hold, and so forth.

[*clapping her hand into* SIR FRANCIS'S]

SIR FRANCIS: [*aside*] Oh, the dear rogue, how I dote on her!

MIRANDA: And advise his impertinence to trouble me no more, for I prefer Sir Francis for a husband before all the fops in the universe.

MARPLOT: Oh lord, oh lord! She's bewitched, that's certain: here's a husband for eighteen – here's a shape – here's bones rattling in a leathern bag. [*turning* SIR FRANCIS *about*] Here's buckram³¹ and canvas to scrub you to repentance.

SIR FRANCIS: Sirrah, my cane shall teach you repentance presently.

MARPLOT: No faith, I have felt its twin brother from just such a withered hand too lately.

MIRANDA: One thing more; advise him to keep from the garden gate on the left hand; for if he dare to saunter there about the hour of eight, as he used to do, he shall be saluted with a pistol or blunderbuss.

SIR FRANCIS: Oh monstrous! Why chargie, did he use to come to the garden gate?

MIRANDA: The gardener described just such another man that always watched his coming out, and fain would have bribed him for his entrance. – Tell him he shall find a warm reception if he comes this night.

MARPLOT: Pistols and blunderbusses! Egad, a warm reception indeed; I shall take care to inform him of your kindness, and advise him to keep farther off.

³¹*buckram*: stiff fabric

MIRANDA: [*aside*] I hope he will understand my meaning better than to follow your advice.

SIR FRANCIS: Thou hast signed, sealed, and ta'en possession of my heart forever, chargie, ha, ha, ha! And for you, Mr Saucebox, let me have no more of your messages, if ever you design to inherit your estate, gentleman.

MARPLOT: Why, there 'tis now. Sure I shall be out of your clutches one day – well guardian, I say no more, but if you be not as arrant a cuckold, as e'er drove bargain upon the Exchange, or paid attendance to a court, I am the son of a whetstone;[32] and so your humble servant. [*Exit*]

MIRANDA: Don't forget the message; ha, ha!

SIR FRANCIS: I am so provoked – 'tis well he's gone.

MIRANDA: Oh mind him not, guardie, but let's sign articles, and then –

SIR FRANCIS: And then – adod, I believe I am metamorphosed: my pulse beats high, and my blood boils, methinks –

[*kissing and hugging her*]

MIRANDA: Oh fie guardie, be not so violent: consider the market lasts all the year – well, I'll in and see if the lawyer be come, you'll follow. [*Exit*]

SIR FRANCIS: Aye, to the world's end, my dear. Well, Frank, thou art a lucky fellow in thy old age, to have such a delicate morsel, and thirty thousand pound in love with thee; I shall be the envy of bachelors, the glory of married men, and the wonder of the town. Some guardians would be glad to compound for part of the estate, at dispatching an heiress. But I engross the whole. Oh!

Mihi praeteritos referat si Jupiter annos.[33]

[*Exit*]

SCENE FIVE

A tavern

SIR GEORGE *and* CHARLES *with wine before them*, WHISPER *waiting on them*.

[32]*whetstone*: sharpener
[33]Would Jupiter restore me the years that are fled. [Virgil, *Aeneid*: viii, 560]

SIR GEORGE: Nay, prithee don't be grave Charles: misfortunes
will happen, ha, ha, ha! 'Tis some comfort to have a companion
in our sufferings.

CHARLES: I am only apprehensive for Isabinda; her father's
humour is implacable; and how far his jealousy may transport
her to her undoing, shocks my soul to think.

SIR GEORGE: But since you escaped undiscovered by him, his
rage will quickly lash into a calm, never fear it.

CHARLES: But who knows what that unlucky dog Marplot told
him; nor can I imagine what brought him thither; that fellow is
ever doing mischief; and yet, to give him his due he never
designs it. This is some blundering adventure, wherein he
thought to show his friendship, as he calls it; a curse on him.

SIR GEORGE: Then you must forgive him; what said he?

CHARLES: Said? Nay, I had more mind to cut his throat, than to
hear his excuses.

SIR GEORGE: Where is he?

WHISPER: Sir, I saw him go into Sir Francis Gripe's just now.

CHARLES: Oh! Then he's upon your business, Sir George, a
thousand to one but he makes some mistake there too.

SIR GEORGE: Impossible, without he huffs the lady, and makes
love to Sir Francis.

Enter DRAWER

DRAWER: Mr Marplot's below, gentlemen, and desires to know
if he may have leave to wait upon ye.

CHARLES: How civil the rogue is, when he has done a fault!

SIR GEORGE: Ho! Desire him to walk up. Prithee Charles,
throw off this chagrin, and be good company.

CHARLES: Nay, hang him, I'm not angry with him. Whisper,
fetch me pen, ink and paper.

WHISPER: Yes, sir.   [*Exit*]

Enter MARPLOT

CHARLES: Do but mark his sheepish look, Sir George.

MARPLOT: Dear Charles, don't overwhelm a man — already
under insupportable afflication. I'm sure I always intend to
serve my friends; but if my malicious stars deny the happiness,
is the fault mine?

SIR GEORGE: Never mind him, Mr Marplot; he is eat up with
spleen, but what says Miranda?

MARPLOT: Says – nay, we are all undone there too.

CHARLES: I told you so, nothing prospers that he undertakes.

MARPLOT: Why, can I help her having chose your father for better for worse?

CHARLES: So: there's another of Fortune's strokes. I suppose I shall be edged out of my estate with twins every year, let who will get 'em.

SIR GEORGE: What, is the woman really possessed?

MARPLOT: Yes, with the spirit of contradiction, she railed at you most prodigiously.

SIR GEORGE: That's no ill sign.

Enter WHISPER, *with pen, ink and paper*

MARPLOT: You'd say it was no good sign, if you knew all.

SIR GEORGE: Why, prithee?

MARPLOT: Hark 'e, Sir George, let me warn you, pursue your old haunt no more, it may be dangerous.

[CHARLES *sits down to write*]

SIR GEORGE: My old haunt, what d'you mean!

MARPLOT: Why in short, then since you will have it, Miranda vows if you dare approach the garden gate at eight o'clock, as you used, you shall be saluted with a blunderbuss, sir. These were her words, nay she bid me tell you so too.

SIR GEORGE: Ha! The garden gate at eight, as I used to do! There must be a meaning in this. Is there such a gate, Charles?

CHARLES: Yes, yes: it opens into the Park; I suppose her ladyship has made many a scamper through it.

SIR GEORGE: It must be an assignation then. Ha, my heart springs with joy, 'tis a propitious omen. My dear Marplot, let me embrace thee, thou art my friend, my better angel –

MARPLOT: What do you mean, Sir George?

SIR GEORGE: No matter what I mean. Here, take a bumper[34] to the garden gate, ye dear rogue you.

MARPLOT: You have reason to be transported, Sir George; I have saved your life.

SIR GEORGE: My life! Thou hast saved my soul, man. – Charles, if thou dost not pledge this health, mayst thou never taste the joys of love.

[34]*bumper*: glass of wine

CHARLES: Whisper, be sure you take care how you deliver this. [*gives him the letter*] Bring me the answer to my lodgings.

WHISPER: I warrant you, sir.

MARPLOT: Whither does that letter go? – Now I dare not ask for my blood.

CHARLES: Now I'm for you.

SIR GEORGE: To the garden gate at the hour of eight, Charles, along, huzza!

CHARLES: I begin to conceive you.

MARPLOT: That's more than I do, egad – to the garden gate, huzza! [*drinks*] But I hope you design to keep far enough off it, Sir George.

SIR GEORGE: Aye, aye, never fear that; she shall see I despise her frown; let her use her blunderbuss against the next fool, she shan't reach me with the smoke, I warrant her. Ha, ha, ha!

MARPLOT: Ah, Charles, if you could receive a disappointment thus *en cavalier*,[35] one should have some comfort in being beat for you.

CHARLES: The fool comprehends nothing.

SIR GEORGE: Nor would I have him; prithee take him along with thee.

CHARLES: Enough: Marplot, you shall go home with me.

MARPLOT: I'm glad I'm well with him, however. Sir George, yours. Egad, Charles's asking me to go home with him gives me a shrewd suspicion there's more in the garden gate than I comprehend. Faith, I'll give him the drop, and away to guardian's, and find it out.

SIR GEORGE:
I kiss both your hands. – And now for the garden gate.
It's beauty gives the assignation there,
And love too powerful grows, t'admit of fear.   [*Exit*]

----

[35]*en cavalier*: in a cavalier manner

Act Four

SCENE ONE

Outside the house of Sir Jealous Traffick

Enter WHISPER, PATCH *is peeping out the door*

WHISPER: Ha, Mrs Patch, this is a lucky minute, to find you so readily; my master dies with impatience.

PATCH: My lady imagined so, and by her orders I have been scouting this hour in search of you, to inform you that Sir Jealous has invited some friends to supper with him tonight, which gives an opportunity to your master to make use of his ladder of ropes. The closet window shall be open, and Isabinda ready to receive him; bid him come immediately.

WHISPER: Excellent! He'll not disappoint, I warrant him. But hold, I have a letter here, which I'm to carry an answer of, I can't think what language the direction is.

PATCH: Foh, 'tis no language, but a character which the lovers intend to avert discovery. Ha, I hear my old master coming downstairs, it is impossible you should have an answer; away, and bid him come himself for that. – Begone, we are ruined if you're seen, for he has doubled his care since the last accident.

WHISPER: I go, I go. [*Exit*]

PATCH: There, go thou into my pocket. [*Puts it to her side, and it falls down.*] Now I'll up the back stairs, lest I meet him. Well, a dextrous chamber-maid is the ladies' best utensil, I say.[*Exit*]

Enter SIR JEALOUS *with a letter in his hand*

SIR JEALOUS: So, this is some comfort; this tells me that Senor Don Diego Babinetto is safely arrived; he shall marry my daughter the minute he comes, ha, ha! What's here? [*picks up the letter which* PATCH *dropped.*] A letter! I don't know to make of the superscription, I'll see what's within side. [*opens it*] Humph, 'tis Hebrew, I think. What can this mean? There must be some trick in it; this was certainly designed for my

daughter, but I don't know that she can speak any language but
her mother-tongue. No matter for that, this may be one of love's
hieroglyphics, and I fancy I saw Patch's tail sweep by. That
wench may be a slut, and instead of guarding my honour, betray
it. I'll find it out I'm resolved. Who's there?

Enter SERVANT

SIR JEALOUS: What answer did you bring from the gentlemen I
sent you to invite?

SERVANT: That they'll all wait of you, sir, as I told you before;
but I suppose you forgot, sir.

SIR JEALOUS: Did I so, sir? But I shan't forget to break your head,
if any of them come, sir.

SERVANT: Come, sir! Why did you not send me to desire their
company, sir?

SIR JEALOUS: But I send you now to desire their absence; say I
have something extraordinary fallen out, which calls me abroad
contrary to expectation, and ask their pardon; and d'ye hear,
send the butler to me.

SERVANT: Yes, sir.   [*Exit*]

Enter BUTLER

SIR JEALOUS: If this paper has a meaning, I'll find it. – Lay the
cloth in my daughter's chamber, and bid the cook send supper
thither presently.

BUTLER: Yes, sir, – Heyday, what's the matter now?   [*Exit*]

SIR JEALOUS: He wants the eyes of Argus, that has a young
handsome daughter in this town; but my comfort is, I shall not be
troubled long with her. He that pretends to rule a girl once in her
teens, had better be at sea in a storm, and would be in less danger;
          For let him do or counsel all he can,
          She thinks and dreams of nothing else but Man.   [*Exit*]

SCENE TWO

Isabinda's chamber

ISABINDA *and* PATCH

ISABINDA: Are you sure nobody saw you speak to Whisper?

PATCH: Yes, very sure, madam; but I heard Sir Jealous coming
downstairs, so clapped his letter into my pocket.

                                        [*feels for the letter*]

ISABINDA: A letter? Give it me quickly.

PATCH: Bless me! What's become on't – I'm sure I put it –

[*searching still*]

ISABINDA: Is it possible thou could'st be so careless? – Oh! I'm undone forever, if it be lost.

PATCH: I must have dropped it upon the stairs. But why are you so much alarmed? If the worst happens, nobody can read it, madam, nor find out who it was designed for.

ISABINDA: If it falls into my father's hands, the very figure of a letter will produce ill consequences. Run and look for it upon the stairs this moment.

PATCH: Nay, I'm sure it can be nowhere else –

[*As she is going out of the door, she meets the* BUTLER *entering*]

PATCH: How now, what do you want?

BUTLER: My master ordered me to lay the cloth here for his supper.

ISABINDA: [*aside*] Ruined, past redemption –

PATCH: You mistake sure: what shall we do?

ISABINDA: I thought he expected company tonight – Oh! Poor Charles! Oh, unfortunate Isabinda!

BUTLER: I thought so too, madam, but I suppose he has altered his mind. [*lays the cloth, and exit*]

ISABINDA: The letter is the cause; this heedless action has undone me. Fly and fasten the closet-window, which will give Charles notice to retire. Ha! My father! Oh confusion!

Enter SIR JEALOUS

SIR JEALOUS: Hold, hold, Patch, whither are you going? I'll have nobody stir out of the room till after supper.

PATCH: Sir, I was going to reach your easy chair. – Oh, wretched accident!

SIR JEALOUS: I'll have nobody stir out of the room. I don't want my easy chair.

ISABINDA: [*aside*] What will be the event of this?

SIR JEALOUS: Hark ye, daughter: do you know this hand?

ISABINDA: As I suspected – hand do you call it, sir? 'Tis some school-boy's scrawl.

PATCH: Oh invention! Thou chamber-maid's best friend, assist me.

SIR JEALOUS: Are you sure you don't understand it?

[PATCH *feels in her bosom, and shakes her coats*]

ISABINDA: Do you understand it, sir?

SIR JEALOUS: I wish I did.

ISABINDA: [*aside*] Thank heaven you do not. — Then I know no more of it that you do, indeed, sir.

PATCH: Oh lord, oh lord, what have you done, sir? Why the paper is mine, I dropped it out of my bosom.

[*snatching it from him*]

SIR JEALOUS: Ha! Yours mistress?

ISABINDA: [*aside*] What does she mean by owning it?

PATCH: Yes, sir, it is.

SIR JEALOUS: What is it? Speak.

PATCH: Yes, sir, it is a charm for the toothache. — I have worn it these seven years; 'twas given me by an angel for aught I know, when I was raving with the pain; for nobody knew from whence he came, nor whither he went. He charged me never to open it, lest some dire vengeance befall me, and heaven knows what will be the event. Oh! Cruel misfortune, that I should drop it, and you should open it. — If you had not opened it —

ISABINDA: [*aside*] Excellent wench!

SIR JEALOUS: Pox of your charms and whims for me; if that be all, 'tis well enough; there, there, burn it, and I warrant you no vengeance will follow.

PATCH: [*aside*] So, all's right again thus far.

ISABINDA: [*aside*] I would not lose Patch for the world — I'll take courage a little. — Is this usage for your daughter, sir? Must my virtue and conduct be suspected for every trifle? You immure me like some dire offender here, and deny me all the recreations which my sex enjoy, and the custom of the country and modesty allow; yet not content with that, you make my confinement more intolerable by your mistrusts and jealousies; would I were dead, so I were free from this.

SIR JEALOUS: Tomorrow rids you of this tiresome load — Don Diego Babinetto will be here, and then my care ends, and his begins.

ISABINDA: Is he come then? [*aside*] Oh how shall I avoid this hated marriage.

Enter SERVANTS *with supper*

SIR JEALOUS: Come, will you sit down?

ISABINDA: I can't eat, sir.

PATCH: [*aside*] No, I dare swear he has given her supper enough. I wish I could get into the closet —

SIR JEALOUS: Well, if you can't eat, then give me a song whilst I do.

ISABINDA: I have such a cold I can scarce speak, sir, much less sing. [*aside*] — How shall I prevent Charles coming in?

SIR JEALOUS: I hope you have the use of your fingers, madam. Play a tune upon your spinnet, whilst your woman sings me a song.

PATCH: [*aside*] I'm as much out of tune as my lady, if he knew all.

ISABINDA: I shall make excellent music.

[ISABINDA *sits down to play*]

PATCH: Really sir, I'm so frighted about your opening this charm, that I can't remember one song.

SIR JEALOUS: Pish, hang your charm: come, come, sing anything.

PATCH: [*aside*] Yes, I'm likely to sing truly. — Humph, humph; bless me I cannot raise my voice, my heart pants so.

SIR JEALOUS: Why, what does your heart pant so, that you can't play neither? Pray what key are you in, ha?

PATCH: [*aside*] Ah, would the key were turned of you once.

SIR JEALOUS: Why don't you sing, I say?

PATCH: When madam has put her spinnet in tune, sir? Humph, humph —

ISABINDA: [*rising*] I cannot play sir, whatever ails me.

SIR JEALOUS: Zounds sit down and play me a tune, or I'll break your spinnet about your ears.

ISABINDA: What will become of me?   [*sits down and plays*]

SIR JEALOUS: Come mistress.

PATCH: Yes, sir.   [*sings, but horribly out of tune*]

SIR JEALOUS: Hey, hey, why you are a-top of the house, and you are down in the cellar. What is the meaning of this? Is it on purpose to cross me, ha?

PATCH: Pray, madam, take it a little lower, I cannot reach that note — nor any note I fear.

ISABINDA: Well begin — Oh! Patch, we shall be discovered.

PATCH: I sing with the apprehension, madam – humph,
   humph –   [*sings*]
   [CHARLES *pulls open the closet door*]

CHARLES:
   Music and singing.
   'Tis thus the bright celestial court above
   Beguiles the hours with music and with love.
   Death! her father there!
   [*The women shriek.*]

CHARLES: Then I must fly –   [*Exit into the closet*]
   [SIR JEALOUS *rises up hastily, seeing* CHARLES *slip back in
   the closet*]

SIR JEALOUS: Hell and furies, a man in the closet! –

PATCH: Ah! A ghost, a ghost – he must not enter the closet –
   [ISABINDA *throws herself down before the closet door, as in
   a swoon.*]

SIR JEALOUS: The devil! I'll make a ghost of him I warrant you.
                                                [*strives to get by*]

PATCH: Oh sir, have a care, you'll tread upon my lady. – Who
   waits there? Bring some water. Oh! This comes of your opening
   the charm. Oh, oh, oh, oh.   [*weeps aloud*]

SIR JEALOUS: I'll charm you, housewife, here lies the charm
   that conjured this fellow in, I'm sure on't; come out you rascal,
   do so. Zounds, take her from the door, or I'll spurn her from it,
   and break your neck downstairs.

ISABINDA: Oh, oh, where am I – [*aside to* PATCH] He's gone, I
   heard him leap down.

PATCH: Nay, then let him enter – here, here madam, smell to
   this; come, give me your hand: come nearer to the window, the
   air will do you good.

SIR JEALOUS: I would she were in her grave. Where are you
   sirrah? Villain, robber of my honour! I'll pull you out of your
   nest.   [*goes into the closet*]

PATCH: You'll be mistaken, old gentleman, the bird is flown.

ISABINDA: I'm glad I have 'scaped so well. I was almost dead in
   earnest with the fright.

   Re-enter SIR JEALOUS *out of the closet*

SIR JEALOUS: Whoever the dog were, he has escaped out of the
   window, for the sash is up, But though he has got out of my

reach, you are not. And first Mrs Pander, with your charms for the toothache, get out of my house, go, troop; yet hold, stay, I'll see you out of my doors myself, but I'll secure your charge ere I go.

ISABINDA: What do you mean, sir? Was she not a creature of your own providing?

SIR JEALOUS: She was of the devil's providing for aught I know.

PATCH: What have I done, sir, to merit your displeasure?

SIR JEALOUS: I don't know which of you have done it; but you shall both suffer for it, till I can discover whose guilt it is. Go, get in there, I'll move you from this side of the house [*Pushes* ISABINDA *in at the door, and locks it: puts the key into his pocket.*] I'll keep the key myself; I'll try what ghost will get into that room. And now forsooth I'll wait on you downstairs.

PATCH: Ah, my poor lady – downstairs, sir! But I won't go out, sir, till I have looked up my clothes.

SIR JEALOUS: If thou wer't as naked as thou wer't born, thou should'st not stay to put on a smock. Come along, I say! When your mistress is married, you shall have your rags, and everything that belongs to you; but till then –

[*Exit, pulling her out*]

PATCH: Oh! Barbarous usage for nothing!

PATCH *and* SIR JEALOUS *re-enter at the lower end of the stage*

SIR JEALOUS: There, go, and come no more within sight of my habitation these three days, I charge you.

[*slams the door after her*]

PATCH: Did ever anybody see such an old monster?

Enter CHARLES

PATCH: Oh! Mr Charles, your affairs and mine are in an ill posture.

CHARLES: I am inured to the frowns of Fortune: but what has befallen thee?

PATCH: Sir Jealous, whose suspicious nature's always on the watch; nay, even while one eye sleeps, the other keeps sentinel; upon sight of you, flew into such a violent passion, that I could find no stratagem to appease him; but in spite of all arguments, locked his daughter into his own apartment, and turned me out-of-doors.

CHARLES: Ha! Oh, Isabinda!

PATCH: And swears she shall neither see sun or moon, till she is Don Diego Babinetto's wife, who arrived last night, and is expected with impatience.

CHARLES: He dies: yes, by all the wrongs of love he shall; here will I plant myself, and through my breast he shall make his passage, if he enters.

PATCH: A most heroic resolution. There might be ways found out more to your advantage. Policy is often preferred to open force.

CHARLES: I apprehend you not.

PATCH: What think you personating this Spaniard, imposing upon the father, and marrying your mistress by his own consent.

CHARLES: Say'st thou so, my angel! Oh could that be done, my life to come would be too short to recompense thee. But how can I do that, when I ne'er know what ship he came in, or from what part of Spain; who recommends him, or how attended?

PATCH: I can solve all this. He is from Madrid, his father's name Don Pedro Questo Portento Babinetto. Here's a letter of his to Sir Jealous, which he dropped one day. You understand Spanish, and the hand may be counterfeited. You conceive me, sir.

CHARLES: My better genius, thou hast revived my drooping soul: I'll about it instantly. Come to my lodgings, and we'll concert matters.   [*Exeunt*]

SCENE TWO

A garden gate, open. SCENTWELL *waiting inside*

Enter SIR GEORGE AIRY

SIR GEORGE: So, this is the gate, and most invitingly open. If there should be a blunderbuss here now, what a dreadful ditty would my fall make for fools! And what a jest for the wits! How my name would be roared about street! Well, I'll venture all.

SCENTWELL: [*entering*] Hist, hist! Sir George Airy –

SIR GEORGE: A female voice! Thus far I'm safe, my dear.

SCENTWELL: No, I'm not your dear, but I'll conduct you to her; give me your hand: you must go through many a dark passage and dirty step before you arrive –

SIR GEORGE: I know I must before I arrive at Paradise; therefore be quick, my charming guide.

SCENTWELL: For aught you know; come, come, your hand and away.

SIR GEORGE: Here, here, child, you can't be half so swift as my desires.   [*Exeunt*]

SCENE THREE

Inside the House

Enter MIRANDA

MIRANDA: Well, let me reason a little with my mad self. Now don't I transgress all rules to venture upon a man without the advice of the grave and wise? But then a rigid knavish guardian, who would have married me! To whom? Even to his nauseous self, or nobody. Sir George is what I have tried in conversation, enquired into his character, am satisfied in both. Then his love! Who would have given a hundred pounds only to have seen a woman he had not infinitely loved? So I find my liking him has furnished me with arguments enough of his side; and now the only doubt remains, whether he will come or no.

Enter SCENTWELL

SCENTWELL: That's resolved, madam, for here's the knight.

[*Exit*]

SIR GEORGE: And do I once more behold that lovely object, whose idea fills my mind, and forms my pleasing dreams!

MIRANDA: What! Beginning again in heroics! – Sir George, don't you remember how little fruit your last prodigal oration produced? Not one bare single word in answer.

SIR GEORGE: Ha! the voice of my Incognita. – Why did you take ten thousand ways to captivate a heart your eyes alone had vanquished?

MIRANDA: Prithee no more of these flights, for our time's but short, and we must fall to business. Do you think we can agree on that same terrible bugbear, Matrimony, without heartily repenting on both sides!

SIR GEORGE: It has been my wish since first my longing eyes beheld ye.

MIRANDA: And your happy ears drank in the pleasing news, I had thirty thousand pounds.

SIR GEORGE: Unkind! Did I not offer you in those purchased minutes to run the risk of your fortune, so you would but secure that lovely person to my arms?

MIRANDA: Well, if you have such love and tenderness, (since our wooing has been short) pray reserve it for our future days, to let the world see we are lovers after wedlock; 'twill be a novelty –

SIR GEORGE: Haste then, and let us tie the knot, and prove the envied pair –

MIRANDA: Hold, not so fast, I have provided better than to venture on dangerous experiments headlong. – My guardian, trusting to my dissembled love, has given up my fortune to my own disposal; but with this proviso, that he tomorrow morning weds me. He is now gone to Doctor's Commons[36] for a licence.

SIR GEORGE: Ha, a licence!

MIRANDA: But I have planted emissaries that infallibly take him down to Epsom, under pretence that a brother usurer of his is to make him his executor; the thing on earth he covets.

SIR GEORGE: 'Tis his known character.

MIRANDA: Now my instruments confirm him this man is dying, and he sends me word he goes this minute; it must be tomorrow ere he can be undeceived. That time is ours.

SIR GEORGE: Let us improve it then, and settle on our coming years, endless, endless happiness.

MIRANDA: I dare not stir till I hear he's on the road – then I, and my writings, the most material point, are soon removed.

SIR GEORGE: I have one favour to ask, if it lies in your power, you would be a friend to poor Charles, though the son of this tenacious man: he is as free from all his vices, as nature and a good education can make him; and what now I have vanity enough to hope will induce you, he is the man on earth I love.

MIRANDA: I never was his enemy, and only put it on as it helped my designs on his father. If his uncle's estate ought to be in his

[36]*Doctor's Commons*: London's law centre

possession, which I shrewdly suspect, I may do him a singular piece of service.

SIR GEORGE: You are all goodness.

Enter SCENTWELL

SCENTWELL: Oh, madam, my master and Mr Marplot are just coming into the house.

MIRANDA: Undone, undone, if he finds you here in this crisis, all my plots are unravelled.

SIR GEORGE: What shall I do? Can't I get back into the garden?

SCENTWELL: Oh, no! He comes up those stairs.

MIRANDA: Here, here, here! Can you condescend to stand behind this chimney-board,[37] Sir George?

SIR GEORGE: Anywhere, anywhere, dear madam, without ceremony.

SCENTWELL: Come, come, sir; lie close –

[*They put him behind the chimney-board.*]

Enter SIR FRANCIS *and* MARPLOT, SIR FRANCIS *peeling an orange.*

SIR FRANCIS: I could not go, though 'tis upon life and death, without taking leave of dear Chargie. Besides, this fellow buzzed in my ears, that thou might'st be so desperate to shoot that wild rake which haunts the garden gate; and that would bring us into trouble, dear –

MIRANDA: [*frowning at Marplot, aside*] So Marplot brought you back then; I am obliged to him for that, I'm sure –

MARPLOT: By her looks she means she's not obliged to me, I have done some mischief now, but what I can't imagine.

SIR FRANCIS: Well, chargie, I have had three messengers to come to Epsom to my neighbour Squeezum's, who, for all his vast riches, is departing.   [*sighs*]

MARPLOT: Aye, see what all you usurers must come to.

SIR FRANCIS: Peace ye young knave! Some forty years hence I may think on't – But, chargie, I'll be with thee tomorrow, before those pretty eyes are open; I will, I will, chargie, I'll rouse you, i'faith. – Here Mrs Scentwell, lift up your lady's chimney-board, that I may throw my peel in, and not litter her chamber.

MIRANDA: Oh my stars! What will become of us now?

---

[37] *chimney-board*: Piece of wood placed in front of fireplace in summer to stop downdraughts

SCENTWELL: Oh, pray sir, give it me; I love it above all things in
nature, indeed I do.

SIR FRANCIS: No, no, hussy; you have the green-pip[38] already,
I'll have no apothecary's bills.

> [*goes towards the chimney-board*]

MIRANDA: Hold, hold, hold, dear guardie, I have a, a, a, a, a,
monkey, shut up there; and if you open it before the man comes
that is to tame it, 'tis so wild 'twill break all my china, or get away,
and that would break my heart; [*in a flattering tone*] for I'm fond
on't to distraction, next thee, dear guardie.

SIR FRANCIS: Well, well, chargie, I won't open it; she shall have
her monkey, poor rogue; here, throw this peel out of the
window.   [*Exit* SCENTWELL]

MARPLOT: A monkey! Dear madam, let me see it; I can tame a
monkey as well as the best of them all. Oh how I love the little
miniatures of man!

MIRANDA: Be quiet, mischief, and stand farther from the
chimney. — You shall not see my monkey — why sure —

> [*striving with him*]

MARPLOT: For heaven's sake, dear madam, let me but peep, to
see if it be as pretty as my Lady Fiddle-Faddle's. Has it got a
chain?

MIRANDA: Not yet, but I design it one shall last its lifetime. Nay,
you shall not see it! — Look, guardie, how he teases me!

SIR FRANCIS: [*getting between him and the chimney*] Sirrah,
sirrah, let my chargie's monkey alone, or Bambo shall fly about
your ears. What, is there no dealing with you?

MARPLOT: Pugh, pox of this monkey! Here's a rout: I wish he
may rival you.

>   *Enter a* SERVANT

SERVANT: Sir, they put two more horses to the coach, as you
ordered, and 'tis ready at the door.

SIR FRANCIS: Well, I am going to be executor, better for thee,
jewel. Bye chargie, one buss! — I'm glad thou hast got a monkey to
divert thee a little.

MIRANDA: Thank'e dear guardie. — Nay, I'll see you to the coach.

SIR FRANCIS: That's kind, adod.

---

[38]*green-pip*: anaemic disease of adolescent girls

MIRANDA: [*to* MARPLOT] Come alone, Impertinence.

MARPLOT: [*stepping back*] Egad, I will see the monkey now. [*lifts up the board, and discovers Sir George*] Oh lord, oh lord! Thieves, thieves, murder!

SIR GEORGE: Damn'e, you unlucky dog! 'Tis I; which way shall I get out! Show me instantly, or I'll cut your throat.

MARPLOT: Undone, undone! At that door there. But hold, hold, break that china, and I'll bring you off.

[*He runs off at the corner, and throws down some china.*]
Re-enter SIR FRANCIS, MIRANDA *and* SCENTWELL

SIR FRANCIS: Mercy on me! What's the matter?

MIRANDA: Oh you toad! What have you done?

MARPLOT: No great harm, I beg of you to forgive me. Longing to see the monkey, I did but just raise up the board, and it flew over my shoulders, scratched all my face, broke yon china, and whisked out of the window.

SIR FRANCIS: Was ever such an unlucky rogue! Sirrah, I forbid you my house. Call the servants to get the monkey again. I would stay myself to look it, but that you know my earnest business.

SCENTWELL: Oh my lady will be the best to lure it back; all them creatures love my lady extremely.

MIRANDA: Go, go, dear guardie, I hope I shall recover it.

SIR FRANCIS: Bye, bye, dearie. Ah, mischief, how you look now! Bye, bye. [*Exit*]

MIRANDA: Scentwell, see him in the coach, and bring me word.

SCENTWELL: Yes, madam.

MIRANDA: So, sir, you have done your friend a signal piece of service, I suppose.

MARPLOT: Why look you, madam, if I have committed a fault, thank yourself; no man is more serviceable when I am let into a secret, nor none more unlucky at finding it out. Who could divine your meaning? When you talked of a blunderbuss, who thought of a rendezvous? And when you talked of a monkey, who the devil dreamt of Sir George?

MIRANDA: A sign you converse but little with our sex, when you can't reconcile contradictions.

Enter SCENTWELL

SCENTWELL: He's gone, madam, as fast as the coach-and-six can carry him.

    Enter SIR GEORGE

SIR GEORGE: Then I may appear.

MARPLOT: Dear Sir George, make my peace! On my soul, I did not think of you.

SIR GEORGE: I dare swear thou didst not. Madam, I beg you to forgive him.

MIRANDA: Well, Sir George, if he can be secret.

MARPLOT: Ods heart, madam, I'm as secret as a priest when I'm trusted.

SIR GEORGE: Why 'tis with a priest our business is at present.

SCENTWELL: Madam, here's Mrs Isabinda's woman to wait on you.

MIRANDA: Bring her up.

    Enter PATCH

MIRANDA: How do'e Mrs Patch? What news from your lady?

PATCH: That's for your private ear, madam. Sir George, there's a friend of yours has an urgent occasion for your assistance.

SIR GEORGE: His name.

PATCH: Charles.

MARPLOT: Ha! Then there's something a-foot that I know nothing of. I'll wait on you, Sir George.

SIR GEORGE: A third person may not be proper, perhaps; as soon as I have dispatched my own affairs, I am at his service. I'll send my servant to tell him I'll wait upon him in half-an-hour.

MIRANDA: How come you employed in this message, Mrs Patch?

PATCH: Want of business, madam: I am discharged by my master, but hope to serve my lady still.

MIRANDA: How! Discharged! You must tell me the whole story within.

PATCH: With all my heart, madam.

MARPLOT: [*aside*] Pish! Pox, I wish I were fairly out of the house. I find marriage is the end of this secret: and now I am half mad to know what Charles wants him for.

SIR GEORGE: Madam, I'm double pressed by love and friendship: this exigence admits of no delay. Shall we make Marplot of the party?

MIRANDA: If you'll run the hazard, Sir George; I believe he means well.

MARPLOT: Nay, nay, for my part, I desire to be let into nothing; I'll be gone, therefore pray don't mistrust me.   [*going*]

SIR GEORGE: So, now he has a mind to be gone to Charles. But not knowing what affairs he may have upon his hands at present, I'm resolved he shan't stir. – No, Mr Marplot, you must not leave us, we want a third person.   [*takes hold of him*]

MARPLOT: I never had more mind to be gone in my life.

MIRANDA: Come along then; if we fail in the voyage, thank yourself for taking this ill-starred gentleman on board.

SIR GEORGE:

> That vessel ne'er can unsuccessful prove,
> Whose freight is beauty, and whose pilot Love.   [*Exeunt*]

Act Five

SCENE ONE

Enter MIRANDA, PATCH *and* SCENTWELL

MIRANDA: Well, Patch, I have done a strange bold thing; my fate is determined, and expectation is no more. Now to avoid the impertinence and roguery of an old man, I have thrown myself into the extravagance of a young one; if he should despise, slight, or use me ill, there's no remedy from a husband but the grave; and that's a terrible sanctuary to one of my age and constitution.

PATCH: Oh fear not, madam, you'll find your account in Sir George Airy; it is impossible a man of sense should use a woman ill, endow'd with beauty, wit and fortune. It must be the lady's fault, if she does not wear the unfashionable name of wife easy, when nothing but complaisance and good humour is requisite on either side to make them happy.

MIRANDA: I long till I am out of this house, lest any accident should bring my guardian back. Scentwell, put my best jewels into the little casket, slip them into thy pocket, and let us march off to Sir Jealous's.

SCENTWELL: It shall be done, madam.   [*Exit* SCENTWELL]

PATCH: Sir George will be impatient, madam: if their plot succeeds, we shall be received; if not, he will be able to protect us. Besides, I long to know how my young lady fares.

MIRANDA: Farewell, old Mammon, and thy detested walls: 'twill be no more 'Sweet Sir Francis'; I shall be compelled to the odious talk of dissembling no longer to get my own, and coax him with the wheedling names of 'my precious', 'my dear', 'dear guardie'. Oh Heavens!

Enter SIR FRANCIS *behind.* MIRANDA *starts with fright*

SIR FRANCIS: Ah, my sweet chargie, don't be frighted. But thy poor guardie has been abused, cheated, fooled, betrayed, but nobody knows by whom.

MIRANDA: [*aside*] Undone! Past redemption.

SIR FRANCIS: What, won't you speak to me, chargie?

MIRANDA: I am so surprised with joy to see you, I know not what to say.

SIR FRANCIS: Poor dear girl! But do'e know that my son, or some such rogue, to rob or murder me, or both, contrived this journey? For upon the road I met my neighbour Squeezum well, and coming to town.

MIRANDA: Good lack! Good lack! What tricks are there in this world.

    Enter SCENTWELL, *with a diamond necklace in her hand, not seeing* SIR FRANCIS.

SCENTWELL: Madam, be pleased to tie this necklace on, for I can't get into the –   [*seeing* SIR FRANCIS]

MIRANDA: The wench is a fool, I think! Could you not have carried it to be mended, without putting it in the box?

SIR FRANCIS: What's the matter?

MIRANDA: Only dear'e, I bid her, I bid her – Your ill-usage has put everything out of my head. But won't you go, guardie, and find out these fellows, and have them punished? And, and –

SIR FRANCIS: Where should I look them, child! No, I'll sit me down contented with my safety, nor stir out of my own doors till I go with thee to a parson.

MIRANDA: [*aside*] If he goes into his closet, I am ruined. Oh! Bless me, in this fright, I had forgot Mrs Patch.

PATCH: Aye, madam, I stay for your speedy answer.

MIRANDA: [*aside*] I must get him out of the house. Now assist me Fortune.

SIR FRANCIS: Mrs Patch! I profess I did not see you. How dost thou do, Mrs Patch? Well, don't you repent leaving my chargie.

PATCH: Yes, everybody must love her – but I came now –[*aside to* MIRANDA] – Madam, what did I come for? My invention is at the last ebb.

SIR FRANCIS: Nay, never whisper, tell me.

MIRANDA: She came, dear guardie, to invite me to her lady's wedding, and you shall go with me, guardie, 'tis to be done this moment, to a Spanish merchant: old Sir Jealous keeps on his humour, the first minute he sees her, the next he marries her.

SIR FRANCIS: Ha, ha, ha! I'd go if I thought the sight of

matrimony would tempt chargie to perform her promise. There
was a smile, there was a consenting look with those pretty
twinklers, worth a million. Ods-precious, I am happier than the
Great Mogul, the Emperor of China, or all the potentates that
are not in the wars. Speak, confirm it, make me leap out of my
skin.

MIRANDA: When one has resolved, 'tis in vain to stand, shall I
shall I; if ever I marry, positively this is my wedding-day.

SIR FRANCIS: Oh! Happy, happy man. – Verily I will beget a
son the first night, shall disinherit that dog Charles. I have estate
enough to purchase a barony, and be the immortalising the
whole family of the Gripes.

MIRANDA: Come then, guardie, give me thy hand, let's to this
house of Hymen.

My choice is fixed, let good or ill betide.

SIR FRANCIS: The joyful bridegroom I,

MIRANDA: And I the happy bride.   [*Exeunt*]

SCENE TWO

Enter SIR JEALOUS *meeting a* SERVANT

SERVANT: Sir, here's a couple of gentlemen enquire for you; one
of them calls himself Senor Diego Babinetto.

SIR JEALOUS: Ha! Senor Babinetto! Admit 'em instantly! –
Joyful minute: I'll have my daughter married tonight.

Enter CHARLES *in a Spanish habit, with* SIR GEORGE
dressed like a merchant

SIR JEALOUS: Senor, beso las menas vuestra merced es muy
bien venido en esta tierra.[39]

CHARLES: Senor, soy muy humilde, y muy obligado cryado de
vuestra merced: mi padre embia a vuestra merced, los mas
profondos de sus respetos; y a commissionada este Mercadel
Ingles, de concluyr un negocio, que me haze el mas dichoso
hombre del muhndo, haziendo me su yerno.[40]

---

[39]Sir, I kiss your worship's hands; you are most welcome to this country.

[40]Sir, I am most humbly obliged for your worship's greeting. My father sends
your worship his deepest respects. To settle the business he has commissioned this
English merchant whom I consider the most trustworthy man in the world to have
come to my notice.

SIR JEALOUS: I am glad on't, for I find I have lost much of my Spanish. Sir, I am your most humble servant. Senor Don Diego Babinetto has informed me that you are commissioned by Senor Don Pedro, etc., his worthy father.

SIR GEORGE: To see an affair of marriage consummated between a daughter of yours and Senor Diego Babinetto his son here. True, sir, such a trust is reposed in me, as that letter will inform you. [*aside*] I hope 'twill pass upon him.

[gives him a letter]

SIR JEALOUS: Aye, 'tis his hand.   [*seems to read*]

SIR GEORGE: [*aside*] Good – you have counterfeited to a nicety, Charles.

CHARLES: [*aside*] If the whole plot succeeds as well, I'm happy.

SIR JEALOUS: Sir, I find by this, that you are a man of honour and probity; I think sir, he calls you Meanwell.

SIR GEORGE: Meanwell is my name, sir.

SIR JEALOUS: A very good name, and very significant.

CHARLES: [*aside*] Yes faith, if he knew all.

SIR JEALOUS: For to mean well is to be honest, and to be honest is the virtue of a friend, and a friend is the delight and support of human society.

SIR GEORGE: You shall find that I'll discharge the part of a friend in what I have undertaken, Sir Jealous.

CHARLES: [*aside*] But little does he think to whom.

SIR GEORGE: Therefore, sir, I must entreat the presence of your daughter, and the assistance of your chaplain; for Senor Don Pedro strictly enjoined me to see the marriage rites performed as soon as we should arrive, to avoid the accidental overtures of Venus!

SIR JEALOUS: Overtures of Venus!

SIR GEORGE: Aye, sir, that is, those little hawking females that traverse the Park, and the play-house, to put off their damaged ware – they fasten upon foreigners like leeches, and watch their arrival as carefully as the Kentish men do a ship-wreck. I warrant you they have heard of him already.

SIR JEALOUS: Nay, I know this town swarms with them.

SIR GEORGE: Aye, and then you know the Spaniards are naturally amorous, but very constant, the first faces fixes 'em; and it may be very dangerous to let him ramble ere he is tied.

CHARLES: [*aside*] Well hinted.

SIR JEALOUS: Pat to my purpose. – Well, sir, there is but one thing more, and they shall be married instantly.

CHARLES: [*aside*] Pray heaven that one thing more don't spoil all.

SIR JEALOUS: Don Pedro writ one word in his last but one, that he designed the sum of five thousand crowns by way of jointure for my daughter; and that it should be paid into my hand upon the day of marriage –

CHARLES: [*aside*] Oh! The devil.

SIR JEALOUS: – in order to lodge it in some of our funds in case she should become a widow, and return for England.

SIR GEORGE: [*aside*] Pox on't, this is an unlucky turn. What shall I say?

SIR JEALOUS: And he does not mention one word of it in this letter.

CHARLES: [*aside*] I don't know how he should.

SIR GEORGE: Humph! True, Sir Jealous, he told me such a thing, but, but, but, but, – he, he, he, he, – he did not imagine you would insist upon the very day; for, for, for, for money you know is dangerous returning by sea, an, an, an, an, –

CHARLES: [*aside*] Zounds, say we have brought it in commodities.

SIR GEORGE: And so, sir, he has sent it in merchandise, tobacco, sugars, spices, lemons, and so forth, which shall be turned into money with all expedition. In the mean time, sir, if you please to accept of my bond for performance –

SIR JEALOUS: It is enough, sir. I am so pleased with the countenance of Senor Diego, and the harmony of your name, that I'll take your word, and will fetch my daughter this moment. Within there!

   Enter SERVANT

SIR JEALOUS: Desire Mr Tackum, my neighbour's chaplain, to walk thither.

SERVANT: Yes, sir.   [*Exit*]

SIR JEALOUS: Gentlemen, I'll return in an instant.

CHARLES: Wondrous well, let me embrace thee.

SIR GEORGE: Egad that five thousand crowns had like to have ruined the plot.

CHARLES: But that's over! And if Fortune throws no more rubs in our way —

SIR GEORGE: Thou'lt carry the prize. — But hist, here he comes.

Enter SIR JEALOUS, *dragging in* ISABINDA

SIR JEALOUS: Come along, you stubborn baggage you, come along.

ISABINDA:
Oh, hear me, sir! Hear me but speak one word:
Do not destroy my everlasting peace:
My soul abhors this Spaniard you have chose,
Nor can I wed him without being cursed.

SIR JEALOUS: How's that!

ISABINDA:
Let this posture move your tender nature.   [*kneels*]
Forever will I hang upon these knees:
Nor loose my hands till you cut off the hold,
If you refuse to hear me, sir.

CHARLES: [*aside*] Oh that I could discover myself to her!

SIR GEORGE: [*aside*] Have a care what you do. You had better trust to his obstinacy.

SIR JEALOUS: Did you ever see such a perverse slut? Off, I say! Mr Meanwell, pray help me a little.

SIR GEORGE: Rise, madam, and do not disoblige your father, who has provided a husband worthy of you, one that will love you equal with his soul, and one that you will love when once you know him.

ISABINDA: Oh! Never, never! Could I suspect that falsehood in my heart, I would this moment tear it from my breast, and straight present him with the treacherous part.

CHARLES: [*aside*] Oh my charming faithful dear!

SIR JEALOUS: Falsehood! Why who the devil are you in love with? Don't provoke me, or by St Iágo I shall beat you, huswife.

CHARLES: Heaven forbid; for I shall infallibly discover myself if he should.

SIR GEORGE: Have patience, madam! And look at him: why will ye prepossess yourself against a man that is master of all the charms you would desire in a husband?

SIR JEALOUS: Aye, look at him, Isabinda. Senor pase vind adelante.[41]

[41]Come forward, sir.

CHARLES: My heart bleeds to see her grieve, whom I imagined would with joy receive me. Senora obligue me vuestra merced de su mano.[42]

SIR JEALOUS: [*pulling up her head*] Hold up your head, hold up your head, huswife, and look at him: is there a properer, handsomer, better-shaped fellow in England, ye jade you? Ha! See, see the obstinate baggage shuts her eyes; by St Iägo, I have a good mind to beat 'em out.   [*pushes her down*]

ISABINDA:
      Do, then, sir, kill me, kill me instantly.
      'Tis much the kinder action of the two;
      For 'twill be worse than death to wed him.

SIR GEORGE: Sir Jealous, you are too passionate. Give me leave, I'll try by gentle words to work her to your purpose.

SIR JEALOUS: I pray do, Mr Meanwell, I pray do; she'll break my heart. [*weeps*] There is in that, jewels of the value of £3000 which were her mother's, and a paper wherein I have settled one half of my estate upon her now, and the whole when I die; but provided she marries this gentleman; else by St Iägo I'll turn her out-of-doors to beg or starve. Tell her this, Mr Meanwell, pray do.   [*walks off*]

SIR GEORGE: Ha! This is beyond expectation! – Trust me, sir, I'll lay the dangerous consequence of disobeying you at this juncture before her, I warrant you.

CHARLES: [*aside*] A sudden joy runs through my heart like a propitious omen.

SIR GEORGE: Come, madam, do not blindly cast your life away just in the moment you would wish to save it.

ISABINDA: Pray, cease your trouble, sir, I have no wish but sudden death to free me from this hated Spaniard. If you are his friend, inform him what I say: my heart is given to another youth, whom I love with the same strength of passion that I hate this Diego; with whom, if I am forced to wed, my own hand shall cut the Gordian knot.[43]

SIR GEORGE: Suppose this Spaniard, which you strive to shun, should be the very man to whom you'd fly?

---

[42]Madam, oblige me with the favour of your hand.
[43]*Gordian knot*: a difficult situation

ISABINDA: Ha!

SIR GEORGE: Would you not blame your rash resolve, and curse your eyes that would not look on Charles?

ISABINDA: Oh Charles! Oh, you have inspired new life, and collected every wandering sense. Where is he? Oh! Let me fly into his arms. [*rises*]

SIR GEORGE: Hold, hold, hold. 'Sdeath, madam, you'll ruin all; your father believes him to be Senor Babinetto: compose yourself a little pray, madam.

[*he runs to* SIR JEALOUS]

CHARLES: [*aside*] Her eyes declare she knows me.

SIR GEORGE: She begins to hear reason, sir; the fear of being turned out of doors has done it.

[*runs back to* ISABINDA]

ISABINDA: 'Tis he! Oh, my ravished soul!

SIR GEORGE: Take heed, madam, you don't betray yourself. Seem with reluctance to consent, or you are undone.

[*runs to* SIR JEALOUS]

SIR GEORGE: Speak gently to her, I'm sure she'll yield, I see it in her face.

SIR JEALOUS: Well, Isabinda, can you refuse to bless a father, whose only care is to make you happy, as Mr Meanwell has informed you? Come, wipe thy eyes, nay prithee do, or thou wilt break thy father's heart. See, thou bring'st the tears in mine, to think of thy undutiful carriage to me. [*weeps*]

ISABINDA: Oh! Do not weep, sir, your tears are like a poignard[44] to my soul; do with me what you please, I am all obedience.

SIR JEALOUS: Ha! Then thou art my child again.

SIR GEORGE: 'Tis done, and now, friend, the day's thy own.

CHARLES: The happiest of my life, if nothing intervene.

SIR JEALOUS: And wilt thou love him?

ISABINDA: I will endeavour it, sir.

Enter SERVANT

SERVANT: Sir, here's Mr Tackum.

SIR JEALOUS: Show him into the parlour — Senor tome vind

---

[44] *poignard*: dagger

sueipora; cette momento les juntta les manos.⁴⁵

[*gives her to* CHARLES]

CHARLES: Oh transport! – Senor yo la reciba como se devo un tesero tan grande.⁴⁶ Oh! My joy, my life, my soul.

[*they embrace*]

ISABINDA: My faithful everlasting comfort.

SIR JEALOUS:

Now, Mr Meanwell, let's to the parson.
Who, by his art, will join this pair for life,
Make me the happiest father, her the happiest wife.

[*Exeunt*]

SCENE THREE

The street before Sir Jealous's door

Enter MARPLOT, *alone*

MARPLOT: I have hunted all over the town for Charles, but can't find him; and by Whisper's scouting at the end of the street, I suspect he must be in the house again. I am informed too, that he has borrowed a Spanish habit out of the play-house: what can it mean?

Enter a SERVANT *of Sir Jealous's to him, out of the house*

MARPLOT: Hark'e, sir, do you belong to this house?

SERVANT: Yes, sir.

MARPLOT: Pray can you tell me if there be a gentleman in it in Spanish habit?

SERVANT: There's a Spanish gentleman within, that is just a-going to marry my young lady, sir.

MARPLOT: Are you sure he is a Spanish gentleman?

SERVANT: I am sure he speaks no English, that I hear of.

MARPLOT: Then that can't be him I want; for 'tis an English gentleman, though I suppose he may be dressed like a Spaniard, that I enquire after.

SERVANT: [*aside*] Ha! Who knows but this may be an imposter? I'll inform my master; for if he should be imposed upon, he'll

---

⁴⁵Sir, take your wife; from this very moment your hands are joined.
⁴⁶Sir, I welcome her to me as befits a treasure so great.

beat us all round. – Pray, come in, sir, and see if this be the person you enquire for.

SCENE FIVE

Inside the house

Enter MARPLOT

MARPLOT: So, this was a good contrivance: If this be Charles, now will he wonder how I found him out.

Enter SERVANT *and* SIR JEALOUS

SIR JEALOUS: What is your earnest business, blockhead, that you must speak with me before the ceremony's past? Ha! Who's this?

SERVANT: Why this gentleman, sir, wants another gentleman in a Spanish habit, he says.

SIR JEALOUS: In Spanish habit! 'Tis some friend of Senor Don Diego's, I warrant. Sir, I suppose you would speak with Senor Babinetto –

MARPLOT: Heyday! What the devil does he say now! – Sir, I don't understand you.

SIR JEALOUS: Don't you understand Spanish, sir?

MARPLOT: Not I, indeed, sir.

SIR JEALOUS: I thought you had known Senor Babinetto.

MARPLOT: Not I, upon my word, sir.

SIR JEALOUS: What then, you'd speak with his friend, the English merchant Mr Meanwell?

MARPLOT: Neither, sir, not I.

SIR JEALOUS: [*in an angry tone*] Why, who are you then, sir? And what do you want?

MARPLOT: Nay, nothing at all, not I, sir. Pox on him! I wish I were out. He begins to exalt his voice, I shall be beaten again.

SIR JEALOUS: Nothing at all, sir! Why then, what business have you in my house? Ha!

SERVANT: You said you wanted a gentleman in Spanish habit.

MARPLOT: Why, aye, but his name is neither Babinetto, nor Meanwell.

SIR JEALOUS: What is his name, then, sirrah? Ha? Now I

look at you again, I believe you are the rogue that threatened me
with half a dozen Myrmidons – Speak, sir, who is it you look
for? Or, or –

MARPLOT: A terrible old dog! – Why, sir, only an honest young
fellow of my acqaintance – I thought that here might be a ball,
and that he might have been here in a masquerade; 'tis Charles,
Sir Francis Gripe's son, because I know he used to come hither
sometimes.

SIR JEALOUS: Did he so? – Not that I know of, I'm sure. Pray
heaven that this be not Don Diego – If I should be tricked now –
ha? My heart misgives me plaguily. – Within there! Stop the
marriage! – Run, sirrah, call all my servants! I'll be satisfied that
this is Senor Pedro's son, ere he has my daughter.

MARPLOT: Ha! Sir George! What have I done now?

Enter SIR GEORGE *with a drawn sword between the scenes*

SIR GEORGE: Ha! Marplot here – oh the unlucky dog! – What's
the matter, Sir Jealous?

SIR JEALOUS: Nay, I don't know the matter, Mr Meanwell –

MARPLOT: [*going up to* SIR GEORGE] Upon my soul, Sir
George –

SIR JEALOUS: Nay, then, I'm betrayed, ruined, undone:
thieves, traitors, rogues! [*offers to go in*] Stop the marriage, I
say –

SIR GEORGE: I say go on, Mr Tackum – Nay, no entering here, I
guard this passage, old gentleman; the act and deed were both
your own, and I'll see 'em signed or die for't.

Enter SERVANTS

SIR JEALOUS: A pox on the act and deed! – Fall on, knock him
down.

SIR GEORGE: Aye, come on scoundrels! I'll prick your jackets
for you.

SIR JEALOUS: Zounds, sirrah, I'll be revenged on you.

[*beats* MARPLOT]

SIR GEORGE: Aye, there your vengeance is due: ha, ha!

MARPLOT: Why, what do you beat me for? I han't married your
daughter.

SIR JEALOUS: Rascals! Why don't you knock him down?

SERVANT: We are afraid of his sword, sir; if you'll take that
from him, we'll knock him down presently.

Enter CHARLES *and* ISABINDA

SIR JEALOUS: Seize her then.

CHARLES: Rascals, retire; she's my wife, touch her if you dare, I'll make dogs-meat of you.

SIR JEALOUS: Ah! Downright English: — Oh, oh, oh, oh!

Enter SIR FRANCIS, MIRANDA, PATCH, SCENTWELL *and* WHISPER

SIR FRANCIS: Into the house of joy we enter without knocking. Ha! I think 'tis the house of sorrow, Sir Jealous.

SIR JEALOUS: Oh, Sir Francis! Are you come? What, was this your contrivance to abuse, trick, and chouse me out of my child!

SIR FRANCIS: My contrivance! What do you mean?

SIR JEALOUS: No, you don't know your son there in Spanish habit?

SIR FRANCIS: How! My son in Spanish habit! Sirrah, you'll come to be hanged; get out of my sight, ye dog! Get out of my sight.

SIR JEALOUS: Get out of your sight, sir! Get out with your bags? Let's see what you'll give him now to maintain my daughter on.

SIR FRANCIS: Give him? He shall never be the better for a penny of mine — and you might have looked after your daughter better, Sir Jealous. Tricked, quotha! Egad, I think you designed to trick me. But look ye, gentleman, I believe I shall trick you both. This lady is my wife, do you see; and my estate shall descend only to the heirs of her body.

SIR GEORGE: Lawfully begotten by me — I shall be extremely obliged to you, Sir Francis.

SIR FRANCIS: Ha, ha, ha, ha! Poor Sir George! You see your project was of no use. Does not your hundred pound stick in your stomach? Ha, ha, ha!

SIR GEORGE: No faith, Sir Francis, this lady has given me a cordial for that.   [*takes her by the hand*]

SIR FRANCIS: Hold, sir, you have nothing to say to this lady.

SIR GEORGE: Nor you nothing to do with my wife, sir.

SIR FRANCIS: Wife sir!

MIRANDA: Aye really, guardian, 'tis even so. I hope you'll forgive my first offence.

SIR FRANCIS: What, have you choused me out of my consent, and your writings then, mistress, ha?

MIRANDA: Out of nothing but my own, guardian.

SIR JEALOUS: Ha, ha, ha! 'Tis some comfort at least to see you are over-reached as well as myself. Will you settle your estate upon your son now?

SIR FRANCIS: He shall starve first.

MIRANDA: That I have taken care to prevent. There sir, is the writings of your uncle's estate, which has been your due these three years.   [*gives* CHARLES *papers*]

CHARLES: I shall study to deserve this favour.

SIR FRANCIS: What, have you robbed me too, mistress! Egad I'll make you restore 'em – huswife, I will so.

SIR JEALOUS: Take care I don't make you pay the arrears, sir. 'Tis well it's no worse, since 'tis no better. Come young man, seeing thou hast outwitted me, take her, and bless thee both.

CHARLES: I hope, sir, you'll bestow your blessing, too, 'tis all I'll ask.   [*kneels*]

SIR FRANCIS: Confound you all!   [*Exit*]

MARPLOT: Mercy upon us, how he looks!

SIR GEORGE: Ha, ha! Ne'er mind his curses, Charles; thou'lt thrive not one jot the worse for 'em. Since this gentleman is reconciled, we are all made happy.

SIR JEALOUS: I always loved precaution, and took care to avoid dangers. But when a thing was past, I ever had philosophy enough to be easy.

CHARLES: Which is the true sign of a great soul; I loved your daughter, and she me, and you shall have no reason to repent her choice.

ISABINDA: You'll not blame me, sir, for loving my own country best.

MARPLOT: So, here's everybody happy, I find, but poor Pilgarlick.[47] I wonder what satisfaction I shall have, for being cuffed, kicked, and beaten in your service.

SIR JEALOUS: I have been a little too familiar with you, as things are fallen out; but since there's no help for't, you must forgive me.

---

[47]*Pilgarlick*: muggins

MARPLOT: Egad, I think so – but provided that you be not so familar for the future.

SIR GEORGE: Thou hast been an unlucky rogue.

MARPLOT: But very honest.

CHARLES: That I'll vouch for; and freely forgive thee.

SIR GEORGE: And I'll do you one piece of service more, Marplot. I'll take care that Sir Francis makes you master of your estate.

MARPLOT: That will make me as happy as any of you.

PATCH: Your humble servant begs leave to remind you, madam.

ISABINDA: Sir, I hope you'll give me leave to take Patch into favour again.

SIR JEALOUS: Nay, let your husband look to that, I have done with my care.

CHARLES: Her own liberty shall always oblige me. Here's nobody but honest Whisper and Mrs Scentwell to be provided for now. It shall be left to their choice to marry, or keep their services.

WHISPER: Nay then, I'll stick to my master.

SCENTWELL: Coxcomb! And I prefer my lady before a footman.

SIR JEALOUS: Hark, I hear the music, the fiddlers smell a wedding. What say you, young fellows, will you have a dance?

SIR GEORGE: With all my heart; call 'em in.

A Dance

SIR JEALOUS: Now let us in and refresh ourselves with a cheerful glass, in which we will bury all animosities; and:

> By my example let all parents move,
> And never strive to cross their children's love;
> But still submit that care to Providence above.